Praise for *The Mythological Dimensions o...*

"*The Mythological Dimensions of Neil G...*
interested in the history and development of fantasy. Its fifteen intelligent, scholarly, and very readable essays examine Gaiman's work in light of the literary, mythic, and pop-cultural influences that have shaped him as a writer as well as his own on-going influence on the field of fantastic literature."

—Delia Sherman, author of *The Freedom Maze*

"A marvelously erudite and impressive compendium of insightful glosses to and upon mythmaker Neil Gaiman's splendid work."

—Patricia Kennealy-Morrison, author of *The Keltiad* fantasy series and *Strange Days: My Life With and Without Jim Morrison*

"It is a brilliant conceit to view Gaiman's work through such filters as Tolkien, *Beowulf*, and even *Doctor Who*. Through these divergent lenses, we gain a deeper understanding of his contribution to storytelling, myth, and the creation of worlds. It would be easy to simply touch upon influences; *Dimensions* goes deeper, as each chapter fills in a grand world view that gives us context to the man and his words. A tremendous insight into one of our best modern writers."

—Sam Balcomb, Rainfall Films, Director/Producer

"*The Mythological Dimensions of Neil Gaiman* fills a key gap in the study of this prolific fantasist by exploring how Gaiman both recasts myth from many cultural traditions and creates his own new set of myths for the twenty-first century. The editors have compiled a broad array of incisive and entertaining essays spanning Gaiman's varied career and touchstone works such as *The Sandman* graphic novel series, his seminal novels *American Gods* and *Anansi Boys*, his award-winning books for young adults such as *The Graveyard Book* and *Coraline*, his short fiction, and even his scripts for classic SF/fantasy films and television series such as *Beowulf*, *Babylon 5*, and *Doctor Who*. This volume situates Gaiman's myth-making in the tradition of other writers from George MacDonald to C. S. Lewis and J. R. R. Tolkien, and examines how Gaiman finds his own voice and constructs his own unique mythic universes. This will be an important collection for all scholars, students, and fans of Gaiman and contemporary fantasy literature."

—David D. Oberhelman, Professor, Oklahoma State University Library; member of the Council of Stewards for the Mythopoeic Society

The
Mythological Dimensions
of
NEIL GAIMAN

The Mythological Dimensions *of* NEIL GAIMAN

Edited by

Anthony Burdge
Jessica Burke
Kristine Larsen

The Mythological Dimensions of Neil Gaiman

Copyright© Anthony Burdge, Jessica Burke, Kristine Larsen
April 2012

All rights reserved. No part of this book may be reproduced in any form without the expressed written permission of the publisher, except by a reviewer.

Printed in USA.　First printing 2012, Kitsune Books.
Second printing 2013, CreateSpace.

Cover art by Catherine Sparsidis

Disclaimers:
The opinions expressed in individual essays are solely those of the authors and not necessarily those of the editors or the publisher.

Dedication

We dedicate this volume in loving memory
of our friend & mentor
Alexei Kondratiev

CONTENTS

Acknowledgments • 11

Foreword by Matthew Dow Smith • 12

Preface by Lynnette Porter • 15

Title Abbreviation Conventions • 20

The Authors and the Critics: Gaiman, Tolkien & Beowulf • 21
  Jason Fisher

The Problem with Bod: Examining the Evolution of Neil Gaiman's Response to C.S. Lewis's *The Last Battle* in "The Problem of Susan" and *The Graveyard Book* • 35
  Chelsey Kendig

Ravens, Librarians and Beautiful Ladies: Bakhtinian Dialogueism in the Gothic Mythology of Neil Gaiman and George McDonald • 49
  Melody Green

What Ever Happened to the Time Lord? Mythology and Fandom in Neil Gaiman's Contributions to Unfolding Texts • 64
  Matthew Hills

So Long and Thanks for all the Dents! A Guide for the Hitchhiker through the Worlds of Douglas Adams and Neil Gaiman • 81
  Anthony S. Burdge

Consorting with the Gods: Exploring Gaiman's Pan-Pantheon • 94
  Harley J. Sims

Gaiman: The Teller of Tales and the Fairy Tale Tradition • 109
Leslie Drury

The Best Things Come in Threes: The Triple Goddess in the Works of Neil Gaiman • 125
Tony Keen

Women's Magic: Witches and the Works of Neil Gaiman • 141
Jessica Burke

Fables and Reflections: Doubles, Duality and Mirrors in the Fiction of Neil Gaiman • 173
Samuel Brooker

Through a Telescope Backwards: Tripping the Light Fantastic in the Gaiman Universe • 186
Kristine Larsen

The Eternal Carnival of the Myth: Or How to Kill Myths and Live Happy • 199
Camillo A. Formigatti

"It Starts with Doors" Blurred Boundaries and Portals in the Worlds of Neil Gaiman • 208
Tanya Carinae Pell Jones

The End of the World as We Know It: Neil Gaiman and the Future of Mythology • 223
Lynn Gelfand

The Playful Palimpsest of Gaiman's Sequential Storytelling • 239
Colin B. Harvey

Contributors • 253

Bibliography • 258

Index • 279

ACKNOWLEDGMENTS

Anthony, Jessica, and Kristine would like to thank our Editors at Kitsune Books, Anne Petty and Lynn Holschuh, for having faith in us to produce another collection that continues the publisher's "Mythological Dimensions" series.

The editors are indebted to Brie Alsbury, for her keen eye and for taking the time to review the manuscript.

Anthony is appreciative for the help of Shield Bonnichsen, creator and webmaster of The Neil Gaiman Visual Bibliography. His assistance in providing scans of everything Neil Gaiman wrote about Douglas Adams, for magazines, was a tremendous boost in research material. Shield's website is a must stop for all things Neil Gaiman.

Anthony and Jessica would like to thank their dear friend Catherine Sparsidis, cover art illustrator. Cat is a long-time friend and artist for The North East Tolkien Society. Her art has graced numerous covers and pages of society journals, has been featured in the society calendar, and on various incarnations of the society website. We are devotees of her creative vision which serves to open portals between worlds.

Lastly, and most importantly, the editors would like to thank Neil Gaiman. This collection is, of course, dedicated to his work, but the editors are indebted to Mr. Gaiman for spreading the word of our Call for Papers on his blog and in Twitter posts. It is his support for and interaction with his fan community that is admirable, and so very much appreciated.

Now for that pint of Shoggoth's Old Peculiar...

FOREWORD

The Muse in the Black Leather Jacket: A Kind of Introduction

Matthew Dow Smith

It's nearly impossible to talk about author, screenwriter, comic book writer, poet, and occasional songwriter Neil Gaiman without touching on the subject of myths and legends in one way or another. Whether it's the modern mythology of superheroes, the gods and monsters of ancient myths, or the folklore of cultures past and present, there is almost always a mythological component to Gaiman's work, in any medium.

Then there's the fact that Neil Gaiman has become a bit of a myth in his own right, a legendary figure in Fantasy circles, with an ever-expanding group of devoted fans who follow him from project to project, medium to medium, praising his work on their blogs and message boards, recommending his books to friends and strangers alike. And when Gaiman makes public appearances—always in his trademark black leather jacket, black jeans, and black t-shirt—his fans present him with dolls and sculptures inspired by his stories, or paintings they've done of characters from his books, and speak of how being exposed to his work changed their lives.

Many of these same fans have gone on to write stories of their own, some even becoming quite famous themselves; and it is no overstatement to say that few living authors have ever inspired so many others to write. His name is almost universally cited as a major influence by writers in the Urban Fantasy field, not to mention the wider Fantasy genre, the Science Fiction genre, and more than a few Mystery writers, as well.

If not a god among other, far more mortal Fantasy writers, Neil Gaiman has at the very least become a kind of modern muse, lighting a spark of creativity in a surprisingly wide portion of his audience.

Like many people, I first came across the name Neil Gaiman on the cover of a comic book—in my case, DC Comic's *The Sandman* #8. This was early in his career, before the novels, before the television shows and movies, but even then, the signature Gaiman elements were in place. In the issue, we see the figure of Death re-envisioned as a young-looking woman who claims the newly dead with love and respect instead of gloom and menace. No black cloak, no scythe, just a Goth girl with pale skin, heavy eye makeup, and an ankh necklace. And instead of a slow build-up to a fight between spandex-clad superheroes, we are presented with a 22-page conversation between Death and her brother Dream that touches on the human condition and what it means to be alive.

This was a new kind of mythology, built on classic themes and ideas, even characters, but filtered through the modern world in a way that made the drab, sometimes confusing reality around us seem a little more magical, if you only knew where to look. In its own way, it fulfilled the reverse function of traditional mythology. Instead of explaining how the world came to be, it showed us what the world would be like if all those myths were true. It would be a world much like our own, but somehow better, more interesting, more magical.

That first dip into Gaiman's blend of the mundane and the magical was only the beginning. As *The Sandman* series continued, Gaiman worked an ever increasing pantheon of gods and monsters into the narrative—creatures from Greek myths stood side by side with Norse gods like Thor and Odin, and even forgotten characters from the more recent mythology of the DC comic book universe found their way into the story, playing their own small part in a narrative that grew into an unabashed celebration of stories and myths on a grand scale I had never seen before.

Gaiman carried this same almost promiscuous exuberance for mythologies well known and obscure with him as he moved from comics to television, then to books, and later into movies: sometimes placing ancient gods in modern settings, as in novels like *American Gods* and *Anansi Boys*; sometimes re-presenting our oldest stories in exciting and accessible new ways, as in his script with Roger Avary for the film, *Beowulf*; and even occasionally creating mythologies of his own, steeped in the folklore and fairy tales of our past, as in his novels *Coraline* and *The Graveyard Book*. You will find discussions of the mythological aspects to all these in the essays collected here in this book, along with examinations of Gaiman's work as it relates to authors such as Tolkien, Lewis, and Lovecraft, as well as myths and fairy tales in general.

I can't pretend to be capable of producing the kinds of insights present in these essays, but even now, nearly twenty years after that first encounter with Neil Gaiman's work in the pages of *The Sandman*, I find myself in awe of the staggering depth and breadth of his mythological knowledge and his ability to weave that knowledge into new, entertaining forms. It may not be a unique gift—I'm thinking here of Gaiman's long-time friends, Kim Newman and Alan Moore, both of whom have tapped into modern and ancient mythologies to one degree or another in their work—but I would argue only Gaiman has cast so wide a net. One need only look at the penultimate *Sandman* storyline, *The Wake*, to see just how many cultures' folklores Gaiman can appropriate at the same time. Even the shared universes of Philip Jose Farmer's Wold Newton novels and Moore's *League of Extraordinary Gentlemen*, chock full as they are with characters from a wide array of pulp novels, movies, and comic books, seem almost limited in scope when compared with the eclectic pantheon of Gaiman's *American Gods*.

The question of which author can fit the greatest number of pantheons—whether characters from fiction or the gods and monsters of our ancient myths—into a single story aside, Neil Gaiman has clearly captured the imagination of a generation of fantasy readers, including the authors featured in this book. Did their first exposure to Gaiman's work change their life? I wouldn't dare speak for them, but I will speak for myself...

By the time I had finished reading that issue of *The Sandman* all those years ago, my life really did change. I had decided to write and draw my own comic books.

The muse in the black leather jacket had ignited another spark.

—Matthew Dow Smith
Delmar, NY
2012

PREFACE

Magic and Dreams and Good Madness

Lynnette Porter

For New Year 2001, Neil Gaiman wished "magic and dreams and good madness" for his legions of readers. A little more than a decade later, his hope for us all in 2012 is that we "make mistakes....Make glorious, amazing mistakes"—because that means we are making something new: "you're Doing Something."[1] The decade-separated wishes might seem incongruous, but then Gaiman's work has never been limited to one culture, time period, franchise, story world, or medium. Why should the content of his New Year's messages be any different?

Yet Gaiman's New Year's wishes and plethora of published works all revolve around the very essence of what makes us human: the realm of the mind. Gaiman encourages us to think and to expand our range of experiences. Both dreams and mistakes determine who we are and how we respond to the glories and challenges of life. For all that he writes about death (or Death), Gaiman and his art are "amazing" and life affirming. Perhaps that is one reason why he has won so many awards—16 alone (including the Newberry Medal and Hugo Award) for *The Graveyard Book* and dozens more for *Coraline, American Gods,* and *The Sandman* series.

He creates realistic modern characters: thinking, feeling beings who are called to respond in marvelous ways that they could never have predicted. They touch us because they are lively and force us to interact with them, whether they reside in worlds far way in an interplanetary future or a fictionalized terran past, whether they are human, hybrid, or immortal. Gaiman understands the modern mind and forces us to contemplate our lives and society. Instead of providing mere escapist entertainment, he holds up a mirror so we can discover ourselves.

Modern man Gaiman also is a wizard who conjures new tales made from myth and folklore, not only from his own culture but myriad others around the world and throughout history. He dissects familiar fables and intriguingly re-combines their elements into new tales.

Gaiman, like me and, I suspect, most people who read this book, is a fan of classic stories first discovered in childhood that continue to influence us as adults. He pays homage to the stories others have developed over the years but is still true to his style when asked to play in someone else's cinematic or literary backyard. In 2011, for example, Gaiman not only wrote one of my all-time favorite *Doctor Who* episodes, "The Doctor's Wife," but he added a new layer to the series' mythology that is compatible with the franchise's nearly 50-year history of episodes. Similarly, Gaiman's most recent pastiche of Sherlock Holmes ("The Case of Death and Honey") and his 2004 story "A Study in Emerald" bookend the life of the venerable detective and allow us to consider Holmes, and his scientific methods, in a different way. Even if Gaiman had not revisited several of my favorite authors and fandoms, I would find his insights into the characters and myths that shape our culture fascinating, both from a fan and an educator's perspective. Similarly, the following essayists offer us new ways to consider Gaiman's works.

For example, Jason Fisher's "The Authors and Critics: Gaiman, Tolkien, and Beowulf," compares Gaiman's and Roger Avary's script for the 2007 film *Beowulf* with Tolkien's interpretation of the epic poem. As a humanities teacher, I have used *Beowulf* the movie to introduce students to the title character and the art of adaptation. My students also study the poem and Tolkien's "Beowulf: The Monsters and the Critics," both discussed in Fisher's chapter. They then look at the ways that the Gaiman/Avary script presents images found in the poem but that also are seen in another adaptation—Peter Jackson's *Lord of the Rings* films. Just as Tolkien's descriptions of the Rohirrim reflect *Beowulf*'s influence, so does the 2007 film resonate not only with the original epic, but Tolkien's stories and their adaptations, as well as Gaiman's understanding of the historic text and mythology in general. After reading Fisher's chapter, I will include it as a text when my students next study *Beowulf* and adaptation. In this way, this volume's essayists analyzing Gaiman's themes and methods, authors and adaptors of myth (like Tolkien and Gaiman), and I (along with, other educators) form a continuing cycle of passing on ancient stories and adapting them for the next generation.

New interpretations of mythic characters and themes are a cultural necessity, something that Gaiman well understands. As Colin B. Harvey notes in the final chapter ("The Playful Palimpsest of Gaiman's Sequential Storytelling"), Gaiman excels in the "continuance and transformation of myth," which, as Lynn Gelfand reminds us in her chapter ("The End of the World as We Know It"), "must fit the changing social, economic, and technological requirements of a society." Gaiman continues a myth by transforming mythic beings so they can live in our world, or we in theirs, but he also meets those technological requirements of making myth accessible. He tells stories through a variety of media—printed comic books, graphic novels, stories, children's books, novels, and poems as well as television, film, and even song. Gaiman recognizes the importance of interacting with an original tale, discovering something unique to reveal (in his case, through writing about it), and then creating a new artwork based on the reinterpretation of myth, folklore, or more recent authors' classics. This creative process is analyzed in the following chapters, allowing us to learn more about the writer as well as what has been written.

The older I become, the more clearly I can see the interconnections among my diverse interests and analyses of a wide range of texts. Not surprisingly, Gaiman is way ahead of me in this exploration of the connections between literature and modern experience, philosophy and action, and authors and characters. His works are, as Anthony S. Burdge suggests in "So Long and Thanks for All the Dents!", a portal through which we explore other realities and thus make sense of our own.

The "magic and dreams and good madness" of Neil Gaiman's many works are reflected in the following 15 chapters. Like Gaiman, these essayists force us to reconsider familiar works from a different perspective and to interact with what we read. Although I have long been a fan of *Beowulf*, Sherlock Holmes, and *Doctor Who*, for example, Gaiman and these essayists make me rethink my interpretation of beloved stories. Perhaps that is Gaiman's, and this book's, greatest strength. These chapters, like Gaiman's work, should surprise and inspire us.

The essayists analyze three types of connections: those between Gaiman and other authors, those between Gaiman and myth or folklore, and those among Gaiman's works. They reflect on Gaiman's most famous as well as least discussed stories and cover traditional prose as well as comics, television franchises, and film.

Gaiman's Link to Other Authors

Chelsey Kendig ("The Problem with Bod") explains how Gaiman's childhood fondness for C. S. Lewis' *Narnia* books eventually led to his "fix" of sorts to Lewis' expulsion of Susan Pevensie from Narnia (or heaven). Gaiman's "The Problem of Susan" is a precursor to *The Graveyard Book,* in which, as Kendig shows us, original character Bod can be compared with Lewis' Susan.

Although Gaiman may not be as clearly a fan of George MacDonald's stories as he is of Tolkien's or Lewis', Melody Green ("Ravens, Librarians, and Beautiful Ladies") illustrates connections between Gaiman's character of Death in *The Graveyard Book* and Death of the Endless in *The Sandman* series with the North Wind in *At the Beck of the North Wind,* written by "father of the fantasy genre" MacDonald. Green analyzes where

mythology involving ravens and librarians might possibly fit into the ways MacDonald and Gaiman "create new spaces in which old ideas can be challenged and explored."
Gaiman not only interacts with authors of the past but with his contemporaries, such as Douglas Adams. As Burdge notes in his aforementioned chapter, the two influenced each other, personally and professionally, but, more significantly, they are catalysts to inspire the writers who follow them. If we, as Burdge wonders, may be living in one of the parallel universes these authors described, then we are indeed fortunate that ours has intersected with both Gaiman's and Adams'.

Gaiman, Myths, and Folklore

The early chapters of this book often explore Gaiman-as-fan, but the author is an expert on ancient myths as well as twentieth-century stories. Harley J. Sims shows Gaiman "Consorting with the Gods" and creating a "pan-pantheon." A later chapter, Camillo A. Formigatti's "The Eternal Carnival of the Myth," indicates ways that Gaiman challenges our ideas about immortal gods and the way they really might interact with modern humans.

Folklore is another part of Gaiman's literary repertoire. Leslie Drury looks at Gaiman as "The Teller of Tales and the Fairy Tale Tradition." Fables likewise are crucial underpinnings to Gaiman's works, and Samuel Brooker discusses the "Doubles, Duality and Mirrors" in the author's fiction.

Powerful female characters, whether from myth or folklore, include goddesses and witches, and Gaiman makes both the traditionally idealized as well as the more frequently feared seem normal. Tony Keen notes that "The Best Things Come in Threes"—such as the Triple Goddess (e.g., three as one, or three separate beings) found in Gaiman's writings. In "Women's Magic: Witches and the Work of Neil Gaiman," Jessica Burke analyzes the ways that the author writes about witches without stigmatizing them as evil.

Connections Among Gaiman's Works

Although several essayists stick with Gaiman's print stories, Matt Hills ("Whatever Happened to the Time Lord?") celebrates the value of Gaiman's contributions to the *Babylon 5*, Batman, and *Doctor Who* franchises. Although Gaiman's scripts often allow him to play in the universes of other creators, these stories may have been considered less significant than those involving Gaiman's original characters. Hill refutes this notion, asserts that "mythology and fandom are insistently interconnected in Gaiman's work as a producer-fan," and explains why the stories created by Gaiman-the-fan are important to franchises' ongoing myth making and the evolution of fandom. Gaiman's stories often skew linear time and, as Hills illustrates in a discussion of *Doctor Who*, beginnings and endings are often presented in reversed order. Four essayists—Kristine Larsen ("Through a Telescope Backwards"), Tanya Carinae Pell Jones ("'It Starts with Doors'"), Lynn Gelfand, and Colin B. Harvey—discuss the beginnings and endings of worlds, atypical storytelling sequences, and eternal themes, as presented by Gaiman.

When delving into these essayists' analyses of Gaiman's stories and characters, we are bound to gain a deeper understanding of a single work and its place within popular culture, as well as a greater appreciation of the awe-inspiring breadth of Gaiman's subject matter. Even long-time fans may, as did I, discover a previously unread or unseen gem and go off to find it. This book provides a fitting tribute to Gaiman's collection of multimedia stories. It illustrates how deeply Gaiman is embedded in our cultural consciousness and just why he receives all those awards.

Because Gaiman understands the nature and purpose of myth and modern story, he can re-interpret or create characters and worlds so that they are at once fresh and familiar. He forces us to admit our links to each other and the mythic past while challenging us to make new connections with ideas and to defy societal expectations. He asks us to think, to dream, and to do, even if we make mistakes. As the many Gaiman stories analyzed in this book attest, our entertainment and intellectual lives are never the same once we read or hear his words, and if we follow his example, we too can bring magic to our madness.

---

1 Gaiman, Neil. "My New Year Wish." 31 Dec. 2011. Web. 8 Jan. 2012. <http://journal.neilgaiman.com/>

TITLE ABBREVIATION CONVENTIONS

American Gods—Gods
Anansi Boys—Anansi
Batman: Whatever Happened to the Caped Crusader?—Batman
Don't Panic: Douglas Adams and The Hitch-Hiker's Guide to the Galaxy—Don't Panic
Death: The High Cost of Living—High Cost
Fragile Things: Short Fictions and Wonders—Fragile
Good Omens—Omens
The Graveyard Book—Graveyard
Mr. Punch: The Tragical Comedy or Comical Tragedy—Mr. Punch
Odd and the Frost Giants—Odd
The Sandman (series as a whole)—Sandman
The Sandman I: Preludes and Nocturnes—Preludes
The Sandman II: The Doll's House—Doll's House
The Sandman III: Dream Country—Country
The Sandman IV: Season of Mists—Mists
The Sandman V: A Game of You—Game
The Sandman VI: Fables and Reflections—Fables
The Sandman VII: Brief Lives—Brief Lives
The Sandman VIII: World's End—World's End
The Sandman IX: The Kindly Ones—Kindly Ones
The Sandman X: The Wake—Wake
The Sandman: The Dream Hunters—Hunters
Smoke and Mirrors: Short Fictions and Illusions—Mirrors

The Authors and the Critics: Gaiman, Tolkien, and Beowulf

Jason Fisher

"Legend is always false and always true. History invents facts; but legend can only invent or transpose details [...]."[1]

For many, the lure of *Beowulf* is irresistible. In spite of occasional complaints by students at being made to labor through the epic poem (the same complaints that have been made against Homer, Virgil, Dante, and so on), there is no denying that readers have found *Beowulf* compelling for centuries. It is a work that has survived the trials of time and taste—the only surviving copy was almost lost in a fire in 1731[2]—and it continues to captivate and transport readers today. In many ways, *Beowulf* can be seen as a progenitor of modern fantasy literature. Not only does *Beowulf* itself feature swords and sorcery, monsters and heroes, kings and villains, but the poem has had a profound influence on some of the giants of twentieth-century fantasy literature. It is not uncommon for readers to discover *Beowulf* through their favorite fantasy author, or to discover new fantasy authors through *Beowulf*. This certainly reflects my own experience.

In this essay, I propose to consider two of the twentieth century's best-loved authors, J.R.R. Tolkien and Neil Gaiman, and their respective responses to and borrowings from the oldest surviving English poem. Seventy-five years ago—almost to the very day as I write these words—J.R.R. Tolkien described *Beowulf* as

> not a 'primitive' poem; it is a late one, using the materials (then still plentiful) preserved from a day already changing and passing, a time that has now for ever vanished, swallowed in oblivion; using them for a new purpose, with a wider sweep of imagination, if with a less bitter and concentrated force.[3]

Another way of putting this is to say that *Beowulf* is both old and new. It is a work perennially renewed and recontextualized. It is perennially fresh because of ongoing reinterpretation in the light of our evolving culture, and yet it stands as a perpetual reminder of where we came from. It moors us to our past while yet pointing to new and distant shores. *Beowulf* feels almost inaccessibly remote; yet somehow it remains fresh, exciting, and vibrantly *human*. To this last point, it is in their striking contrast with the monsters and other supernatural elements in the poem that its kings and thanes seem the most like us. We can relate to their fears and aspire to their courage. The poem has earned a primacy in the Western canon that simply refuses to diminish.

Tolkien's *Beowulf*

It would be difficult to overestimate the importance of *Beowulf* to Tolkien and of Tolkien to *Beowulf*. It is scarcely exaggerating to suppose that without either one, we might not have had the other; at least, not as we know them. Of course, Tolkien the man would have lived and breathed without *Beowulf*, but he might never have become the academic and fantasy writer remembered today. Likewise, *Beowulf*, the Anglo-Saxon text, would have existed without Tolkien, but it might never have come to be appreciated as a work of art, indeed one of the greatest works of art ever made in English.

From our perspective today, with Tolkien's impact on *Beowulf* studies taken for granted, this is a difficult possibility to grasp. Isn't it inevitable, we might ask, that *Beowulf* would have come to be recognized for the work of art that it is? But this did not look inevitable at all before the first half of the twentieth century. Poetic works of the type and period as *Beowulf*, perhaps even particularly typified by *Beowulf*, were once regarded as "a raving or rambling sort of wit or invention, loose and flowing, with little art or confinement to any certain measures or rules," which "served [...] to charm the ignorant and barbarous vulgar;" but "the true flame of poetry was rare among them, and the rest were but wild-fire that sparked and crackled a while, and soon went out with little pleasure," no more than "a sort of jingle that pleased the ruder ears."[4]

This was the view about a century before Tolkien encountered *Beowulf*. But surely the latter part of the nineteenth century brought new appreciation for the poem? Well, yes and no. As difficult as it might be for those with a post-Tolkienian perspective to believe it, this impression was not much improved by the time Tolkien was preparing to enter the fray. The emergence of comparative philology over the course of the nineteenth century had brought a new appreciation for *Beowulf*, but this appreciation was mainly limited to deconstructing the poem for what it could reveal about the Old English language. It was not much more than an extended glossary to further the aims of comparative philologists. It is almost single-handedly thanks to Tolkien that the tide in *Beowulf* studies turned. How did this happen, and why?

Tolkien first encountered *Beowulf* while in secondary school at King Edward's in Birmingham. Under the tutelage of George Brewerton, an anglophile if ever there were one,[5] Tolkien's interests broadened from Latin, Greek, French, and German to Welsh, Old English, Old Norse, Middle English. He began to read anonymous medieval romances, Chaucer—and *Beowulf*, which he found, even as a teenager, "to be one of the most extraordinary poems of all time."[6] He studied the poem even more closely as an undergraduate at Exeter College, Oxford, and then he lectured on *Beowulf* at Leeds and Oxford. Around the same time, C.S. Lewis was embarking on his own teaching career. Lewis understood the difficulty of the material and intuited the most effective way to approach it, perhaps rather better than Tolkien,[7] to whom it came so naturally. Around 1928, Lewis began organizing "Beer and Beowulf" evenings, where his undergraduates "chanted Beowulf aloud, and passed around the beer jug."[8] He had met Tolkien a couple of years before, and one must imagine that Tolkien participated in at least a few of these *béorscipan*.[9]

Just a few years prior, Tolkien had undertaken his own translation of *Beowulf*. By 1926, Tolkien had completed a prose translation and had made another, incomplete translation in alliterative verse.[10] By the 1930's, with his translations and a series of lectures behind him, Tolkien had formed a cogent theory of *Beowulf*, a theory which suggested that the critics before him were all wrong about the poem. This theory, embodied in the lecture "*Beowulf*: The Monsters and the Critics," proposed that the poem should be regarded as art, and indeed a masterwork, rather than merely a quarry for digging up Old English words and nuggets of history. Moreover, Tolkien suggested that the monsters and other fantastical elements—the very elements most critics had been inclined to dismiss as "matter that is really not worth serious attention"[11]—were in fact the centerpiece of the poem and an essential part of its greatness. The lecture was published in 1936, and *Beowulf* criticism was forever changed. When you boil the argument down, part of what Tolkien is doing is explaining his own literary tastes and justifying fantasy literature at the same time.

Tolkien's own literary invention was profoundly influenced by *Beowulf* as well. His fiction and poetry are interlarded with allusions to and borrowing from the great Anglo-Saxon poem. There is no need to attempt an exhaustive survey here, but a few examples will help to set the stage. I'll mention a few lesser-known works first, both to whet the reader's appetite as well as to demonstrate the breadth of inspiration Tolkien drew from *Beowulf*. So, before I come to Tolkien's novels, *The Hobbit* and *The Lord of the Rings*, let me describe a poem, a painting, and a short story. All of these date from a period of rich and varied work before and just after the publication of *The Hobbit*.

The poem, "Iumonna Gold Galdre Bewunden," was titled and based on a single line from the Old English poem. The earliest version was probably written in 1922, but the poem was published forty years later as "The Hoard" in *The Adventures of Tom Bombadil* (1962). The title (and the line from *Beowulf*) means "gold of men of yore, wound in enchantments," and in the poem, a hoard of enchanted gold brings about the demise first of a dwarf, then the dragon who killed him, then the young warrior who killed the dragon, now an old king. It is cursed, like the dragon's hoard in *Beowulf*. The painting, dated 1927, likewise has an Old English title drawn directly from *Beowulf*: "Hringboga Heorte Gefysed." It depicts a dragon, coiled and ready to strike, and it means "the coiled dragon's heart was stirred" to come out and do battle over his hoard of gold. The short story dates to the first part of the 1940s. In "Sellic Spell" (still unpublished), Tolkien sought to retell the folkloric and mythical aspects of the Beowulf story, cutting out all of the historical and religious interpolations made by the *Beowulf* poet. It was a kind of experiment to reconstruct an earlier, purely pagan version of the tradition. Its hero was therefore called "Beowolf."[12]

And so we come to *The Hobbit* and *The Lord of the Rings*, Tolkien's masterworks. Again, I could easily spend an entire essay tracking down and spotlighting allusions, borrowings, and parodies from *Beowulf*, but a few representative examples will have to suffice.[13] In *The Hobbit*, the most obvious example comes toward the end of the novel, when Bilbo faces the dragon and the stolen hoard of the dwarves. As readers will recall, Bilbo the would-be burglar creeps into the mountain through a secret entrance and steals "a great two-handled cup, as heavy as he could carry."[14] Virtually the identical episode occurs in *Beowulf*. About a year after *The Hobbit* was published, a reader asked Tolkien whether his own cup-stealing scene came from *Beowulf*, to which Tolkien replied:

> *Beowulf* is among my most valued sources; though it was not consciously present to the mind in the process of writing, in which the episode of the theft arose naturally (and almost inevitably) from the circumstances. It is difficult to think of any other way of conducting the story at that point. I fancy the author of *Beowulf* would say much the same.[15]

One cannot help but suspect that Tolkien is being a bit coy about not having *Beowulf* consciously in mind. But even if we take him at his word, the poem was by this time so familiar to him, it would certainly have come *unconsciously* to mind as he penned the scene—"almost inevitably," as it were.

The dragon Smaug himself owes an imaginative debt to *Beowulf*.

In this case, there is perhaps a greater debt to the Norse *Fáfnismál*, but I will set that aside for now. In his lecture, "*Beowulf*: The Monsters and the Critics," Tolkien wrote that "Beowulf's dragon [...] is not to be blamed for being a dragon, but rather for not being dragon enough, pure plain fairy-story dragon." Rather, his depiction "approaches *draconitas* rather than *draco*."[16] Tolkien himself decided to attempt to remedy the *Beowulf* poet's failure, and as Tom Shippey has shown, Tolkien put a real, honest-to-goodness dragon at center stage in his own novel, *The Hobbit*.[17]

In *The Lord of the Rings*, by far the most obvious borrowing from *Beowulf* lies in the characterization of Rohan and the Rohirrim. Meduseld, the seat of Théoden in Edoras, appears modeled directly from Heorot, where Hrothgar ruled the Spear-Danes. Many of the names in Rohan are found also in *Beowulf* —Éomer, Gárulf, Guthláf, Gúthwinë, Háma, Helm, Théoden, and still more besides. And it isn't merely the names, but the architecture, the armor and weaponry, the language, and the culture itself that were borrowed—though as in his answer to the query about *The Hobbit* and the cup-stealing episode, Tolkien is circumspect. But Tom Shippey unmasks him:

> You remember, no doubt, the footnote, in one of the Appendices, where Tolkien says you mustn't think that the Riders [of Rohan] resemble the ancient English in any except accidental respects. Absolutely untrue! Tolkien covering his tracks yet again! The Riders of Rohan resemble the Old English down to minute detail. Their names are all Old English [...] but they also behave that way. All the habits which he talks about like [...] piling arms outside, not being allowed in to see the king with weapons in your hand, the counsellor sitting at the feet of the king, all these come straight out of *Beowulf*, down to minute detail. The actual things they say are said by characters in *Beowulf*, very often.[18]

It is also worth noting that the name Froda occurs in *Beowulf* (though not solely in *Beowulf*), and this is certainly part (though again, not all) of the history of Tolkien's character, Frodo Baggins. Gollum likewise resembles Grendel in many respects. Both are characterized as half-man, half-monster, cannibals creeping about in the dark under a curse, both stronger and more cunning than other men, and so forth. Gríma Wormtongue, too, bears similarities to Grendel. The blades that pierce the Nazgûl melt before the hobbits' eyes, just as the blade with which Beowulf decapitates Grendel melts away before his. As I say, I could go on, but let that suffice as we must now turn to our attention to Neil Gaiman.

Gaiman's *Beowulf*

Neil Gaiman's work reveals a double-edged influence: the direct impact of *Beowulf* as well as the influence of J.R.R. Tolkien, and through him the secondary, more indirect influence of *Beowulf* again. The most obvious example of Gaiman's engagement with the tradition came in his and Roger Avary's screenplay for the 2007 computer-animated film adaptation of *Beowulf*, but the story actually begins much earlier than this.

After co-writing a string of cult hits with Quentin Tarantino in the early 1990s — *Reservoir Dogs* (1992), *True Romance* (1993), and finally *Pulp Fiction* (1994), for which they shared an Academy Award — Roger Avary was looking for a project of his own. In 1995, he wrote a treatment for *Beowulf*. The dramatic core of his proposed film came from a series of questions Avary had asked himself about the poem more than a decade earlier:

> If Grendel is half-man, half-demon ... then who is his father?

> Why does Grendel never attack Hrothgar, the king?

> How does Beowulf hold his breath for days on end during the fight with Grendel's Mother? Maybe he wasn't fighting her? Or maybe he isn't human?

> When Beowulf goes into the cave to kill Grendel's Mother, why does he emerge with Grendel's head instead of hers? Where's the proof that the mother was killed? [19]

These are probing questions! Reading between the lines—in this case literally—Avary decided that "[alt]hough it's not in the poem, clearly, Grendel was Hrothgar's bastard son [...] sired [...] in exchange for worldly wealth and fame."[20] But in spite of his novel interpretation, Avary continued to struggle with how to adapt the "odd two-act structure"[21] of *Beowulf* into a cohesive feature film. It was Neil Gaiman who provided the final insight: "Roger, don't you see? If Grendel is Hrothgar's son, the dragon surely must be Beowulf's son—come back to haunt him."[22] The two decided to work together on a full-length screenplay, and the result was hammered out over two weeks in June, 1997. Owing to the vagaries of the motion picture industry, it would take another decade, and a second draft of the screenplay, before their vision of *Beowulf*, remade "as a sort of Dark Ages *Trainspotting*, filled with mead and blood and madness,"[23] would finally reach the public. But Gaiman was not content merely to wait on Hollywood.

In 1998, sometime not long after he and Avary wrote their first draft of the *Beowulf* screenplay, Gaiman published a poem called "Lawrence Talbot: BAY WOLF" in the multicontributor anthology, *Dark Detectives*. The poem is an obvious adaptation of the basic *Beowulf* story; it hardly needs pointing out that the title is a clever twist on the name of the Anglo-Saxon hero. Moreover, the poem exhibits some of the same unique interpretations that characterize the film adaptation (and a few new ones).

The poem was reprinted — retitled simply "Bay Wolf" (remember Tolkien's adaptation of the character as "Beewolf") — in Gaiman's own collection, *Smoke and Mirrors*, in the same year, and Gaiman chose a telling epigraph for his new book: "But where there's a monster there's a miracle," from a poem by Ogden Nash entitled "Dragons are Too Seldom." It may not be a coincidence that this recalls Tolkien's 1936 lecture on *Beowulf*, discussed above. Remember, Tolkien charged that the dragon in *Beowulf* was not quite dragon enough — *real* dragons are too seldom, we might say. Gaiman, in his transformation of the dragon into more than just a dragon, but Beowulf's bastard son, was very much in sympathy with Tolkien here. This epigraph could also serve as a rallying cry for every fan of fantastical literature, from those enthralled by the *Beowulf* poet a millennium ago to the teaming hordes of present-day fantasy fans.

In the poem, Gar Roth is a Venice Beach kingpin, running an all-night hot spot full of sex, drugs, and rock and roll. Grand Al is just a neighbor turned vigilante—not necessarily a bad guy himself; but Gar Roth was keeping him up all night with the noise. Beowulf is Lawrence Talbot, a noirish "adjuster" for hire, and a man who (it seems) can transform into a wolf. The battle between the Bay Wolf and Grand Al transpires much as in Gaiman's source material, but Grendel's motives are more like those in the Avary/Gaiman screenplay. Talbot pursues Grand Al to his mother's lair, where he encounters the monster's mother. Here again, the novel interpretation in the screenplay is apparent: "whether I loved her or killed her... [w]hat we did is no business of yours."[24] The subtext is obvious. One can almost see the seductive ghost of Angelina Jolie.

"Bay Wolf" does not proceed as far as the dragon episode, perhaps for the same reason that Roger Avary originally found *Beowulf* hard to adapt (its "odd two-act structure"). But it's pretty clear that the solutions that Gaiman and Avary worked into their screenplay were behind much of Gaiman's appropriately poetic reinvention of *Beowulf*: the noise as a motive for Grendel's predation, Grendel's mother as the original MILF, Beowulf as part-monster himself, and so on. "Bay Wolf" is a clever adaptation in many other ways as well, recalling the Venice Beach gang wars of Baz Luhrmann's *Romeo + Juliet*, just two years before. It is full of imaginative language and witty turns of phrase (*e.g.*, "fearmoans and whoremoans" for pheromones and hormones).[25]

The idea that Beowulf was a skinchanger of some kind, as we see in the poem "Bay Wolf," has a basis in philology. In the second draft of the screenplay (and in the final film), Grendel's mother greets Beowulf with the following words:

> Are you the one they call Beowulf? The Bee-Wolf. The bear. Such a strong man you are. With the strength of a king. The king you will one day become. [...] I know that underneath your glamour you're as much a monster as my son Grendel. Perhaps more.[26]

In the first draft, Grendel's mother makes the accusation even more directly: "And you're a monster too. Part bear, part wolf, all monster."[27] Gaiman and Avary are making veiled references to etymologies proposed for the name Beowulf, in which it was theorized that Beowulf was Old English *béo* "bee" + *wulf* "wolf," and bee-wolf was a kenning for bear, a "wolf or ravager of the bees."[28] In the original medieval context, this was probably merely metaphorical, but Gaiman and Avary have taken the etymology literally. In either case, this philological touch would have appealed very much to Tolkien, and it's even possible that it was Tolkien's indirect influence which prompted Gaiman and Avary to include such an academic detail in their screenplay.

Remarking and Remaking the Tradition

The changes that Gaiman and Avary made to the underlying story of *Beowulf*, along with its departures from the tone or style of the original, stirred up swift irritation among medieval scholars and literati. The film was called "a great cop-out on a great poem" (Bonnie Wheeler), "some kind of monster" (Jeff Sypeck), "Anglo-Saxons of the Caribbean" (Gary Kamiya), and "a weird cross between a serious attempt to envision the Northern early medieval past and 'Ye Olde Medieval Worlde' of *Shrek*" (Michael Drout), to give just a taste. "Dr. Virago" (a pseudonym) shares a more nuanced, but still highly critical opinion in a lengthy online review. It was, she writes, like "a sloppy disaster of disorganization, hastiness, illogic, and misreading," though with "moments of insight;" it was "a mess of a movie,"[29] but she

> could see some of the seemingly odder choices were still informed choices—they were attempts at doing something based on interpretation rather than the literal elements of the poem—but in going so wrong, those choices were all the more disappointing.[30]

And Richard Scott Nokes "didn't like the snotty way in which it called the poem into question, while leaving its own telling above suspicion."[31]

But is all of this righteous indignation really justified? Anyone has a right to his or her opinion, of course, especially in the subjective judgment of art. But reactions in the scholarly community tended, almost universally, toward offense that anybody would dare alter the story of *Beowulf*. I take a rather different view myself, as it would seem the *Beowulf* poet himself did. Far from being set in rune-stone, the story was once quite fluid and only came to be fixed over time. One feature of the poem that serves to reinforce the idea of its inviolability is the fact that it survives in only a single manuscript. That is to say, unlike many other relics of centuries bygone, there are no competing versions of *Beowulf* with equal provenance from the Middle Ages. There once were several copies separating the poet's original and the extant manuscript, and like a game of Chinese Whispers, these must have differed—but none survive.[32] This leaves an understandable lay perception that the poem was always fixed as it exists today, but scholars should—and do—know better.

Today's authors—Tolkien, Gaiman, and anyone else besides—have as much right to respond to and adapt the story as did the *scops* and scribes of Anglo-Saxon England. After all, the story of Beowulf itself was deliberately altered in order to incorporate explicitly Christian elements. To put it simply: *Beowulf* is already a kind of adaptation, in this case a Christian adaptation of earlier pagan material. "Out of such old lays of Beowulf's adventures, our poet selected, combined, and retold a complete story from his own point of view."[33] It is an amalgam of historical facts, remarkably accurate under the circumstances; legend and folk-tale plot elements, with an underlying mythology only hinted at; and the imposition of Christianity, a theological mantle draped rather carelessly over the backbone of the earlier (heathen) belief system. For all the apparent disharmony of this literary chimaera, *Beowulf* was, and is, regarded as great art.

It would be wrong to lionize the poet or to insist that *Beowulf* has no faults. Many scholars agree that it has some very definite faults (though the poem overcomes these and succeeds in spite of its defects).

> Had Christianity not come to Britain and controlled the activity of its poets, we might have had a *Beowulf* with a heathen mythology, like the lays of the *Poetic Edda*. [...] It is a blemish on the Anglo-Saxon epic that the newly learned Christian piety crowded this out, not only because of the incongruity of representing the wilder heroes [...] swayed by the gentle precepts of the Church, but because this is on the whole so awkwardly done. The religion of the characters seems imposed upon them rather than natural to them.

> The poorest and weakest parts of the poem are to be found among the definitely Christian passages. The only thing that is naïve about the poem is its theology. Here is untried material, and a childlike attitude toward a new faith. Tradition had not yet taught the poet how to treat it with technical assurance. [...] The real vitality of the poem lies in its paganism.[34]

And if the *Beowulf* poet could be permitted to freely choose, reject, and reassemble, cobbling together a whole which succeeds at certain points and fails at others, why not Tolkien or Gaiman? Indeed, both authors dissect out — or at least attenuate — the explicitly Christian elements and place a greater emphasis on the stronger, more vital elements of paganism and the supernatural. How can they be faulted for seeking to right the wrongs — I might say re-*write* the wrongs — of the original?[35]

At the heart of both Tolkien's and Avary and Gaiman's adaptations and responses to *Beowulf* lie the monsters and other supernatural elements. As with the question of the legitimacy of adaptation, this too has authority in the original manuscript. The surviving manuscript[36] contains more than just *Beowulf* itself, promoting the primacy of the monsters. Preceding *Beowulf*, the codex contains three prose works which all deal with monsters: a homily on the life of a "dog-headed St. Christopher [,] twelve fathoms tall;" a description of the "Wonders of the East," with "dragons [...] a hundred and fifty feet long" and "monsters [...] so numerous and so varied that strangely tall men are among the lesser marvels;" and a "Letter of Alexander the Great to Aristotle," which describes "a great battle between men and water monsters, *nicras.*"[37] Indeed,

> *Beowulf* was perhaps esteemed and recopied in the Anglo-Saxon period for quite other reasons that those for which we prize it today. [The prose works] describe marvels fitly to be grouped with Grendel and his dam, with the dragon and water-monsters of *Beowulf*.[38]

Significantly, then, both Tolkien and Gaiman have each in his own way promoted a view of the poem that is more in keeping with its original context than the laity views the work today, and their attenuation of the religious elements and emphases on the monsters are perfectly appropriate. The Avary and Gaiman screenplay does *precisely* this — as does Tolkien's short story, "Sellic Spell," though we also have scattered examples of various kinds through his poetry and fiction.

Gaiman has said that "[t]he biggest motivation was creating a film that would be satisfying as a story. *Beowulf* is a remarkable, powerful story.

It's the oldest story in the English language that we have. But, it's always been considered incredibly problematic, from a literary and critical point of view [...]."[39] Avary and Gaiman then elaborate on this:

> AVARY: If you read it, keep in mind that it existed as an oral tradition for maybe 700 years before it was written down, and when the Christian monks put it down onto the document, they added their own flare to the storytelling, and they added their elements of Christianity to it. What we did was look at the existing translations and realized that there were hints and elements of the story [that were left out].
>
> GAIMAN: For example, when Beowulf goes off to fight Grendel's mother, he heads down into that lair, all on his own, disappears, is gone for eight days fighting her, and comes back with Grendel's head. Eight days is an awful long time to fight a monster, and why didn't he bring *her* head back? And so, we are actually very faithful to what happened. We're just implying that maybe there was other stuff that happened as well.

These are very legitimate questions. And while Gaiman and Avary are clearly interpolating, they are doing so with a solid foundation and perfectly reasonable intentions.

The dragon episode in *Beowulf* offers a lacuna of a similar nature. Stuart Lee and Elizabeth Solopova observe that "the narrative describing the treasure, its history, the dragon and the theft is cursory and leaves much to the imagination. The last survivor, for example, is a mysterious figure, and we know little about the dragon and even less about the fugitive who stole the cup." Such gaps, they note, "appeal to the imagination and may have inspired Tolkien to approach as a writer what puzzled him as a scholar."[40] We might make an analogous statement about Roger Avary and Neil Gaiman: that they were intrigued by the omissions and wished to read between the lines and recover explanatory elements they felt might have been omitted.

A Closing Word

The year after *Beowulf* came to the silver screen, Neil Gaiman wrote the introduction for a new edition of Bram Stoker's seminal vampire novel, *Dracula*. In it, he made several pronouncements which seem applicable to *Beowulf* and his attitude toward it. "I suspect," he writes, "that the reasons why *Dracula* lives on, why it succeeds as art, why it lends itself to annotation and to elaboration, are paradoxically because of its weaknesses as a novel," reasons which, *mutatis mutandis*, are just as pertinent to *Beowulf*. "*Dracula* is," like *Beowulf*,

> a book that forces the reader to fill in the blanks, to hypothesize, to imagine, to presume. [...] The story spiderwebs, and we begin to wonder what occurs in the interstices. [...] [Y]ou might find yourself, almost against your will, wondering about things in the crevices of the novel, things hinted at, things implied. And once you begin to wonder, it is only a matter of time before you will find yourself waking in the moonlight to find yourself writing novels or stories about the minor characters and offstage events [...].[41]

This is what Tolkien did, and this is what Gaiman has done again a half-century later. They are not the only authors to confront the critics and scholars, taking *Beowulf* in new directions, breathing new life into a work already more than a thousand years old, nor will they be the last. John Gardner's *Grendel*, Michael Crichton's *Eaters of the Dead*, and Parke Godwin's *The Tower of Beowulf* all play in the same space. While the 1981 film *Clash of the Titans* is given a scaffolding of Ancient Greek settings and mythology, its plot structure is clearly a calque on *Beowulf*: the hero faces three monstrous foes, with Calibos, Medusa, and the Kraken obvious analogues of Grendel, his mother, and the dragon.

There is something special about *Beowulf* that inspires adaptation, that makes authors and artists want to sub-create within that world. At the same time, the epic poem exhibits certain flaws and gaps that call out for correcting and for filling. It is apparent from their body of work—a body which is still growing through posthumous publications of Tolkien's earlier works, and through Gaiman's powerful and unabated imagination—that both authors have successfully stood up to the critics and brought readers new and existing treatments of the traditional Beowulf story, a story which, thanks to Tolkien and to Gaiman, remains both ancient and brand new.

---

1 Gummere, 4.
2 "During the 18th century, the Cotton manuscripts were moved for safekeeping to Ashburnham house at Westminster. On the night of 23 October 1731 a fire broke out, in which many of the manuscripts were damaged, and a few completely destroyed. *Beowulf* escaped the fire relatively intact [the edges of some pages scorched] but it suffered greater loss by handling in the following years, with letters crumbling away from the outer portions of its pages. Placed in paper frames in 1845, the manuscript remains incredibly fragile, and can be handled only with the utmost care." (British Library, "Beowulf").
3 (Tolkien, *Monsters*, 33). Tolkien delivered the Sir Israel Gollancz Memorial Lecture to the British Academy on November 25, 1936. That lecture, "*Beowulf*: The Monsters and the Critics," was subsequently published in Volume 22 of the *Proceedings of the British Academy* and has been reprinted many times. It has been called "the single most influential article ever written on *Beowulf* in the poem's 200-year critical history" (Drout, "Seventy-five Years Later", 6).

4 Temple, 428–9.
5 George Brewerton was "an energetic man [...], one of the few assistant masters at the school who specialized in the teaching of English literature. [...] Always a fierce teacher, he demanded that his pupils should use the plain old words of the English language. If a boy employed the term 'manure' Brewerton would roar out: 'Manure? Call it muck! Say it three times! *Muck, muck, muck!*'" (Carpenter, *Tolkien*, 27–8; italics original).
6 Carpenter, *Tolkien*, 35.
7 *Beowulf* and the language in which it is written are difficult for undergraduates, and nowadays even for graduate students. But in Tolkien's view, "Old English (or Anglo-Saxon) is not a very difficult language, though it is neglected [...]"; however, he admitted that "the idiom and diction of Old English verse is not easy" (Tolkien, *Monsters*, 51). This is perhaps an understatement, and one suspects that Lewis's approach might have found more success with the average college student.
8 Hooper, 749.
9 *Béorscipe* is an Old English word for a feast or revel. These events were a centerpiece in medieval English culture, as typified by the unflagging revels at Heorot in *Beowulf*. The first element in the word means "beer," which shows that the Anglo-Saxons had their priorities straight!
10 Scull and Hammond, 84–5.
11 Tolkien, *Monsters*, 14.
12 Scull and Hammond, 85–6.
13 For more, interested readers may consult Fisher, Bolintineanu, Christensen, among many other essays on the subject.
14 Tolkien, *Hobbit*, 228.
15 Tolkien, *Letters*, 31.
16 Tolkien, *Monsters*, 17.
17 Shippey, *Road*, 90.
18 Shippey, "Tolkien Society Annual Dinner" 15.
19 Gaiman and Avary, 5; italics original.
20 Gaiman and Avary, 5.
21 Gaiman and Avary, 10.
22 Gaiman and Avary, 10.
23 Gaiman, "Astonishingly".
24 Gaiman, *Mirrors*, 196.
25 Gaiman, *Mirrors*, 191.
26 Gaiman and Avary, 58 [screenplay pagination].
27 Gaiman and Avary, 87 [screenplay pagination].
28 (Sweet, 202). This theory has been joined by several others over the history of *Beowulf* scholarship, but it remains the most popular. Even if the etymology "bee-wolf" is correct, this might not be a kenning for bear after all, but rather woodpecker (see Skeat, 163).
29 Dr. Virago [pseudonym]. "A diminished Beowulf, a shrinking Grendel, a wussy Wealhtheow, and Grendel's MILF."
30 Ibid.
31 Nokes, Richard Scott. "Beowulf Movie Review."
32 Stanley, 105.
33 Gummere, 2–3.
34 Lawrence, 9.
35 At the same time, the *Beowulf* poet had a clear agenda to promote the new faith, while Gaiman clearly did not. Tolkien probably falls somewhere in between. The goals of the *Beowulf* poet are clear, and while some may consider them to be artistic faults, they should not be regarded as *thematic* ones. "When early scholars traced the mythological parallels of *Beowulf*, they did not reckon with the mind of a poet well-versed in Christian apologetic techniques against the pagans, deliberately using, and diminishing the stature of, older myths for his Christian didactic purposes; an imaginative explorer who obliterated most of the tracks of his journey; an ingenious craftsman creating from strangely assorted stones of native tradition a mosaic of symbolic design. Yet the assumption of such a mind, and such a context, would do much to explain the enigmas of *Beowulf*." (Dronke, 325). Moreover: "[a]lthough the Christian veneer seems the least admirable part of the poem, from a literary point of view, it may, by a curious irony, have saved the whole from destruction, in days when many a bonfire of old manuscripts

was lit for the faith" (Lawrence, 15).

36 *Beowulf* is part of the Nowell Codex (named for Laurence Nowell, Dean of Litchfield, died 1576, the first known owner of the manuscript). The Nowell Codex is itself one of two manuscripts bound together in Codex Vitellius, A, xv, part of the famous Cotton Library, now a part the British Library. *Beowulf* is the next to last work in its codex.

37 Stanley, 105–6.
38 Lawrence, 14.
39 Roberts, "Cast of Beowulf Interview".
40 Lee and Solopova, 109.
41 Stoker, xvi–iii.

The Problem with Bod:
Examining the Evolution of Neil Gaiman's Response to C.S. Lewis's *The Last Battle* in "The Problem of Susan" and *The Graveyard Book*

Chelsey Kendig

As children's books, *The Chronicles of Narnia* and Neil Gaiman's *The Graveyard Book* partake of literary traditions that are as old as the art of storytelling itself."[1] The stories most deeply embedded in Western Culture are those that were told to children: Bible stories, Greek myths, and fairy tales. In *Children's Literature: A Reader's History from Aesop to Harry Potter,* Seth Lerer documents the ways in which Greek and Roman children were taught using the texts of Homer and Virgil. Children of the American Revolution toted hornbooks featuring Bible quotes, and scholar Jack Zipes has put endless time and energy into examining the ways in which fairy tales were manipulated to have the most didactic power.

Gaiman seems to be very aware of the power of children's books. In his short story "The Problem of Susan," the main character is a professor of children's literature, and she comments on this phenomenon, when she discusses "the Victorian notion of the purity and sanctity of childhood [which] demanded that fiction for children should be made…well…pure…and sanctimonious."[2] This observation is important, because this story is focused on exploring the issues in C.S. Lewis's *The Chronicles of Narnia*, and through it Gaiman illustrates that Lewis's beliefs seem to be similar to the Victorians. Gaiman himself has said he believes in the "remarkable power of children's literature."[3] *The Chronicles of Narnia* certainly seem to have had power, or at least influence, over Gaiman.

Everywhere in literature, but perhaps most pronouncedly in children's literature, there is a visible progression from era to era. The popular books of the previous generation are passed down and influence the writing of the next generation of authors. In the way that Elizabethan children studied Roman classics, and then as adults alluded to these classics in their writings, so do today's children read authors such as Tolkien and C.S. Lewis. These works become, in a way, modern myth—referenced explicitly and implicitly by later authors. Neil Gaiman noted he read *The Chronicles of Narnia* hundreds of times as a boy, and then "aloud as an adult, twice, to my children,"[4] and "there is so much in these books I love."[5]

His works show this familiarity and this love, but they also question *The Chronicles of Narnia*—questions that lead to the next addition to the myths that build cultural conscious.

The Narnia tales are centered on the four Pevensie siblings who discover another world in the back of a magical wardrobe found in a relative's country house. Peter, Susan, Edmund, and Lucy are not the only ones to have adventures in Narnia, but they are the central figures of the seven tales, and known as High Kings and Queens of Narnia. Lewis's tales are, on the surface, moralistic adventure books that headed the trend of children's fantasy for years afterward—but they also rely heavily on Christian allegory, which Gaiman and other critics frequently take issue with. This is particularly important in the final book of the series, *The Last Battle*, where all the High Kings and Queens of Narnia are admitted back into the magical world—which symbolizes heaven—after they die in the real world—all except Susan. The designation of *The Chronicles of Narnia* as modern myth can be seen in the way readers, particularly Gaiman, question Susan's expulsion from heaven. First, critics such as David Downing and Laura Miller attempted to explain Susan's exile with what is known about her in the books, and about Lewis in the writing of them, but this leads to further complications. Then comes "The Problem of Susan" wherein Gaiman creates a fix—a story of sorts, one that highlights the problems of Susan's exile within the world of *The Chronicles* and within the "real world." These explicit examinations aren't enough, though. In the way that the Romans adapted Greek myth to incorporate their own beliefs and worldviews, and in the way that the New Testament adapts for a changed world, *The Graveyard Book* is a children's book aimed at a contemporary audience that serves to solve—whether done intentionally or not—the problem of Susan.

Before one can understand the way this is done, one must understand what the problem of Susan is and the depths of the attempts that have been made to solve it.

Before delving into the depths of Lewis's controversial decision to ban Susan from Narnia, I will first acknowledge that in a letter to a reader dated 22 January 1957 he says that:

> ....the books don't tell us what happens to Susan. She is left alive in this world at the end, having by then turned into a rather silly, conceited young woman, but there is plenty of time for her to mend and perhaps she will get to Aslan's country in the end in her own way.[6]

He qualifies this, saying, "I think that whatever she had seen in Narnia she *could* (if she was the sort that wanted to) persuade herself, as she grew up, that it was all nonsense."[7] This quote illustrates what Lewis *believes* he is doing by keeping Susan out of Narnia. Lewis is punishing her for not "learn[ing] to know [Aslan] by that name"— meaning Jesus, which was "the reason why you were brought to Narnia that by knowing me here for a little you may know me better there."[8] Thus, one assumes that the way to be exiled from Aslan's country at the end of the book would be to prove unfaithful during the time in the other world. What causes Gaiman and other scholars to question this is that Lewis is not consistent enough with his characterization of Susan for this insistence upon her lack of faith to be supported.

David C. Downing in *Into the Wardrobe: CS Lewis in the Narnia Chronicles* believes that at the end of *The Last Battle*, "Lewis took the Christian doctrine of salvation and applied it to each person's spiritual journey as a whole."[9] Does he do so with Susan? Certainly, Susan is shown to be the most doubting character in the books. Upon first entering Narnia she says, "I—I wonder if there is any point going on. I wish we'd never come," but she quickly adds, "but I think we must do something for Mr. Whatever-His-Name-Is—I mean the faun,"[10] showing her willingness to adapt her thinking. In *Prince Caspian*, she also has a moment of doubt wherein she "really believed it was him—he I mean—yesterday, and I really believed it was him tonight when you woke us up. I mean, deep down inside. Or I could have, if I'd let myself."[11] This admission reveals much about Susan's desire to be certain, her attention to exactness in her correction of her grammar, and her willingness to listen to doubt and fear.

However, these doubts are *part* of her overall journey, and she is forgiven for them. Immediately after she admits them Aslan says: "come let me breathe on you. Forget [your fears]. Are you brave now?"[12] Downing believes that in doing this, "Aslan expresses his spirit in breathing upon his creatures,"[13] thus after this moment Susan is given strength from the Holy Spirit. Is this redemption still not enough for Lewis? Even when he admits to a reader in a letter dated 27 April 1956—the same year *The Last Battle* was released—that "people do find it hard to keep on feeling as if you believed in the next life, but then it is just as hard to keep on feeling as if you believed you were going to be nothing after your death. I know this because in the days before I was a Christian I used to try."[14] Did he think Susan was falling victim to this difficulty? That her doubts were strong enough to undermine the power of Aslan's spirit and her own willingness to accept Aslan? Perhaps. And perhaps he set out to do this from the start. When Susan first hears the name Aslan she "felt as though some delicious smell or some delightful strain of music had just floated by her,"[15] implying that she's set up not to completely grasp Aslan, but always have him floating by her.

But Susan's lack of faith and willingness to doubt do not emerge in the conversation wherein the Kings and Queens of Narnia discuss Susan's exclusion from Narnia.

"My sister Susan," answered Peter shortly and gravely, "Is no longer a friend of Narnia."

"Yes," said Eustace "and whenever you've tried to get her to come and talk about Narnia she says 'What wonderful memories you have! Fancy your still thinking about all those games we used to play as children.'"

"Oh Susan!" said Jill. "She's interested in nothing nowadays except nylons and lipsticks and invitations. She was always a jolly sight too keen on being grown up."

"Grown up indeed!" said Lady Polly. "I wish she would grow-up. She wasted all her school time wanting to be the age she is now and she'll waste all the rest of her life trying to stay that age. Her whole idea is to race on to the silliest time of one's life as quick as she can and then stop there as long as she can."

"Well, don't let's talk about that now," said Peter. "Look! Here are some lovely fruit trees..."[16]

Eustace does point out that Susan no longer believes in Narnia, but it is not tied to a lack of faith, but rather to a different transgression—the desire to "grow up." Not only has this desire been established in Narnian canon,[17] but it deviates wildly from the established idea that Aslan's Country is an allegory for Heaven. It is never acknowledged that the other Pevensies were particularly religious in the real world, except for Lucy's statement that "In our world too, a stable once held something in it that was bigger than the whole world."[18] It is assumed that they are, and if this passage had been omitted it might have been assumed that Susan was not faithful to God, and this was why she was excluded from Narnia. But Lewis chose to include this passage, and he chose to write the rest of the novels allegorically, and so the disparity remains, which eventually led to the idea for Neil Gaiman's short story "The Problem of Susan."

Feminist critic Laura Miller comments on Susan's damnation in her book *The Magician's Book: A Skeptic's Adventures in Narnia*. Like Neil Gaiman, she read and loved *The Chronicles of Narnia* as a child, but encountered difficulties with them once she'd grown up. She says, "I *wanted* to grow up didn't I? As a child I'd always thought Lewis was on my side in that, as a young adult I realized he'd disappointed me."[19] Miller focuses on Lewis's purportedly anti-female line, summarizing his attitude toward Susan's plight as "if she keeps on as she has been, preoccupied with feminine nonsense, this alone will be enough to bring her to a bad end."[20] After an interview with Neil Gaiman she states that "[Gaiman] maintains [that] there was a level on which, of course [Susan] doesn't get to heaven because she's just like the witches, and they wear dresses and they're pretty,"[21] suggesting that Lewis is anti-female. Certainly, many of his villains are beautiful women—the witches mentioned in Gaiman's quote. On the other hand, during the third novel in the *Chronicles*, *The Horse and His Boy*, Susan is described as being "the most beautiful woman he had ever seen" by Shasta, the main character, and there are no negative implications tied to this. Gaiman, too, seems to realize this, or at least move past this explanation for Lewis's damnation of Susan, because vanity is a small issue in "The Problem of Susan."

Lewis's letters suggest his prejudice isn't necessarily toward women or the idea of beauty. It's toward adolescence — or at least the idealization of adolescence in society. This bias emerges several times in his letters, most often in his correspondence with a nameless American woman whom he'd never met, but to whom he wrote regularly. In a letter dated August 1, 1953 Lewis writes:

> Yes, I think there is lots to be said for no longer being young...it is just as well to be past the age at which one expects or desires to attract the opposite sex. It's natural enough in our species, as in others, that the young birds should show off their plumage—in the mating season. But the trouble is that there's a tendency to rush all the birds on to that age as soon as possible and then keep them there as late as possible, this the real value of the *other* parts of life in a senseless, pitiful attempt to prolong what, after all, is neither its wisest, its happiest, or its most innocent period.[22]

This reasoning is almost the exact sentiment he has Polly express about Susan, although Polly's statement lacks the sympathetic admission that flashy behavior is allowed "in the mating season." It's impossible to say definitively why Lewis became so steadfast in this view in the three years separating the letter from *The Last Battle*, but perhaps had to do with a realization that his readers were approaching the period of life he so disliked. In 1962 a child with whom he'd often exchanged correspondence informed him of her choice of college, and he says, "I should however have thought you could have found what you wanted nearer home."[23]

Lewis shows disdain for the adventuresome nature of adolescence —fine, apparently for children— and the message he obviously felt he needed to impart. Miller says "Lewis remarked that asking yourself 'what do modern children need?' can never produce a good story,"[24] but he wished to impart to modern children the idea that adolescent desires were to be frowned upon, and he didn't care that he contradicted the nature of the character he'd created to do so.

In *The Last Battle,* Aslan assures Lucy that:

> ...there was a real railway accident...your father and mother and all of you are—as you used to call it in the Shadowlands—dead. The term is over and the holidays have begun. The dream is ended. This is the morning.[25]

This gels with Lewis's belief that "there is nothing discreditable in dying,"[26] but does not acknowledge the brutality of the death and the effect on the one left behind. It is this oversight that Gaiman latches on to in "The Problem of Susan."

The story is superficially that of an aged children's literature professor who is interviewed by a young journalist on the night before her death. The professor's first name is never given, but she is Susan, truly all-grown-up. Her profession allows for a meta-examination of *The Chronicles of Narnia*. The young interviewer sums up the issue with Susan's treatment: "All the other kids go off to Paradise and Susan can't go. She's no longer a Friend of Narnia because she's too fond of lipsticks and nylons and invitations to parties,"[27] the incongruous explanation—both religious and anti-feminist:

> [S]he still had time while she lived to repent...not believing, and the sin of Eve...there must have been something else wrong with Susan...otherwise she wouldn't have been damned like that—denied the heaven of further up and further in. I mean, all the people she had ever cared for had gone on to their reward in a world of magic, and waterfalls, and joy. And she was left behind.[28]

In a way, this character represents Laura Miller, the young woman who has become disillusioned by Narnia. However, the old professor represents the far deeper truths of Susan being denied heaven.

"She was available to identify her brothers' and her little sister's bodies,"[29] Susan says, and makes the point that "I doubt there was much opportunity for nylons and lipsticks after her family was killed. There certainly wasn't for me. A little money—less than one might imagine—

from her parents' estate to lodge and feed her. No luxuries."[30]

Did Lewis think of this? Considering his disdain for hedonism, would he have considered the simple life a punishment, or a form of lesson teaching? Either way, it makes the actuality of what the *Last Battle* implies even darker, especially when Gaiman further illustrates the professor remembering "I was taken to a nearby school—it was the first day of term,"[31] which harkens back to Aslan's metaphor about term being over for the Friends of Narnia. For Susan, it would have just begun, and started with this memory of her dead brothers and sister. Was she supposed to be forced into fate by the hope that she would have "seen their bodies, and thought, they're on holiday now?"[32] This would be unlikely for a doubtful, reasonable girl. Gaiman predicts her belief manifesting itself more likely in the thought that, "A god who would punish me for liking nylons and parties by making me walk through that school dining room, with the flies, to identify Ed, well...he's enjoying himself a bit too much isn't he? Like a cat getting the last ounce of enjoyment out of a mouse."[33] This highlights the absurdity of transposing the tenants of a land where the Son-of-God is a lion into the "real world."

Through this statement, Gaiman highlights the two flaws in Lewis's scenario. Not only does leaving Susan with the loss of her entire family make her less inclined to have faith in the Aslan-of-another-name in her world, it also shows the differences between the real world and Narnia. In Lewis's Narnia, obviously created for children, you do not see the consequences of the brutalities, which Gaiman points out when he depicts Susan's dream of "standing...on the edge of the battlefield... her eyes flick to the cut throat, and the sticky red-black pool that surrounds it, and she shivers."[34] In Narnia these consequences do not seem to exist, and yet Lewis affects the real world with a train crash that kills not only the Friends of Narnia, but presumably the others that were on the train.

Gaiman's mastery of Susan's character and thus his ability to speak on the subject is shown in the next part of the conversation wherein the professor corrects herself, realizing that the correct term would be a gram of enjoyment, rather than an ounce. She corrects herself in the same way Susan did in *The Last Battle*. A similar detail is shown when the professor notes that:

> She smells like her grandmother smelled, like old women smell and for this she cannot forgive herself, so on waking she bathes in scented water and naked and towel dried dabs several drops of Chanel toilet water beneath her arms and neck. It is, she believes, her sole extravagance.[35]

Thus in no way does he deny the claims Lewis makes about Susan. She doesn't want to get old, to reach the age Lewis puts on a pedestal. She is somewhat vain. However, Gaiman's presentation of her beliefs suggests that the truth of what Lewis is objecting to could be said to be—and Miller believes it is—sexuality. Sexuality is objectionable in a Christian worldview, but the children's novel does not allow for the full exploration of this sin, and so Lewis's objections to "lipsticks and invitations" seem petty.

In the format of Gaiman's story, a view of Narnia from the "real world," Gaiman illuminates the problems with Lewis's punishment of Susan for her form of being "grown up." The scenario that Gaiman describes seems far too innocuous to be punishable by exclusion from Paradise, except for actually being sexual, which Lewis does not even allude to. Of Susan's youth Gaiman says:

> ...she had spent an evening once, kissing him, in a summerhouse.... It was, she decides, Charles and Nadia Reid's house in the country. Which meant that it was before Nadia went away with the Scottish artist and Charles took the professor with him to Spain....This was many years before people commonly went to Spain for their holidays; it was an exotic and dangerous place in those days...and he took what was left of her virginity on a blanket on a Spanish beach....She was twenty years old, and had thought herself so old.[36]

Here Gaiman highlights the transitory nature of what Susan is being punished for. It is particularly necessary to remember that Susan has a history of seeing her own lack of faith and correcting it, as she does in *Prince Caspian*, as Gaiman seems to do. Lewis seems to forget Susan's ability to come back to her faith after questioning it. He states in a letter that "she *could* (if she was the sort that wanted to) persuade herself as she grew up that it was all nonsense."[37] Perhaps he is merely determined to condemn Susan's period of silliness, as Gaiman seems to think.

Gaiman picks up on the threads of faith that Lewis drops and at least acknowledges that they are a part of Susan's story. When Greta, the student, mentions that she discussed the leaving-behind of Susan with her English teacher, the teacher said "[Susan] still had time while she lived to repent...Not believing, I suppose. And the sin of Eve."[38] This explanation seems to fit more with the explanation that makes more sense within the Christian doctrine that weaves itself in and out of the tale of Narnia. Certainly lack of faith is a reason for not being allowed into Heaven, and Susan is said to have denied Narnia. It also makes more sense with Lewis' assertion that Susan could convince herself that it was all nonsense, merely because she could keep not believing whether or not she was 'silly.' Indeed, to have her family torn away from her in the way that they were would, to most, be a satisfactory reason for not believing. The true problem of Susan is that Lewis does not emphasize this.

Susan's punishment and the fairness thereof is only one aspect of *The Chronicles of Narnia* explored in Gaiman's short story. He examines the "remarkable power of children's literature...."[39] Although Gaiman obviously respects children's literature, "The Problem of Susan" does suggest a certain contempt of the idea that it should be used to teach any sort of religious lesson. In a dream, assumedly after her death, the professor reads an "unpublished" Mary Poppins novel wherein "Jane and Michael follow Mary Poppins on her day off, to Heaven. They meet the boy Jesus, who is still slightly scared of Mary Poppins, because she was his nanny....'There's no making her do anything, not her. She's Mary Poppins....Not her' said God the Father....I didn't create her. She's Mary Poppins."[40] There is much to be gathered from this passage. First, there's the somewhat laughable and flawed God who does not have power over this staple character of children's literature. This idea emphasizes the dangers of explicitly embedding religion into children's books. The idea, though, that Jesus might be afraid of Mary Poppins is something to note. Is it possible that ideas in children's stories embed themselves as deeply into their readers as religious doctrine might?

Lewis may have thought so; he designed his stories to be a primer, of sorts, to Christian faith, going so far as to assert to a reader's mother that her son's belief in Aslan was in its way a belief in Jesus.[41] Gaiman himself was so moved by a book read in childhood that he crafted this story in response. And even if one sees "The Problem of Susan" as more literary response than sparked by embedded belief, I contend that children's stories such as *The Chronicles of Narnia* are able to become part of the mythos, and did so particularly in the case of Neil Gaiman. After all, a few years after publishing "The Problem of Susan," Gaiman penned *The Graveyard Book*, a novel that builds upon questions asked and themes introduced in *The Chronicles of Narnia,* and has the potential to stand under the umbrella of modern myth.

I do not seek to claim that Gaiman asked himself "suppose there was a boy who lived in a graveyard, and suppose he solved the problem of Susan being exiled from Narnia" the way Lewis claims he created *The Chronicles of Narnia—that is,* by saying he thought "let us suppose that there were a land like Narnia and that the Son of God, as He became a man in our world, became a lion there."[42] In fact, to do so would be to negate both books' placement in the evolutionary ladder of myth. Rather, the themes of *The Chronicles of Narnia* have become so important to Gaiman, whether consciously or unconsciously, that *The Graveyard Book* responds to them.

In the novel, Nobody "Bod" Owens is a young boy who, not unlike Susan, has lost his entire family. In this case, however, he is the one to gain entrance to a "magical" land when the denizens of the local graveyard save him from his family's murderer. They grant him "the Freedom of the Graveyard,"[43] meaning he has the ability to fade, to enter graves, and most importantly to see ghosts. He is raised by Mr. and Mrs. Owens, a ghostly couple who never had children of their own. Bod has numerous adventures in the graveyard, climaxing in his triumph over the man who killed his family.[44]

One of the main themes in the novel, similar to one of Lewis's stated beliefs that may or may not have been transferred to *The Chronicles of Narnia*, is that death is not something to be feared. Rather, it is to be respected. The dead live on, either as the graveyard's specters or in memory as Bod's family does. Death herself is personified as the "Lady on the Grey,"[45] which highlights the fact that death is neither ultimately good nor bad, neither black nor white. It just is. And though Bod does voice a desire to ride the horse (presumably to die and/or stay in the graveyard) he is promised that he will ride her one day. There are no caveats to this; nothing required of him. Death is an equalizer. In the lullaby Bod's mother sings to him before he leaves the graveyard, she entreats him to "Kiss a lover/Dance a measure/Find your name/and buried treasure" and also "face your life/ its pain its pleasure/leave no path untaken,"[46] quite a contrast from Aslan who tells his followers only to have faith while they are gone, so they might return. Here is the essential theme of living life to the fullest rather than ending it to stay somewhere comfortable.

In fact, the two characters who have died young, the witch Liza Hempstock and the boy Thackery Porringer, have unfinished business and rather unpleasant personalities. Bod solves Liza's problem for her by making her a headstone, but it is still obvious from her interest (perhaps romantically) in Bod that she did not have a complete life. Thackery is exaggeratedly attached to the copy of *Robinson Crusoe,* which he was buried with,[47] showing a desire for adventure he never got to fulfill.[48] Thus, Gaiman does away with the romantic notion of children dying early to access the magical land (graveyard).

Moreover, in the last lines of the novel there is a huge contrast to the end of Narnia. Lewis ends *The Last Battle* with the assertion that:

> All their life in the world and all their adventures in Narnia had only been the cover and the title page. Now at least they were beginning chapter one of the Great Story which no one on earth has read, which goes on forever, in which every chapter is better than the one before."[49]

This quote emphasizes the importance of the afterlife, the return to the magical land, and belittles the life, howsoever short, the children have led in "The Shadowlands." It allows Lewis to be disdainful of the adolescence his readers are approaching in favor of his old age, where one is approaching this theoretical "great story."

The tone of this passage is reflected at the end of *The Graveyard Book*. Bod goes through the gates of the cemetery with:

> [A] passport in his bag, money in his pocket. There was a smile dancing on his lips, although it was a wary smile, for the world is a bigger place than a little graveyard on a hill, and there would be dangers in it and mysteries, new friends to make, old friends to rediscover, mistakes to be made and many paths to be walked before he would, finally, return to the graveyard or ride with the Lady on the back of her great grey stallion.
>
> But between now and then, there was Life, and Bod walked into it with his eyes and his heart wide open.[50]

Bod's journey more closely resembles that of Gaiman's Susan than Lewis's heroes, and also more realistically reflects the life of a potential reader. Bod will live life, make mistakes, have adventures. Nowhere does Gaiman suggest disdain for the idea of growing up, for the adventuresome nature of Bod's impending adolescence, nor does he so much as suggest that Bod could do something which would deny him reentry into his home.

The parallels between the endings speak to the way in which the *Chronicles* have become etched into the mind of the next generation. Whether or not Gaiman intended Bod's journey to be a response to Lewis, or a solution to the problem of Susan (and I prefer to think that he didn't), it speaks to the power of a work that engenders such a response from readers years after they were part of the intended audience. Lewis is a part of the children's literature mythos, and more than being a part of the canon for an author who sets out to write a fantasy for children, it is, in its own right, a form of the Greek myth drawn upon by Joyce and the Roman archetypes drawn on by Shakespeare. It is modern myth.

Lewis wanted Narnia to be "a 'fairy tale' because he had something to say that could only be expressed in this way. He didn't offer much detail as to what that something was.[51] Although the "something" he wanted to express probably refers to the allegory that has caused such controversy, the designation of "fairy tale" is, in fact, the most accurate way of describing the way in which *The Chronicles of Narnia* fit the designation of modern myth, especially in terms of Neil Gaiman's reaction to them. There have been many, many after-the-happily-ever-after short stories explaining away elements of fairy tales that become problems as time passes. Then thematic and structural pieces of the fairy tales are recycled in other works, well-woven, but still recognizable.

Of course, Lewis was in turn adapting older stories to a modern world. The world changed so drastically in the early part of the twentieth century when Lewis was writing, as reflected in his setting the first Narnia story in World War II. Writers and readers alike were searching for a way to explain the modern world, wherein machines had torn up the countryside and man had been killing man almost non-stop for forty years. For Lewis, the answer was to highlight the myths that came before, but to cushion them in idealizing what was lost—a love for nature and animals—to try to slow down the changes. Gaiman's generation was the one who devoured these books, trying to make sense of the changes that had been made, of the world as their ancestors saw it, a world that was not as different as the modern from the ancients, but incredibly changed nonetheless. Maybe this is how Lewis became part of modern myth so quickly, because this generation had little else to draw on to explain the world.

The world is still moving incredibly quickly. At least one member of the generation that latched onto *The Chronicles of Narnia* has questioned it and created the next fairy-tale, one that incorporates more contemporary beliefs. What once took thousands of years to create, question, alter, and embed is taking a single generation. One wonders what will come next in line, what questions *The Graveyard Book* will raise with readers, and how they will examine Neil Gaiman as a result.

Gaiman is known for his investigations into the power of mythical figures in adult works such as *American Gods*. One wonders if, in the future, his less explicit explorations will be the ones remembered. C.S. Lewis is most well-remembered for *The Chronicles of Narnia*, even though in his time he was celebrated for being a writer of Christian thought. Will *The Graveyard Book* be what Gaiman is known for? Perhaps. Like the Chronicles, Bod's story is a children's book, which draws heavily on myths that came before and changes them to reflect the author's thoughts (intentionally and unintentionally). On the back of the U.K. hardcover edition of *The Graveyard Book*, the late Diana Wynne Jones's blurb asserts that *The Graveyard Book* is "the best book Neil Gaiman has ever written." This is, of course, a matter of opinion, but the book's popularity and the accolades it has received, as well as relation to its canonical forebears, puts it in a better position to become part of modern myth, and therefore be remembered as such.

1 Miller, 8.
2 Gaiman, *Mirrors*, 246.
3 Gaiman, Introduction to *The Sandman: Endless Nights*, xxv.
4 Ibid.
5 Ibid.
6 Lewis, *Letters to Children*, 67.
7 Ibid.
8 Lewis, *The Dawn Treader*, 270. This instruction was given to Lucy and Edmund, but I believe it's safe to assume Aslan said much the same thing when he spoke to Peter and Susan at the end of *Prince Caspian* judging by Peter's assertion that it's "all rather different than I thought" (Lewis, *Caspian*, 236).
9 Downing, 83.
10 Lewis, *The Lion, The Witch and the Wardrobe*, 65.
11 Lewis, *Prince Caspian*, 161.
12 Lewis, *Prince Caspian*, 162.
13 Downing, 71.
14 Lewis, *Letters to Children*, 61.
15 Lewis, *The Lion, The Witch and the Wardrobe*, 74.
16 Lewis, *The Last Battle*, 169.
17 With the possible exceptions of Susan's correcting of her own grammar, her observation is that she'd never heard a grown-up "talk like the professor and didn't know what to think" (Lewis, *The Lion, The Witch and the Wardrobe*, 52). When he speaks of Narnia and the fact that in *The Horse and His Boy* she is a grown-up having to deal with royal suitors and not considered silly. Indeed, perhaps her longing for adulthood could be seen as a chance to return to this Golden Age of Narnia, though Lewis doesn't acknowledge it.
18 Lewis, *The Last Battle*, 177.
19 Miller, 142.
20 Miller, 162.
21 Miller, 130.
22 Lewis, *Letters to an American Lady*, 19.
23 Lewis, *Letters to Children*, 106.
24 Miller, 65.
25 Lewis, *The Last Battle*, 228.
26 Lewis, *Letters to an American Lady*, 67.
27 Gaiman, *Mirrors*, 245.
28 Ibid.
29 Ibid.
30 Ibid.
31 Ibid.
32 Gaiman, *Mirrors*, 244.
33 Gaiman, *Mirrors*, 246.
34 Gaiman, *Mirrors*, 236.
35 Gaiman, *Mirrors*, 240.
36 Ibid.
37 See note 8.
38 See note 29.
39 See note 3.
40 Gaiman, *Mirrors*, 248.
41 Lewis, *Letters to Children*, 53.
42 Lewis, *Letters to Children*, 45.
43 Gaiman, *Graveyard*, 31.
44 Interestingly, this man is called "Jack Frost," making winter a villain in this book similar to the way it is in Narnia with The White Witch.
45 Gaiman, *Graveyard*, 160.
46 Gaiman, *Graveyard*, 306.
47 (Gaiman, *Graveyard*, 174) —a nod to an early, influential, children's book?

48 Thackery Porringer could not read; however, whether his focus on the novel represents the unattained goal of literacy, or the impossibility of Thackery adventuring the way Crusoe did, it still shows the limitations he now faces. The extreme popularity of *Robinson Crusoe*, itself part of the children's literature mythos, makes me believe he would have had an idea of the adventure within the book, and feeds his desperation to possess it.
49 Lewis, *The Last Battle*, 228.
50 Gaiman, *Graveyard*, 307.
51 Miller, 9.

Ravens, Librarians, and Beautiful Ladies: Bakhtinian Dialogueism in the Gothic Mythology of Neil Gaiman and George MacDonald

Melody Green

The similarities between the work of the contemporary fantasist Neil Gaiman and the Victorian novelist and Pastor George MacDonald are at times quite striking. Writing roughly 100 years after MacDonald, Gaiman uses some of the same mythological images, characters, and motifs to explore the same questions that MacDonald did. In some places, these two writers bring their readers to very similar conclusions, while in others, differences are sharply drawn. These similarities involve images and beliefs surrounding death, the nature of evil, and the possibility of forgiveness. One of the most striking of these similarities is the anthropomorphization of death as a beautiful woman, while another is the particular way that both use images of ravens, libraries, and the Lilith story along with Adam and Eve to explore issues relating to the meaning of life and the nature of both evil and forgiveness.

While he is not read frequently today, MacDonald has often been called the founder of the fantasy genre. In his essay "Fantasy," C. W. Sullivan argues that George MacDonald was the first fantasy writer to not simply retell older stories, but to use images, motifs, and other aspects of ancient tales to create new stories of his own.[1] Sullivan argues that MacDonald's stories therefore shaped the fantasy genre that followed it.[2] In her article "Cosmic and Psychological Redemption in George MacDonald's *Lilith*," Bonnie Gaarden claims that MacDonald "wrote the first fantasy novels for adults in English."[3] More importantly, G. K. Chesterton, C. S. Lewis, and J. R. R. Tolkien, who have also been credited with shaping the fantasy genre as it is known today, all acknowledge in various places that MacDonald influenced their writings in one form or another.[4] The similarities between MacDonald and Gaiman could possibly be simply a matter of inheritance. In his Guest of Honor speech at Mythcon 35, Neil Gaiman, acknowledged the influence that Tolkien, Lewis, and Chesterton have had on his own work.[5] One could talk about the influence of MacDonald on Gaiman simply because MacDonald influenced people who in turn influenced Gaiman, but the similarities between the works of MacDonald and Gaiman are much more striking than those of MacDonald and any of these other three. For the purpose of this discussion, Russian literary critic Mikhail Bakhtin's concept of the dialogic nature of literature may shed light on the implications of the similarities between the works of these two writers. In multiple texts, most notably in *The Dialogic Imagination*, Bakhtin claims that every literary production, whether a novel, a poem, or any other genre, exists in dialogue with writings that had been created earlier. Each text, he argues, is a commentary on, response to, or continuation of texts and stories that came before it. Therefore, reading a contemporary text and an older text that deal with similar issues or concepts changes the way that the reader understands both. Read in this light, Neil Gaiman's use of mythological images and ideas in his fiction can be seen as existing in dialogue with the gothic fantasies of George MacDonald. Both, in turn, can be viewed as existing in dialogue with specific stories that lend motifs, concepts, and even specific characters to their writings.

While both MacDonald and Gaiman are clearly working in dialogue with specific myths, their shared approach to a concept that is quite important in every mythological system is a vital starting point. Both authors have written stories involving an anthropomorphic Death. Examples of living, breathing symbols of death can be found throughout mythology, including the Greek god Hades and the Norse goddess Hel, both of whom rule over the land of the dead in their own mythological systems. Another example would be from Jewish Midrash tradition, where the personification of death is an angel named Azrael. These mythological anthropomorphisms often have beautiful aspects, but they can also be quite disturbing. Both MacDonald and Gaiman work toward eliminating the disturbing part of death, to present visions of death that are calm, orderly, and playful. MacDonald's *At the Back of the North Wind*, as well as Gaiman's *Sandman* series and *The Graveyard Book*, portray Death as a beautiful woman. Instead of being distant goddesses, these versions of Death actually meet and talk to individuals, and can be friendly, kind and even, at times, fun.

Of these, Gaiman's *The Graveyard Book* presents the most traditional image of Death. This Death often appears on a grey horse; at one point she and her horse ride across the sky, creating a striking image for those who witness it.[6] Images of Death arriving on a horse occur in multiple mythologies, both Pagan and Christian. Her horse, however, is the most traditional thing about her. The Lady on the Grey has a laugh that is described as "the chiming of a hundred tiny silver bells."[7] At another point, she dances with the boy Bod, and tells him that someday, he will ride with her on her horse, in the way one promises a special treat to a child.[8]

Like Bod in *The Graveyard Book,* the little boy Diamond in George MacDonald's *At the Back of the North Wind* also spends time with Death. This stranger is, when he first meets her, little more than a voice outside of his wall that sounds both playful and plaintive. Their first conversation has a touch of humor, since Diamond mistakenly calls her "Mr. North Wind," and it takes him a few moments to realize why she teasingly finds that offensive. Throughout the text she is both funny and playful, but she has a morbid job and has already begun to do her work on the child. As the Lady on the Grey in *The Graveyard Book* does with Bod, this woman Diamond calls "North Wind" talks to Diamond about the future. Unlike the Lady on the Grey, however, she begins to take the child on trips with her. After each trip he is a little sicker, a little weaker. But Diamond does not quite understand who his friend is, not even when at one point she leaves him behind because she must go sink a ship. While she never tells him her exact name, many hints are dropped to help readers discover it for themselves. She calls herself Diamond's friend, but warns him that he, like most people, does not understand her real identity:

> People call me by dreadful names, and think they know all about me. But they don't. Sometimes they call me Bad Fortune, sometimes Evil Chance, and sometimes Ruin; and they have another name for me which they think the most dreadful of all.[9]

That name the reader is left to guess. But after she sinks ships and gives children fatal diseases, it becomes clear that her other name is Death. This Death can change sizes and shapes, but in Diamond's mind, his friend is always beautiful. At one point, he reflects: "The face of the North Wind was so grand! To have a lady like that for a friend— with such long hair, too!"[10] Even though the little boy eventually dies in the story, his death is presented as a gentle thing. Sad, yes, but not fearful or terrifying because Diamond has simply left with a friend he knows well.

MacDonald's North Wind also has much in common with Death of the Endless in Gaiman's *Sandman* series. Both are supernatural beings, deathless themselves, and beautiful. Whereas MacDonald's readers first meet North Wind in a playful mood, teasing the little boy Diamond about what he should call her and what he should call the hole in his wall (she insists that it is not a hole, but a window that she can use to look at him through), Death first appears in *The Sandman* series as a perky teenage Goth girl who tries to get her younger brother, Dream, to laugh by telling him a joke from the movie *Mary Poppins,* then continues to use words like "Peachy Keen," "cute," and "fantabulous."[11] After this cheery introduction, she takes her brother with her as she goes to work just as North Wind takes

Diamond. Dream watches his older sister apologize to some of the people she takes, observes her talking kindly to others while he talks her job over with her, and finds his sister describing one as "sweet."[12] Just as Diamond thought North Wind was beautiful, many find this humanized Death beautiful as well. For example, when a teenage boy named Franklin has a brush with her, her physical appearance and slightly flirtatious manner leads him, like Diamond, to look forward to their next meeting. Of course, he does not understand what their next encounter will entail. Another example occurs in *The World's End*, when a man sees Death as she walks behind her brother's funeral procession. She looks up at him, and in that moment, he falls in love with her. He explains, "I'll always love her. All my life."[13]

Not only do both North Wind and Death appear to be fun, beautiful women, but their method of bringing people into the afterlife is similar. At one point, Diamond hears from a preacher about a land that exists "at the north wind's back," and he asks his friend to take him there. Significantly, at this point in the story Diamond has had headaches, is frequently tired, and has been described as "not looking well."[14] North Wind explains to him that while technically that land is her home, she has never been there herself. She cannot go to the land at the back of the north wind, because that would undo her. But she does "allow" the curious Diamond to visit this land. In order to do this, she gives him a specific command: "you must go through me [...] you must walk on as if I were an open door, and go right through me."[15] The boy does exactly that: as he walks toward her, he puts one hand on her knee, but instead of meeting solid flesh, he passes into her. She is described as being an "intense cold," a cold that "stung him like fire."[16] Eventually, her cold "got into his heart, and he lost all sense."[17] After losing consciousness, Diamond passes into the land at her back: the land that she herself can never reach.

In the world of the Sandman, Death, like North Wind, draws people close to herself so that they can pass onto wherever they will go after life. Death, in this series, is one of seven undying anthropomorphizations who each rule over a concept in the same ways that ancient gods rule over specific aspects of life. In the first volume of *The Sandman*, Death's brother Dream—who is himself also known as the Sandman, the King of Dream, and Morpheus—describes hearing the sound of wings each time she takes a soul. Like North Wind, Death clearly believes that people go somewhere after she has taken them, but unlike North Wind, the place is made less clear to the reader. When one old man hints that he is not sure if heaven exists, instead of answering him, she says, "Now's when you find out, Harry."[18] Later in the series, it is revealed that people tend to receive what they expect in the afterlife. This is made most clear when Lucifer decides to empty out hell and give the keys to Dream.

Both Gaiman and MacDonald anthropomorphize death in the way that they do in order to challenge attitudes about death, a concept that has long been a topic addressed by myth. At the same time, both also understand that within the culture that they are working in, there is one main reason people fear death. The fear of death is the fear of the unknown. In order to make death less fearsome, both authors understand that it is not enough to simply change the anthropomorphic metaphor that they are using; they must also reduce the fear itself.

One common way that the fear of death is symbolized in western culture is in the concept of hell. The concept of hell comes from the Christian tradition, in which it is believed people go to hell in order to suffer the just punishment of their wrongdoing. There are, in different Christian traditions, different ways to get out of being sent to hell. Hell is discussed in the Bible; for example, in the gospels Jesus warns his followers that it is better to be physically maimed than to have a whole body but end up in hell.[19] The New Testament books of 2 Peter and Revelation both describe hell as a place of punishment devised for rebellious angels, but John Milton's *Paradise Lost* presents hell as the home of Satan and his followers. Milton's Satan and demons punish the humans who are sent by God to hell. Ultimately, *Paradise Lost* has done more than the Bible to shape both Victorian and popular contemporary understandings of this ancient concept. Both Gaiman and MacDonald engage in a Bahktinian dialogue with these older texts in order to work toward a removal of the fear of death. The Scottish minister does this by retaining names but rejecting images from the earlier texts; Gaiman, on the other hand, embraces these images.

In MacDonald's novel *Lilith*, Mr. Vane, who owns a large mansion in England, travels through a mirror and finds himself in another world. When he asks Mr. Raven, his guide into this other world, to explain what has happened, Mr. Raven assures him that he has not really left home at all, but has entered "the region of the seven dimensions."[20] At one point in this other world, Mr. Vane watches two skeletons argue fiercely with each other. When Mr. Vane asks Mr. Raven what is going on, he replies, "'You are not in hell [...] neither am I in hell. But those skeletons are in hell!'"[21] Upon being pressed for more information, Mr. Raven further explains that those two skeletons, since they were once a married couple whose love had turned to hate, were condemned to stay with each other until "they must grow weary of their mutual repugnance, and begin to love one another."[22] When this happens, they will regain flesh and eventually, they will no longer be skeletons. They will also no longer hate each other, and ultimately, they will no longer be in hell. Hell, in MacDonald's *Lilith*, is a state of being that people bring with them; it is not a place one is condemned to because of bad behavior. Most importantly, Mr. Raven explains, everyone who is living in hell has the hope of personal improvement: they can, like the skeletons whose argument Mr. Vane witnessed, eventually find themselves living in heaven simply because they have changed their own attitude and approach to the world. Hell, in *Lilith*, is a personal condition that one can grow out of.

Even though Hell is not a place in its own right in this text, Satan, the fallen angel once known as Lucifer and who in *Paradise Lost* is presented as the ruler of Hell, makes an appearance. This Satan is called "The Shadow," and makes his appearance at the end of the story. At one point he attempts to keep Mr. Vane from accomplishing a mission he has been given. This Shadow, however, proves to be nothing more than what his name suggests: a mist that Mr. Vane can easily walk through, and even though Satan, the old enemy of man, looks frightening, he has no power.

Gaiman's method of weakening the power of hell involves a more direct approach. Instead of denying hell any existence of its own, in *The Sandman* series ideas of hell presented in the epic poetry of both Dante and Milton are embraced. In the first volume, *Preludes and Nocturnes*, Dream goes to hell in order to retrieve his helmet, which has fallen into the hands of a demon. While traveling through a hell complete with prison cells, demons in all shapes and sizes, and images straight out of *The Inferno*, Dream encounters a woman he himself sent to hell. In an enigmatic moment, she asks if he still loves her; he responds, "yes, I still love you. But I have not yet forgiven you."[23] Later, in *Season of Mists*, Death confronts her brother, insisting that it was wrong for him to send someone to hell simply because she refused to love him. Later in the series, the Sandman regrets having damned the woman Nada, and decides that he must go back and set her free. This story of Dream's condemnation and eventual change of heart was written by Gaiman, and it directly confronts a system of beliefs that MacDonald was quite familiar with. MacDonald was raised in a strict Calvinist home. This Calvinism, Rolland Hein explains in *The Harmony Within: The Spiritual Vision of George MacDonald*, taught that all humans deserve to burn in hell, but God, for reasons of his own, chooses some people to go to heaven, instead. The rest of humanity, the young MacDonald was taught, was condemned and could do nothing to change it.[24] Richard Reis explains in *George MacDonald's Fiction: A Twentieth Century View* that throughout his life, MacDonald found this particular view not only of God, but of humanity itself, to be "repulsive."[25] Out of this repulsion, MacDonald creates his idea that hell is a state of being instead of a place. Here is one of the points at which a dialogic view of the work of these two writers reveals something interesting: while MacDonald rejects this concept, it is Gaiman who creates the images and characters that directly weaken this view of the afterlife. Gaiman's Dream, like the Calvinist God, sends people (or at least, a person) to hell for reasons of his own. Gaiman's Death is the one who voices the injustice of this scenario—an injustice that MacDonald cannot as effectively address in the structure he has created.

Just as the character Satan is met in *Lilith*, throughout *The Sandman* series, the Dream king and his siblings have multiple encounters with Lucifer Morningstar. Since the Bible describes Lucifer as a fallen angel, this series presents him not as the goat-footed, horned-headed, tail wagging demon that is often used to represent him. Instead, this Lucifer, when first met, is shown dressed as a traditional angel: a gown and big wings. In Miltonian fashion, this Lucifer rules over hell, but he has the option of leaving it. He uses his power to set the prisoners of hell free. The result of this, ironically, shows a possible need for a concept of hell: all of the scary things need to be kept somewhere where they can't hurt anyone outside of their own realm.

Intriguingly, in both stories, the power of hell is pitted against the power of dreams. The Sandman, at one point, is confronted by Lucifer. Lucifer challenges the idea that dreams have any power in hell. His response is that if those who lived in hell could not dream of heaven, then hell would lose its power.[26] In *Lilith*, however, in "the region of the seven dimensions," dreaming is also important: people are brought here to lie down and go to sleep, in order to dream until the time of their own awakening. Those who, like the arguing skeletons Mr. Vane listens to, have brought hell with them cannot lay down to dream. They must first become human again.[27]

Just as Lucifer makes his appearance in both Gaiman's *The Sandman* series and in MacDonald's *Lilith*, other characters from the Judeo-Christian story of the Creation and Fall play important roles in a world other than our own. In *The Sandman*, this occurs in the land ruled by the Sandman, Dream. This place is inhabited not only by the creatures that occur in the dreams that people have at night, but also of the stories that people tell to each other. In *Lilith*, it is the region of seven dimensions. Placing these characters in alternate worlds assists the reader in viewing these old, familiar characters, and thus, old, familiar concepts, differently. In *Lilith*, this is expressed directly to Mr. Vane as he is told, "You cannot understand your own world until you have visited another."[28] Not only are old familiar characters shown in a new light when they have been placed in a different world, but new characters can easily be added who, in their turn, help the reader think differently about what they are encountering.

In both of these alternate worlds, the Adam and Eve story is presented in close association with a librarian who is also a raven. Their shared use of this striking image places Gaiman and MacDonald not only in dialogue with texts that present images of hell, but also in dialogue with each other. While neither ravens nor librarians occur in the Adam and Eve story, both of these raven/librarian characters play an important role in the text in which they occur. This role, in both cases, directly relates to the mythological significance of the raven, as well as the typical role of the librarian.

Ravens, while not appearing in the story of Adam and Eve, do play a significant role throughout mythology. For example, in Haida and Tlingit (Native American tribes found in the northern west coast) mythology, Raven created the world.[29] More importantly, in many cultures, ravens are closely associated with death. Deities who frequent battlefields such as the Morrígan or Odin are often accompanied by ravens, who will, in turn, devour the dead flesh of fallen warriors. In *The Prose Edda*, Odin is even called "The Raven God" because of his two ravens, Huggin and Munnin, "thought" and "memory."

The names of these two ravens suggest exactly why scavengers of the battlefield are also, in the fiction of both George MacDonald and Neil Gaiman, librarians. Libraries, of course, hold books, and books, in turn, are traditionally items in which history is stored and ideas are explained. In other words, libraries store memory and thought, and librarians are the guardians and caretakers of these items.

The libraries these ravens have charge of are in huge, old homes, and include some unusual books. Gaiman's library exists in Dream's home, while MacDonald's library sits in an old home that holds a tenuous relationship to the real world. Gaiman's librarian, Lucien, has charge over every book that was never written. Some of these are books that people dreamed about writing but never wrote, while others are books that people began to write, but never finished.[30]

As Dream's librarian, Lucien is on friendlier terms with the Sandman than many others, and is often seen chatting with Dream's raven, whose name is Matthew. Later in the series, however, Matthew discovers that he is not Dream's first raven. In *The Kindly Ones*, the tenth volume of the *Sandman* series, Matthew learns that Dream has had ravens before him. Understandably concerned, the bird asks what happened to them. Dream responds by saying that Lucien the librarian, a friend of Matthew's, is "the first raven of them all."[31] Dream's librarian, then, is none other than the first winged death-symbol. His familiarity with death becomes obvious when Death arrives at Dream's home on business, and Lucian offers to find her a book she might like to read.[32]

In the first chapter of *Lilith*, the reader is informed that the old home in which the story takes place is haunted by the ghost of a librarian, a man named Mr. Raven. According to local legend, Mr. Raven's library consisted "not of such books only as were wholesome for men to read, but of strange, forbidden, and evil books."[33] Like Lucien, he has charge of an unusual library. While Lucien used to be a raven and is now a human-looking librarian, at times Mr. Raven appears as quite literally, a raven. At other times, however, he takes on a distinctly different appearance: "he was no longer a raven, but a man of middle height with a stoop, very thin, and wearing [sic] a long black tail coat."[34] Later, while discussing Mr. Raven's role, Mr. Vane calls Mr. Raven not only a librarian, but "the sexton of all he surveyed."[35]

While the librarian is a non-canonical addition to both stories, more traditional Judeo-Christian characters show up as well. As the prime actors (aside from God himself) in the Genesis story, the characters Adam and Eve must be discussed together. In *The Sandman*, Cain and Abel frequently show up, as do Eve and Lilith, who while not strictly canonical herself, entered the Jewish story through Assyrian mythology.[36] Adam, however, only appears in a story that Eve tells to a baby named Daniel and the raven Matthew. This audience is significant: the story of how sin entered the world is told to a young child at the beginning of his life, and a raven, a symbol of death. Eve tells these two a story of how Adam had not one, but three wives: Lilith, who desired domination during intimate moments and was therefore kicked out of the Garden of Eden alone; a second wife, who never had a name but who disgusted Adam because of how she was made; and Eve, the woman who is telling the story. Eve does not tell the child and bird what happened to Adam, but she does explain what she knows of the fate of the three women. Lilith "gave birth to the Lilim, the children of Lilith, who have haunted the nights of the sons of Adam ever since." The second wife was either forgotten or destroyed by her creator, while the third, Eve, "lived to be older than any woman, who in the end did not die, but who retreated to her cave. Blamed for sin. For misery. For the Fall."[37]

In *The Sandman*, Eve tells the story of Adam, Eve, and Lilith while visiting the house shared by the brothers Cain and Abel. During this visit, Eve denies that Cain is her son, and when he counters by declaring "you're everybody's mother," she responds, "that is a matter of opinion."[38] This Eve willingly admits that she is the one blamed for all sin, sorrow, and sadness, but refuses the one bit of honor that religious traditions leave to her: she will not let herself be called the Mother of All. This Eve lives alone in a cave, occasionally visited by the raven Matthew, and points out that she "dwells in nightmares."[39] Like the children of Lilith, this Eve is also a creature that haunts the night.

While Adam never makes a personal appearance in *The Sandman* series, in MacDonald's *Lilith*, he plays a vital role. Mr. Vane, the man who has inherited the house haunted by the librarian who is also a raven, eventually learns that his shape-changing librarian-raven-ghost also happens to be Adam, the Father of All. Whereas Gaiman's Adam disappears from the story after making the important decisions regarding which of the three women he really wanted, MacDonald's Adam watches over his children, putting them down to "sleep" at the end of their earthly lives. This sleep is, of course, death, but these children of Adam sleep only to first, dream, and then to wake again into a new and glorious life. Mr. Vane, when he begins to understand Adam's role, calls him the "lord of all that was laid aside."[40] He calls Adam's home "the burial-ground of the universe."[41] In this way, MacDonald's librarian is as closely associated with death as Gaiman's. At the same time, however, MacDonald's Adam does not disappear after three failed attempts to gain the perfect wife, but instead takes responsibility for the people that he has brought into the world, even if it is a grim responsibility. Just as a librarian does with his books, Adam carefully makes a place for the people he refers to as "all of my children."[42] After making a place for them, he carefully puts each one away in his or her rightful place, to wait until, like a library book, they are called for.

While Gaiman's Adam appears to no longer have any sort of a relationship with his third wife, MacDonald's Adam has a strong relationship with his current wife. The first time Adam brings Mr. Vane to his home, he declares "here is my wife's house! She is very good to let me live with her!"[43] Their home is peaceful and their interactions with each other are gentle and kind. Both MacDonald's and Gaiman's Eves are very much traditional women who mostly stay in their homes. Gaiman's Eve happens to make her home in nightmares, while MacDonald's Eve lives with a husband who loves her in a house full of her sleeping children. Gaiman's Eve is still suffering for her crime of disobedience, while MacDonald's Eve has, in the words of Mr. Raven, "repented, and is now beautiful as never was woman or angel."[44]

Another character from this story that both work with is Lilith. Lilith comes into the story not through the Bible, as the others do, but through Midrash. She first appears in ancient Assyrian/Babylonian myth, but is not presented as Adam's first wife until the Talmudic-midrash *Aleph Bet of Ben-Sirach*, which was written sometime between 800 and 1000 CE.[45]

In *The Sandman* series, Eve describes Lilith as a proud, strong woman with many children who all torment the dreams of Adam's descendents. Like Adam, Lilith has disappeared. Her ultimate fate is less important to this story than her original role: she rebelled, Adam did not want her, she gave birth to monsters. After all, it is Eve who tells both Adam's and Lilith's stories, and she has a good reason to not care about Lilith's eventual fate.

The Lilith presented by MacDonald, however, plays a very different role. Like Gaiman's Lilith, she was Adam's first wife, but in this case, it is Adam, not Eve, who explains the nature of Lilith's rebellion:

> ...she counted it slavery to be one with me, and bear children for HIM, who gave her being. One child, indeed, she bore; then, puffed with the fancy that she had created her, would have me fall down and worship her! Finding, however, that I would but love and honour, never obey and worship her, she poured out her blood to escape me.[46]

This Lilith ran from Adam and joined herself to "The Great Shadow," who, in turn, made Lilith the queen of hell.[47] She now rules over a city of people whose dislike of each other is only outdone by their dislike of strangers, and she drinks the blood of infants born into that city. Those infants are not her children, but the children of Adam. Like both the Lilith and the Eve of *Sandman*, she is a creature closely associated with nightmare. Ultimately, however, this Lilith is bound by an army of children and delivered to the house in which Adam and Eve live. Adam greets them at the door "almost merrily," while Eve looks at her and declares her "The mortal foe of my children!"[48] Lilith, like the descendants of Adam, must lie down and sleep, but her sleep serves a different purpose. The Shadow, to whom she long ago aligned herself, now wishes to destroy her, and her only salvation is forgiveness and sleep. Where Gaiman's Lilith and Eve are both left with open-ended stories, MacDonald's Eve and Lilith both receive forgiveness, and, through forgiveness, peace.

Thus far, Gaiman and MacDonald's dialogic interaction has been, primarily, one of agreement. Both agree that an important step toward reshaping an understanding of death involves the creation of a new anthropomorphic character; both agree that raven librarians who are associated with death introduce an element of calmness and order to the idea. Viewing these texts as being in Bahktinian dialogue, however, reveals something important about the parts of the stories that are markedly different. In the case of Eve and Lilith, this shows something about how both authors bring culturally-shaped attitudes to the conversation they are having with ancient myth. The fate of MacDonald's characters reflects attitudes of the Victorian England in which he wrote. Many writers discussing Victorian attitudes have pointed out that there was a strong belief at the time when MacDonald lived and wrote that humans were in a process of continual improvement, and that scientific, political, and social advances were going to make the world a much better place.[49] The fate of MacDonald's Lilith and Eve reflect this confidence in human improvement. The fate of Gaiman's Eve and Lilith, however, do not share the same hope. Instead, they reflect the postmodern thought of the era in which they were created. Postmodern thought, as Jacques Lyotard explains in *The Postmodern Condition*, is not self-assured, has little hope in ideological structures and is, in many ways, the exact opposite of Victorian thought.[50] These two writers have, therefore, brought their own cultures into this ongoing dialogue about death.

In both MacDonald's and Gaiman's texts, Lilith has a daughter. In *The Sandman: Season of Mists,* Lucifer introduces Mazikeen, a denizen of Hell, as "A daughter of Lilith."[51] When Lucifer decides to "close down" hell and let everyone go, Mazikeen chooses to stay with him. One half of Mazikeen's face is beautiful, while the other half has no skin. Her muscles and brain are exposed, as are her teeth. Like MacDonald's Lilith, Mazikeen chooses to side with the evil one. But while The Shadow wanted to keep Lilith for himself, Lucifer tells Mazikeen that she may not go with him. She disobeys and follows him anyway. Eventually, Lucifer opens a club at which Mazikeen works (while wearing a mask so as not to frighten the customers), and when he ultimately chooses to close it, she promises again that she will follow him. This evil one does not choose her, but she chooses him and he allows her to trail along. The evil he presents in this relationship is not the desire to possess, as the Shadow does in MacDonald's Lilith, but is simple indifference.

Where Gaiman's daughter of Lilith aligns herself with the Lord of Hell and follows him wherever he goes, MacDonald's daughter of Lilith plays a vital role in her mother's ultimate release from Satan's power. At the beginning of her story, Lona, like Mazikeen, has no interaction with her mother. But where Mazikeen's broken relationship may be because her mother is, like the lord of hell that she follows around, simply indifferent to her existence, Lona's mother hates her with a passion. At one point when she confronts Adam, MacDonald's Lilith declares that if she has the chance, she will drink her own daughter's blood. Lona's army of children, however, overcomes Lilith and takes her prisoner. First they take her to the house of Mara, a daughter of Adam and Eve whose job it is to teach people the meaning of sorrow. After this, Lona leads the army of children as they take their victim to the home of their first parents. During this procession, Lilith experiences a change of heart toward her daughter.

At the home of Adam and Eve, Lilith finds, however, that she cannot let go of The Shadow herself. A long debate ensues, from which it is ultimately determined that Adam must cut off Lilith's hand with the sword that once guarded the gates of Eden. Cutting off her hand is a physical symbol of Lilith's break with Satan, and it is vital that her former husband be the one to bring about this break. And yet it is not a renewed love for

Adam, but her new-found love first for her daughter, then the children that her daughter rescued, that saves Lilith. Lona, the daughter of Lilith, is also important because Mr. Vane, the human whose own adventures have mixed dangerously with Lilith's, falls in love not with a daughter of Eve, but a daughter of Lilith. And when Lilith lies down to sleep, so does her daughter, and so, ultimately, does Mr. Vane. All three accept the peace that is offered in Adam's house, not the peace of a hopeless death, even though death is what they have accepted, but the peace of sleep that will end in the awakening of a new and glorious dawn. Whereas Gaiman's daughter of Lilith is caught in a story that has no closure, MacDonald's has found the closure she needs in forgiving her mother, getting to know her father, and laying down to sleep in hope. The fates of both Lona and Makizeen, like Eve and Lilith before them, again bring cultural attitudes of the eras in which they were created to the conversation at hand.

While Adam, Eve, Lilith, and the children of Adam and Lilith appear in both stories, the two canonical sons of Adam and Eve only appear in *The Sandman* series. In MacDonald it may simply be that they, like many others, eventually found forgiveness and slept, but in Gaiman's text, they play a very different role.

Cain and Abel live in Dream's country because they are a part of the oldest story ever told. As a part of the story that shaped much of human thought and dreams, they have a contract with the Lord of Dreams. The contract is, essentially, this: throughout all time, Abel offends Cain (sometimes by doing something directly, sometimes simply by existing), Cain kills Abel, Abel comes back to life again, the brothers live together in peace for a while, and then the cycle repeats itself. Abel tells the story of the original contract to the child Daniel shortly after Eve tells him the story of Lilith. After Cain killed Abel because "the Land's Creator" liked Abel's sacrifice better than Cain's, Dream and Death both approached Abel and offered to let him live in the new gardens that they were creating.[145] Death makes him no promises, but Dream promises him a house and the job of telling stories. Dream gives Abel a "letter of commission," and eventually, the Lord of Dreams allows Cain to join his brother.[53] The commission that Cain has says that Cain, because of the mark he has received, cannot be killed by anyone, and Abel can only be killed by Cain. The Mark of Cain protects him from everyone, while Abel's contract protects him from everyone except Cain. Near the end of *The Sandman* series, Abel is killed not by Cain, but by the Fates. Cain therefore takes his letter of commission to the Sandman himself for retribution. Cain kills his brother, but he also loves him in a tortured way.

Gaiman's use of the story of Cain and Abel is another of the places where the difference between MacDonald and Gaiman's approaches interact dialogically. MacDonald's text apparently does not find these two characters worth mentioning, while Gaiman's engages them as part of the oldest story ever told in order to invoke the mythological nature of their story. Both Gaiman and MacDonald place characters from the Judeo-Christian creation story in an alternate world that is, at times, visited by all people from our world. In this sense, they both are working in dialogue with the first few chapters of the *Book of Genesis*. Gaiman and MacDonald ask the same question: "now what?" When looking at Gaiman and MacDonald together, however, it becomes clear that they give two starkly different answers to this question. Gaiman's sequel leaves the story open-ended: Cain forever kills Abel, the daughter of Lilith forever follows Lucifer, and Eve forever lives in the world of nightmares. In Gaiman's world, there is no reprieve for these characters. They simply must live out the results of their actions or their choices, never deviating from the roles given them in their own stories. In MacDonald's sequel to the story of Adam and Eve, however, there is closure for everyone. Each character receives forgiveness and reconciliation, and that forgiveness leads to both personal growth and peace.

This, then, is where a dialogic reading of these texts brings the reader. Both Gaiman and MacDonald have taken on the same essential issues using the same basic images. Both are concerned with mythical presentations of death, the afterlife, and the relationship between these and the concepts of wrongdoing and forgiveness. Presented side by side, it becomes clear that one story uses Adam, Eve, Lilith, and their children to present a vision of hope, while the other presents a vague hopelessness. One provides escape from one's mistakes; the other suggests a lack of any such escape route. Reading these two stories not only in light of myth, but in light of each other, as well, reveals that not only do they reinvent old imagery, but that both embrace new images. In both cases, the raven librarian and the playful, feminine anthropomorphic death help to create new spaces in which old ideas can be challenged and explored, rejected or possibly even embraced.

---

1 Other writers than George MacDonald have been called the first to write this sort of fantasy, including H. P. Lovecraft, Lord Dunsany, and William Morris. For the purpose of this article, Sullivan's claim is being used because MacDonald's first fantasy novel of this sort, *Phantastes*, was published in 1858, while Lovecraft was not born until 1890, and Dunsany, 1878. The claim that Morris was the first to write such stories is more substantial, since his prose romance *The Hollow Land* was published in 1856, two years before *Phantastes*. Whether or not *The Hollow Land* can be considered the same genre, however, is debatable, since this story can also be read as an allegory about the dominance of art over all other aspects of life.
2 Sullivan, "Fantasy," 420.
3 Gaarden, "Cosmic," 20.
4 While each of these writers acknowledges the influence of MacDonald on their work in several places,

examples include C. S. Lewis's Preface to *George MacDonald, an Anthology*; Chesterton's Preface to *George MacDonald and his Wife*, by Greville MacDonald, and Tolkien's Letter on January 16, 1938, to the editor of *The Observer*, in which he states that George MacDonald is the only Victorian writer who influenced the writing of *The Hobbit*.
5 Gaiman, Mythcon.
6 Gaiman, *Graveyard*, 31.
7 Gaiman, *Graveyard*, 30.
8 Gaiman, *Graveyard*, 161,162.
9 MacDonald, *At the Back of the North Wind*, 357.
10 MacDonald, *North Wind*, 17.
11 Gaiman, *Preludes*, 215.
12 Gaiman, *Preludes*, 225.
13 Gaiman, *World's End*, 157.
14 MacDonald, *North Wind*, 91, 103.
15 MacDonald, *North Wind*, 111.
16 MacDonald, *North Wind*, 112.
17 MacDonald, *North Wind*, 112.
18 Gaiman, *Preludes*, 224.
19 Matthew 5:29-30; Mark 9: 43-45.
20 MacDonald, *Lilith*, 21.
21 MacDonald, *Lilith*, 93.
22 MacDonald, *Lilith*, 94.
23 Gaiman, *Preludes*, 113.
24 Hein, *The Harmony Within*, 15.
25 Reis, *George MacDonald's Fiction: A Twentieth Century View*, 33.
26 Gaiman, *Mists*, 129.
27 MacDonald, *Lilith*, 21.
28 MacDonald, *Lilith*, 25.
29 MacDonald, *Lilith*, 9.
30 Gaiman, *Seasons*, 40.
31 Gaiman, *Kindly Ones*, part 11, page 15.
32 Gaiman, *Kindly Ones*, part 12, page 20.
33 MacDonald, *Lilith*, 9.
34 MacDonald, *Lilith*, 14.
35 MacDonald, *Lilith*, 27.
36 Geduld, "The Lineage of Lilith," 58.
37 Gaiman, *Fables*, 216.
38 Gaiman, *Fables*, 212.
39 Gaiman, *Fables*, 204.
40 MacDonald, *Lilith*, 27.
41 MacDonald, *Lilith*, 27.
42 MacDonald, *Lilith*, 40.
43 MacDonald, *Lilith*, 27.
44 MacDonald, *Lilith*, 148.
45 Stern, *Rabbinic Fantasies*, 168.
46 MacDonald, *Lilith*, 148.
47 MacDonald, *Lilith*, 148.
48 MacDonald, *Lilith*, 213.
49 While discussions of this common Victorian attitude can be found in many texts, a standard starting place for such a study of Victorian attitudes would be J. H. Buckley's *The Victorian Temper: A Study in Literary Culture*.
50 For more information, see Lyotard's *The Postmodern Condition*.
51 Gaiman, *Mists*, 85.
52 Gaiman, *Fables*, 220.
53 Gaiman, *Fables*, 220.

Whatever Happened to the Time Lord? Mythology and Fandom in Neil Gaiman's Contributions to Unfolding Texts

Matthew Hills

The mythological dimensions of Neil Gaiman's work are nothing if not multiple. One might, for instance, consider how Gaiman's *Sandman* series approximates to a Campbellian mythic structure,[1] or how it posits ontology of the Endless standing behind prior myths-as-stories.[2] Or one might address the "explicit mythology" of *American Gods*, *i.e.*, how the novel appropriates scenarios and figures from classic myths in order to rework them in and for the present day.[3] Whether affirming models of myth, or acting as meta-mythic reconfigurations, Neil Gaiman has repeatedly and self-consciously engaged with myth in his fantastic fabulations. In this chapter, however, I want to consider yet another mythological dimension, and one which has been less explored in scholarly studies of Gaiman's creative output.

My focus will be less on Gaiman as primary auteur-creator, and more as a contributor to media franchises creatively led by others. For example, Gaiman has contributed episodes to the TV series *Babylon 5* (executive produced, created, and lead-written by J.M. Straczynski) and *Doctor Who* (under show runner Steven Moffat). He has also contributed to the Batman mythos, *e.g.*, in the "last Batman story" *Whatever Happened to the Caped Crusader*. Previous critical work has tended to marginalize these works within Gaiman's oeuvre; *The Neil Gaiman Reader* offers no sustained study of Gaiman's *Babylon 5* episode, despite some contributors[4] equating Gaiman's craft with that of U.S. stage magicians (and guest stars in his *Babylon 5* episode, "Day of the Dead") Penn and Teller.[5] I would suggest that scholarship tackling Gaiman has displayed a tendency to celebrate his authorial persona, thereby rendering his franchise contributions of secondary importance. These supposedly cannot be read as straightforward expressions of Gaiman's authorial vision, and are assumed instead to be hemmed in by the requirements of writing for others' characters and others' narrative universes. Of course, the line I am drawing here can be challenged: it might be countered that the Sandman was not Gaiman's own character, but was instead a "revisionist" reworking of an established character.[6]

However, thought of as a revisionary comic book writer, Gaiman's authorial agency has been stressed. By radically transforming the Sandman, Gaiman promotes — and is able to agentively control — his vision of the character.[7] By strong contrast, Gaiman borrows the Batman temporarily, weaves a one-shot *Doctor Who* story, and shapes an interlude in a run of 61 consecutive *Babylon 5* episodes from creator Joe Straczynski.[8]

I want to argue that these franchise contributions deserve attention as "mythological" texts alongside the more frequently studied and celebrated canon of *Sandman*, *American Gods*, and so on. To leave "The Doctor's Wife" or "Day of the Dead" to one side runs the risk of reproducing an art versus commerce binary, where Gaiman's (graphic) novels deserve literary decoding, but his franchise entries are implicitly devalued or seen as less artistically worthy. Lance Parkin makes a related point when he discusses contemporary media franchises shaped by a series of producers:

> [E]ven decades after "the death of the author," a text written by one person is still most commonly seen as inherently more impressive and worthy of study than one that is the work of many hands. The terminology used is often disparaging. The most popular U.S. term for ongoing narratives, "franchise," places them in the realm of burger joints and pretzel stands, rather than art or academia... I will use a less emotive term, coined in the title of the first academic analysis of *Doctor Who*: "unfolding text."[9]

I shall follow Parkin's lead here, focusing on Gaiman's contributions to a range of "unfolding texts." Parkin defines an unfolding text as a "fiction based around a common character, [or] set of characters...that has had some form of serial publication," noting that although this can have a single author, unfolding texts are "typically written by many" as well as having decentred, multiple narratives: "most contain a number of distinct series, in different media, usually with different creators and even intended audiences."[10] Unfolding texts can run over many years. For instance, *Batman* began in 1939, while *Doctor Who* started in 1963. And their continuity can evolve and shift across different eras (*e.g.*, the "pre-Crisis" Batman; the first Doctor), with new production teams or lead creatives taking charge periodically.

Parkin suggests that despite these diachronic variations, unfolding texts are understood by readers and viewers to follow certain rules:

> In his study of Batman, Will Brooker[11] suggests... that a Batman story... has a core set of concepts... readers and viewers understand

them as "rules"... This may apply more to unfolding texts that were always the work of many hands – or it may be that "written by a particular person" is one of the core concepts for some unfolding texts.[12]

The latter point brings *Babylon 5* into my discussion, since unlike *Batman* and *Doctor Who*, this unfolding text was very much linked to a single creator, J.M. Straczynski. *Babylon 5* is thus less multiple, and somewhat less "unfolded," if you like, than *Batman* and *Doctor Who*. But Gaiman's contribution to this narrative universe, similar to his work with characters such as the Doctor and the Batman, nevertheless has to fit into perceived "rules" and established continuity.

Parkin makes the provocative case that unfolding texts and their "rules" are themselves akin to mythologies: "Throughout history there have been unfolding texts; Robin Hood, King Arthur, and the classical myths, for example, have all the characteristic of an unfolding text."[13] He is not alone in reaching this conclusion; writing of superhero continuity in comic books, Richard Reynolds also equates contemporary superheroes with mythology. Reynolds argues that "serial continuity," which is how continuity develops over time, and "hierarchical continuity," or the configuration of superhero continuity at a given moment, combine to form what's called structural continuity:

> ...structural continuity embraces more than the sum total of all the stories and canonical interactions.... Structural continuity also embraces... actions which are not recorded in any specific text, but inescapably implied by continuity.... If superheroes are to have any claim at all to be considered the bearers of a 'modern mythology' and in some ways comparable to the pantheons of Greek or Native American or Norse mythology, then this extra-textual continuity *is a vital key to the way in which the mythology of comic books is articulated in the mind of readers*.[14]

For Reynolds, then, structural continuity becomes "metatextual," *i.e.*, it does not exist in any one text, nor in any series of texts, but is in fact a production of fan reading and knowledge: "The ideal fan is capable of envisaging an ideal DC or Marvel metatext: a summation of all existing texts plus all the gaps which those texts have left unspecified."[15] Such "metatextual structural continuity" is not merely a set of "rules" or learnt facts about a superhero character. It also includes "gaps" in the narrative universe—material that is not shown or given to fans, but nevertheless implied as a present absence. Superheroes become mythological through their "interaction with the audience," and specifically the fan audience: "metatextual structural continuity... is the strategy through which superhero texts most clearly operate as myths."[16]

Reynolds' work on comic book heroes resonates with my own work on cult TV and especially *Doctor Who*, where I have posited a similar process of continuity formation, termed *hyperdiegesis*.[17] Like Reynolds, I emphasise the significance of textual gaps and implications, describing hyperdiegesis as "the creation of a vast and detailed narrative space, only a fraction of which is ever directly seen or encountered within the text, but which nevertheless appears to operate according to the principles of internal logic and extension."[18] Piers Britton, writing recently in *TARDISbound*, argues that the "maintenance, ordering and enhancement of the *Doctor Who* hyperdiegesis have almost entirely been the work of fans,"[19] with fan writers and latterly producer-fans attempting retroactively to re-order— or at the very least acknowledge[20]—contradictions and tensions between the show's different iterations. Britton suggests that as a result of changes in production team, and changes in format, "*Doctor Who*'s hyperdiegetic framework is at best rickety. With its time-travel premise, *Doctor Who* was not conceived with an eye to internal coherence."[21]

Reynolds on comic book superheroes; Britton on *Doctor Who*; Parkin on the likes of *Batman* and *Doctor Who*—all argue in a variety of ways for the importance of fan activations of the "structural continuity" or "hyperdiegesis" of unfolding texts, themselves conceptualised as contemporary mythologies. This role for fandom now clearly extends into professional media production:

> ...production teams of long-running shows are frequently now themselves (as they are inevitably described in interviews) "self-confessed fans." Fans reading an Internet interview or attending a convention want reassurance that the producer "understands the show" (usually a thinly veiled euphemism for that fandom's specific preferences).[22]

This is important not just to reassure fan cultures that TV shows, and much-loved characters, are in safe hands. It also means that producer-fans have an understanding of "metatextual structural continuity," thus being able to coherently build on, or bring to coherence, the "rickety" hyperdiegesis making up, for instance, *Doctor Who*'s mythological dimensions.[23] I argue that fan knowledge is similarly privileged in Neil Gaiman's contributions to *Babylon 5*, *Batman*, and *Doctor Who*. Gaiman positions himself as a producer-fan, relating to these unfolding texts through the lenses of lived fandom, and/or as a writer self-consciously drawing on fan knowledge via research and testing of story ideas. And as Lance Parkin has argued, "each new *Doctor Who* story... is inevitably part of something much larger and more enduring, something greater than the sum of its parts. This privileges the returning audience (particularly the fans) for an unfolding text."[24] Fandom is likewise emphasised in Gaiman's working practices when he contributes to unfolding texts. Here, he is structurally placed in the position of a "tie-in writer,"[25] not having control over ongoing story arcs and developments planned by show runners/creators, and instead having to pitch and refine story ideas which fit into, and do not contradict or duplicate, developing mythologies.

Gaiman's work on *Babylon 5*, *Batman*, and *Doctor Who* shares a common focus on fan knowledge, and on exploiting and exploring the "gaps" in coherent, fragmented, or rickety hyperdiegetic narrative worlds. Gaiman thematically gathers together hyperdiegetic present absences (the return of dead characters in "Day of the Dead," as well as fleshing out Rebo and Zooty); suspends hyperdiegetic coherence in order to acknowledge different iterations of an unfolding text (in *Whatever Happened to the Caped Crusader*); and creates synthetic continuity, *i.e.*, building a new coherence across rickety, disarticulated eras of *Doctor Who* (in "The Doctor's Wife.") Each adds adroitly to established mythology, and each positions Gaiman in relation to fan knowledge, further blurring the line between producer and fan by offering up "fan service" (content aimed at garnering fan approval and appreciation). More than this, however, I will suggest that fan readings (and writings) tend to emphasise a character's or a TV show's mythology—that is to say, fandom activates an unfolding text as mythological. The mythological dimensions of *Babylon 5*, *Batman*, and *Doctor Who* do not coincidentally intersect with fan knowledge/receptions; they are generated and sustained via fan cultural capital[26] whether this belongs to "Big Name Fans," assorted fan readers, published scholar-fans, or celebrated producer-fans such as Gaiman himself. In short, one game that fandom characteristically plays with its beloved texts is the game of learning, retelling, and reading-for the mythological dimensions of unfolding texts.

Ritualized Mythology: The Dead Speak Aboard Babylon 5

Neil Gaiman's episode of *Babylon 5*, "Day of the Dead," has been published in annotated script form by DreamHaven Books. In itself, this is unusual for a freelance contribution to a TV series, and the publication enables Gaiman to highlight exactly what he was responsible for, and what was amended, tweaked, or written by show runner Joe Straczynski. In one sense, this demystifies the collective production practices of television, but at the same time it enables attributions of authorship to be made. Gaiman notes that it was Straczynski who added in the episode's mysterious, prophetic message for Sheridan: "The original draft of the script said 'Joe— give me a message for here.'" And he did."[27] Rather than depicting the show runner's addition—premised on textual control over ongoing story arcs— as an imposition, Gaiman discursively frames it as an invitation on his own part. Rather than representing his authorial position as hemmed in, then, or as secondary in relation to Straczynski, Gaiman consistently emphasises his authorial agency.

Elsewhere, Gaiman has recounted having to pitch his *Babylon 5* story idea, receiving approval first from Straczynski and then the show's producers. Again this process is represented as one which enabled Gaiman's creativity rather than imposing the TV industry's need for an outline.[28] Despite this discourse of enabled authorship that downplays the "limited textual power" of a freelance contributor to an unfolding text,[29] Gaiman's *Babylon 5* script works in a series of ways that can be read as self-reflexively incorporating the position of the hired hand. Firstly, Gaiman is contributing here to a series with a carefully protected coherence in terms of its "hyperdiegetic" continuity—something which meant that the show could be positioned and validated by SF fans as "novelistic."[30] As such, there were relatively few diegetic gaps that Gaiman could explore without impacting on *Babylon 5*'s ongoing arc, but his script nevertheless proved to be adept at exploiting a specific series of present absences, or textual implications, within what Reynolds would call "structural continuity." Gaiman rewarded fan loyalty, and played to longer-term fan knowledge, by temporarily bringing back a range of deceased characters—servant of the Shadows, Mr. Morden; Londo's former lover Adira; and the soldier, Dodger, who had propositioned Garibaldi.

This device allowed Gaiman to offer fan service without conflicting with the show's seriality, since he purposefully used characters who had been written out, playing on both fans' and lead characters' memories of these figures. Sharing the typical work practices of a "tie-in writer," Gaiman acknowledges that he drew on fan knowledge during his research for the episode, observing: "The Shoggren were my tip of the hat to my friend John Sjogren, who played the part of my 'As a rabid *Babylon 5* fan—is this cool?' tester from the beginning."[31] Gaps within continuity used by Gaiman are thus the present absences of deceased characters, given voice again for one episode only. Where other gaps might form part of Straczynski's intended arc,[32] characters firmly belonging to the show's past can be safely returned to for one-shot "special appearances."

Gaiman also reworks *Babylon 5*'s format to permit a more fantasy-oriented tale; the return of the dead remains a mystery and is not explained in scientific or (techno-babble-oriented) science-fictional terms. This temporary retooling of the show's hyperdiegesis is achieved by setting a ritualised boundary to the event; part of Babylon 5 is sold to the Brakiri race for just a few hours. Jan Johnson-Smith has argued that the station Babylon 5 acts as a post-modern confusion of spatial coordinates, seeming to be mapped (blue sector, red sector, etc.) but actually never clearly being linked together as a series of diegetic spaces.[34] Following this theme, Johnson-Smith reads "Day of the Dead" as a further symptom of such spatial confusion:

> In "Day of the Dead," a whole sector of the station goes missing. Bought by the Brakiri Ambassador for a set period of time, it becomes a physical and spiritual part of the Brakiri homeworld, cut off from the rest of the station from Brakiri dusk until dawn... *Babylon 5* has sets with which we become familiar... but their actual location and the corridors linking them are a mystery.[35]

However, I would argue that Gaiman's narrative device—displacing a section of Babylon 5—does more than recap post-modern thematics. "Day of the Dead" is careful to emphasise that the Brakiri will not be satisfied with "renting" space on Babylon 5. Part of the station must become theirs, being owned by them outright for the period of their ritual. Bounded in space and time, certain sleeping quarters are literally demarcated within a Brakiri line, and only until planetary sunrise on the Brakiri homeworld. Gaiman's Brakiri therefore stand-in textually for the freelance writer's extra-textual position. Not content with borrowing or "renting" characters just for the duration of one script, Gaiman wants to make part of *Babylon 5* "his" within the bounded confines of one episode. The Brakiri ritual thus reflexively incorporates the situation of the freelance writer contributing to an unfolding text, a text that will otherwise be read by fans as the property of "the Great Maker" (the God-like term accorded to Straczynski):

> Many fans perform the role of follower of the Great Maker, asking him specific information [online and at conventions] about Babylon 5. He presumably answers with the authority of one who knows... [fans' questions] would normally circulate within fandom. The competing answers among fans would constitute the only critical discourse on the *Babylon 5*. Straczynski, however, apparently answers nearly every question asked by fans. His answer[s]... silence... apparent inconsistency.[36]

As a freelance scriptwriter, Gaiman's authorship is subordinated to that of the "Great Maker" and his assumed authority over the show's hyperdiegesis. "Day of the Dead" effectively dramatizes Gaiman's structural position within the show's production. It represents a shift in the narrative rules of *Babylon 5*, and a temporary change in ownership over the station (the Brakiri taking charge just as Gaiman assumes temporary ownership of characters). Both of these are, though, knowingly bounded as rituals fixed in space and time, meaning that *Babylon 5* reverts to its standard ontology at planetary sunrise, and its standard continuity at episode's end. The episode even visually demarcates its ritually transformed zone of meaning (and zone of authorship) through the distinctive use of red lighting and CGI distortion effects.

What I'm terming *ritualized mythology* means contributing to an unfolding text's "structural continuity"—where other creatives have overall or discursive authority—by deliberately and self-reflexively making temporary, bounded and hence ritualistic changes to an otherwise coherent hyperdiegesis. The Brakiri section of Babylon 5 becomes, for just one episode, a space outside typical realism (even by the standards of SF TV), also shifting closer to Gaiman-esque fantasy or dream logic. By contrast, Gaiman's landmark contribution to Batman's unfolding text, in *Whatever Happened to the Caped Crusader*, situates itself very differently in relation to Batman's mythological dimensions.

Indeterminate Mythology: The Batman Says Goodbye

Although Parkin groups together a range of unfolding texts, I would argue that the hyperdiegesis of *Babylon 5* is relatively coherent, having been planned "novelistically" by its showrunner. By contrast, *Batman* and *Doctor Who* have far less hyperdiegetic consistency. *Who* is "rickety"[37] or "flexible, even on the fundamentals of the show's mythology."[38] And the Batman likewise

> reveals an impulse toward fragmentation. Since his creation in 1939, numerous editors, writers, artists, directors, scriptwriters, performers and licensed manufacturers have "authored" the Batman... the Batman has no primary urtext... but has rather existed in a plethora of equally valid texts constantly appearing over [many decades].[39]

Unlike his contribution to *Babylon 5*, then, Gaiman is positioned very differently as a freelance contributor to the *Batman* mythos. There is far less sense of having to ritualistically draw a line around his work, distinguishing it as a temporary, bounded sector within someone else's narrative universe. And there is no absolute or clear "urtext" to fit into, though there are evidently still specific "rules" of Batman's mythology.[39] Another difference is that in this instance, Gaiman directly represents himself as a producer-fan:

> *Whatever Happened to the Caped Crusader?* An Introduction, or a Love Letter... I love Batman. There are other characters I like. There may be other characters I like better. And there are characters I invented, and I love all of them like children. But I loved, and still love Batman, unshakeably, unquestioningly, as one loves a parent. He was the first. He's always been there.[41]

More than merely expressing fannish love for Batman, here Gaiman inverts the binary of valorised "single-authored" work versus devalued, commercial "franchise" labour. In his familial simile, Batman is given creative and affective primacy: he is the generative "parent" in contrast to Gaiman's own created characters who are figured as "children." With *Whatever Happened to the Caped Crusader?* Gaiman was tasked with punctuating Batman's existence by writing "the last Batman story:"

> Batman had survived many eras, and would, undoubtedly, survive many more. If I were going to tell the last Batman story it would have to be something that would survive Batman's current death or disappearance, something that would still be the last Batman story in twenty years, or a hundred. ...In my head, the story was simply called *Batman: The End*, but the first time DC Comics' people talked about it, they described it as "Whatever Happened to the Caped Crusader?" and the title sort of stuck.[42]

Gaiman's authorial persona[43] has been strongly linked to his work on *The Sandman* comic book series, leading academics such as Henry Jenkins to note that "Vertigo ...made its reputation as the place where DC does everything but superheroes. That's where someone like Neil Gaiman rules supreme (and he would clearly be in the bidding for best contemporary comics writer if I excluded the superhero modifier)."[44] It is perhaps not surprising, therefore, that Gaiman inter-textually cites his own ending to the Sandman story in his Batman "ending." *Sandman: The Wake* involved the mourning of Dream, one of the Endless, who is ultimately reborn in a mythic cycle of renewal.[45] And what Gaiman conceptualised as *Batman: The End* echoes this, featuring the mourning of Batman, and concluding with the character's rebirth and cyclical return to the beginning of his life. *The Sandman Companion* suggests that *Sandman: The Wake* "book-ended the whole series. The very first line of *Sandman*, at the top of page 1 in *Preludes and Nocturnes*, is: "Wake up, sir. We're here." Similarly, issue 72 closes the series down with "you woke up."[46] *Whatever Happened to the Caped Crusader?* resonates with this classical structuring of myth as a "circuitous quest,"[47] or as "an eternally recursive system in which endings are relativized and beginnings insubstantial."[48] Knowing that Batman will enter into a new narrative "iteration"[49] after this tale,[50] Gaiman avoids his "last" story being immediately superseded by relativizing Batman's end. At the same time, this (in)conclusive move creates new inter-textual links between Gaiman's Batman and the Sandman—links that had already been present, as for example in Batman's cameo in *The Wake*,[51] and in the use of white-on-black speech balloons for both characters in Gaiman's work.[52] Batman's "wake" also playfully cites the Endless when Gaiman concludes his *Batman* #686 strip with an unknown narrator (later identified as Bruce Wayne's mother) pointing out, "I don't think death is a person, Bruce."[53]

When summing up *The Wake* in an afterword, Gaiman suggests that "I have always been bad at goodbyes. In many ways, that's what these stories are about: the process of saying goodbye. ...The Ten Volumes of Sandman, of which this is the last, comprise a story about stories."[54] The exact same words could be taken to sum up *Whatever Happened to the Caped Crusader?* just as well. This too features a series of goodbyes as Batman embraces his fate, and what proves to be his rebirth: "Goodnight house. Goodnight, batcave. ...Goodnight, batmobile. Goodnight, Alfred. ...Goodnight, Bat-signal... Goodbye."[55]

And Gaiman's producer-fan "love letter" to the Batman is also a "story about stories." It accommodates "divergent expressions" of the character by allowing for "ambiguous constructions" of meaning and continuity.[56] Different characters such as Selina Kyle and Alfred the "gentleman's gentleman"[57] recount conflicting narratives about Batman's death, contradicting one another and externally conflicting with established iterations of—albeit already fragmented—continuity. Gaiman makes no attempt to resolve continuity fragments into newfound coherence, something which I would argue Grant Morrison's Batman does attempt, by psychologizing and thus reclaiming disavowed continuity elements such as Bat-mite, the Bat Radia, and the Zur En Arrh Batman into a new Bat-ontology. Instead, Gaiman allows all of Batman's history to co-exist, implying that "mutually exclusive metaphysics... stand in relief in the same way a text like *Batman: The Killing Joke* suspends Batman's fictional continuity."[58] Joe Chill can be both dead, and attending the very "end" of Batman's tale; Alfred can be the Joker, yet this development can simultaneously be dismissed as "impossible."

This strategy for engagement with an unfolding text can be termed *indeterminate mythology*; unlike Gaiman's carefully bounded and ritualized take on *Babylon 5*, this producer-fan re-interpretation instead emphasizes and promotes the free play, and the never-ending cycle, of retellings. Gaiman blurs together his fandom and his professional authorship[59] by positioning Batman as inter-textually enmeshed with *The Sandman*, while also valorising the "constant renewal" of an unfolding text.[60] As Laurence Coupe has argued, "'[i]ntertextuality' is not the problem but the solution" to inspiring new activations of mythological meaning.[61] Gaiman intertextually adds "another layer of continuity"[62] by audaciously transforming Alfred into the Joker, and by near-magically transforming the Bat-signal into a midwife's hands as Bruce Wayne is born. This new layer co-exists with Batman's fragmented continuity; it's neither clearly "in" continuity nor obviously "out of continuity" as an "Elseworlds"-type story. In fact, Gaiman deconstructs the very notion of presenting a coherent tale that cleanly "fits" continuity, or which steps to one side, by configuring Batman's hyperdiegesis as indeterminate: the life of the Batman is dream-like, capable of holding together contradictions. Or it is an eternal recurrence, always being relived, and always being retold by its protagonists, as well as by fans and producer-fans.

I have contrasted Gaiman's approach to Batman against Grant Morrison's in this instance, suggesting that the former refutes a precise ontology for the character's mythology, whereas the latter seeks to piece together disparate continuities, and different eras of Batman's real-world history, into a newly psychologised jigsaw. This approach to an unfolding text—seeking to shape new coherence out of hyperdiegetic fragments—can be characterised as *synthetic mythology*, and I will illustrate how Gaiman deploys this mode in his producer-fan work on *Doctor Who*, despite eschewing it in *Whatever Happened to the Caped Crusader?*

Synthetic Mythology: The TARDIS Says Goodbye... and Hello

Just as he has para-textually stressed *Batman* fandom in his work with the character, Gaiman has also testified to a lifelong *Doctor Who* fandom in forewords,[63] interviews,[64] and on his blog. It is thus Gaiman's fan status that is offered up as the motivation and the key context for his contributions to these unfolding texts.[65] Pretransmission publicity for "The Doctor's Wife" noted of the episode that "it'll be one the fans will love. It's a real love letter to the fans."[66] If *Whatever Happened to the Caped Crusader?* is a "love letter," then so too is Gaiman's contribution to *Who*, marking out his authorship of unfolding texts as recurrently linked to fan service, and to giving fans something they'll appreciate as an outstanding manipulation of mythology. Gaiman's *Doctor Who* fan affect and knowledge are articulated here with his professional creativity:

I had become infected by the idea that there are an infinite number of worlds, only a footstep away. And another part of the meme was this: some things are bigger on the inside than they are out on the outside. And, perhaps, some people are bigger on the inside than they are on the outside, as well ...[T]he shape of reality— the way I perceive the world—exists only because of *Doctor Who*. Specifically, from *The War Games*, the multipart series that was to be Patrick Troughton's swansong.[67]

Batman is granted a primacy and a generative status, and *Doctor Who* is similarly described as defining Gaiman's imaginative sense of the real; the TV series is positioned as underpinning his own later work as a fantasy novelist.[68] Once more inverting hierarchies of "original" and "franchise" fiction, Gaiman blurs fandom and professional identity in the way that M.J. Clarke suggests is characteristic of "tie-in" writers (and hired contributors to unfolding texts). Clarke points out the need to "eliminate anything that may overlap with previous or upcoming [TV] episodes" when tie-in pitches are considered.[69] Gaiman's situation reverses this scenario: his initial TV episode idea was apparently amended as a result of being too similar to a tie-in novel.[70] He then refocused on the notion of exploring the TARDIS:

> I still liked the idea of going deeper into the TARDIS and making the TARDIS dangerous—but if you're going to make the TARDIS dangerous, you have to ask yourself questions. What's made the TARDIS dangerous? The TARDIS' soul is no longer the TARDIS' soul? Okay, so where *is* the TARDIS' soul? Well, it's *in somebody*. And at that point, that was all I needed to start making a story... We've known really since *The Edge of Destruction*—so William Hartnell's third story—that the TARDIS was intelligent. In drafts of the script where we needed Idris to say more, one of the lines she actually said, she quoted William Hartnell: "The machine is not intelligent as we think it is intelligent...."[71]

Gaiman's approach to *Doctor Who*'s program mythology[72] bears all the hallmarks of the sociology of culture examined by Clarke, who argues that contributors to unfolding texts face the "paradoxical situation"[73] of needing to "add value" by creating something new, at the same time as fitting into established continuity. Clarke suggests that:

> The solution... is to exploit the "unexplored gems" of the series... "filling in the blanks... that they don't flesh out too much in the TV

show"... Tapping the unexplored gem means drawing on elements implied in the on-air series, but not directly addressed... Although the use of unexplored gems solves the paradox of value-added tie-ins, this practice is predicated precisely upon... forms of research [using or drawing upon detailed fan knowledge].[74]

The TARDIS can be identified as one such "unexplored gem," having accompanied the Doctor on his travels through time and space since 1963. Giving it a consciousness and a persona for the first time in "The Doctor's Wife" enables Gaiman to create synthetic mythology, drawing a new coherence out of disparate eras of the program and its "rickety" hyperdiegesis.[75] Gaiman has conceded that his childhood fandom proved insufficient for furnishing hyperdiegetic details about the TARDIS from 1963 to the present day. Interviewed for *SFX* magazine, Gaiman was asked: "You're dealing with the mythology of the show. Did you need to research it or was it all there in your head?"[76] His response indicated the importance of using fan research in order to create synthetic mythology:

> Mainly in my head, but there was definitely some researching. I asked a friend of mine named Steve Manfred... I'd say, "Steve, is there anywhere that I can go for a list of every part of the TARDIS that has ever been named and referenced throughout the entirety of 50 years of *Doctor Who*?" And he'd just type them all out for me... The funny thing is that almost all of that research wound up in drafts of scripts and then fell out again.[77]

This again resonates with Clarke's work on the practices of producer-fandom: "In addition to tapping their own fandom... writers also mine the fandom of others, using fan-created artifacts as shortcuts in their own research processes."[78] Drawing on his own and Manfred's extensive fan knowledge, Gaiman selectively edits and recombines aspects of established continuity so as to simultaneously add to *Doctor Who* — giving voice to the TARDIS in an unprecedented manner — and fit his work into gaps, implications and details ranging across the program's history. Synthetic mythology lends newfound coherence to a fragmented or rickety hyperdiegesis. It shares this reworking-for-consistency with a mode of fan reading or "retconning," albeit enacting this within an official text rather than in fan reception.[79]

However, synthetic mythology remains a "limited textual power"[80] insofar as it has to avoid contradicting or significantly altering program mythology. Gaps and implications can be developed, but established continuity cannot be transgressed or markedly rewritten. Gaiman has stated that he would have radically reworked *Doctor Who* were he to have been granted authorial control over it pre-2005:

> In my head the Time Lords exist, and are unknowable—primal forces who cannot be named, only described: the Master, the Doctor, and so on. All depictions of the home of the Time Lords are, in my head, utterly non-canonical. The place in which they exist cannot be depicted because it is beyond imagining: a cold place that exists only in black and white. It's probably a good thing that I've never actually got my hands on the Doctor. I would have unhappened so much.[81]

But when he eventually gets to write for the TV series, Gaiman does not have the situated agency of a show runner; he is unable to "unhappen" major aspects of mythology, though it should be noted that he is on record as broadly approving of Russell T. Davies' retooling of the program.[82] Nevertheless, "The Doctor's Wife" is restricted to *re-happening Doctor Who*. Writing in *Doctor Who Magazine*, David Bailey teases the reader: "it... makes you wonder what world-shaking events will unfold now that [Neil Gaiman]... finally, *actually* has his hands on our beloved series."[83] The reality is that synthetic mythology, or rereading/rewriting for consistency, does not shake the world of "structural continuity" so much as affectively play with selected aspects of it.

As with his work on *Babylon 5* and *Whatever Happened to the Caped Crusader?,* Neil Gaiman also incorporates a number of characteristic strategies into his *Doctor Who* episode. Like *Babylon 5*, he self-consciously places a boundary around his contribution, making the Junkyard planet not just a referencing of Totter's Lane from the first ever *Doctor Who* story in 1963,[84] but also part of a "bubble universe" that can therefore function in an even more fairy tale-like and whimsical manner than the standard Whoniverse, as well as playing with fan desires and expectations for a return of the Time Lords. Less exaggeratedly than in "Day of the Dead," Gaiman nonetheless again ritualistically bounds his contribution, providing a narrative rationale for his own brand of fantasy.

And "The Doctor's Wife" also echoes Gaiman's book-ending of *The Sandman* series by portraying the TARDIS's humanized form, Idris, in a cyclical, looping manner. She says "goodbye" upon first meeting the Doctor and "hello" as she leaves his life to be restored to her machine form. Again, and also akin to *Whatever Happened to the Caped Crusader?*, the "process of saying goodbye"[230] is picked over and rendered in mythic form; endings and beginnings are relativized, or displaced in time and relative dimensions, perhaps, by virtue of being chronologically muddled. Finally, Gaiman's subordination to an ongoing story arc under the show-runner's control—this time, Steven Moffat—is brought home by virtue of the fact that a prophetic message is inserted into his *Doctor Who* episode. *Babylon 5*'s "Day of the Dead" included J.M. Stracsynski's addition of Kosh's message, whilst "The Doctor's Wife" includes Moffat's addition of "the only water in the forest is the river."[85] Otherwise, Gaiman's contributions to these TV series act as temporary breaks from ongoing story arcs.

In all of Neil Gaiman's additions to unfolding texts that I've considered here—whether deploying ritualized, indeterminate, or synthetic mythology—his work is "tested" on a "rabid... fan" by way of research (*Babylon 5*), draws on his own professed fandom (*Batman*), or combines personal fandom with other fan research (*Doctor Who*). Gaiman's manipulations of "structural continuity" hence repeatedly draw on and privilege modes of fan reading, either by returning to gaps in the text (*e.g.*, dead characters), recognizing all forms of continuity while playfully offering up outrageously transgressive narrative possibilities (*e.g.*, the helper as lead villain), or seeking to create coherent retroactive continuity (voicing the TARDIS). Mythology and fandom are insistently interconnected in Gaiman's work as a producer-fan, suggesting that reading unfolding texts as myths is a key part of fan cultural capital and fan interpretation. Blanket descriptions of these texts as "mythic," or as having mythological dimensions, may thus miss the mark somewhat. Unfolding texts can act as myths; they can be specifically read and activated *as* mythic by fan cultures and by professional authors making use of their own (and others') fan affects, knowledge, and identities. Yet the hyperdiegetic universes of contemporary TV and comic books are not objectively given as mythologies. Instead, they are affectively engaged with, and read-as-mythology, by communities of fan readers. Mythology might validate fan investment, and legitimate popular culture, but it is also actively produced through fan (re)interpretations and producer-fan (re)tellings. Mythology is, perhaps, the ultimate fan service.

---

1 Rauch, 11-21.
2 Klock, 126.
3 Reynolds, 53.
4 Lundberg, 122.
5 Dowd, 105.
6 Brooker, "The Best Batman Story," 42.
7 Baker, 21-22.
8 Lancaster, 7.
9 Parkin, "Truths Universally Acknowledged," 13.
10 Ibid.
11 Brooker, *Batman Unmasked*.
12 Parkin, "Truths," 18.
13 Parkin, "Truths," 22.
14 Reynolds, 41 and 43, my italics.
15 Reynolds, 43.

16 Reynolds, 45.
17 Hills, *Fan Cultures*, 131.
18 Hills, *Fan Cultures*, 137.
19 Britton, 21.
20 Hills, *Triumph of a Time Lord*.
21 Britton, 22.
22 Parkin, "Truths," 21.
23 Britton, 25.
24 Parkin, "Truths," 23.
25 Clarke, 434-56.
26 Hills, *Fan Cultures*.
27 Gaiman, *Day of the Dead*, 50.
28 Baker, 51-2.
29 Clarke, 450.
30 Lancaster, 8.
31 Gaiman, *Day of the Dead*, 21.
32 Keane, 15.
33 Johnson-Smith, 216.
34 Johnson-Smith, 215.
35 Lancaster, 24.
36 Britton, 22.
37 Parkin, "Truths," 13.
38 Uricchio and Pearson, 184-5.
39 Brooker, *Batman Unmasked*.
40 Gaiman, *Batman*, no page numbers given.
41 Gaiman, *Batman*, n.p.
42 Joan Gordon, 84.
43 Jenkins, 21.
44 Rauch, 17-8.
45 Bender, 221.
46 Coupe, *Myth: 2nd Edition*, 64.
47 Silverstone, 112.
48 Umberto Eco, 117.
49 Klock, 5.
50 Bender, 225.
51 Brooker, *Batman Unmasked*, 275.
52 Gaiman, *Batman*, n.p., final panel of issue #686 reprint.
53 Gaiman, *Wake*, 185.
54 Gaiman, *Batman*, n.p.
55 Uricchio and Pearson, 192.
56 Gaiman, *Batman*, n.p.
57 Klock, 126.
58 Clarke, 443.
59 Coupe, 173.
60 Coupe, 173.
61 Klock, 21.
62 Gaiman, "Foreword: The Nature of the Infection," 7-10.
63 Setchfield, 80-2.
64 Gaiman, "Production Notes," 4.
65 Marcus Wilson, quoted in Guy Haley, 11.
66 Gaiman, "Foreword: The Nature," 8.
67 Gaiman, "Foreword: The Nature," 9.
68 Clarke, 450.
69 David Bailey, "A Boy and His Box," 32.
71 Hills, "Mythology Makes You Feel Something," 198-215.
72 Clarke, 447.

73 Clarke, 447.
74 Britton, 22.
75 Setchfield, 82.
76 Ibid.
77 Clarke, 444.
78 Britton, 21.
79 Clarke, 450.
80 Gaiman, "Foreword: The Nature," 9.
81 Bailey, "In Gaiman's Terms," 48.
82 Ibid.
83 Setchfield, 80.
84 Gaiman, *Wake*, 185.
85 Neil Gaiman, *The Guardian*, TV & Radio Blog: Live Q&A with Neil Gaiman."

So Long and Thanks for All the Dents!
A Guide for the Hitchhiker
Through the Worlds of Douglas Adams and Neil Gaiman

Anthony S. Burdge

It may be safe to say that if you are currently holding a print or Kindle version of the volume in which this chapter is contained, then you the reader may be from the same version of the Earth where Neil Gaiman and Douglas Adams have co-existed. Is this the same Earth destroyed by Vogons, you may ask? There is a chance, along the axis of probability, that this is possible. The stories by Gaiman and Adams have recorded the adventures of various life forms that have entered dreams, alternate realities, and parallel dimensions. With my attempt at humor aside, I believe there are relative questions to ask regarding the comparison of stories by these two beloved authors.

For purposes of expanding entries on Gaiman and Adams for *The Guide*, (more on that in a moment), we must examine who these two beings are and what instruction they both provide for travelers to other worlds and dimensions—including the effects of this type of travel. By meddling with the minds of their audiences, Gaiman and Adams may have already caused instabilities in the axis of space-time. Or are they themselves complex beings who have caused dimensional probabilities to arise in the Whole Sort of General Mish Mash?[1] Before we attempt to address the complexity of this probability, the axis of space-time and its effects on the simple human mind, let us see what we need to expand upon regarding Neil Gaiman.

Gaiman, Neil is a descendent of primitive ape life forms that have inhabited an "utterly insignificant little blue green planet," called "Earth," for really far too long.[2] However, the entry for Neil Gaiman in *The Hitchhikers Guide to the Galaxy*[TM3] states: "Dreamer. Harmless Writer." The reader may already know that this particular Harmless Writer, with an unusually large amount of hair on his head, has been known to state that there have been key inspirational role models within his life and his body of work. A few of these key figures have been, yet are not limited to, J.R.R Tolkien, C.S Lewis, and G.K Chesterton[4]. For the purpose(s) of Mega Dodo Publications[5] we will focus on but one of these inspirational figures, that of another carbon-based ape descendent from the same utterly insignificant little blue-green planet who went by the name of Douglas Adams.

Adams, classified as "Hoopy Explainer. Mostly Harmless Writer," was an editor and primary author of the Earth- based version of *The Guide*. Now *The Guide* has many permutations and variations, constructed by Adams for the purpose of your entertainment via radio, television, cinema, and print. Each of these variations concerns a book about a book. However, this present chapter will be absent of any comic boings, technological bleeps, bloops, and whizzes, or any other audio effects you may have become accustomed to in previous variations and explorations. Throughout the varied versions of these stories by Adams, we are presented with the story of Arthur Dent, who, alongside his traveling companion and contributor for *The Guide*, Ford Prefect, both routinely consult *The Guide*.[6] Every reader of *Hitchhiker's* knows that his or her representative in the fantastical worlds Adams explores is that very ordinary ape man named Arthur Dent. Dent has been the odd and dull Everyman, the person we can relate to, and through whose eyes we have seen all the strange things happening throughout all of the narrative incarnations of *Hitchhiker's*.[7] *The Guide*, by Adams, offers insight into the events of Arthur's adventures in the narrative, which I feel fits the varied samplings I have included in this chapter.

> Those who are regular followers of the doings of Arthur Dent may have received an impression of his character and habits which, while it includes the truth and, of course, nothing but the truth, falls somewhat short, in its composition, of the whole truth in all its glorious aspects. And the reasons for this are obvious: editing, selection, the need to balance that which is interesting with that which is relevant and cut out all the tedious happenstance.[8]

Gaiman's stories possess numerous memorable everyday characters, neither entirely odd, nor dull, and whom you may recall when having a good time at the pub, but more importantly those who have similarly experienced the strange and alien such as Richard from *Neverwhere*, Joey Harker of *Interworld*, and several we shall sample from *The Sandman* series.

Gaiman is quoted as being an "enormous fan"[9] and after numerous interviews with Adams, wrote *DON'T PANIC: Douglas Adams and the Hitchhikers Guide to the Galaxy*.[10] Gaiman states: "As a young man, I wrote the *Hitchhiker's Guide to the Galaxy* companion, *Don't Panic*, which was enormously fun. Every 25-year-old should get to work with Douglas Adams."[11] After writing *DON'T PANIC*, Gaiman turned down numerous offers[12] to write about the lives of other celebrities and felt his future did not lie with writing books about other people. Without stating the overly zarqing obvious, Gaiman's friendship and work with Adams left a "lasting influence"[13] on his own life and work. Adams told Gaiman, as recorded in *DON'T PANIC*, "So my job was to make the fantastical and dreamlike appear to be as real and solid as possible, that was always the crux of *Hitchhiker's*."[14] As well received as Adams' work has been, it appears he succeeded in this accomplishment.

Gaiman stated of Adams:

> I think that perhaps what Douglas was was probably something we don't even have a word for yet. A Futurologist, or an Explainer, or something one day they'll realize that the most important job out there is for someone who can explain the world to itself in ways that the world won't forget.[15]

I, your humble narrator, feel what Gaiman shares about Adams is also applicable to Gaiman's own work. Both writers, in many unforgettable and successful ways, have succeeded in explaining the world, to the world.[16] Many of Gaiman's stories, if not all in some way, illustrate the recordings of characters who have traveled throughout the realms of Dream, crossed into parallel dimensions, met alternative versions of themselves, slipped into the realm of Faerie, explored fantastical Underground cities, and opened doors to darker versions of "normal reality." As chapters in the present volume discuss, Gaiman's own work greatly illustrate the reality of the fantastical and dreamlike.

Readers of Gaiman's work, similar to that of Tolkien's sub-created world, may feel the worlds they enter via the narrative, are as real as the one you, the reader of this volume, currently inhabit. Tolkien discusses the mechanics of how his story was transmitted to him "from the channels the creator is known to have used already [as] the fundamental function of 'sub-creation.'"[17] As an aside, if you are expecting any extensive commentary on a Creator Being, the Almighty Bob,[18] other assorted gods, minor deities from the Halls of Asgard, or the Great Prophet Zarquon,[19] then you are certainly looking in the wrong place. In no fashion whatsoever will these beings stick their pesky faces into any of this chapter; not only do they tend to involve themselves in the daily lives of humans, and make a mess of them, they absolutely cannot be trusted.[20] This author feels the same about elves and fairies—none of them now, my precious.

Tolkien's world of Middle-earth and many other dimensions intersect, turning upside down and inside out the explorers' sense of perception about what is "real."[21] Those who possess a copy of *The Hitchhikers Guide to the Galaxy*,[22] "the most remarkable, certainly the most successful book ever to come out of the great publishing companies of Ursa Minor,"[23] may already realize these concepts were a key staple for Douglas Adams, unless of course you have been hiding out with a mattress on Sqornshellous Zeta.[24]

Gaiman's characters tend to begin their journey similar to that of an Earth-based shamanic exploration of the mind, the mind being the bridge to an infinite amount of internal dream worlds. One example is Barbie's journey to the Land[25] after receiving the Porpentine from a dying Martine Tenbones in *A Game of You*.[26] By contrast, the catalyst for Adams' characters has been the external heroic journey, an equally organic, natural, human process. The fantastical and dreamlike worlds these silly, semi-evolved simians explore appear at first to them, and the reader, quite extraordinary and foreign. This ability to explore internal and external worlds has been a part of human evolution since they first came down out of the trees and walked upright. It has remained a part of the evolution of Homo Sapiens through to their current state. However, the Earth and its inhabitants, with its infinitely multitudinous probabilities as part of a Plural Zone, should not tamper with travel to parallel worlds and dimensions. If you are a life form originating from a Plural Sector, such as you the reader, then hyperspace travel should not be attempted as you may be prone to experience inter-dimensional foul ups. This, as you may already be familiar, has been quite problematic for Arthur Dent.

Readers shall hopefully also be informed of how these concepts are applicable to their own lives and world when a Vogon Constructor Fleet arrives[27] to make way for a hyperspace bypass, or helping them recall where their towel is.

Are dreams real? Do we need instructions?

In his short story collection *Fragile Things,* Gaiman provides "Instructions" on the behaviors a traveler should exhibit when entering other worlds. In the enlightening previous chapter by Matt Hills, Gaiman is cited to have come to understand the shape of reality, and an infinite amount of worlds, by his watching of *Doctor Who*. So either a) the author himself is such as his character Door from *Neverwhere* and is himself a portal to other worlds, or b) by the telling of stories he is a guide for his audience to these worlds. Yet by the transmission of said stories some may question reality relative to their own.

> Remember your name.
> Do not lose hope—what you seek will be found.
> Trust Ghosts. Trust those that you have
> helped to help you in their turn
> *Trust dreams*

Trust your heart, and trust your story.[28]

    So are we to question or distrust the validity of these instructions? By entering these worlds of dream we must trust that they are indeed real and not entirely hypothetical set in motion by a weaver of myth.[29] Gaiman, the Harmless Writer, states quite matter of factly about Adams in his Introduction to M.J. Simpson's biography of Douglas Adams, "This is a book filled with facts about someone who dealt in dreams."[30] Since Gaiman went from writing a book about Douglas Adams to introducing us to the world of Dream in *The Sandman* series, Gaiman may have indeed been inspired by this notion concerning Adams and dreams.

    Elsewhere in this volume Tanya Jones states, "We consciously create boundaries and imaginary lines and borders to keep us safe and grounded in reality, especially globally and socially."[31] So as the reader how do you know these dream worlds do not exist beyond the page upon which they are written? Are you creating mental boundaries because it questions your sense of reality? Does your head hurt? Good — because it should.

    In *The Sandman: Preludes and Nocturnes* Gaiman presents Doctor Destiny, alternatively known as John Dee. While conversing during their drive, Dee asks Rosemary:

> [Dee] "Do you know what Dreams are made of, Rosemary Kelly?"
> [Rosemary] "Made of? They're just Dreams..."
> [Dee] "NO. They aren't. People think Dreams aren't real because they aren't made of matter, Of particles. Dreams ARE Real. But they are made of viewpoints, of images, of memories and puns and lost hopes."[32]

Indeed, then we can safely assume that Dreams are Real, this commentary by Dee is coupled with insight on The Ruby, or Dreamstone belonging to Morpheus, which is in the hands of Dee who illustrates how he can manipulate the reality of dreams with it. It is interesting that Gaiman utilizes the viewpoints of Doctor Destiny (John Dee), to illustrate the world in which he is working. Destiny states in *Preludes and Nocturnes,* which is a nod to the John Dee of your world, "I'm a Hermetic Philosopher and Scientist too."[33] Dr. John Dee, consultant to Queen Elizabeth I, straddled the world of science and magic, immersing himself in magic, astrology, Kabbalah, Hermeticism, while attempting to commune with angels in order to learn the universal language of creation. The science of the Jewish people, Kabbalah, deals with utilizing the mind as a bridge to access sub-created worlds within the *Etz Chaim*, The Tree of Life, or more appropriately the worlds of the *Sefirot*. Each of these divine centers upon the Tree, and within the human energy system, deals with various aspects of creation governed by an angelic hierarchy. It is a way of understanding the relationship between the microcosm and the larger matrix of the Macrocosm.[34] Dee's use of magic and its relation to the universe can be further defined by the instructor of Joey Harker's Practical Thaumaturgy class, or Magic 101: "'Magic' is simply a way of talking to the universe in words that it cannot ignore."[35] Within the worlds of *The Sandman* and DC Comics, Doctor Destiny is a parallel version of Queen Elizabeth's consultant who did all of these things alongside the manipulation of dreams through the Ruby, which belonged to Dream.

Upon the Earth of Gaiman and Adams, dreams are the stuff of the mind, and humanity apparently has the ability to access these worlds built right into it.

So how did humanity get this way?!

Let us briefly look at what Adams tells us about the Earth and humanity. If you plan on learning anything from *The Hitchhikers Guide to the Galaxy* then it is that you, the reader, and your fellow inhabitants of the planet Earth all form a matrix that is a part of an organic computer called Earth, "...you see the mice set up the whole Earth business as an epic experiment in behavioral psychology, a ten million year program..." said Slartibartfast to Arthur Dent when he visited the planet Magrathea.[36] Additionally, we learn from these events that the mice are "merely protrusions into our dimensions of vast hyper-intelligent pan-dimensional beings, the whole business with the cheese and squeaking is just a front...and they control quite a large sector of the Universe in our dimension."[37] So which is it? Do humans have access to worlds through dreams and sub-creation via Tolkien's theories of Creation, utilizing arcane, occult knowledge and ritual magic of John Dee, thereby allowing them to cross over to a parallel universe where Gaiman is actually the author of *The Lord of the Rings*?[38] Or, as Adams tells us, are we merely crossing into dreams via our created nature for the benefit of the mice? You may have already surmised the answer. Gaiman has cleverly hidden many nuggets of instruction and wisdom in his work, which concern humanity and its relation to its multidimensional nature. For example:

> The In-Between is a dangerous place. There are—creatures—that live here, or partly here. We call 'em 'mudluffs.' That's an acronym, MDLF, standing for multi-dimensional life-form. Which is kind of a pointless label, I know—*we're all multidimensional life-forms*, right?[39]

Since Adams has told us the Earth was created by pan-dimensional beings, the mice, as an organic computer matrix to find the Ultimate Question, of which the answer is 42, then it is not a far stretch that the human brain is hard-wired for pan-, trans-, or intra-dimensional activity.

> [Zaphod] Hey, will you get this, Earthman? You're a last-generation product of that computer matrix...and you were right up to the moment your planet got the finger, yeah?
> [Arthur Dent] Er...
> [Ford Prefect] So your Brain was an organic part of the Penultimate Configuration of the Computer Program
> [Arthur Dent] Organic? But I've never felt an organic part of anything![40]

The initial shock of opening up to these ideas does not entirely wear off for Arthur Dent throughout the events of his travels, "I seem to be having tremendous difficulty with my lifestyle."[41] However, for Joey Harker, "It felt good, it felt *right*, to *use my mind* to open the In-Between, to pass from world to world to world."[42] Additionally, when Joey Harker was commissioned to be the Walker for his team, and they commenced upon an intra-dimensional excursion, he "...took a deep breath, [and] opened a door into madness with [his] mind."[43]

For those of us who have moved beyond thinking their digital watches are still a pretty neat idea, into contemplation of their own mental state and its relation to multi-dimensional travel, let us look at how some reactions to the actual travel to other worlds and dimensions before you, the reader, create a mess of the Universe by attempting any such foolishness on your own.

If you find yourself entering a world beyond your normality...

> "My God," complained Arthur, "you're talking about a positive mental attitude and you haven't even had your planet demolished today. I woke up this morning and thought I'd have a nice relaxed day, do a bit of reading, brush the dog...It's now four in the afternoon and I'm already being thrown out of an alien spaceship six light-years from the smoking remains of the Earth!"
> "All right," said Ford, "just stop panicking!"
> "Who said anything about panicking?" snapped Arthur. "This is still culture shock. You wait till I've settled down into the situation and found my bearings. *Then* I'll start panicking!"[44]

For Neil Gaiman, entering dream worlds, subterranean cities, or parallel worlds may be second nature as he speaks quite casually about them in his online journal, whether it's slipping into a parallel universe where everything is reversed,[45] slipping into one while reading an interview,[46] viewing photographs from a parallel universe[47] or admitting knowledge of a parallel earth.[48] In the author's note that opens his novel *InterWorld*, Gaiman states:

> This is a work of fiction. Still, given an infinite number of possible worlds, it must be true on one of them. And if a story set in an infinite number of possible universes is true in one of them, then it must be true in all of them. So maybe it's not as fiction as we think.

In light of this comment by Gaiman, the reader should take some ease as they adjust to the idea of worlds and parallel universes beyond their own. In one way this reflects what Adams wrote in the synopsis of *Hitchhiker's*: "Not to worry about the Earth...there are an infinite multiplicity of parallel universes in which the Earth is still alive and well."[49] The ease with which Gaiman speaks of parallel universes and dream worlds in his stories may be due to the "deep physics," and "weighty SF/cosmological scientific questions," within the thinking process of Douglas Adams.[50] But for people such as Arthur Dent and Richard Mayhew, there is a genuine struggle with accepting the change to their lifestyle and perception of 'reality.' As we sympathize with Arthur's lifestyle difficulty, culture shock, and imminent danger of being tossed out an airlock on an alien spaceship, we can equally do so with Richard. According to the diary entry Richard writes in his mind:

> *Dear Diary,* he began. *On Friday I had a job, a fiancée, a home, and a life that made sense. (Well, as much as any life makes sense) Then I found an injured girl bleeding on the pavement, and I tried to be a Good Samaritan. Now I've got no fiancée, no home, no job, and I'm walking around a couple of hundred feet under the streets of London with the projected life expectancy of a suicidal fruitfly.*[51]

When you are thrust into an alien environment, or it dawns on you that there is a whole different world under the streets of London, humanity tends to yearn for the creature comforts that bring them a sense of normalcy such as the closeness of a loved one, a dog, a home, a good cup of tea, and a steady job. These socially programmed conditions do not allow room for the human mind, for the most part, understanding beyond their creation of mental borders, which provide a safe standard of what is normal to them. The average human may not even know what the catalyst will be that allows their entry into these worlds. For Arthur Dent it was Ford Prefect who had received a signal on his Sub-Etha Sense-O-Matic concerning the arrival of the Vogons.[52] For Richard it was assisting a face down on the sidewalk, hurt and bleeding Door.[53] With Barbie in *A Game of You*, she witnesses the death of Martin Tenbones who had ventured into her own world to hasten her return to The Land, which she had previously thought of as dream adventures and not part of her 'reality.'[54]

To what advantage, or disadvantage, is all of this…

So, you may indeed be wondering, as the thought of venturing upon this type of travel dawns on you, to what advantage would it be, or disadvantage.

Well to begin, you could be Rose Walker who discovers that not only is she a very rare Dream Vortex, but when she dreams that her dreams are incredibly real and vivid. Additionally, she learns that "each mind creates and inhabits its own world, and each world is but a tiny part of that totality that is the dreaming."[55] To Rose's disadvantage she learns that one of the rules of protecting the Dreaming is that Dream must terminate her existence.[56]

For Richard Mayhew, assisting a young girl who was hurt, bloodied and face down in the street, which is honorable unto itself, finds that helping her causes him to lose his job, fiancée, be no longer recognized by his co-workers,[57] or be allowed to withdraw money from an ATM.[58] Upon this realization that he may be stuck with Door and her strange world, he reluctantly accepts the quest of assisting her. This has some advantages, particularly in regard to finding a heroic side. Not only does Richard defeat the Beast,[59] but he also is able to face and overcome the Ordeal of the Key.[60] This in the end leaves him back on the right side of his perfectly normal world and soon after with a choice to return to the Underside of London.

If you have dreams of large wolflike dogs, talking parrots, rats dressed as Inspector Gadget and a land in which you are referred to as a Princess, then like Barbie, you may realize soon enough that those dreams are real. Barbie, lying down upon her bed, enters The Land via her mind and dreams, and finds herself on an adventure with Luz, Wilkinson, and a variety of other beings.[61]

According to the infinitely varied *Hitchhiker's Guide to the Galaxy*, readers will find Arthur Dent in very similar situations. His planet is destroyed, he cannot find a good cup of tea, learns that there is a 15-mile-high statue of him, ends up on the planet Lamuella finding work as their Sandwich Maker, discovers he has a daughter, finds himself on an alternate Earth with his love Fenchurch, who disappears while traveling off planet and who Arthur rediscovers at Milliways, the Restaurant at the End of the

Universe. As this all may indicate, the stories of these characters may not entirely specify they are from your Earth, galaxy, or universe. If you find that you are not from the Earth of Gaiman and Adams, or that of Arthur Dent, Barbie, Richard Mayhew, or Joey Harker, then you must realize that:

> ...the universe we exist in is just one of a multiplicity of parallel universes which co-exist in the same space but on different wavelengths, and in millions of them the Earth is still alive and throbbing much as you remember – or very similar at least – because every possible variation of the Earth also exists.[62]

This may indeed work to your advantage if you are seeking to get away for a while, from you daily humdrum routine activities and live a little. Keep in mind there are plenty of disadvantages of a human being from a Plural Sector deciding to travel beyond the boundaries of his or her semi-evolved simian mental capacity. If said human decides to take it upon his or herself to do so, then remember one thing: Know Where Your Towel Is.

Concluding Remarks

From all of this discussion there are many ways to enter a parallel world, whether it is through the mind and dreams, helping a hurt young girl, discovering you have a team of alternate selves, using the universal language of creation, or merely by having your planet destroyed. Additionally, we have learned via Gaiman and Adams of the existence of many dimensions, many parallel worlds, and many versions of the Earth to consider. From the authoritative insight of these authors, we have learned how many beings can travel from one world to another and the advantages and disadvantages should you choose to travel yourself. On one version of the Earth, some people believe in a Creator Being that brought forth humanity out of a universal language. John Dee was such an individual and this was his ticket to exploration.

However, one highly evolved ape descendent named Terence McKenna, believed that humanity's transformation occurred with the incorporation of the *Psilocybe cubensis* mushroom in the diet of the early ancestors of Homo Sapiens. This is the very same mushroom that today is referred to as the "magical" kind, which is a potent psychedelic that improves visual acuity and stimulates sexual activity. According to McKenna, this effect would have definitely proved to be of evolutionary advantage to humans' omnivorous hunter-gatherer ancestors that would have stumbled upon it "accidentally," and the discovery of which would make it easier for them to hunt.[63]

For our purposes, we already know that one version of the Earth, purported to be created by a Judeo-Christian Creator Being, was in fact the product of mice seeking to find the Ultimate Question. It is of interest to note here that McKenna also suggested that intelligence on Earth may have spread due to these spore-bearing life forms, (*i.e.*, magic mushrooms). These spores, being of a species of high intelligence, arrived on Earth after migrating through outer space in order to establish a symbiotic relationship with human beings. From this symbiosis, McKenna theorized that the mushroom's potency promotes linguistic thinking.

This theory may throw the proverbial monkey wrench—no pun intended toward understanding the mechanics of traveling between worlds as it relates to the ape descendents— into humanity. Has humanity developed with pan-dimensional abilities from mice? As suggested in Gaiman's *InterWorld,* we can open the In-Between with our minds— but is it because of mice, a Creator Being, or mushroom spores? This theory may then further put in jeopardy your understanding of the masterful use of narrative language by Adams and Gaiman, which may assist you to enter another dimension. Whether it is true of your Earth, or another version, then all of the previous discussion isn't worth a load of dingo kidneys and humanity's intelligence and ability is not the product of a Creator Being, not of mice, but of unidentified aliens who have spread their magical spores throughout the cosmos.

This ends my update for *The Guide* with concern to Neil Gaiman and Douglas Adams but still begs the question: What version of the Earth, or realm of Dream, are you from?

---

1 The Whole Sort of General Mish Mash (WSOGMM) found with the pages of Adams' *Mostly Harmless*, "…is the sum total of all the different ways that exist of looking at thing, or more specifically, all the different probabilities that exist through which you could look at things…[it] is a metaphor created to help people better understand a part of the complex concepts presented by the complicated web of probabilities (parallel universes, one could say) presented by created…" http://hitchhikers.wikia.com/wiki/Whole_Sort_of_General_Mish_Mash
This is also referred to by the Doctor (10th) as "a Big Ball of Wibbly Wobbly Timey Wimey…stuff."
2 This version of the Earth may no longer exist, depending upon which universe, or dimension, you currently inhabit.
3 Since you, the reader, exist in the time and space you do, the version of the Guide that is being updated is not the future, second, and more powerful version of the Guide created by Infinidim Enterprises for the Vogons (see *The Guide* for a definition of what a Vogon is), which stretched across all dimensions, perceived everything, and had unfiltered perception. Since there is much wrangling of physics to do here, in order to understand first how I know this since The Guide Mark II exploded and destroyed all versions of the Earth and we both are scratching our heads as to why we exist at all— we shall leave it as part of the Whole Sort of General Mish Mash.
4 Mythcon 35 Guest of Honor Speech http://www.mythsoc.org/mythcon/35/speech
5 Not Kitsune Books, you ask? Mega Dodo Publications is the Galactic Publication Overseer that optioned Kitsune Books to unravel the quandaries that lie within the being calling himself "Neil Gaiman," as explained in great detail within the present volume you now hold.

6 A bit of sympathy for any confusion. Adams wrote a book about a book, which narrates itself in different versions—with different outcomes. Adams wrote a radio play that became a book that became a television series, interspersed with more books, a film, and more radio series—oh and comics too—all of which differ. If you happen to own an actual Guide, then you may understand a bit more than the average Earth-bound being.
7 Gaiman, *DON'T PANIC*, 142.
8 Adams, *The Ultimate Hitchhiker's Guide to the Galaxy*, 568.
9 Neil Gaiman hitchhikes through Douglas Adams' hilarious galaxy (Interview by Kathie Huddleston). http://web.archive.org/web/20040216101052/http://scifi.com/sfw/advance/24_interview.html
10 Mega Dodo Publications and Neil Gaiman are still wrangling the legalities of his use of "DON'T PANIC," which as you may know is boldy displayed in large friendly written letters upon the front of *The Hitchhikers Guide to the Galaxy*.
11 <http://www.neilgaiman.com/p/About_Neil/Interviews/Neil_Gaiman's_Otter_Tricks_by_Chris_Bolton,_Powells.com_(August,_2005)>
12 Many of these offers came from such esteemed publications as *PlayBeing, Mega Dodo*, and *Eccentric Gallumbits*.
13 See note 9.
14 Gaiman, *DON'T PANIC*, 141.
15 <http://journal.neilgaiman.com/2008/04/remembering-douglas-1.html>
16 Gaiman states of Adams, "But I do think that everything Douglas did that was really successful consisted of trying to explain the world to the world." I felt such praise is also applicable to Gaiman. (Huddleston Interview).
17 Carpenter, *Letters*, 188.
18 (Adams, *The Ultimate Hitchhiker's Guide to the Galaxy*, 728). The god being of the inhabitants of the planet Lamuella.
19 Adams, *The Ultimate*, 228.
20 If you absolutely have need to consult an intellectual guide on Neil Gaiman and his consorting with gods, then please refer to the brilliant chapter by Harley Sims in the present volume.
21 The question of What is Real? is as problematic as a Vogon Fleet circling your planet to make way for an Interstellar ByPass—neither of which will be dissected at the present time.
22 The narrative version, often paperback edition, by Douglas Adams, "not the galactic, large pocket calculator sized version having upon its face over a hundred flat press-buttons and a screen about four inches square, upon which any one of over six million pages can be summoned almost instantly and comes in a durable plastic cover upon which the words DON'T PANIC are printed in large friendly letters."
23 (Gaiman, *Don't Panic*, 158)
24 Adams, *The Ultimate*, 349.
25 In *A Game of You*, the fantastical realm Barbie travels to is simply called "The Land."
26 Gaiman, *Game*, 36.
27 The author of this chapter does sincerely hope the reader is able to gain some clarity on the matter of which he writes because Mega Dodo Publications and the police of Jazzlebrix Minor have threatened to throw him in the Total Perspective Vortex, which lies between a fairy cake and cranky old woman, if he does not.
28 Gaiman, *Fragile*, 193, italicized for emphasis.
29 See Sims in the present volume.
30 This introduction can be found by searching Gaiman's website/journal at http://journal.neilgaiman.com /2008/04/remembering-douglas-1.html
31 See Jones' chapter in the present volume.
32 Gaiman, *Preludes*, 16.
33 Gaiman, *Preludes*, 16.
34 There is an abundant amount of material available on Kabbalah, which gives this basic premise of the Tree of Life. See works by Aaron Leitch, Israel Regardie, Dion Fortune & Aryeh Kaplan.
35 Gaiman & Reaves, *InterWorld*, 179.
36 Adams, *The Original Hitchhiker Radio Scripts*, 73.
37 Adams, *The Original Hitchhiker Radio Scripts*, 73, 82,
38 Gaiman, Mythcon 35 Guest of Honor Speech: "I came to the conclusion that *Lord of the Rings*

was probably, the best book that ever could be written, which put me in something of a quandary...I wanted to write *The Lord of the Rings*. The problem was that it already had been written..." <http://www.mythsoc.org/mythcon/35/speech>

39 Gaiman & Reaves, *InterWorld*, 63, italic stress my own,
40 Carnell & Leialoha, *The Hitchhiker's Guide to the Galaxy: The Authorized Collection Graphic Novel*, 130.
41 Adams, *The Ultimate*, 128.
42 Gaiman and Reaves, *InterWorld*,157, second italic stress is my own.
43 Gaiman and Reaves, *InterWorld*, 118.
44 Adams, *The Ultimate*, 48.
45 Gaiman notes: "Also, I think I have slipped into a parallel universe in which everything is reversed." <http://journal.neilgaiman.com/2008_03_01_archive.html>
46 And again: "There was a very odd moment in the middle of reading the Dame Darcy interview at Bookslut.com where I thought I'd slipped into a parallel universe...." <http://journal.neilgaiman.com/2004/04/millions-and-billions-and-trillions.asp>
47 And not for the last time: "Bill Stiteler sent me this link to a set of photographs from a prallel universe...." <http://www.flickr.com/photos/williamhundley/sets/72157594235409275/>
48 Finally, for us at present: "And finally, another one from, I suspect, a parallel earth." <http://journal.neilgaiman.com/2008_10_01_archive.html>
49 Gaiman, *DON'T PANIC*, 241.
50 Gaiman, *DON'T PANIC*, 186.
51 Gaiman, *Neverwhere*, 135.
52 Adams, *The Ultimate*, 20.
53 Gaiman, *Neverwhere*, 24.
54 Gaiman, *Game*,36.
55 Gaiman, *Doll's House*, 195-197.
56 Gaiman, *Doll's House*, 202.
57 Gaiman, *Neverwhere*, 59.
58 Gaiman, *Neverwhere*, 66.
59 Gaiman, *Neverwhere*, 314.
60 Gaiman, *Neverwhere*, 253.
61 Gaiman, *A Game of You*, 51
62 Gaiman, *DON'T PANIC*, 40.
63 Terence McKenna, *Food of the Gods: The Search for the Original Tree of Knowledge*.

Consorting with the Gods: Exploring Gaiman's Pan-pantheon

Harley J. Sims

[Mister Pinkerton:] "There's a theory that for a human to be killed by a god is the best thing that could possibly happen to the human under discussion. It eliminates all questions of belief, while manifestly placing a human life at the service of a higher power. Where do you stand on this theory?"
[Carla:] "I--I don't believe in God."
[Mister Pinkerton:] "You don't have to believe in God. But what about gods? Eh? The plurality of powers and dominions. The lords and ladies of field and thorn, of asphalt and sewer, gods of telephone and whore, gods of hospital and car-crash?"
[Carla:] "This is crazy."

—*The Sandman: The Kindly Ones*[1]

It is unclear whether Carla ever learns who Mister Pinkerton truly is; in the same panel where he declares his identity, the young woman is engulfed by the conflagration that kills her. Like Low Key Lyesmith in *American Gods*, Mister Pinkerton of *The Sandman* is a pseudonym for the Old Norse trickster-god Loki, a being who, as Neil Gaiman postulates and Odin specifies earlier in *The Sandman* series, is properly "the child of giants, but Aesir [properly Æsir, the dominant clan of Norse gods] by right of blood-brotherhood."[2] In both *The Sandman* and *American Gods*, the machinations—and, ultimately, the manipulation—of Loki serve as engines of the plot, involving the gods and spirits of numerous traditions ancient, modern, and invented.

In this involvement, no single work of Gaiman's is incompatible with another; in *Sandman* as in *American Gods*, *Anansi Boys*, *Neverwhere*, and *Stardust*, deities and creatures from various mythic and folkloric traditions—European, Middle-eastern, African, Asian, North American, and others—coexist and interact, all ageless if not immortal, and bearing different attitudes towards their fall from popular belief. From a Lucifer who quits Hell to play the piano, to a Thor who blows his head off out of depression, Gaiman portrays both an otherworld and an underworld of fallen idols and icons, an alternate über-reality where the deities born to peoples continents away and historically unacquainted with one another now rub shoulders as surely as they do in modern dictionaries of gods and myth. Gaiman's particular approach to mythological tales and figures exemplifies what is perhaps the dominant impulse of modern Fantasy—the desire to explore the imaginary on its own soil. Gaiman treats the stuff of myth as possessing a hypothetical reality of its own, a reality to be developed as an active explorer rather than reiterated as a passive reteller. The purpose of that exploration is, in turn, to add grand, new dimensions to preexisting material, reinvigorating ancient texts and icons with modern relevance even as the original material elevates Gaiman's own creations. Through this symbiosis, Gaiman places himself upon the web of story, spinners ever poised, never a witness but always a weaver. In doing so, he sets an example of the most decorous manner in which to engage imaginative material— imaginatively, but invested with the sense of reality that makes any and all things believable. This chapter will examine some of the elements, implications, and achievements of what might be called Gaiman's *mythism*, in particular those of his magnum opus *Sandman* series. Projects such as *Neverwhere*, *American Gods*, *Anansi Boys*, *Stardust*, the *Death* graphic novels, and various shorter works are effectively treated as tributaries and offshoots, if not as evidence of a world shared with and established by *The Sandman*.

Gaiman's works illustrate his method in many ways, but no more so than with his vision of a cosmic backstage where the deities and spirits of all cultures and historical periods continue in secret to influence human affairs. Such a backstage might be called a 'pan-pantheon' and whose pertinence to Gaiman's portrayal of the gods is fitting. The word 'pantheon' seems to have been adopted into the English language twice, once in the fourteenth century and again in the seventeenth.[3] Both times it came from Latin sources, though the word is Greek in origin: *pántheion* (πάνθειον) (from *pan* [παν] 'all' + *theîos* [θεῖος] 'of or sacred to a god' [θεός]). According to extant literature, the word had meanings ranging from "all embracing divinity" (*cf.* modern pantheism) to, as Aristotle used it in his *Mirabilia*, a "temple or place consecrated to all gods."[4] Its first documented use in English refers to the Roman Pantheon and other sacred buildings of its sort,[5] where all the deities of a people are identified and honored. The second time the word entered English, it was in the context of theological debate, and referred—most familiar to the modern sense of the term—to "[a] habitation of all the gods; the assemblage of all the gods; the deities of a people collectively."[6] Though this definition appears preemptive and all-embracing, it was common practice from the beginning of its use to specify pantheons by region or religion, distinguishing the Roman Pantheon from the Greek, for example, even though the ancient and Classical worlds saw much adoption and conflation of deities among peoples.

More importantly for our purposes here, and as John Clute has observed, "[p]antheons are part of the furniture of much genre fantasy,"[7] involving fantasy writers' use of historical deities, as well as the invented deities of Secondary worlds. The Valar of J.R.R. Tolkien's Secondary world Arda are often referred to as a pantheon,[8] while the gods of Wizards of the Coast's pulp-fantasy series *Dragonlance* and *Forgotten Realms* are routinely catalogued in sourcebooks as the pantheons of Krynn and Faerûn, respectively. While a person might refer to the plurality of pantheons in Gaiman's works in terms of a single body—*The Sandman* pantheon, for one—the term *pan-pantheon* ('all of the collections of deities') has here been adopted to emphasize Gaiman's particular plurality, and most of all its inclusive and open-ended basis in imagination.

Though it is clear from the first appearance of Cain and Abel in *The Sandman* story "Imperfect Hosts" that Gaiman's narratives embrace numerous mythical and spiritual traditions, the word 'pantheon' itself appears several times in Gaiman's works, most notably (and aptly) in *The Sandman* title *The Season of Mists*. In this volume, Dream has unwillingly inherited the keys to Hell—as Death calls it, "the most desirable plot of psychic real estate in the whole order of created things"[9] — prompting the god, figures, and personified archetypes of the multiverse to come soliciting. At the banquet on the first night of their arrival, Loki describes the Shinto deity Susano-o-no-mikoto (Susano-wo)[10] as "a lone member of his ancient pantheon."[11] Later, in a private meeting with Dream, the Japanese god himself explains that "[t]he gods of Nippon [...] are expanding—assimilating other pantheons, later gods, new altars and icons."[12] These particular gods and pantheons are not always represented or made clear as the assemblage awaits Dream's decision over the future of Hell. A white-bearded figure in a pointy, star-spangled hat—the classic Renaissance wizard, possibly Merlin, or Prospero[13]—mentions to his literally-faceless companion that he is "surprised not to see a representative from the Greek gods here."[14] He might well have said 'pantheon,' for it is clear by this point that the gods and figures are organized by original civilization rather than, say, their particular ministry or sphere of influence.[15] For example, Loki explains to Odin that Susano-o-no-mikoto is "a storm god, like your son [Thor],"[16] but Thor and Susanowo appear either unacquainted with or uninterested in one another, suggesting that, as with the murderous new gods in *American Gods*, and like political parties in non-coalition governments, only one cabinet has jurisdiction somewhere at any one time.

The deities, god-like beings, and supernatural figures that appear or are mentioned in Gaiman's works number in the hundreds, and are listed and indexed online, in many books, and elsewhere. To attempt to reproduce such a resource here would be redundant, but it would also misrepresent both the pan-pantheon and the inclusiveness of Gaiman's imaginary world. Even when they appear in droves, as in *The Sandman* volumes *Season of Mists* and *The Wake*, as well as in *American Gods*, these mythical figures are as much allusion as presence, their names effectively hypertext linking them to the traditional bodies of story from which they derive.

Encounters in *The Sandman* with Calliope, Orpheus, Hades, and Persephone necessarily evoke the eight other Muses, Zeus, Hera, Hestia, Poseidon, Demeter, Hercules, the Titans, and potentially everyone else in a dictionary or other collection of Greek myths, relatively few of whom are actually portrayed in the world of *The Sandman*, yet all of whom must be up to something elsewhere. Whether with Ishtar of the Assyro-Babylonian pantheon, Anansi of the African Ashanti people, Czernobog of prehistoric Slavonic belief, or several other sole specimens of assumed pantheons such as Easter,[17] Gaiman employs both well-known and hardly-known figures, and in mutually beneficial fashion borrows from their mystery and tradition even as his own narratives promote and develop them as individual characters. Such involvement is not restricted to the figures of ancient, defunct, and obscure religions and pantheons. To represent the Angel Islington in the London Below of *Neverwhere*, Aziraphale the angel of the Eastern Gate of Eden in *Good Omens*, and the celestial representatives Dumas and Remiel in *The Sandman* is to recruit the living lore of the Abrahamic holy books and their apocrypha, material in which—along with forces such as Order and Chaos[18]—many millions of people in the industrialized world still believe. Such recruitment goes hand-in-hand with Gaiman's use of historical figures such as Maxmilien Robespierre, Shakespeare, Marco Polo, and Caius Julius Caesar Octavius, though it should be acknowledged that, compared to more political comic-book writers such as Alan Moore and Frank Miller, Gaiman's involvement of real-life figures and affairs, at least in outwardly real-life contexts, is quite modest. His major players are celestials, infernals, and other outsiders—beings largely immune from, though potentially influencing, the day-to-day affairs of the human mainstream.

    No matter how overwhelming the preexisting ocean of story might seem when channeled into the margins of a single body, Gaiman deepens it further by developing its mythic traditions in three fundamental ways. The first is by inventing new figures for existing historical cultures, a long-standing custom of creative mythography often practiced by fantasy writers, but also by celebrated English poets; Leigh Hunt's catalogical poem "The Nymphs," for example, coins several new varieties of the feminine wood spirits, including Ephydriads, Limniads, Napeads, and Nepheliads.[19] Gaiman engages in this sort of invention with Aziraphale in *Good Omens*[20] and in *The Sandman*, with several demons, but also by attaching the Endless— including Destiny, Death, Destruction, Desire, Despair, and Delirium, but especially the eponymous Dream—to several historical pantheons, most notably that of the Greeks. In *The Sandman*, Orpheus is the child of Dream and the muse Calliope, a parentage that is an invention of Gaiman's in the sense that existing mythology attributes his fatherhood to Apollo, or possibly to the Thracian Oeagrus.[21] In "The Song of Orpheus, Chapter One" in *Fables and Reflections*, all seven of the Endless appear at the wedding of Orpheus and Eurydice, and are fitted with Greek names.[22] That the most detailed involvement of Dream and the Endless is with the Hellenic tradition is unsurprising, as the idea of a dream-deity is most associable with the Greek god Morpheus, one of the thousand children of Hypnos, god of sleep, according to the mythography of Homer, Pausanius, and Ovid. Not only is Dream often called 'Morpheus' in *The Sandman*, but he is also once summoned by its recitation into the waking world, suggesting it is in fact his True Name.[23]

Another way in which Gaiman develops mythical traditions is by developing pantheons previously invented. Though the Endless serve as an example of this as well—through, for instance, the attachment of mythical archetypes such as Death and Dream to the more specialized creations of Despair and Delirium—there are more clear-cut examples, and beyond *The Sandman*'s weighty precedents. *The Books of Magic* explored many of the mythological and enchanted elements of the DC Universe, developing the pluralistic world of gods, spirits, and super powered beings which has remained central to Gaiman's imaginary realities.[24] His original work with Todd McFarlane's *Spawn* comic series was to introduce both Angela, an evil angel, as well as to provide a back-story to the Hellspawn legacy that complicated the previously static and satanic Malebolgia who created Spawn himself.[25] In the same vein, Gaiman's contributions to H.P. Lovecraft's Cthulhu mythos were to add biographical depth to several of the Old Ones and their spawn,[26] figures usually left in the shadows of the mythos's imaginary world. The apparent predilection on the part of Gaiman to reach for the background of any portrait he touches is striking, suggesting his desire to manipulate not simply the characters, but also the cosmologies and cosmogonies that determine the significance of those characters' thoughts and actions.

Finally, Gaiman invents new pantheons entirely. The Endless of *The Sandman* again provide a good case, but there are subtler and more intricate examples, some where Gaiman works by allusive implication, and other times where he organizes preexisting figures into coherent social and political bodies. When, in "The Passengers," Dream appears to Martian Manhunter in pursuit of the Dreamstone, the Martian sees Dream as L'Zoril—"a *very* old god," presumably of Mars[27]—implying not only that a number of gods were known to the Martians of the DC Comics universe, but also that certain gods to some peoples are different gods to others[28] (or, in the case of the Endless, that they are sometimes worshipped as gods when they are in fact a different class of being). Perhaps the best example, however, lies with Gaiman's portrayal of Faerie and its government, which is presided over by the Shakespearean aspects of Titania and Auberon/Oberon from *A Midsummer Night's Dream*. Rooted as it is in Shakespeare's most celebrated comedy, and first portrayed in *The Sandman* story of the same name, Gaiman's conception of the Seelie Court is unmistakably English. Though he and Shakespeare employ the same combination of English and Classical figures, their otherworldly society is cohesive and their aristocracy stately. British folklorist Thomas Keightley describes the fusion as follows:

> Shakspeare *[sic]*, having the Faerie Queene before his eyes, seems to have attempted a blending of the Elves of the village with the Fays of romance. His Fairies agree with the former in their diminutive stature…in their fondness for dancing, their love of cleanliness, and their child-abstracting propensities. Like the Fays, they form a community, ruled over by the princely Oberon and the fair Titania. There is a court and chivalry.[29]

That said, there seems more of Edmund Spenser's *Faerie Queene* than of Mab in Gaiman's Titania—though Mab and Titania are later suggested to be one[30]—and as Faerie and its administration continue to be developed throughout *The Sandman*, they appear more like the Renaissance monarchy of the Classical woodlands (as in Spenser and Shakespeare) and less the anarchy of the English countryside's folkloric superstitions.

Gaiman's engineering of the fairy pantheon is further demonstrated by its two most prominent characters, Cluracan and Nuala. The names of both belong to traditional Irish figures who bear little direct resemblance to their namesakes in *The Sandman*; a clúracán is a class of solitary fairy—another of which is the leprechaun—and is described as small and withered, while characterized as a layabout and a lone drunkard.[31] Nuala, meanwhile, is no less than a form of Finnguala or Úna, wife of the Irish fairy-king Finnbheara, and so a version of Titania in her own right. In *The Sandman*, however, Cluracan is an individual—a foppish emissary of Titania—and Nuala is his sister, a diffident and lugubrious sprite. In *A Season of Mists*, Cluracan represents Titania at the court of Dream and offers Nuala in exchange for Hell. When Dream effectively returns the infernal realm to its Creator, Nuala is relinquished nonetheless, becoming a listless but loyal servant in Dream's house and eventually playing a minor role in his fate. The fealty of these lone Irish figures[32] to the English Titania suggests the sort of Hiberno-English or Anglo-Celtic amalgam that has become common to fairy folklore—an aboriginal pan-pantheon, so to speak—but it demonstrates yet again Gaiman's urge to reshape, recast, and/or reorganize the mythic materials he adopts.

The ultimate example of Gaiman's mythological inventiveness, however—a figure who represents all three methods just described—belongs to the mysterious god Pharamond who first appears in *The Sandman* volume *Brief Lives*. When readers first meet him, he is head of a successful global travel company, and is called upon by Dream to provide means of transportation as he and he sister Delirium seek their wayward brother Destruction on Earth. The necessity of the old gods and spirits to change, branch out, and adapt to new times and modes of worship is leitmotif in Gaiman's mythological works, and is central to Pharamond's role:

> [Dream:] "You are well, Pharamond?"
> [Pharamond:] "Oh, yes. Keeping busy. I'm the last of my pantheon, you know."
> [Dream:] "I know."
> [Pharamond:] "I suppose you would, wouldn't you? I wasn't thinking. Diversification. *That's* the secret. You were right about that."[33]

Unlike Susanowo, the last figure to voice these sentiments, the pantheon to which Pharamond belongs is unclear. His name seems to be that of a legendary fifth-century Frankish king.[34] There are encouraging etymological considerations—especially the Germanic *fara-mann* 'travel man' or *fara-mund* 'travel protection'—that make sense because Pharamond is a travel agent when Dream meets him in the late twentieth century. Nevertheless, there is reason to believe that neither the Roman alphabet nor the Germanic language in which his name is recorded yet existed when he and Dream last met, in Babylon.[35] Furthermore, Pharamond is unlikely to be a Babylonian deity—not only because the Babylonians borrowed most of their pantheon from the Sumerians, but also because the Akkadian language included no 'f' sound.[36]

Whereas, Pharamond claims to be the last of his assembly, the goddess Ishtar is still alive when he says this, at least for the moment.[37] In a conversation with Delirium, Dream reveals that Pharamond was already in decline when they last met,[38] suggesting that, like the witch Thessaly/Larissa of *A Game of You* and *The Wake*, the lawyer Bernie Capax in Chapter Three of *Brief Lives*, and the nameless, buffalo-headed figure Shadow dreams constantly in *American Gods*,[39] Pharamond may have hailed from a time and place long before living or written memory. Pharamond's name presents several other possibilities, most notably that of the island of Pharos on which the lighthouse of Alexandria once stood, the Jewish Pharisees, and, of course, the Egyptian Pharaohs, to which Pharamond has a certain racial resemblance. One could go on with such speculation, but it is of course fruitless to presume to study empirically something that exists only within the imagination. As Samuel R. Delaney's introduction to *A Game of You* pretends, "[w]hat—? You don't know what sort of a goblin a Tantoblin is? Well, neither do I. What's more, the OED won't help us."[40]

Despite these uncertainties and potential inaccuracies, Pharamond is a credible character, and he works as a historical figure in the same way he works as a mythical one. To understand this operation, one must understand the sense of reality that is essential to the worlds of comic books and other collaborative franchises including bodies of myth,[41] and to appreciate the idea that Gaiman's narratives are not simply oriented by that sense of reality, but that they exploit it. Only the briefest of outlines is possible here,[42] but it is important to admit that all fictional worlds are imaginary, and that a world does not need to be alternate to be fictional; the London of Gaiman's *Neverwhere* is a product of fiction, as is The Dreaming in *The Sandman*. The foremost distinction between these two examples is the degree of fictive space each affords—effectively, how much the writer can get away with before the reader's suspended disbelief begins to reassert itself. A literary world's *fictionality*—the quality of or capacity to possess fictive space—is determined for the most part by the reader's knowledge of and ability to investigate that world. Unlike The Dreaming, London possesses basic credibility, which means that the reader will recognize the world as part of his or her own so long as the narrative does not contradict the reader's knowledge thereof; this is one of the reasons why Gaiman's modern human characters exist primarily on the fringes of society, and not at its heart. On the other hand, truly alternate worlds such as The Dreaming afford the greatest amount of fictive space simply because the objective accuracy of its narrative development cannot be investigated. Only its consistency can be verified in such a way—and The Dreaming is an inconsistent place. This is also one of the reasons why Gaiman's portrayal of alternate worlds such as Hell and Asgard focuses on the movers and shakers.

Where comic-book and collaborative-franchise realities surmount this basic relationship, and how Gaiman succeeds in making his invented ancients credible, is through dimensional proliferation, where contradictory realities not only coexist, but potentially overlap. In comics, as in myths, lives are infinite, timelines navigable, and possibilities endless. Dead characters can come back to life or be revisited at a time or in a dimension where they never died; purportedly longstanding influences can be introduced and retroactively streamlined. As Delaney says of *The Sandman*, "[in] these narratives, the whole world is haunted and mysterious. There is no solid status quo, only a series of relative realities, personal to each of the characters, any and all of which are frail, and subject to eruptions from other states and conditions."[43] Nothing can be erroneous in a world of possibilities because the gaps required for fictive space can be introduced and inflated wherever necessary, much like airbags before a potentially violent impact. For a number of years in the late 1980s, for example, Marvel Comics offered a 'No-prize' to those who could spot potential fallacies and continuity errors in their stories, and who could then pose explanations or episodes that would rationalize them.[44] Because they are constrained by neither time nor space, gods and other divine, magical, or extra-dimensional beings are the very embodiments of such correctives; consider the episode of *The Simpsons* where Lucy Lawless explains to a sceptical fan that every time an inconsistency occurs in *Xena*, "a wizard did it."[45] They are what Fantasy Studies calls 'liminal beings,'[46] and they are often as anachronistical as they are powerful; examples include the Genie of Disney's *Aladdin*, Q of *Star Trek: The Next Generation*, and the Merlin of T.H. White's Arthurian tales. If, then, comic-book worlds afford the most permutable flow of events, the gods of these worlds represent their most liberated inhabitants—beings so immune to the idea of inaccuracy as to be close to pure fictionality itself.

The gods are liminal beings within liminal worlds, and it is because of this that even the most problematic of Gaiman's mythical characters, such as Pharamond of *The Sandman*, work. They work not simply because they can always be explained, but because they can always be excused.

It is from this perspective that Gaiman neither rewrites nor truly contradicts the myths from which they derive, rather that he choreographs and reconciles their many traditions in the light of a single, grand, and boundless production—a sort of mono-mythic reality within which our own world is a small dimension. The original, disparate stories he treats as sort of rudimentary glimpses—peeks stolen through a cosmic curtain which he himself is determined to sweep wide open. In this way, Gaiman does not distort the myths on which he draws, but instead combines and elaborates them through appropriation and retelling, exploiting the imaginative and multidimensional potential that is the very essence of story. This is not to say that he does not ever change things—he has, some of which he has apologized for[47]—nor to say that his work is without errors, some more pedantic than glaring. His conflation, for example, of Samael and Lucifer in *The Sandman* poses an angelogical quagmire,[48] while the pronunciation of Loki he posits in *American Gods*—"Low Key"—is inaccurate according to the Old Norse–Icelandic record (Loki rhymes with *hockey*).[49] Furthermore, the Anglo-Saxon language in the *Beowulf* film that Gaiman co-wrote with Roger Avary is nightmarish, at least to a student of Old English. Nevertheless, the liberties of Gaiman's inventiveness are indulged primarily in the fictive spaces between and behind the traditions he combines, and not in their midst, a procedure encouraged and bolstered by the unobstructable continuity of comic-book reality. David Bratman notes that:

> ...with *Sandman*, Gaiman aimed to use a comics-based mythos to expand on, interact with, and *deepen* classical legends of mythology and popular history. On one hand, this approach might seem like merely another clever postmodern ruse, taking old Greek and Norse myths, European and Asian and Islamic folk tales, plus scenarios from Dante, Blake, Milton and Dore, and mixing them with 20th-century comics and horror elements. Still, Gaiman made it all work, and on his own terms. His tales of the Endless... resounded as works of both grand invention and wondrous apocrypha. Which is to say, sure, you could see the modern-day sensibility in it all—the fun subterfuge of deities and comics characters sharing the same space, the same dilemmas. At the same time, it was as if you had discovered a timeless trove of fascinating lost legends and mysteries: missing vellums that revealed how so many different people shared so many similar patterns of fable and providence in their disparate histories of storytelling.[50]

It should seem amusing to consider that no writer or publishing house holds the copyright to the gods; they are, in many ways and for all their power, the most vulnerable characters in fiction. No better illustration of their public ownership exists than the fact that the same pantheons appear in both the DC and Marvel Universes. As Bratman argues, however, Gaiman's narratives are memorable not because the gods simply appear, but because their cosmologies are assembled and re-constelled so intricately. The originals need not fall for the new stories to stand; as the Icelandic Odin says of his American aspect Wednesday in *American Gods*, "[h]e was me, yes. But I am not him."[51]

So far, this paper has spoken primarily of the presence of mythical figures in Gaiman's works. The number of artistic uses to which these figures are put, including the roles they play, is potentially infinite, limited only by the imagination and argumentation of the reader. Among the many ways Gaiman seeks to invest his pan-pantheon with realistic traits and tendencies, however, sexuality and reproduction are crucial, fertilization being perhaps the most substantial form of engagement and appropriation one world can have with another. An introductory comment by director Robert Zemeckis from the *Beowulf* DVD well illustrates this aspect of Gaiman's writing: "This has nothing to do with the *Beowulf* you were forced to read in Junior High School. It's all about eating, drinking, killing, and fornicating."[52] The original Old English poem *Beowulf* has plenty of eating, drinking, and killing. It is overt fornication that it lacks, and which therefore most differentiates the film that Gaiman co-wrote, one which makes Hrothgar and Beowulf the lovers of Grendel's mother, and the respective fathers of Grendel and the dragon. The use of sexuality to make the imaginative seem more real is by no means exclusive to Gaiman's work, nor limited to the fantasy genre. For example, its constant and often gruesome involvement in the storylines of such successful television crime franchises as *CSI*, *Criminal Minds*, and *Law and Order* suggests that its basis in biology, combined with its complex scientific, psychological, and cultural ramifications, makes it an extremely effective hook for engaging secular audiences. Gaiman's use of sexuality has similarly disturbing examples,[53] but the manner in which his writings unite the elements of sex and mythology has far greater effect than gritty credibility. In Pygmalion-like fashion, Gaiman's imagination first sculpts then embraces his most important mythical figures, to the extent that many of his central human protagonists and other characters are only partially human. These include Shadow of *American Gods*, Charlie Nancy of *Anansi Boys*, Tristran Thorn of *Stardust*, and, to varying degrees, Rose Walker, Jed Walker, and Daniel Hall of *The Sandman*. As one of the Three tells Calliope in *The Sandman*, "[t]here are few of the old powers willing or able to meddle in mortals' affairs in these days,"[54] but of those obsolescent gods and spirits who seek to remain active and known in the modern day, their most powerful form of intervention seems to be intercourse. Whether through the offspring it produces or the conflicts it creates, this communication in many ways moves Gaiman's narratives towards their conclusions, and illustrates the various states of lordship and slavery in which the gods find themselves vis-à-vis humankind.

When Death and John Constantine performed a public-service announcement about sexually transmitted diseases and the importance of using condoms in *Death: The High Cost of Living*,[55] The Endless may be said to have finally jumped the shark. The announcement nevertheless confirmed the prominence of—if not comfort with—sexuality in Gaiman's *Sandman* franchise, as well as its involvement with mythical and otherwise supernatural elements and themes. This quality is established within the opening pages of volume one *Preludes and Nocturnes*, where a woman named Unity Kincaid unwittingly sets in motion the central thread of *The Sandman* story. Falling asleep the night Dream is imprisoned by occultists, she like many others falls victim to a sleeping sickness that rarely sees her awake. She is impregnated while asleep—raped by an unnamed assailant—and it is not until *The Doll's House*, fifty years later in the story, that we meet Rose Walker, her grand-daughter, a generation removed from the crime. She turns out to be what Dream calls a Dream Vortex, a person capable of disrupting the order of The Dreaming and potentially destroying entire worlds. It is a lamentable tradition that Dream must kill the Dream Vortex when it arises in order to prevent chaos, though Unity Kincaid intervenes and rightfully takes Rose's place.[56] Dream then realizes that Unity's rapist—and Rose's grandfather—must have been Desire, presumably one of the "little games" that only Despair, Desire, and Delirium of the Endless play.[57] Dream calls Rose Walker one of his own blood,[58] someone he could not kill without dire consequences, and his confrontation with Desire is marked by this remonstration:

> We of the Endless are the servants of the living—we are NOT their masters. WE exist because they know, deep in their hearts, that we exist. When the last living thing has left this universe, then our task will be done. And we do not manipulate them. If anything, they manipulate us. We are their toys. Their dolls, if you will. And you—and Despair, and even poor Delirium—should remember that.[59]

Nevertheless, Desire *has* manipulated them, and the results of that action will move far beyond the events of *The Doll's House*. The plot is as intricate and as labyrinthine as only a long-lasting serial title can be, but Rose Walker's brother Jed, who is also a scion of the Endless, is in many ways responsible for Daniel Hall, whom Dream claims as his own after his mother spent years gestating in The Dreaming. Once Daniel has been taken—not, however, by Dream—the vengeance of his mother Hippolyta raises the ire of the Three, who pursue vengeance on Dream when he breaks some sort of celestial law after ending the life of his son Orpheus. The final panel of *The Doll's House* states that Desire, alone in its (his/her) realm with mannequin-castle arms-upraised, "feels nothing like a doll. / Nothing like a doll at all,"[60] suggesting that the Endless are not so impotent as Dream assumes.

Orchestrated births are a feature in several other of Gaiman's works, though in more concerted a narrative fashion than *The Sandman*. The birth of Shadow in *American Gods*, for example, is revealed to be part of Loki and Wednesday's scheme to resecure their divine ascendance, while Tristran Thorn in *Stardust* is both the child of Lady Una of Stormhold, as well as the agent of her liberation and accession of the throne. There are, furthermore, offspring of the gods whose lives are more consequential than sequential to a grand design; Charlie Nancy, son of the Ashanti trickster Anansi in *Anansi Boys*, leads a mediocre existence for the most part, seemingly the result rather than the instrument of his father's antics. There are, furthermore, numerous sexual encounters between mythical figures and humans—especially in *American Gods*—which are not necessarily about offspring; in "Calliope" in *American Gods*, two writers successively imprison and rape the Muse of epic poetry in order to achieve literary inspiration and fame.

The mixing of sexuality and mythology is in many ways analogous to Gaiman's prolific storytelling. Though *The Sandman* series with its many gods and spirits has long been concluded, Gaiman's use and reuse of myths, legends, and other bodies of story has branched out into all media and genres—from television through box-office films to children's books and superhero comics in both the DC and Marvel universes. The coexistence of all these figures and traditions within a single imaginative reality is always conceivable if not explicit, and puts Gaiman in league with the likes of Stephen King, Anne Rice, H.P. Lovecraft and many others who have woven their works into single mythos. Literature from all historical periods has developed and reshaped the myths of preexisting traditions, but the pan-pantheon is a remarkably modern development, and one which Gaiman handles preeminently. Owed to a combination of modern secularism, multiculturalism, and relativism—not to mention the countless encyclopaedias, dictionaries, and studies of world myths and legends—the ancient practice of subsuming and streamlining belief systems has given way to a fully pluralistic and accretive understanding of myth. As for the originals from which his stories draw, and despite the success he has enjoyed through retellings, there is humility to be found in many of Gaiman's public reflections, and even in the mouths of his characters. When in *The Sandman* story "Men of Good Fortune," Hob Gadling mentions a version of *King Lear* with a happy ending, Dream says "[t]hat will not last. The Great Stories will always return to their original forms."[61] Nevertheless, and as Death tells Urania Blackwell in "Façade," "[m]ythologies take longer to die than people believe. They linger on in a kind of dream country that affects all of you."[62]

---

1 Gaiman, *Kindly Ones*, 23.
2 (Gaiman, *Mists*, 112). Gaiman's position that Loki is Æsir only by blood-brotherhood exploits the ambiguity of the original literary sources; reportedly sired by a giant, Loki is listed in the Edda of Snorri Sturluson as being simply "numbered among the Æsir," which, as elucidated by John Lindow, means he may not in fact be one of them. See Lindow, 216.
3 *Dictionary of English Etymology*, 647.
4 *Greek-English Lexicon*, 1298.

5 The original Pantheon is now known as the Santa Maria Rotunda; it has been a place of worship of the Roman Catholic Church since 609 CE.
6 *The Oxford English Dictionary*, 2nd ed., s.v. "pantheon" (def. 2) 149.
7 *The Encyclopedia of Fantasy*, 744.
8 Tolkien makes it reasonably clear, however, that the Valar are not, in fact, gods, but are created beings of a lesser order than their maker, Eru. "Valaquenta" states that "Men have often called them gods" (Tolkien, *Silmarillion*, 23); Tolkien puts the word in quotations ('gods') when referring to the Valar in his letters (Tolkien, *Letters*, 193).
9 Gaiman, *Mists*, 102.
10 The standard name—and headword—for the god, as opposed to the honorific Susano-o-no-Mikoto, which is His Brave Swift Impetuous Male Augustness. Susano-Wo spells this out himself (Gaiman, *Mists*, 112); it is also elaborated in Turner and Coulter, 445.
11 Gaiman, *Mists*, 148.
12 Ibid.
13 The character Prospero appears in a remarkably similar aspect in Gaiman, "The Tempest." (Gaiman, *Wake*, 157).
14 (Gaiman, *Mists*, 170). The Greek gods are absent here, but readers met the Muse Calliope in the eponymous story in *Dream Country*, while Orpheus, Hades, and Persephone appear in *Fables and Reflections*. The Fates—both in person and in influence—are ubiquitous throughout *The Sandman* stories, appearing as an aspect of the Three.
15 Some dictionaries of gods and goddesses index their entries by sphere of influence as well as national origin: see Jordan, 301-9.
16 Gaiman, *Mists*, 148.
17 Examples are from the following sources: Ishtar appears in "Chapter 4," *Brief Lives*; Anansi is in both *American Gods* and *Anansi Boys*; Czernobog and Easter appear in *American Gods*.
18 Physical manifestations of these forces appear in Gaiman, *Mists*, 101.
19 Hunt, 213-24.
20 The name goes unmentioned in Gustav Davidson's *Dictionary of Angels*; it is assumed to be a pseudo-Hebraic invention of Gaiman and Terry Pratchett.
21 See "Orpheus" in March, 572.
22 *potmos* (destiny); *teleute* (the Last [one]); *oneiros* (dream); *olethros* (destruction); *epithumia* (desire); *aponoia* (desperation); *mania* (madness); the choice to translate Death as Teleute is likely to avoid confusion and/or conflation with the existing Greek figure Thanatos, whose name means "Death," and who is traditionally the twin brother of Hypnos. See "Thanatos" in March, 738.
23 See Gaiman, "Collectors," *Doll's House*, 168-9. Glob also warns Brute that saying Morpheus's name could allow him entry into their pocket dimension of the Dreaming; see Gaiman, "Playing House," *Doll's House*, 96.
24 Gaiman, *The Books of Magic*, passim.
25 Gaiman. *Spawn*, passim.
26 Gaiman, "I, Cthulhu," as well as Gaiman, "Shoggoth's Old Peculiar" in *Smoke and Mirrors*, 147-59.
27 Gaiman, "Passengers," *Preludes*, 147.
28 Though Gaiman's pan-pantheon is pluralistic, there are conflations and overlaps. Consider, for example, the shifting identities of the Three in "Imperfect Hosts," *Preludes*, 73. Compare as well the coexistence of the Greek realm (and god) of Hades (see Gaiman, "The Song of Orpheus, Part 3," *Fables*, 182-6) with the name of Hades as a synonym for the Hell ruled by Lucifer (Gaiman, *Mists*, 39, 43).
29 Keightley, 325.
30 Gaiman, *Worlds' End*, 46, 49.
31 The being is a common entry in many resources. See, for example, "cluricaune" in MacKillop, 92.
32 It should be acknowledged, however, that two of the Three in *The Sandman* imply themselves to be aspects of the Morrígan and possibly Morgaine (Gaiman, "Imperfect Hosts," *Preludes*, 73); in *American Gods*, meanwhile, and besides the appearance of the Morrígan, the leprechaun Mad Sweeney is a prominent character.
33 Gaiman, *Brief Lives*, 12.
34 See Wood, 36-7.
35 It is never made clear when exactly Pharamond and Dream met in Babylon, but the city was utterly desolate and historically obscure at least a century before the birth of Christ. By the time of the Frankish

king Pharamond, it can hardly be said to have existed at all. It can only be assumed—in keeping with the theme of *Brief Lives*—that Pharamond and Dream met at the height of Babylon, as long as four thousand years ago (Gaiman, *Brief Lives*, 20).
36 See Huehnergard and Woods, 230.
37 Ishtar meets her end in Gaiman, *Brief Lives*, 20-4.
38 Gaiman, *Brief Lives*, 21.
39 See, variously, Gaiman, "I Woke Up and One of Us Was Crying," *Game*, 171, where Thessaly says, upon being asked how old she is, that she was born "in the day of the greatest darkness, in the year the bear totem was shattered." In Gaiman, *Brief Lives*, Bernie Capax recalls not having smelled a mammoth since he was a child (2-3). Shadow's first dream-encounter with the buffalo-headed man in *American Gods*, happens, as the creature describes, "[i]n the earth and under the earth [...] where the forgotten wait," 18.
40 Delaney, Introduction. *A Game of You* [10].
41 A collaborative franchise may be defined as any body of characters and their stories that is developed by numerous writers, particularly over many years, and resulting in the loss of continuity. At best, development may be steadily accretive, but such coherence is unlikely save with a single author and/or a brief period of development. Evidence from franchises in all eras—including Classical myth, Arthurian legend, and even *Star Trek*—demonstrates that accumulative treatments of a tradition most often create an incoherent web of material, including divergent accounts of similar episodes, as well as various episodes of uncertain relationships with one another.
42 For a comprehensive outline of this subject, as well as a configuration of reality, fiction, and imagination, see Iser, ix-xix, 1-21.
43 Delaney, [8].
44 For an outline, see <http:// http://en.wikipedia.org/wiki/No_prize>.
45 "Treehouse of Horror X," *The Simpsons*.
46 See "liminal beings" in *The Encyclopedia of Fantasy*, 581-2.
47 "[B]ut students of folklore must simply find it in their hearts to forgive me for, at one stroke of my pen and my heart, changing [Rev. B. W.] Ashton's Hototogisu bird into a raven." Gaiman, "Afterword," *The Dream Hunters*, [128]. Gaiman also speaks in terms of a potential crime committed when he and Roger Avary's screenplay for *Beowulf* neglected to send Beowulf back to his homeland, and instead had him become king of Denmark; see "The Origins of Beowulf," *Beowulf. Director's Cut*.
48 See entries "Samael," and "Lucifer" in Davidson, 255, 176. *The Sandman* does not ever nominate Lucifer as 'Satan' or 'the Devil', but for a defense of the gradual interchangeability of Lucifer and other names for the Devil, see Russell, 247.
49 Odin—which is properly spelled Oðinn and pronounced Othinn (with the th voiced as in clothe) is another example, though its pronunciation, like Loki, has been conventionalized. See Orchard, where it is insisted that the more accurate headwords might seem pedantic in the face of longstanding conventions [17].
50 Gilmore, 10.
51 Gaiman, *Gods*, 587.
52 "A Hero's Journey: The Making of Beowulf," in *Beowulf. Director's Cut*.
53 Perhaps no more so than in Gaiman, "24 Hours," *Preludes*, though also in "Calliope," *Dream Country*, where two writers rape the Muse to receive her inspiration (also considered below).
54 Gaiman, "Calliope," *Dream Country*, 19.
55 Gaiman, *High Cost*, 95-101.
56 Unity claims—and Dream agrees—that she would have been the vortex if he hadn't been imprisoned, and the Dreaming interrupted. Gaiman, "Lost Hearts," *Doll's House*, 216.
57 Despair makes the remark to Desire one page before Rose Walker is introduced in Gaiman, "The Doll's House Part 1," *Doll's House*, 44.
58 Gaiman, "Lost Hearts" *Doll's House*, 225-227.
59 Ibid.
60 Ibid.
61 Gaiman, "Men of Good Fortune," *Doll's House*, 132.
62 Gaiman, "Façade," *Dream Country*, 109.

Gaiman: The Teller of Tales and the Fairy Tale Tradition

Leslie Drury

> What is important is to tell the stories anew,
> and to retell the old stories.
> They are our stories, and they should be told.[1]

Neil Gaiman's work is rich with allusions and re-envisioning of familiar myths, folk and fairy stories, especially in his short fiction collections. The collection becomes less about the specific sources for the tales and more about their function as a group—where the transmission of the tales becomes central to their meaning. Gaiman's stories tend to share certain elements as he digests and reworks these structures from fairy tales and folklore, oral tradition and literary pedigree: they form a new relationship between reader and tale as Gaiman presents the role as author as primarily that of the storyteller.

The history of folklore and fairy tale in the western literary tradition lends itself to this type of exploration of meta-narrative issues.[2] Given the genre's roots in oral tradition, critical work on folk and fairy tales through the centuries indicates the importance of the interchange between teller, tale, and audience as a constantly evolving process that suits the needs of each new telling. As Marina Warner says, "For these are stories with staying power, as their antiquity shows, because the meanings they generate are themselves magical shape-shifters, dancing to the needs of their audience."[3] Many critics see the setting down of fixed literary versions of fairy tales as an ossifying process in which the move from oral forms to literary texts has altered the natural flexibility of the tales. However, Gaiman's approach to fairy tale shows that the conversation between tale teller and audience can be an ongoing process, and he develops this understanding of the importance of the oral associations with fairy tale as they have evolved over time. He says,

> The stories that people had told each other to pass the long nights had become children's tales. And there, many people obviously thought, they needed to stay.

But they don't stay there. I think it's because most fairytales, honed over the years, work so very well. They feel right. Structurally, they can be simple, but the ornamentation, the act of retelling, is often where the magic occurs. Like any form of narrative that is primarily oral in transmission, it's all in the way you tell 'em.[4]

In working with stories from the canon of classic fairy tales and folklore, Gaiman utilizes their familiarity and associations with social repetition in order to explore human experience, emotion, and sexuality through the act of tale telling. Fairy tales pervade much of Gaiman's work, but in this essay I will be exploring a few specific adaptations from his short fictions that deal directly with familiar folk and fairy tales. The short story "Snow, Glass, Apples" and the poems "The White Road" and "Locks" show Gaiman utilizing familiar stories from the fairy tale tradition in a manner that self-consciously highlights their relationship to the act of storytelling as a creatively generative process.

"Snow, Glass, Apples"

The story "Snow, Glass, Apples"[5] shows Gaiman reworking the "Snow White" tale into a recognizable but perverse version of itself. Most of the story elements from the original are present—the Princess follows her generic description, the Queen orders the girl's heart cut out, the girl survives in the forest amongst dwarves, the poisoning by apple occurs, the prince finds the seeming dead Princess, she is revived, and the Queen is executed—but the way the reader perceives these events is dramatically altered. This effect is achieved in two key ways: through a decisive twist in the perspective of the story, by using the Queen as narrator, and, through this new narrative voice, reworking key motifs from the original tale. Both of these contribute to a version of events that is both profoundly familiar in the way that fairy tales often are and profoundly unsettling in the way it recasts the familiar material in a way that shows a very adult and very dark aspect of the story.

Crucial to this reworking is a shift in the narrative voice. Like most fairy tales, "Snow White" is classically represented in the third person with narrative favoring Snow White herself as the (passive) protagonist. However, Gaiman's version shifts the narrative to the first person, in the perspective of a heretofore unknown version of the Queen.[6] Without altering most of the key portions of the plot, Gaiman presents an unsettling new version by showing the Queen's motivations and justifications of her actions in the face of the vampiric evil that is the young Princess.[7]

The way that Gaiman has shifted some of the central signifiers in the plot is crucially linked to his choice of narrator: this is the *Queen's* story.

The Queen makes several mentions of the lies that the Princess and Prince have told of her, implicating the traditional tale and making the original a competing narrative to the Queen's own version. Mathilda Slabbert argues that the Queen is an unreliable narrator. She notes that the Queen's presentation of her story is complicated by her capability for violence, power struggles, and sexual manipulation.[8] In addition to this, the Queen's belated acknowledgement of the glamour she has used on the King in their courtship adds to the sense of distrust by the reader. Despite these qualifiers, however, it is worth exploring the way the Queen's construction of her own narrative functions in its competition with the original story. For example, speaking of the idea that the Queen was given an animal's heart when she ordered that the Princess's heart be brought to her, she says:

> ...they say I was fooled. And some say (but it is *her* lie, not mine) that I was given the heart, and that I ate it. Lies and half-truths fall like snow, covering the things that I remember, the things I saw. A landscape, unrecognizable after a snowfall; that is what she has made my life.[9]

This image of snow as the narratively obliterating influence of the Princess's competing tale indicates the way the Queen plays upon key icons from the original tale to subvert the meaning of the original.

Gaiman uses the familiarity of the fairy tale elements of the Snow White story in order to firmly establish some of the altered meanings of the key touchstones of the story. As the title indicates with "Snow, Glass, Apples," the story picks up on several iconic elements from the tale. This tale is originally iconized by the girl's coloring and its associations with particular items. The Princess's skin is white as snow and, as the Queen echoes the original, "Her eyes were as black as coal, black as her hair; her lips were redder than blood."[10] In the original, Snow White's name and descriptors function as a guiding principle in the story, originally indicating her exceptional beauty, and thus goodness, and leading to the Queen's jealous machinations. In such a way, Gaiman has pricked out the key elements of the story that have been generously discussed critically— the snow of her mother's wish and the tone of the girl's skin, the glass of the Queen's magic mirror and the girl's coffin, and the apples of the Witch Queen's curse and Snow White's false death—and pivots these same elements into new meaning. In this crucial way, Gaiman keeps the story fully recognizable structurally and iconically but twists its meaning through the new perspective of the Queen's version. The Princess is now an evil creature whose "snow white" skin is indicative of her unnatural life and cold flesh and her "lips as red as blood" exhibit her vampiric nature.

In particular, Gaiman makes extensive use of snow and apple imagery throughout the story in order to present the Queen's narrative as one that posits the Princess as a deadly force of wintry deprivation and the Queen as a conscientious ruler who utilizes a counteracting force for preparation and provision.

The Queen speaks of such provision, saying:

> Autumn is a time of drying, of preserving, a time of picking apples, of rendering the goose fat. Winter is the time of hunger, of snow, and of death; and it is the time of the midwinter feast, when we rub the goose fat into the skin of a whole pig, stuffed with that autumn's apples; then we roast it or spit it, and we prepare to feast upon the crackling.[11]

These images of autumnal preparation and wintertime hunger, "when fresh food is a dream of warmth and sunlight,"[12] are repeatedly evoked in the story to reinforce the Princess's role as a deathly influence and to show the Queen in her, ultimately ineffective, efforts to ward off this influence.

Snow becomes the ultimate setting for the influence that the Princess has on the world around her. Contrasted with the Queen's golden description of her royal courtship and her connection with the Spring Fair in her earlier years, her time at the castle and under the influence of the Princess is marked by a passing of the years that always falls heavily on wintertime — emblematized by falling snow. The pervasive imagery of a snowy winter is the context for the Queen's first vampiric encounter with the girl, for the false peace after the girl's heart is hung, for the Queen's bewitching of the apples, and for her being prepared for execution. In Snow White's iconic name and in the cold skin that indicates her unfeeling existence, we see the embodiment of a singularly focused seasonality that can only mean deprivation and hunger for the people of the Queen's kingdom.

As is indicated by the Queen's discussion of apples as involved in autumn's preparations for winter, the apple is deeply associated with the Queen's role in storing and preparing against hunger. Apple imagery is also used throughout to develop the meaning of the relationship between the Queen and the Princess as complements in a relationship of provision and deprivation as signified by the unnatural gluttony of vampirism. The poisoned apple known from the original story already carries with it the conflicted coding of sustenance and death but Gaiman's tale adds to this with the context of the Princess's vampirism. The Queen infusing the apple with her own blood to achieve the spell of poisoning and as a draw for the Princess's vampirism changes the iconically red fruit's codification.

The connection between the Queen's offer of an apple and the exchange of blood with the vampiric Princess is one that Gaiman develops earlier in the story that is not present in prior versions. When the six-year-old Princess comes to the Queen insisting she is hungry, the Queen offers one of the apples drying from her bedroom ceiling. As the girl eats the apple, a momentary display of physical affection from the Queen allows the girl to bite the Queen's hand and the girl sucks the Queen's blood in a scene of terrifying mesmerism. Beyond the two instances of apple consumption being conflated with vampirism, the image is further reinforced as the Queen has hung the Princess's heart, "from the roof beam, with the apples and ham and the dried sausages."[13] By linking apples as provisions and the Princess's taking of others' lives through blood, Gaiman taints the former beauty of the crimson shade of the fruit and makes it an icon for the danger all are in when near the Princess.

The image of a heart hanging amongst drying apples and hams also highlights the final way that the Queen employs these concurrent images in her power struggle between autumnal plenty and wintertime deprivation. This is done through the image of the "whole pig, stuffed with that autumn's apples."[14] The connection between apples and the pig for the midwinter feast becomes the final use of apple imagery as the Queen is led to her death, which is drawn from an English variant to the story's end in which the Queen is "roasted alive in the king's brick-kiln (sic)."[15] Using this conclusion and adding in the imagery of the Queen as a greased roast pig, already associated as being stuffed with apples, serves as a final flourish to the way that imagery of winter, apples, and the Princess's vampiric urges in the story function. With the cannibalistic undertones to the Queen's roasting (whether there is an implicit actual feast to follow or not) her being prepared as a roast pig ironically highlights the Queen's ultimate failure to provide for her people against the influence of the wintry Snow White. These uses of snow and apple imagery support the larger theme that Gaiman develops in regard to a seasonality in the story that seems deeply connected with what the Queen represents as her benign witchery and her failure to counteract Snow White's barren influence.

The cannibalistic implications of this final scene are also highlighted by the Queen as she says that "They have told the people bad things about me; a little truth to add savor to the dish, but mixed with many lies."[16] This image of a dish savored with lies, brings together the Queen's representation of the Princess as a perverse consumer with the importance of controlling the narrative. As the Queen faces her death in the kiln, it is revealed that her story has been told as the heat builds around her and that such a story will be lost when she dies. She says, "They will have my body, but my soul and my story are my own, and will die with me."[17] The Queen's thoughts upon her death rework the way that the Princess has affected how she will be perceived and indicate the importance of considering the way their two narratives compete with each other.

As she looks out from the kiln, the first and only mention of the Queen looking at her own reflection is when she sees it in the passive eyes of the Princess as the girl watches the Queen roast to death. The Queen says, "She looked at me though; and for a moment I saw myself reflected in her eyes."[18] Slabbert offers the idea that this reflective moment indicates the women's mutual potential for horrific violent action against each other[19] but it also seems to implicate the way narration functions as we have competing versions of the story. Like Slabbert's idea of mutual violence, the reflection of the Queen in Snow White can also mean mutual negative portrayal: as the Queen has here represented her version of the story, the Princess will go on to represent the Queen as a vindictive witch, continuing to tell "bad things" about her in what will become the classic version of the tale. This recognition of the alternate version of the events as represented through the original tale we are all familiar with is reinforced by the Queen's use of familiar language in her final words. She says, "I think of her hair black as coal, her lips, redder than blood, her skin, snow-white."[20] This final line is the one and only time that the iconic name of the Princess is used in the story. By finishing the Queen's story with the familiar refrain and completing the flourish with the acknowledgement of Snow White's name, this ending has the effect of realigning the story the reader has become absorbed in with the original version of the fairy tale in a jarring manner. Re-emphasizing the icons that have been modified in the Queen's narrative in this final line serves to remind the reader of how much their viewpoint has been altered in the course of the story.

The pivotal pressure that Gaiman applies to this familiar fairy tale is one that yields a disturbing yet enjoyable result. The tale is still strangely familiar yet wholly refreshing. Gaiman says of his desire in this retelling that, "In *Smoke and Mirrors* there are definitely stories where I just wanted to try to essentially do a magic trick—it's 'Snow White,' but I'm going to show it to you in a mirror so you've never seen it like this before. And you'll never be able to think of it in the same way ever again."[21]

Gaiman accomplishes this goal through showing a Queen that constructs a deeply problematic narrative. There is room for doubt in her version, yet at the same time the purpose of her version is to instill doubt regarding the original tale. Thus how we ultimately judge the Queen's narrative is of less importance than that her story has been allowed to escape from the kiln at all. Through exposure to the competing narrative of the Queen's experience, the touchstones of the famous fairy tale are constantly available for re-evaluation and doubt. And it is that ongoing doubt in the face of the original tale, that act of unsettling what the reader believed they knew and the tainting of a previously singular narrative, that is one of the main achievements of Gaiman's version.

"The White Road"

In the poem "The White Road,"[22] Gaiman draws upon the English tale of Mister Fox and related stories and condenses them into a scene of tale-telling that unsteadies our expectations and reevaluates the way narrative functions in constructing reality. The tale of Mister Fox fits within a broader category of murderous husband tales, such as The Robber Bridegroom and Bluebeard,[23] where a young heroine is endangered by a fiancé or new husband who has secretly murdered her predecessors or women very much like her. In "The White Road," Gaiman takes up these themes of secrecy, sexuality and violence, but amplifies the story's signification as a *told* tale and uses the context of narration to dramatically alter our understanding of what these tales mean. By placing the entirety of the poem within a storytelling setting and changing crucial details from the original tale, Gaiman presents a story that is chilling like its source material, but in a wholly new manner.

The central Mister Fox tale that Gaiman uses in his poem typically involves storytelling as crucial to its resolution. The girl engaged to Mister Fox travels to her fiancé's home, witnesses the terrors of his secret homicidal life, returns to her home and, at a storytelling event with all gathered, recounts her experience as though it were a dream and only at the end reveals that this "dream" truly happened. This is usually accomplished by revealing the finger or hand of a woman whose murder she secretly witnessed and recounted in the dream and those in attendance summarily kill Mister Fox based on the evidentiary hand. Gaiman's tale includes the girl's recounting of her "dream" in a richly embellished version, but he omits the first half of the original tale as there is no narration of the girl's "actual" experiences at Mister Fox's home until she tells of them herself. In Gaiman's version, the story begins *in media res* with the common refrain of the man asking his beloved to visit him at his house. The narrator, Mister Fox, begins the poem by saying, "...I wish that you would visit me one day, / in my house. / There are such sights I would show you."[24] We are already at the storytelling event where, in the original tale, the tale-telling contest will end with the girl's reveal, which condemns the murderous Mister Fox. This focus in Gaiman's poem upon narration rather than direct action is incredibly important to the way the poem functions.

In the original, the retelling of the events of the girl's experience as its own story *within* the larger tale is crucial to its resolution; the reader or listener of the original will hear the same story twice in a row but to very different effect—*i.e.*, first with suspense and unknown terror, then with foreknowledge and anticipation of the conclusion of justice. By omitting the duplicate nature of the original, Gaiman makes this version solely about the telling of the story without the anchor of unbiased narration to validate the girl's tale for the reader. As the storytelling event nestled within the larger structure is crucial to the resolution of the larger tale, Gaiman uses the potential of narration as an act to dictate the direction his encompassing tale takes.

It is important to note that there is nothing that contradicts Mister Fox's guilt until the very end of the poem. By using the reveal of what should be a human hand but is only a fox's paw at the conclusion of the fiancée's tale as the pivotal point of *proof* over narrative, Gaiman creates a moment in which the proof of the maiden's tale and the proof of the tale that we are reading are one and the same—yet they do not reach the same conclusion. By saving this form of evidence until the end of the story, allowing the reader to carry the prejudice of previous knowledge of the tale type as Mister Fox's seeming guilt builds through the several Fox tales the women tell, the reveal of his seeming innocence for the reader serves to reinforce the way that narrative creates its own form of truth and that reshifting to a new truth can be shocking or, as within the story, impossible. Despite the unclear and unacknowledged nature of the beloved's evidence, her control of the narrative within his larger narration means that, as Gaiman puts it, "His story is effectively over"[25] without him being able to affect it.

Gaiman takes the opportunity in this storytelling context to add to the central tale by pulling together several variants of the Mister Fox tale type and other thematically related stories to create a new meaning for the core tale.[26] Grouped by their relationship to fox motifs and plots of sexual knowledge and danger, together these tales play with ideas of guilt, concealment, and conclusory judgment but are ambiguous in terms of conclusions regarding these ideas. As the pale woman tells the first tale in the poem, a variant of the Mister Fox tale, it lacks its typically conclusive ending. The girl betrayed by her scholar lover avoids her murder but runs mad and there is no mention of the justice she usually receives in this variant. Conversely, the beloved of Mister Fox presents a richly narrated version of the Mister Fox tale that ends in a contradictory manner: the paw she throws down sows doubt about the justness of her accusation and her lover's death. As the poem moves through the reversals in these stories, determination of guilt and acknowledgment of victimization become problematic concepts. It becomes increasingly unclear who is the fox and who is the victim, who the hunter and who the hunted.

Like "Snow, Glass, Apples," this poem shifts narration from the third person to the first by the former villain of the piece in a manner that drastically changes our relationship to the story. However, where "Snow, Glass, Apples" empowers the reader with a new perspective on the story the shift here to Mister Fox's narration serves to occlude the purpose of the narrative. Rather than being shown a new perspective on the story, we are given an obscured version.

The commandeering of the narrative voice in this story is crucial. After the pale woman's tale is applauded, Mister Fox attempts to tell his own story about trickster foxes in a version that seems poised to switch the gendered power dynamic and trickery of the pale woman's tale by shifting to a different narrative tradition. He begins, "I read that in the Orient foxes follow priests and scholars, in disguise as women, houses, mountains, gods, processions, always discovered by their tails,"[27] but as his story is about to gain momentum he is interrupted by his beloved's father who asks the girl to tell her story. The power of the narrative is displaced from poem's narrator and all are focused upon the girl's story. Gaiman's fantastically rendered version of her tale is riveting for both his reader and her audience. Though Mister Fox is our window into her narration, he contributes little to how we are meant to interpret the tale. Instead there is a great deal of focus on the responses occurring around him, registering the threat through the building focus that the girl's narrative creates. As he says, "All eyes were on me then, not her, though hers was the story."[28] Her captivation of the audience directs their gaze and he is incapable of altering the focus of her narration.

At the crucial climax of her tale, Mister Fox attempts to counteract the effect her tale has with the iconic refrain so well known from the original tale: "It is not so, It was not so, And god forbid it should be so." In the context of the narrative event, it shows him unsuccessfully making an addition to what the narrative means. His final attempt to deny her narrative is interspersed with her assertions of the truth and of her calling him the names of other Mister Fox types: "You Bluebeard," "You Gilles-de-Rais."[29] This dramatic and uneven call-and-response, so reminiscent of the pale woman's ability to lead the room in the clapping song of "A fox went out" but here with much more sinister implications, highlights the way that she has effectively commandeered the narrative potential of the moment. The aggregate power of these inter-textual images of murderous villains lies directly before her reveal of the "proof" of her tale. By seizing the narrative moment, the beloved is able to define the parameters of reality for her audience.

Through the prism of a doubly narrated tale (the man and his beloved) we see the end of his story in a drastically different manner. "The White Road" shows a radically shifted version of the tale of Mister Fox in which the power that the tale-teller wields transforms the meaning of truth, where fiction becomes a death sentence.

Yet despite the beloved's power in this moment, there is one final image before "his tale is effectively at an end."[30] This image is that of the pale woman amusedly leaving and the narrator's recognition of her fox-like nature when he sees "the tail between her legs."[31] This second reveal, in the indication that this woman is a trickster figure recognizable by her concealed tail, hearkens back to Mister Fox's failed attempt to start a story of his own and reiterates his failure at commandeering the narrative. Her newly revealed role as the perhaps ultimately controlling trickster of this piece drastically shifts the way we relate to the hunter/hunted motif and raises questions about the trustworthiness of all of the narrators we are presented with in this story. No one is clearly and unquestionably confirmed guilty and no one is absolved: all we have is a series of intermeshing accusations through story.

The unjustified and complex trust that the maid in the pale woman's story places in her lover, where it is said "she believed him. / Or she believed that she believed,"[32] reflects the way we as readers are asked to ponder how belief interweaves with assertion and how truth and complementary doubt are constructed through narration. In this way, the poem uses the availability of variation in the Mister Fox tales to explore truth as a negotiable concept and the power that the storyteller has in setting the parameters of the experience.

"Locks"

The final piece, the poem "Locks,"[33] is not an adaptation in the sense of the previous two short fictions but is instead a piece about tale-telling itself with a familiar fairy tale at its center. Based around "Goldilocks and the Three Bears," the tale is familiar enough for the reader that basic refrains from the original are all that emanates from the page and the poem becomes an exploration of generations, growing knowledge, and the obligations we share as familial and social creatures as we build ever shifting relationships through story. The poem plays upon the thoughts that a father has as he retells the story of Goldilocks with his two-year-old daughter. It weaves together refrains from the tale itself, his spoken interaction with his daughter, and his own thoughts on this interaction. Gaiman shows a father who sees in the telling of this well-known children's story the opportunity to reflect upon his daughter's future growth and their changing relationships to the perspectives within the story they tell.

As the pair begins telling the story of Goldilocks, the poem shows narration as a negotiable event between father and daughter. The girl insists her details are the way the story is to be told and the father gently acquiesces to her certainty. This emblem of the changeability of the story and the way that we interact through story seems to lie at the heart of the issues that Gaiman explores in this personal image of father and daughter sharing a narrative moment. The negotiation that starts off the poem becomes an appropriate context for the way that we ourselves develop and change, and Gaiman emblematizes his and his daughter's physical and emotional growth through the images of the changeable story.

Through the poem, narrative is shown as changeable, both in the negotiation the daughter creates and in the literary history of the tale itself. Gaiman uses a key change in the form of the story's literary history to contribute to this. In Robert Southey's original literary version of 1837, it was an old woman rather than a young girl who featured in the tale. Over the next seventy-five years, reworkings of the tale changed the main character to the now familiar girl with golden hair.[34] In this change from the original literary version and in the negotiation between father and daughter we see an adaptability in the tale that exemplifies the distinction that folklorists make in regard to the way oral folklore functions.[35]

Despite the move to a young blonde protagonist, the old woman of Southey's version lingers in Gaiman's retelling and this acknowledgement of the changes in the tale provide imagery for the changes from childhood and beyond. Within the poem this manifests itself as a focus upon hair as the image of change and maturation. The narrator says:

> I remember, as I tell it, that the locks of Southey's heroine had silvered with age. The Old Woman and the Three Bears...Perhaps they had been golden once, when she was a child.[36]

This self-conscious inter-textuality as a way to ponder changes in the shifting nature of the story in its own history allows the narrator to explore the future changes in his daughter. As Gaiman says in the introduction, "The form of the story and what happened was right, but people knew that the story needed to be about a little girl rather than an old woman, and when they retold it, they put her in," indicating the importance of the adaptability of these tales as need arises. This is touched upon in the poem in relation to the daughter's growth:

> The repetition echoes down the years. When your children grow, when your dark locks begin to silver, when you are an old woman, alone with your three bears, what will you see? What stories will you tell?[37]

This pondering of his daughter's future experience with her own narrative potential is complicated by the shifting nature of the way they relate to the story as a parallel to their own stage in life. This occurs throughout the poem: the narrator at times identifies both with Baby Bear and Father Bear and likens his own father to a bear.[38] These changing identifications with the story are further highlighted by the potential for understanding the same story lines in a different manner:

> They reach the bedroom. 'Someone's been sleeping in my bed.'[39]
> And here I hesitate, echoes of old jokes, soft-core cartoons, crude headlines, in my head.
> One day your mouth will curl at that line. A loss of interest, later, innocence.
> Innocence, as if it were a commodity.[40]

The concern involved in his daughter's maturation through the loss of innocence as shown here is added to through an additional pun on the idea of the title 'locks.' This occurs directly before considering his daughter's loss of innocence: "The bears go upstairs hesitantly, their house now feels desecrated. They realize what locks are for."[41]

The bears' sense of violation here is directly followed by the idea of the daughter growing into sexual maturity and potential to understand the bears' violation in light of innuendo. The narrator speaks of the wish, repeated from his father, of protecting one's child from the implicit pain of experience: "But we make our own mistakes. We sleep/ unwisely."[42] By playing upon the idea that locks, as hair, are a physical symbol of maturation and that locks, as a form of home security, are a way to ensure (or hope that we have ensured) our family's physical safety, the poem highlights the way in which our family's *emotional* safety cannot be secured. After all, "we make our own mistakes." This is developed at the end of the poem as the narrator continues his vigilance despite these inabilities. He says:

> These days my sympathy's with Father Bear. Before I leave my house I lock the door, and check each bed and chair on my return.[43]

But the deployment of this secondary meaning for 'locks' is complicated by the fact that it places the identification of the narrator and the daughter in different relationships within the story. She is the young girl and will be the old woman, they both have been Baby Bear, and he has been the Father Bear. This creates antithetical viewpoints as they occupy various places in the story. The circularity of perspective here with each new retelling of the story indicates the openness of the narrative opportunity. The way that the telling of the story is an active and recurring event is important to untangling these antithetical perspectives. A told story, a narratively dynamic story, allows for meaning to change in the most meaningful way. This is reinforced by the daughter's call of "*Again. Again. Again,*" asking for the tale to be retold, which is reflected by the father's tripled refrain of "Again" as he checks the security of his home.[44] Because each telling allows the opportunity to occupy a new place in the story, the dynamism of narration is a boon and the relationships that are established as the story is told can evolve as both father and daughter change and grow.

In the introduction to the poem, Gaiman says of fairy tales that:

> They are the currency that we share with those who walked the world before ever we were here. (Telling stories to my children that I was, in my turn, told by my parents and grandparents makes me feel part of something special and odd, part of the continuous stream of life itself.)[45]

The way that tale-telling connects with past generations is one that is directly linked to the nature of repetition in the telling of the tale.

The opening of the poem is "We owe it to each other to tell stories, as people simply, not as father and daughter./ I tell it to you for the hundredth time."[46] Later in the poem, the narrator says "The repetition echoes down the years,"[47] indicating both the repetitive acts of father's wishes for children's and perhaps also the way this is reflected as the familiar refrains of the story are repeated at each new telling.

The generational repetition throughout the poem, and the invocation of a protectiveness that cannot ultimately be successful (the father may check the locks but his daughter will still "make her own mistakes") come together in a way that shows the repeated act of storytelling to be a meaningful way to process these ideas. Through story, there is perhaps a way to rebuild some of the desecration implicit in experience. The repetitive nature of the storytelling and thus the ability for both to join in with the common refrains of the story is employed in a meaningful way in the poem. At one particular point, the two of them contributing to the story takes on the hint of a religious call and response. "'*All up'* you say. A response it is,/ Or an amen."[48] This implication is coupled with the way that experience is presented in the poem as connected with the bears' feeling that "their house now feels *desecrated*."[49] The religious tone of the storytelling repetition here perhaps hints at a redemptive process. In this way, the daughter may lose "the conviction of all two-year-olds"[50] as she grows and changes through experience, as her father has done before her. Despite these inevitable changes, however, there can be a redemptive process in the familiar return to the repetition of shared storytelling.

The tension in these repetitive cycles is maintained through to the end of the poem as every call for 'again' that the daughter makes, is matched by the father's assertion that he will check the locks and beds and chairs "Again. Again. Again." Though the poem doesn't resolve the anxieties implicit in these changing relationships, it does point to the ongoing act of a lifetime of storytelling. Whether this story will be retold between the two of them or, when the girl's locks have "darkened to silver," there is a new audience; the repetition of storytelling through generations will continue to be a meaningful way to express our social relationships.

Conclusion

Through these three short fictions, Gaiman explores the juncture between the fairy tale tradition and the ongoing meaning of storytelling in our lives. Though "Snow, Glass, Apples," "The White Road," and "Locks" deal with this topic in different manners, they all play upon the fertile space between the familiar repetitiveness of well-known tales and the active evolution between teller, audience, and tale. Gaiman draws on the concept of storytelling and a storytelling frame for many of his works, and this is certainly not solely relegated to stories from the classic fairy tale tradition. Conversely, not every fiction of his that evokes fairy tale will necessarily directly engage with issues of tale transmission.

However, within his larger approach to the role of author as storyteller and text as engagement with reader, the fairy tale tradition lends itself to the conversation very readily, and by focusing upon this particular prism we can come to understand some of his thoughts on the topic and how he employs these tales for particular narrative strategies. None of the three resolve their message definitively, and this helps to expose the way that narrative, especially indeterminate narrative, constructs meaning and complicates it. There is a great deal of space in Gaiman's work to further explore the issues touched on here, but, with these short fictions, it has been shown that he utilizes the relationship between fairy tales and storytelling to explore the crucial way that meaning is constructed through the narrative. Gaiman seems to be, in his short fictions at least, intently focused on the act of tale transmission itself and exploits fairy tales from the classic core of the tradition as a particular medium to explore these issues of storytelling as a modern-day act.

In his introduction to "Locks," Gaiman says, "Of course, fairy tales are transmissible. You can catch them, or be infected by them."[51] For "Snow, Glass, Apples" he reiterates a similar idea, saying, "I like to think of this story as a virus. Once you've read it, you may never be able to read the original story in the same way again."[52] In both of these images of tale-telling as a virus the image is one that is inherently about *transmission*. Viral story is a concept that focuses the organic and active nature of a self-replicating process as a means of understanding our own social interactions and the compulsion to continue the familiar repetition of a good story. As Gaiman says in his introduction to "Locks," "I believe we owe it to each other to tell stories. It's as close to a credo as I have or will, I suspect, ever get."[53]

1 Gaiman, "Reflections on Myth," 80-1.
2 Dowd, 103-20, for a discussion of similar themes in Gaiman's graphic novels.
3 Warner, xix-xx. For similar assertions, see: Robert Darnton, 285; Zipes, 9.
4 Gaiman, "Happily Ever After," *The Guardian*.
5 Gaiman, "Snow, Glass, Apples," in *Smoke and Mirrors*, 371-84.
6 For a full discussion of adaptations from the point of view of the Queen, see: David Calvin, 231-245.
7 For a discussion of Gaiman's use of vampire motifs in this story, see: Jessica Tiffin, "Blood on the Snow: Inverting "Snow White,'" 220-230.
8 Slabbert, 77-9.
9 Gaiman, *Mirrors*, 374.
10 Gaiman, *Mirrors*, 372.
11 Ibid.
12 Ibid.
13 Gaiman, *Mirrors*, 380.
14 Gaiman, *Mirrors*, 372.
15 Philip, 109.
16 Gaiman, *Mirrors*, 384.
17 Gaiman, *Mirrors*, 384.
18 Gaiman, *Mirrors*, 384.
19 Slabbert, 79-80.
20 Gaiman, *Mirrors*, 384.
21 Gaiman, "An Interview with Neil Gaiman," in *Smoke and Mirrors*.
22 Gaiman, "The White Road," in *Smoke and Mirrors*, 119-30.
23 Philip, 159.
24 Gaiman, *Mirrors*, 119.
25 Gaiman, *Mirrors*, 22.
26 The Mister Fox variants can be seen in Philip, 158-92. As Gaiman cites Philip's collection as the inspiration for "Snow, Glass, Apples," it is quite possible he was aware of these particular versions from the same collection. A variant of the "A fox went out" song can be seen in Opie, *Nursery Rhymes*, 173-75. The statue of a boy eviscerated by the hidden fox is based upon Plutarch's *Lives*: "So seriously did the Lacedæmonian children go about their stealing, that a youth, having stolen a young fox and hid it under his coat, suffered it to tear out his very bowels with its teeth and claws and died upon the place, rather than let it be seen."
27 Gaiman, *Mirrors*, 122.
28 Gaiman, *Mirrors*, 123
29 Gaiman, *Mirrors*, 128.
30 Gaiman, *Mirrors*, 22.
31 Gaiman, *Mirrors*, 129.
32 Gaiman, *Mirrors*, 120.
33 Gaiman, "Locks," in *Fragile Things*, 233-36.
34 Opie, *The Classic Fairy Tales*,199.
See, for example, Vladimir Propp, "Folklore and Literature," 380. "Folklore also presupposes two agents, but different agents, namely, the performer and the listener, opposing each other directly, or rather without a mediating link. [...] If the reader of a work of literature is a powerless censor and critic devoid of authority, anyone listening to folklore is a potential future performer, who, in turn, consciously or unconsciously, will introduce changes into the work."
35 Gaiman, *Fragile*, 234-5.
36 Ibid.

37 Ibid.
38 Ibid.
39 Gaiman, *Fragile*, 235.
40 Ibid.
41 Gaiman, *Fragile*, 236.
42 Ibid.
43 Ibid.
44 Ibid.
45 Gaiman, *Fragile*, 15.
46 Gaiman, *Fragile*, 233.
47 Gaiman, *Fragile*, 235.
48 Ibid.
49 Ibid. Emphasis added.
50 Gaiman, *Fragile*, 234.
51 Gaiman, *Fragile*, 15.
52 Gaiman, *Mirrors*, 32.
53 Gaiman, *Fragile*, 15-16.

The Best Things Come in Threes: The Triple Goddess in the Works of Neil Gaiman

Tony Keen

"When shall we three meet again?"[1] —Shakespeare, *Macbeth*

That Neil Gaiman is a writer steeped in mythological traditions hardly needs stating at this point.[2] It is obvious from his writings over the past twenty-plus years, and is, of course, explicit in all the contributions to the current volume. This chapter will focus on one particular mythological element in Gaiman's work, his use of the motif of the Triple Goddess.

In many of the mythologies of Western Europe, a motif has been identified that is referred to as the Triple Goddess. This is described as a triad of related goddesses with similar aspects, or a single goddess that appears in three forms. In Greco-Roman mythology, there are many examples (what follows is not a complete list). There are the three Fates, in Greek the *Moirai*, or in Latin the *Parcae* or *Fata*. They are Clotho, Lachesis, and Atropos. There are the Graces (Greek *Charites*, Latin *Gratiae*), Aglaea, Euphrosyne, and Thalia. There are the Furies (Greek *Erinyes*, Latin *Furiae* or *Dirae*), named Alecto, Megaera, and Tisiphone. In one tradition, recorded by the geographer Pausanias (9.29.2),[3] there were only three Muses, Melete, Mneme, and Aoede, rather than the more commonly found nine.[4] Another related Classical deity is Hecate, sometimes depicted with three faces or three bodies.[5] By 1894, Brewer's *Dictionary of Phrase and Fable* was referring to her as an aspect of the Triple Goddess, along with Phoebe and Diana, the latter of which was a moon goddess. Shakespeare describes her as "triple Hecate" in *A Midsummer Night's Dream* (Act V, Scene II), and she appears as the Witches' mistress in *Macbeth* (Act III, Scene V).

Other mythologies have similar figures. Norse mythology has its own version of the three Fates, the Norns, Urðr, Verðandi, and Skuld.[6] Irish mythology has the Morrígan, three warrior women, Badb, Macha, and Nemain, who are sometimes one,[7] and the three Brigits (or Brigids).[8] The Celtic areas of the Roman Empire have produced a number of relief sculptures and small sculptural groups depicting three female figures.[9] These are commonly described as *Matres* ("Mothers") or, when wearing hooded cloaks, *genii cucullati*;[10] but these are modern terms applied to these representations. Though their meaning would no doubt have been obvious to the people who created the images, there is nothing that allows modern scholars to positively identify who these characters are, or even to confirm that the female figures are the same in each representation. It can be suggested that they may represent Hecate, but this remains speculation.

The iconographic grouping of three magical, divine, or semi-divine figures recurs throughout western art and literature. Obviously, this would happen whenever the mythological characters were being represented, but there are also further new variations upon the form. The most famous and influential of these are the three witches of William Shakespeare's *Macbeth*.[11]

In the twentieth century, as theories of mythology were developed, inevitably one emerged to explain the multiple uses of three female figures. The key text here is Robert Graves' *The White Goddess* (1948), who was drawing upon earlier work by James Frazer (*The Golden Bough*, 1890) and Jane Harrison (*Prolegomena to the Study of Greek Religion*, 1903; *Themis*, 1912). This theory identifies the three female figures with three ages of woman, Maiden, Mother, and Crone. It has been enthusiastically adopted by Neo-paganism, and can be seen in the works of D.J. Conway.

Despite the writings of Conway and Marija Gimbutas, much recent work on the theory of myth has tended to raise questions about the Maiden-Mother-Crone version of the Triple Goddess.[12] The Triple Goddess actually covers a wide variety of depictions of female divinities, which do not always fit into the neat divisions offered up by the Maiden-Mother-Crone version. For instance, few of the Classical divinities are differentiated in age. One can make an argument for the Fates, where Clotho spins the yarn of an individual's fate at birth (thus might be the Maiden, symbolic of youth), Lachesis measures it out (thus might be the Mother, symbolic of a life of experience), and Atropos cuts it at the end (thus might be the Crone, symbolic of old age and death). But other Greco-Roman examples fit less well with the most systematized versions of the Triple Goddess. The Graces are all the same age. The Furies were, in origin, not three. When the Athenian playwright Aeschylus put them on stage in the *Eumenides* of 458 BCE,[13] he envisaged there being fifteen of them, as was standard for the Greek tragic chorus of the time (this is, of course, a multiple of three).[14] Only with another playwright, Euripides, some forty years later, did they become three in number,[15] and their names did not appear in literature until the time of Virgil's *Aeneid*, in the first century BCE,[16] although other evidence, from vase painting, etc., shows that the names were evidently known from the fourth century BCE.[17]

It could be argued that these discrepancies are the result of a particular distortion of the Triple Goddess in Greco-Roman myth, but similar questions arise in connection with the other mythologies. It has been, for instance, suggested that the idea that there are three Norns is an importation from the Greco-Roman Fates.[18] Whether the Morrígan is all three of Badb, Macha, and Nemain, or merely one of them, or none of them, varies from text to text. At least one Romano-British relief shows the three *genii cucullati* and a separate mother goddess,[19] and such depictions can be found elsewhere in Celtic and Northern European folklore. It could be argued that the fourfold depiction represents a sequence of Maiden, Warrior, Mother, and Crone, in which the Warrior merges either with the Maiden or Mother; this presupposes a society in which women typically went through a warrior phase.

It may well be that the Triple Goddess is less the representation of an original prehistoric deity, as Gimbutas argued, and more a pattern imposed by nineteenth and twentieth century scholarship upon a wide range of different, but often cross-fertilizing, traditions. Regardless of this, the Triple Goddess retains considerable power as a literary device.[20] For fictional accounts it is not necessary to actually believe in the idea to make use of it.

"Well, I can do next Tuesday"[21]: The Triple Goddess in *The Sandman*[22]

The Triple Goddess is exactly the sort of primal archetype that one would expect to appeal to Neil Gaiman, with the strong sense of mythological heritage that is displayed throughout his work. The fact that the notion has been recognized across different mythologies suits well his interest in the pan-pantheon.[23] It is important to state right from the beginning that in *The Sandman* Gaiman is creating a mythology, and Gaiman is well aware that all mythologies have many inherent contradictions.[24] Why should Gaiman's mythology be any different?[25]

Gaiman first introduced The One who is Three, who come to be referred to as The Three,[26] in the second issue of *Sandman* (18-22). They are, in the first instance, drawn from the pages of DC's continuity. At this point, Gaiman was still doing much of the world-building of *The Sandman* out of preexisting elements of the DC Universe.[27] The Three are Mildred, Mordred, and Cynthia, who were created as "hosts" for a horror/mystery anthology series, *The Witching Hour*, which ran from 1969 to 1978.[28] The use of these characters fits with Gaiman's general theme in this issue, where he introduces into his mythology a number of hosts of DC's anthology series.[29] These include Lucien, who first appeared in *Weird Mystery Tales* 18 (DC, May 1975), Eve, who first appeared in *Secrets of Sinister House* 6 (DC, August–September 1972), and Cain and Abel, who were the hosts of *House of Mystery* and *House of Secrets*.[30] In this, Gaiman was following his friend and mentor, Alan Moore. It had been Moore who had brought Cain and Abel back, in *Swamp Thing* 33, and had introduced the motif of Cain repeatedly murdering Abel, a motif Gaiman used throughout the run of *The Sandman*. At this point, by his own admission, Gaiman had yet to find his own voice.[31] His early comics work was considerably under the influence of Moore.[32] This is hardly surprising; it was, after all, Moore's work on *Swamp Thing* that had brought Gaiman back to reading comics, and Moore who showed Gaiman what a comic script looked like.[33]

Right from his first introduction of them, the Three are much more than the three DC witches who are their immediate source. Dream, the Sandman, meets the Three in a place that resembles the "blasted heath" of *Macbeth*, Act I, Scene I,[34] and the witches are stirring a cauldron. Gaiman introduces them as the Hecateae (18.3).[35] As noted above, Hecate is a possible Triple Goddess, associated with the moon; appropriately Gaiman has the Three emerge when Dream shifts the Dreaming into moonlight.

The witches eventually (19.7) tell Dream to refer to them as Mildred, Mordred,[36] and Cynthia (which is an epithet of the Moon-goddess Artemis/Diana).[37] But before this point is reached, Dream refers to one of them as the Fate Atropos, and to all three as the Graces, and the Three say that they could be referred to as the Morrígan, or Alecto, Magaera (*sic*), and Tisiphone. Lucien previously (16.5) refers to them as "Urth, Verthandi and Skald" (*i.e.*, the Norns). Here, in a characteristic (for him) blending of mythologies, Gaiman gets across the idea that the Three can take on a wide range of personae, and the reader is presumably not expected to think that the names that they have been given so far are the only ones that could be applied. These personae can overlap, and some will be more important at certain points than others. They may even contradict each other. This is a world of fantasy, and importantly, as noted, of mythology. Like everything in *The Sandman*, the Three have their own internal logic—"dream-logic" if you will—but their logic is not susceptible to the more hard-and-fast rules that the reader might attempt to impose.

One of the Three also says "Might as well call us Diana, Mary, Florence and Candy" (19.5). This, of course, is a reference to the original line-up of the Supremes, Motown's leading girl group of the 1960s: Diana Ross, Mary Wilson, and Florence Ballard. "Candy" is perhaps an erroneous reference to Cindy Birdsong, who replaced Ballard in the Supremes in 1967. Birdsong and Ballard overlapped as members in the Supremes for a while, though not performing together. This may be why the Three mentions all four of them. This line is, of course, a joke. But there may be other messages carried along with it. First, that the Three are not necessarily infallible. Secondly, that the Three may not necessarily always be Three—perhaps they can be Four (which would reflect the possibility found in Celtic representations of four deities). The paradigm can shift. Thirdly, possibly the Supremes *are* a manifestation of the Three. It is possible for ordinary humans to manifest as aspects of the Three. Indeed, the next time the Three are seen in any form, in "24 Hours" (16), they are manifesting through three mortal women, Judy (Maiden), Kate (Mother), and Bette (Crone), in a diner, being mentally manipulated by John Dee (the supervillain Doctor Destiny).[38]

Two other points need to be made. First is that Dream has no power over the Three, who are older powers than he is; nor do any of the other Endless, except, as we shall see, Death. In this respect, the Three carry resonances of the position of the Fates in Greco-Roman mythology, where sometimes (though not always), the gods themselves, even the all-powerful Zeus/Jupiter, have to obey the Fates.[39] The other point to note is that the Three shift their personalities from one to another. When the Three first appear (18.2), Mildred is on the left, Mordred in the middle, and Cynthia on the right. In the next panel, Mordred is on the left, Cynthia in the middle, and Mildred on the right. In the three panels on page 19 in which they appear (19.3, 19.5, and 19.5), they are Mildred-Cynthia-Mordred, then Mordred-Mildred-Cynthia, then Cynthia-Mordred-Mildred.[40] Clearly, the reader is meant to think of the Three remaining in one place, but each changing her aspect. It is worth noting, also, that on pages 18-19, each member of the Three goes through the changes in the correct order of Maiden, Mother and Crone, representing the natural progress through the three stages that all women will make. However, though the aspects continue to change on page 20, they no longer do so in the correct order, and the strict order to the changes is not seen in any further appearances. Indeed, when the Three next appear as themselves, rather than manifested as mortals, in *Sandman* 10 (19-20), their aspects do not change in this manner at all, though they do when they appear in *Sandman* 17 (9-10)— but again the changes are not in order. It is difficult to say whether or not Gaiman intends this to indicate the possibility of disruption of the natural progress through Maiden, Mother, and Crone

The general point, however, is clear. The Three, and everything the reader might think they know about them, are constantly in flux. There are rules, but we, as readers, are not privy to precisely what those rules are. Gaiman himself no doubt has some idea how those rules work, but he may well not apply them consistently himself. This inconsistency is part of the mythological aspect of the work that has already been identified.

The Three appear semi-frequently in the early issues. In the first part proper of *The Doll's House* storyline (*Sandman* 10), Rose Walker encounters them in a broom closet in a nursing home in England, where they give her advice; Rose is already unwittingly playing the Maiden in a human trinity, with her mother Miranda playing the Mother, and her newly discovered grandmother Unity Kinkaid as the Crone. In Part 6 of *The Kindly Ones* storyline (*Sandman* 62, 6-7), Rose returns to the nursing home and enters the same broom closet, only to discover that it is merely a broom closet. She then immediately encounters three women, Helena, Amelia, and Magda, who on one level are simply three more residents of the nursing home; but on another level they are the Maiden, Mother, and Crone, and Amelia and Magda have a visual similarity to Mildred and Mordred in "Imperfect Hosts."[41] There is also a further paradigm shift, in that the three are Maiden, Mother, and Crone only in relation to each other; in relation to Rose they are all old women.[42] Moreover, the Maiden here is herself a mother. Indeed, Helena is—though this is not made explicit in the text— Helena Kosmatos, the mother of Hippolyta (Lyta) Hall (née Trevor),[43] and the former superhero called the Fury. Helena herself was a superhero called the Fury, and has, as she tells us (19.1), spent two decades of her life pursuing a blood feud. Here is a link back to another aspect of the Three, the Furies, an aspect which is extremely important to the storyline of *The Kindly Ones*, and which is reinforced for those with a broader knowledge of the DC Universe by the fact that Helena Kosmatos received her powers from the mythological Fury Tisiphone.[44]

In "Calliope," the first of the *Dream Country* stories (*Sandman* 17, 9-10), the Three appear as the Muses recorded by Pausanias (mentioned above), Melete, Mneme, and Aiode (*sic*).[45] In Gaiman's mythology they are the mothers of the Nine Muses,[46] of whom Calliope is one. In *Season of Mists*, the Three appear at the beginning of the story (*Sandman* 21, 2-3), warning Destiny of the Endless of what is to come. They function through many of these stories as oracles (the role also that the three humans manifesting as the Three play for John Dee in "24 Hours"). Nevertheless, despite their largely inactive roles, as observers rather than participants, they are important. This is shown by Gaiman's script for Calliope (as reprinted in *Dream Country*). Gaiman writes (page 14 of the script): "Now we're playing with a running theme in *Sandman*, of the Triple Goddess." Gaiman would slowly build up the importance of the Three through the subsequent issues, ultimately leading to their central role in *The Kindly Ones*.

It would take up too much time to go through every manifestation of the Three in the eight-year run of *Sandman*, and would not be necessary for the purpose of this chapter. However, there are a few that are worth pointing out.

The first is the Three's manifestation in *A Game of You*, and more particularly, the way in which they manifest. By this point in the narrative it has already been established that the Three are associated with the Moon, albeit that this has been shown indirectly, through the use of certain names (*e.g.*, Cynthia, Hecate) and iconography (encountering the Three when the sun is down and the moon is up in "Imperfect Hosts"). It should therefore not be surprising that when the witch Thessaly draws down the Moon in *Sandman* 34 (entitled "Bad Moon Rising"), the Moon turns out to be a Triple Goddess, whom Thessaly names Gorgo, Mormo, and Ereschigal (18.4),[47] nor that the Moon manifests as three faces and three voices blending into one (19.1, 19.3).[48]

What is perhaps a little more surprising is the way in which the Three are manifested in Thessaly herself. When she looks at the Moon (19.2, 19.4) we see the Moon reflected in each lens of her round glasses. Her own round face makes the third of the Moon's three faces. With the pregnant Hazel and Foxglove, who is a lesbian (and therefore a virgin as far as sex with men is concerned),[49] Thessaly then forms a Maiden-Mother-Crone group, and it is this group that sets out on the Moon's Road to find their friend Barbie.[50] In *Sandman* 36, Dream says to Thessaly, "There were more of you then." In Greek and Roman times, the area of Thessaly had been seen as a home for many witches,[51] and Dream's comment may be no more than a reference to that. However, the reader can be forgiven for wondering if in fact Dream means that the last time he encountered Thessaly, she was perhaps accompanied by two more, making her part of another mortal representation of the Three.[52]

The other particularly interesting example is Eve. As already noted, Gaiman introduced Eve as an inhabitant of the Dreaming in *Sandman* 2, when he established that a number of the hosts from DC's 1970s anthology titles were to be found living there. But Gaiman actually created the Eve of *The Sandman* by combining two separate hosts from DC horror comics. Eve had appeared as an old woman with a raven in *Secrets of Sinister House*, where she was been named as such; but an unnamed *young* woman with a raven had appeared in *The Dark Mansion of Forbidden Love* (DC, October 1971). Gaiman formed his Eve by merging the two characters,[53] and so she is a woman with a Raven who sometimes appears old, and sometimes appears young (for examples of her changing her age over a few panels, see Chapter 3 of *Season of Mists*, *Sandman* 24, 18.4-7, and Chapter 1 of *The Wake*, *Sandman* 70, 13-14).

"The Parliament of Rooks" (*Sandman* 40) is an extremely interesting story for this aspect of Eve. In this issue (13-16), she recounts the story of the three wives of Adam. These are Lilith, the Mother, the nameless virgin (the Maiden), and Eve, the Crone. Yet, once again, the paradigm is shifted slightly. The Mother is Adam's first wife, the Maiden his second, and the Crone his third—that seems like the wrong order. Eve is also, as well as being the Crone, the Mother: "You're everybody's mother," Cain says to her (12.6).

In any case, this clearly establishes Eve as an aspect of the Three. So, when the Three are attacking the Dreaming in *The Kindly Ones* (*Sandman* 65), in their aspect as the Furies, they leave Eve alone: "She is, in herself, an aspect of ourselves." (14.2).

At 17.1 in *Sandman* 40, Eve says something very important: "But some say Adam married only once, and they speak truly too." Of course, this is an element of Eve functioning as an aspect of the Three-who-are-One. But Gaiman also establishes here that what might be seen by some as mutually incompatible "truths"—how can Adam have three wives, yet have married only once?—can exist simultaneously in the multiverse of *The Sandman*, and yet both remain "truths." Again, Gaiman is creating a mythology, with all the inherent inconsistency that mythologies have.[54]

All this leads eventually to the thirteen-issue storyline of *The Kindly Ones* (*Sandman* 57-69, February 1994–July 1995). The Three are central to this story, in many aspects.[55] The story takes its name, of course, from the euphemism for the Furies, the Eumenides, which Aeschylus used as the title of the third play in his *Oresteia* trilogy. They appear as the Fates at the beginning and end of the story. And their role as the Furies, and their connection through that to Lyta Hall, who as a superhero took their name, and is the child of another superhero who not only took their name but also took her powers from them,[56] is the driving force for the plot.[57] It also provides a link back to the main DC Universe, from which *The Sandman* was by now increasingly distant.[58]

Furthermore, there are other manifestations of the Three in this story. I have already mentioned the three women in the nursing home. In Part 4 (*Sandman* 60) Lyta Hall encounters the immortal sisters of Medusa, the Gorgons Stheno and Euryale (16). They are an aspiring Three, prevented from achieving their ambitions by the death of their mortal sister. They attempt to make Lyta Hall their third, but again fail.[59] In Part 7 (*Sandman* 62, 23.1-2) there is a brief mention of the Morrígan. In Part 13 (*Sandman* 69) we learn that Rose Walker is working on a book on the Triple Goddess in TV sitcoms (18.3). In Part 4 (15.2), we have already seen some of the materials she is researching—*Bewitched* (USA, 1964-1972), a sitcom about witches, where the triad is Tabitha (once she is born in 1966), Samantha, and Endora, and *Roseanne* (USA, 1988-1997), where the triad is Darlene (why not Becky?), Roseanne, and Roseanne's mother Beverly.[60]

The Kindly Ones also shows the limitations of the Three. They are unable to exact revenge upon Dream for what he has done (or rather, what Lyta believes he has done) to Lyta's son Daniel, only for his killing of his own son (Part 7, *Sandman* 62, 23.5-6, 24.6). And in the end, they are cursorily dismissed by Death (Part 13, 9.4).[61]

After their leading role in *The Kindly Ones*, the Three are largely absent from *The Wake* (though Eve features in that storyline). There is, however, one last manifestation of the Triple Goddess in *Sandman*, in Gaiman's prose story, *The Dream Hunters*.[62] Here the villain of the story, the master of Yin-Yang, keeps in a dilapidated house "three women: one old, one young, and one who was neither young nor old."[63] Clearly here Gaiman once again presents the Maiden, Mother, and Crone; they function as oracles, much as the Three did earlier in the main sequence of *The Sandman*. They are, however, not quite a clear representation of the Three, as they seem to be the servants of the Master of Yin-Yang. Perhaps they are closer to the humans who manifest themselves in aspects of the Three, such as Judy, Kate, and Bette in "24 Hours" (*Sandman* 6) or Foxglove, Hazel, and Thessaly in *A Game of You*.[64] There does seem to be something magical about them, however, as they mysteriously disappear when their house is destroyed.

"They looked like a set of Russian dolls"[65]: The Triple Goddess in Other Gaiman works

Gaiman was not alone in being interested in the motif of the Triple Goddess. At about the same time as Gaiman's earliest issues of *The Sandman* appeared, his friend Terry Pratchett published *Wyrd Sisters* (1989). Pratchett had already introduced the elderly witch Granny Weatherwax in *Equal Rites*, two years previously. In *Wyrd Sisters*, he gave Granny a coven, including the matronly (she has a great many children) Nanny Ogg, and the young novice Magrat Garlick, thus filling the three roles of Crone, Mother, and Maiden.

Whether the two authors had discussed their respective ideas with each other is unclear. However, Pratchett uses his three witches differently from Gaiman. Where, as we shall see, Gaiman's One who is Three are supernatural primal forces, and at least partly symbolic, Pratchett's witches are very much more down-to-earth. Granny Weatherwax does not hold with a great many things, and one suspects that being symbolic is one of these.[66]

Neil Gaiman found his own voice early on in the writing of *The Sandman* (as discussed above), and the creative mode that he employed in that work is something within which he has largely remained for his subsequent writing. Although Gaiman manages to avoid repeating himself in detail, later works such as *Neverwhere*, *Stardust,* and *American Gods* emerge from the same sort of thematic territory as *The Sandman*. There is nothing fundamentally wrong with this, and most writers do it to one degree or another. But it does mean that one should not be surprised to see the Triple Goddess recur through his works. The following section examines some of the more prominent examples of Gaiman using the

Triple Goddess motif. There are other examples, for instance in his short stories, but those have been omitted here for reasons of space.

There are a few mentions in the remainder of Gaiman's work within the DC Universe. In "Notes Towards a Vegetable Theology," written as part of his plans for *Swamp Thing*,[67] Gaiman postulated three May Queens, female earth spirits, who would be in his plans: Black Orchid, the Batman villain Poison Ivy, and Thorn (of Rose and the Thorn).[68] In the *Black Orchid* mini-series, Gaiman's first published work for DC, there were three versions of the main character, the experienced crime-fighter who is killed at the beginning, a mature version who achieves consciousness to replace her, and a child version; this could be another version of the Triple Goddess motif. Surprisingly, however, in *The Books of Magic*, in which Gaiman set out the magical aspects of the DC Universe, there is just one brief explicit reference to the Three in the first chapter, in the context of ancient Greece, where Gaiman mentions the three-faced witch-queen.

The Triple Goddess next becomes significant in *Stardust*, an illustrated fairy tale that draws heavily upon the third chapter of *The Books of Magic* (both were illustrated by Charles Vess).[69] The main antagonist here is the Witch-Queen, who is one of three sisters who call themselves the Lilim (who were in *Sandman* 40 the children of Lilith, first wife of Adam).[70] The Witch-Queen is, in a sense, an aspect of all three of them.[71]

American Gods is another return to the pan-pantheon. It would be very surprising, therefore, if aspects of the Triple Goddess did not manifest themselves in this story. And so they do. The most interesting is where the protagonist of the novel, Shadow, encounters the Slavic Zorya, or Auroras.[72] Unsurprisingly, Gaiman chooses a version of this mythology in which there are three Zorya: Zorya Utrennyaya, the Morning Star, Zorya Vechernyaya, the Evening Star, and Zorya Polunochnaya, the Midnight Star. There are, however, other variants in Slavic myth in which there are only the first two, and indeed, these are the more common versions. According to Mike Dixon-Kennedy,[73] the only named Zorya are Utrennyaya and Vechernyaya. A Midnight Star is found in a few references, but she is quite an obscure figure, never given a name. Of course, Gaiman prefers the less common variant, because it allows him to use the Triple Goddess theme with the Zorya. Gaiman has admitted that Zorya Polunochnaya is at least partially his own invention.[74] What Gaiman does with Zorya Polunochnaya in *American Gods* is to make her a shadowy figure, whom Shadow is not quite sure he has actually met. This reflects the Midnight Star's nebulous presence in Slavic mythology.

Later, Shadow encounters the Norns, before he carries out the vigil for Odin.[75] Other manifestations of the Triple Goddess play minor roles in the work. There is an unremembered three-bodied deity. There is mention of the Brigids. The Greco-Roman Fates appear, as does/do the Morrígan.[76] Kalī, who also appears in this novel, is another aspect of the Triple Goddess. Sancken suggests that she should be seen as such, since she embodies creation, preservation, and destruction.[77] But her role as an aspect of the Triple Goddess is clearer than that. She is an aspect of the goddess Durgā, who is herself an aspect of Pārvatī, and Pārvatī, along with Saraswati and Lakshmī, form the Hindu Tridevi, literally the "three goddesses." It should be noted, however, that Gaiman does not in this novel emphasize the Triple nature of Kalī.

There is one important difference in how Gaiman handles these figures in *American Gods* from how he handles them in *The Sandman*. In *American Gods* the various triples are *not* aspects of each other; rather, each is a separate deity or deities functioning within their own pantheon. It is quite possible in *American Gods* for gods to exist in multiple aspects within pantheons—Shadow encounters an Odin who has traveled across the Atlantic to the United States, but also meets another aspect who has never left Scandinavia. But these aspects do not cross pantheons. This shows Gaiman, as he often does through his career, working through similar concepts to those he has addressed in *Sandman*, but in a manner that allows him to take a fresh look at them.

In the companion volume to *American Gods*, *Anansi Boys*, the protagonist, Fat Charlie Nancy, encounters what could be an aspect of the Triple Goddess, except that in this case, there are four of them. At the wake for his father, Charlie encounters four old ladies, Mrs. Callyanne Higgler, Mrs. Louella Dunwiddy, Mrs. Zorah Bustamonte, and Mrs. Bella Noles. All these names have resonances with other Gaimanic names, if not necessarily with ones used for manifestations of the Triple Goddess.[78] Within their group, they are differentiated by age: "Mrs. Higgler was older than Mrs. Bustamonte, and both of them were older than Mrs. Noles and none of them was older than Mrs. Dunwiddy."[79] Fat Charlie was afraid of Mrs. Dunwiddy in his youth, with some reason, as she was primarily responsible for extracting part of his essence and creating his brother Spider. All four women turn out to be witches, though Mrs. Dunwiddy is the prime mover of the coven. Mrs. Higgler is somewhat differentiated from the others, being introduced in the novel first, as Charlie's father's neighbor, but the ritual that sends Fat Charlie to the beginning of the world is carried out by all four of them.[80] In the novel, Gaiman never really treats Mrs. Dunwiddy, Mrs. Bustamonte, and Mrs. Noles as a Triple Goddess, even if Mrs. Dunwiddy easily fits into the role of crone. It is also worth noting that all four are definitely mortal—Mrs. Dunwiddy dies and is buried at the end of the novel, though there is some implication that she may come back.

Gaiman's most recent published use of the Triple Goddess is in his illustrated children's picture book *Blueberry Girl*, which appeared in 2009, though the original poem had been written in 2000. It begins with an invocation to "ladies of light and ladies of darkness and ladies of never-you-mind." These are depicted by artist Charles Vess as three women, one elderly, one mature (and wearing a wimple), and one younger. How much of this is Vess' imagination and how much Gaiman's is hard to determine. From Gaiman's description of the creative process on this particular work,[81] it is unclear whether Vess was working from anything more than Gaiman's original poem. Though Gaiman is friends with many of his artists, and he and Vess clearly discussed the project in broad terms, it is unclear how detailed these discussions were in terms of what Vess should draw,[82] certainly as compared with the great detail that Gaiman would put into a typical comic script, and Vess may have come up with the imagery himself. But, of course, Vess has worked with Gaiman on many occasions in the past (on *Stardust*, *The Books of Magic*, and several issues of *Sandman*), and would be well aware of Gaiman's interest in the Triple Goddess. It is natural that he would interpret Gaiman's threefold invocation in this manner. The result is quite the most benign version of the Triple Goddess to be found anywhere in Gaiman's work, as befits a children's book. These ladies are not warning of disasters, exacting vengeance, or determining at which point a human life will end. Rather, they are the benevolent source of hope and possibility. Vess' depiction of them as a multi-racial group—the youngest-appearing lady is also non-white—is part of that.

"Three is the magic number"[83]

There are a number of ways in which study of the Triple Goddess in Gaiman's works could be taken further. There is, of course, a link between these three goddesses/witches/spirits/etc., and all the other magical women found in Gaiman's work.[84] It is also worth noting that "threes recur throughout Gaiman's work. *Sandman* 31 is entitled "Three Septembers and a January." Threes are particularly prominent in *Neverwhere*. For example, there are three ordeals to be passed to get the Key that is the central plot device (Alfred Hitchcock's "Macguffin") of the novel, which are passed by three characters, Hunter, Door, and Richard. Three people, Hunter, Richard, and the Marquis de Carabas, confront the Beast of London in the climax of the novel.

But then, Gaiman is hardly alone is making considerable use of threes. It is, after all, as most of the major religions of the planet recognize a magic number. It seems likely that the Triple Goddess will be seen in future work by Gaiman.

1 William Shakespeare, *Macbeth*, Act I, Scene I.
2 Gaiman jokes that the explanation is "When I was four, I was bitten by a radioactive myth" (quoted in Crispin).
3 Levi, 368.
4 Since nine is three times three, it is reasonably easy to see how differing traditions of the Muses could arise. For details of the Fates, Graces, Furies and Muses, see the respective entries in March, 163 (Fates), 165 (Furies), 173 (Graces), 261-2 (Muses).
5 See the entry in March, 179. An example is the *Hecate Chiaramonti* in the Vatican Museums in Rome.
6 See the entry in Orchard, 267.
7 Ó hÓgáin, 307-9.
8 Sjoestedt, 21, 25.
9 Green, 190-204. Examples are known from the Roman fort at Housesteads on Hadrian's Wall, or from Cirencester.
10 Green, 185-7. An example is known from Housesteads.
11 The play was composed c. 1611; the witches first appear in Act I, Scene I.
12 For criticisms of *The White Goddess* and the mythological structure it propounds, see Wood, 22; Morales, 111-14. Morales is working from a feminist perspective.
13 Collard, *Oresteia*, 83-113.
14 See the entry on "chorus" in Howatson and Chilvers.
15 Euripides, *Trojan Women* 457, in Davie, 194.
16 Virgil names Allecto at *Aeneid* 7.324, in West, 150. He does not name the others.
17 See Mackie, 354-6.
18 Westrin, 1480.
19 Green, 186, fig. 83.
20 See Hanes and Sanders, 148.
21 Pratchett, *Wyrd Sisters*, 5.
22 In what follows, I am primarily concerned with the ways in which Gaiman draws together in his work the mythological roots of the Triple Goddess *as Triple Goddess*. For other aspects of how the Triple Goddess is depicted in *The Sandman*, and the implications of that when approached from a feminist critique, see Hanes and Sanders; and for Gaiman's magical women in general, see Jessica Burke in this volume.
23 On Gaiman and the pan-pantheon, see Harley Sims elsewhere in this volume. On one level the pan-pantheon is simply a development of the syncretism that the Greek and Romans performed whenever they encountered anyone else's gods, assimilating them to their own. But it is also something to which comics fans are particularly attracted, having been accustomed from an early age to dealing with such all-encompassing continuities as "the Marvel Universe" or the "DC Universe." Such constructs can be described as "megatexts" (see Marshall, 90 & n. 6, who takes the term from Segal, 48-74), or in Roz Kaveney's formulation, "Big Dumb Narrative Objects" (Kaveney first formulated the term in *From Alien to the Matrix*, 3-4; for its application to the Marvel and DC Universes, see *Superheroes!*, *passim*). Another self-confessed fan of this approach is Gaiman's friend and mentor Alan Moore, whose *League of Extraordinary Gentlemen* series (1999 onwards) is an attempt to turn the entirety of fiction into a single megatext.
24 This is one of the most difficult ideas to get across to students when teaching them myth courses, that there are not necessarily "correct" versions of myths, and that self-contradictory narratives can exist, even within the work of a single author.
25 Clements, 551, takes exception to Gaiman's reluctance to clarify certain issues, such as whether the Endless are "simply ambulatory ideas or are they personalities in their own right?" But to complain about this aspect seems to me to be missing the point.
26 Gaiman refers to them as the Triple Goddess in the text introduction to *The Doll's House* (9). "The Three" is used, e.g., by Thessaly/Larissa in *Sandman* 65, 20.5. From this point on, I will use "the Three" to refer to the characters in *The Sandman*, and "Triple Goddess" for the wider concept.

27 *The Sandman* was unusual in the degree to which it was distanced from DC continuity (for the circumstances that produced that, see Gaiman in Bender, 23-4), but it was never intended to be fully outside it. As the series went on, Gaiman made less and less use of DC characters, beyond those he had introduced in the first twenty issues, and more-or-less made his own.
28 The first nineteen issues are now collected in *Showcase Presents: The Witching Hour.*
29 See Gaiman's "Afterword," *Preludes,* 240.
30 Cain first appeared in *The House of Mystery* 175 (DC, July 1968); Abel was first seen in *DC Special* 4 (DC, July-September 1969), before hosting *The House of Secrets* from issue 81 (DC, August-September 1969). Gaiman also employed another anthology host in *The Sandman,* Destiny (from *Weird Mystery Tales* 1, DC, August 1972), first mentioned in *Sandman* 1 (15.5), but not shown until *Sandman* 7 (15.5). Gaiman brilliantly uses Destiny as the cornerstone of his entire mythological system.
31 In the "Afterword," *Preludes,* 240, he cites *Sandman* 8 as the point at which he was finding his own voice; in Bender, 35, he selects *Sandman* 6.
32 This is particularly noticeable in his 1989 mini-series *Black Orchid.*
33 Gaiman in Bender, 15-18.
34 I think there is no need for the caution of Marshall, 92-3, with regard to identifying echoes of the witches of Macbeth in the Three.
35 I have adopted a reference system for comics that gives the page number followed by the panel number.
36 Which, as the Three hint, is the name of Arthur's son in the Arthurian mythos, and a more appropriate name would be Morgaine, another character who has been identified as a manifestation of the Triple Goddess.
37 Brewer, 694.
38 See Morrow and Hildebrandt, "Issue 6."
39 See the entry in March, 163. As an example of where the Fates are not all-powerful, in Aeschylus' *Prometheus Bound* (Collard, *Persians,* 99-129), the Titan Prometheus possesses knowledge that would allow Zeus to escape his designated fate. This is, of course, an aspect of the clash between the concepts of divine omnipotence and free will that many religions fail to resolve.
40 Moreover, what each one starts eating, the next one finishes; see Morrow & Hildebrandt, "Issues 2."
41 Wagner, Golden and Bissette, 114; Goldfarb and Hildebrandt, <http://www.arschkrebs.de/sandman/annotations/sandman.62.draft.shtml>.
42 Goldfarb and Hildebrandt, ibid.
43 See Gaiman, in Bender, 197.
44 This is explained in *Secret Origins* 12. When Hippolyta Trevor was first introduced, in *Wonder Woman* 300, she was the daughter of the Golden Age (Earth-2) Wonder Woman. After the restructuring of the DC Universe in *Crisis on Infinite Earths* (1985-1986) there never had been a Golden Age Wonder Woman, and so a new Golden Age Fury was created to be Lyta's mother.
45 This is presumably an accidental misspelling.
46 See page 15 of the script to "Calliope," reprinted in *Dream Country.*
47 Gorgo is an alternative spelling of the Greek name usually rendered as "Gorgon," one of three monstrous women (who will appear in *The Kindly Ones*). Mormo is a Greek she-monster (see the entry in March, 261). Ereschigal is a Babylonian deity sometimes identified with Hecate. See Morrow and Hildebrandt "Issue 34."
48 Wagner, Golden and Bissette, 72.
49 Foxglove, it transpires, was the lover of Judy, who plays the role of maiden in "24 Hours."
50 The appearance of Foxglove, Hazel, and Thessaly as Maiden, Mother, and Crone has been recognized on many occasions: see, e.g., Morrow and Hildebrandt, "Issue 34"; Bender, 113; Sanders in Hanes and Sanders, 162-3 (though I question whether Thessaly is as consciously trying to recreate the Triple Goddess as Sanders suggests here); Wagner, Golden and Bissette, 72.
51 For an example of this Roman perception, see the *Metamorphoses,* or *Golden Ass,* of Apuleius, where the hero's troubles begin with a trip to Thessaly and an encounter with witchcraft.
52 For other Triple Goddess elements in *A Game of You,* see Sanders in Hanes and Sanders, 161-5. Further on *A Game of You,* see Bratman, 41-53. At 47-50, Bratman addresses some criticisms that have been made of the story, specifically the deaths of the single black character and the single transgender character, criticisms he feels misplaced. Whilst I appreciate the point of view he takes, I think he is perhaps too dismissive of those criticisms.

53 Gaiman, in Bender, 244-5.
54 The DC Universe as a whole is less accepting of such perceived inconsistencies, and has been "rebooted" on several occasions to eliminate them.
55 I do not intend discussing the entire plot of *The Kindly Ones* in detail here. See Bender, 186-202, and for a discussion of female empowerment (or the lack thereof) in the storyline, see Laity, 65-76.
56 Gaiman never explicitly mentions this, though the Furies do refer to Lyta as "daughter"; but then they tend to refer to all women as "daughter" (as an example, this is how they address Rose Walker in *The Doll's House*).
57 For the Furies in this sequence, see also Marshall, 91-5. The Three also briefly make reference to the three Graeae, old women from Greek mythology possessed of a single eye and a single tooth among them (see the entry in March, 173-4), thus presumably appropriating them as an aspect of the Three (*Sandman* 63, 20.7); arguably this had already been done when Destiny referred to them as the "Grey ladies" in *Sandman* 20 (2.4), "Grey ladies" being a translation of the Latin *graeae*.
58 See note 27 above.
59 Wagner, Golden and Bissette, 119. For the argument that the elf-girl Nuala, Lyta Hall, and Thessaly/Larissa form another manifestation of the Triple Goddess in *The Kindly Ones*, see Sanders in Hanes and Sanders, 165-7.
60 Gaiman, in Bender, 199. I suspect Gaiman may be slightly sending himself up here, especially as another of Rose's Walker's research areas is *The Golden Girls* (USA, 1985-1992), where, of course, there are four principal characters, all of whom are perceived as elderly (though three of the characters are only in their fifties when the show started), and could therefore, in theory, all lay claim to the role of Crone.
61 See Laity, 73.
62 The non-Gaiman spin-offs, *WitchCraft* (DC/Vertigo, June-August 1994) and *The Sandman Presents: The Furies* (DC/Vertigo, 2002), lie outside the purview of this chapter. For the former, see Plowright, 742; for the latter, see Marshall, 95-6 and 97 Figure 6.2.
63 Gaiman, *The Dream Hunters*, 42. See Wagner, Golden and Bissette, 132.
64 In the comics adaptation of the story, P. Craig Russell gives the youngest multiple breasts.
65 Gaiman, *Gods*, 486.
66 This does not mean, of course, that critics cannot still see Pratchett's witches as symbolic. For discussions of Pratchett's witches as manifestations of the Triple Goddess, see Hanes in Hanes and Sanders, 148-58; Hanes, "Weatherwax," 406; Hanes, "Witches," 419. For Pratchett's witches in general, see Sayer; Hanes, "Witches."
67 See Gaiman, *Midnight Days* 16, for the story behind why Gaiman's run on *Swamp Thing* never happened.
68 Gaiman, "Notes Towards a Vegetable Theology," 191.
69 On a purely subjective note, I consider *Stardust* to be quite the finest thing that Gaiman has ever written.
70 Gaiman and Vess, *Stardust*, 61-7; Gaiman, *Stardus*t, 50-4.
71 The movie version (dir: Matthew Vaughn, wri: Jane Goldman, 2007), develops the roles of the other sisters, and names all three as Lamia (the principal witch-queen), Mormo, and Empusa, all female monsters from Greek mythology. Two are names Gaiman has used himself, Lamia in *Neverwhere* and Mormo in *Sandman* 34 (see above).
72 Gaiman, *Gods*, 80-98. According to Dixon-Kennedy, 48, the plural is Zoryi.
73 Dixon-Kennedy, 189.
74 Gaiman and Oswalt, "@ Saban Theater."
75 Gaiman, *Gods*, 485-6.
76 Gaiman, *Gods*, 62, 243, 532, 534, 544.
77 Sancken.
78 Daniel Bustamonte is a victim of the "sleepy sickness" in "Sleep of the Just" (*Sandman* 1).
79 Gaiman, *Anansi*, 31.
80 Gaiman, *Anansi*, 146-9.
81 Gaiman, "This is a prayer for a blueberry girl ..."
82 Not knowing what Vess would do with the book until it was completed may have been attractive to Gaiman. Certainly he has, in his introduction to the graphic novel adaptation of *The Dream Hunters*, identified that as one of the pleasures he got from that project, where P. Craig Russell took Gaiman's

prose story and adapted it without direct reference to Gaiman; thus Gaiman got to experience a new *Sandman* comic in a way that he had not been able to when writing the title.

83 De La Soul, "The Magic Number," 1989.

84 For which see Jessica Burke's chapter in this volume.

Women's Magic: Witches and the Works of Neil Gaiman

Jessica Burke

"Was the gibbet really better than the maypole?"[1]

"Anyway," said Adam, "you've got it all wrong about witches."
.... "My mother said they were just intelligent women protesting in the only way open to them against the stifling injustices of a male-dominated social hierarchy," said Pepper. ... "And she said, at worst they were just free-thinking worshippers of the progenerative principle."
"Who's the progenratty principle?" said Wensleydale.
"Dunno. Something to do with maypoles, I think," said Pepper vaguely.[2]

Neil Gaiman has a knack for making the most unbelievable, believable and the most surreal just two degrees shy of odd. He has challenged boundaries deeply ingrained in fiction and the Western psyche—in regard to female characters and the witch, in particular.

During the New York junket of the publicity tour for the 10th Anniversary of *American Gods,* Gaiman was asked about how he writes his characters. Referring to C.S. Lewis, Gaiman said that writing was basically "the strange events that happen to strange people." Gaiman rebuked Lewis' sentiment because, writing is what happens to "normal characters"—albeit normal characters who sometimes find themselves in odd situations. This level of normalcy makes Gaiman's characters so remarkable, so likeable, and so influential.

Gaiman achieves a state of normal with one of the most maligned characters in Western culture: the witch. In a politically correct world that pinpoints the anti-Semitism in Shakespeare, the racism in Twain, and the homophobia in Hemingway, the witch is still perfectly satisfactory, perched on her broom, black cat and dermatological problems in tow. With perhaps very few exceptions, the image of the witch still serves as a warning. For those who detest the term *bitch*, labeling an unruly, unattractive, unfitting woman as a witch is a great, socially acceptable alternative. Witches of all types—from classic hag to seductive temptress—adorn homes, offices, and schools during Halloween. The witch has been a source of fascination for more than a millennium, but where did this image come from? And why is she so terrifying? Gaiman doesn't merely challenge one representation of the witch—the Hollywood, anti-norm, evil image. Nor does he limit his witches and magical women to the feminist, neo-pagan approach—all hippified, tree-hugging, Girl Power New Agers with crystals and fairy dust. Gaiman takes the images—negative and positive—and addresses them all, in various forms in various pieces of his work. From the witches of the *Malleus Maleficarum*[3] to the Witch in Snow White, he treats them all with an infinitely humane eye—despite the fact that some, like the Lilim, are not human. How are Gaiman's witches different? By their appetite—and intentions.

In his poem, "Instructions," which directs the reader how to maneuver through a fairy tale, Gaiman tells us to "Remember...that witches are betrayed by their appetites...."[4] Appetite is key to determining whether witches presented in Gaiman's work are 'good' or 'evil,' or somewhere in-between. There's a "firm correlation between bodily appetite and the condition of the human soul..."[5] and a woman's appetite—or a witch's—appears more grotesque in Gaiman, more negative, when her intent runs contrary to normative society.

The traditional view of witches presented in *Malleus*, Gaiman delves and satirizes, presenting the grotesque as well as the infinitely human, the humorous and the disturbing. Even in his most stereotypical concepts of the witch, Gaiman allows for normalcy, redemption, and understanding. Perhaps a handful of sorceresses are shown, wholly without deliverance—which stem their function as a lamia or vampire.

What is a witch, really?

That all depends on your source—and your personal belief structure. On the most basic, fundamental level—a witch is a person who traverses boundaries between the waking world and the world of dream, the world of magic. Witches travel a shamanic path, practicing "shamanic traditions" which are:

> ...those that evoke a part of women and men that is natural, primal and wild. A shaman is a person in a tribal culture who confronts the world of the supernatural.[6]

If witches are shamans, then so are storytellers and dreamers. Tellers of story make the *super*natural—that which is beyond the mundane—real, believable, normal. When we dream or create story, we come in contact with the supernatural, and that which is "natural, primal and wild" within each of us. This is a purposefully broad definition of witches, reflecting the potential for magic, for shamanism, and therefore for witchcraft within us all.

Appetite and intent also form part of the normal human potential. We all have them in mundane form—food, affection, money, sex, power, protection, success. When those are no longer commonplace and run contrary to what's normally accepted— deviousness occurs. It is this potential for devious appetite and malicious intent that brands one a witch.

Witches, to the mainstream, are women who practice dark magic, are somehow in league with the forces of Hell, and prance around stark naked brandishing black cats, wearing pointy black hats, and wielding broomsticks. Witches are often portrayed as grotesque old women who frighten –or eat—children, while mumbling into bubbling cauldrons. Throughout we have a layer of appetites unchecked, sexual inadequacy, and sexual deviancy. We have women past their generative prime, women of gender transgression, women with sexual urges, and women with grotesque appetites. As late as the 1970s, academics' theories about witches ranged from unsatisfied women using "unguents and broomsticks for masturbation" to disgruntled women who "felt weaker than men and therefore turned to sorcery."[7]

Outside Neo-Pagan circles, the predominant view of the witch is marked by this grotesque appetite. Inside these circles, witches are shamans—of either sex. But, this view is relatively new and datable to the publications of Margaret Murray (1921) and Gerald Gardner (1955).[8] Definitions of *wicca* or *wicce* that Gardnerians and Murrayites latch onto are predominantly incorrect, etymologically and historically speaking. These misconceptions have been regurgitated by modern Wiccans with regularity. Prior to Gardner and Murray, Witchcraft meant one thing: the practice of negative, harmful magic—*maleficia*— predominantly cast by women.

Witches, Historically Speaking

Habitually, but debatably, the impression of the witch casting *maleficia* traces back to the 1487 publication of the *Malleus*. Kraemer and Sprenger's text ramped up an already booming business in witches—namely location, interrogation, and eradication. For some scholars, the *Malleus* was unique, being the first handbook discussing what witches were—and how to get rid of them. Others argue this text was symbolic of other witch-hunting dogma of the day:

...the *Malleus*, more than any other contemporary treatise on witchcraft, effectively fused theological concerns about demonic magic with popular conceptions of harmful magic (*maleficium*) widely held in European society.[9]

There were, however, precursors to the witch found in *Malleus*. The works of Johannes Nider (1437), the execution of Joan of Arc (1431), texts from the 11th and 12th centuries (the canon *Episcopi* and Burchard of Worms' *Decretum*)[10] and mythology surrounding Thessalian witches are but a few. To the Medieval European mind, the concept of the witch began with so-called *maleficium* or evil deeds, grotesque feminine appetite, and evil intent:

> Prior to the fifteenth century, people spoke in terms of heretics, of *maleficium*, of monstrous female spirits—the *lamiae* and *strigae*, but not of a single composite category, "witch." By the mid-sixteenth century, however, educated men generally agreed upon the definitions of "witch" and "witchcraft," definitions which drew upon, but were clearly distinguished from, older categories.[11]

Generally, there's lateral thinking regarding the foundations for modern views of witchcraft that ignore origins of the term *witch*. Traditions of the malevolent witch with unchecked appetite weren't creations from *Malleus*. As noted previously, reclaiming the term *witch* by modern day Neo-Pagans via Gardner's term *Wica* is a confabulation of history and fancy. According to Gardner,

> Witches were...the Wica, the "wise people", who practise the age-old rites and...herbal knowledge, [who] preserved an occult teaching and working processes which they themselves think to be magic or witchcraft.[12]

Little evidence justifies Gardener's claims linking old folk custom with witchcraft as a unified belief system. The *OED* links the term *witch* etymologically with the Old English term *wicca*, defining a witch as a "man who practises witchcraft or magic...."[13] The first use of the term *wicca* – or *wiccan*—was in the ninth-century *Laws of Ælfred*: "Đa fæmnan, þe gewuniað onfon gealdorcræftigan, & scinlæcan, & wiccan." Translated as— "Do not let women, accustomed to performing incantation and sorcery and witchcraft, live"[14]—akin to "do not suffer a witch to live."[15] By the tumult of the eleventh century, *wiccan* became the antithesis to normally functioning society:

> ...*wælcyrian* and *wiccan* 'witches' are connected as baleful

influences on society in Wulfstan's *Sermo Lupi ad Anglos* (A.D. 1014), which accuses them, in concert with murderers, slayers of kinsmen, and fornicators, of destroying the English nation.[16]

Yet, the term *wælcyrian*, "chooser of the slain, witch, sorceress"[17]—linked to the Norse valkyrie—itself wasn't a negative term, being associated with the Celtic Triple Goddess the Morrígan. For archaeologist Marija Gimbutas, alliances between witches, carrion birds, and goddesses of death and war stretch back into the Proto-Neolithic and Neolithic Ages— discoveries in Zawi Chemi Shandidar in Northern Iraq (10,870 BCE), Çatal Hüyük in central Anatolia (circa 8000 BCE), and Skara Bræ in the Orkney Islands (3100 BCE).[18] But, the witch to Gimbutas was nothing more than a "loathsome caricature" of the once formidable images of "Lady Death...."[19] Ancient Goddesses of Death were deeply associated with fertility—of the earth and of the animals upon it, including humans. Often the destruction of life—as with the "Killer-Regeneratrix" figure, the Morrígan, Hecate, and Kālī—wasn't rooted in animosity, but an intention toward balance, preventing eternally flourishing life.[20] A need for balance is where the concept of appetite emerges: "Witches were greatly feared since they continued to represent the powers of a formidable Goddess on earth."[21] While Christianity gained control in Europe, folk traditions and magic were still practiced; yet these traditions were prosecuted and "considered dangerous" when contrary to normal intentions, normal appetite, and when practiced by women.[22]

Thanks to the schism in the Catholic Church in 1054 and a century replete with war, pestilence, and dissent, Medieval Europe took on a persecutorial atmosphere.[23] Those on the fringes were accused with social destruction, sexual deviancy, malicious intent, and unchecked appetite. Medieval Europe, while in its infancy, began the methodical extermination of undesirables:

> Jews, heretics, and lepers were the first three major categories to fall victim to the persecuting society. ... many of the images and accusations that mainstream Christians attached to one of these three groups were also ascribed to the others: that they were sexually hyperactive and dedicated to luring innocent people into their ranks through their sexual prowess; that they engaged in disgusting anti-human practices, sexual and otherwise; and that they were determined to infiltrate and bring down the larger society around them. ... the idea became popular that one or more vast conspiracies were trying to destroy Christianity from within.[24]

To keep power centralized, dissidents and heretics needed to be identified and dealt with. By 1233, the Inquisition was created, heretics were actively sought and heartily executed: "Western Christianity had become a militant, aggressive faith."[25]

Juxtaposed with this hostility, came the modern concept of demonic forces. As apocalyptic fervor gripped Europe, the Devil took shape as more than an idea; he became an influence—specifically regarding appetites for sex and power. St. Thomas of Aquinas warned that not only could the Devil manipulate even good Christians, demons could have intercourse with humans—of either sex:

> ...demons could appear in male form (*incubi*) or female form (*succubi*) for the purposes of having intercourse with either sex. But Aquinas stopped well short of the later witch stereotype: he did not connect such activity with *maleficia* (evil deeds), or suggest that humans became witches through sexual contact with demons. Still, Aquinas did help to spread and make respectable the idea that demons were active, aggressive creatures who might interact with humans in secret.[26]

The Church became more rigid. *Maleficia* became more of a concern in everyday affairs. Satanic forces became more empowered to tempt and corrupt the faithful, women lost prominence in society, and witches took on a more womanly appearance.

Since the early Church, women were Daughters of Eve, and inheritors of Eve's sin. Tertullian addresses all women in 197 CE:

> And do you not know that you are (each) an Eve? ... You are the Devil's gateway. You are the unsealer of that (forbidden) tree....[27]

This concept didn't initially limit women's social sphere. However, gradually women were prohibited from joining guilds, from practicing midwifery—or indeed any form[28] Women were shunted to the margins; those accused, interrogated, and executed for charges relating to witchcraft were poor women, "itinerant" women, or women who had somehow lost their homes, and position in society.[29]

The shift continued into the Reformation with Martin Luther. Tertullian had established the Daughter of Eve syndrome, which was furthered by the *Malleus*. Women's nature as the doorway to evil was connected to Aristotle's work, "Early modern doctors ...maintained that women were...defective men, and that their smaller craniums indicated smaller mental capacity."[30] Aristotle believed "perfection and spirituality are purely expressed in the male body alone"[31] and that "Women speak the language of idiots...like slaves... are incapable of governing themselves...."[32] This all contributed to Luther's notion of the "good wife." For Luther, the "bad wife" isn't necessarily bound by deviant, aggressive sexual appetites, but by a lack of intellectual capacity and the intent to protect her family. He believed that women were essentially weak and foolish,[33] but that:

> ...women were not evil by nature, but rather by choice: if a woman refuses to marry, or if her married behavior is inappropriate because she loves her family so much that she resorts to magic to protect it, then she renounces the inner moral power that is [also] part of her nature. By refusing to be God's housewife, she becomes a modern witch.[34]

By this definition all women, and all women depicted in Gaiman's work, are witches.

Witches and Appetite

Gaiman's concept of witch hinges on appetite and how it affects normally functioning society, or male society. Despite being a writer who offers a unique and forward-thinking view on and about women, Gaiman intermittently displays a misogynistic tone. In "Feeders and Eaters" we have a cackling old woman who literally feeds on the flesh of men, and the occasional cat. There is no overt use of magic, but Miss Corvier—essentially Miss Crow—is a cannibalistic witch, who eats her familiar and the men she latches onto. By devouring life around her—"Meat"[35]—she absorbs that life into her. But, she doesn't kill her victims outright. After Eddie stumbles upon and dispatches the unlucky feline, Miss Corvier laments:

> He was all I had to keep me going, and you killed him. After all I've done...making it so the meat stays fresh, so the life stays on. After all I've done. I'm an old woman... I need my meat.... I never wanted to be a burden... that was my meat...who's going to feed me now?[36]

The story ends with the image of Miss Corvier renewed, made young—"sort of pretty, in a hungry kind of way."[37] Even as this lamia is invigorated, her male victim like the cat, is nothing but a living carcass. While the term *meat* is a crude allusion to male genitalia, it's also a reference to the cannibalistic witches of the *Malleus*, stealing men's penises and eating children.[38] The old woman made young is a link to stereotypes about women—and about witches—set forth by medieval texts and *Malleus*.

In "Keepsakes and Treasures," we have another disturbing witchlike image of Shahinai, along with an exploration of appetite—male and female—which give stark commentary on gender disparity within society. Opening with a contrasting notion of appetite, the story is in the anonymous voice of an assassin and high-end errand boy for "one of the ten richest men in the world,"[39] Mr. Alice. The speaker's mother is described as having "*clinical nymphomania*"[40] and yet it's clear, this accused promiscuity isn't by choice. She isn't a witch, but a woman trapped in a hell not of her own devising. She had been "locked up for her own protection"[41] —and for the protection of the male society surrounding her. Victim of abuse, rape, and potentially incest, she was institutionalized, tortured, and ultimately committed suicide. Her incarceration reminds us that women outside the bounds of normal society—unmarried, sexually active women—were indicted as witches. The narrator's mother is accused of wanton appetite, but aside from her smiling image leaning "flirtily"[42] against a sports car in an old photo, there is no evidence that the allegation is founded. This nameless woman, despite her imprisonment, claimed the last ounce of control available to her—suicide—rather than continue to be used serving the appetite of men, which victimize and corrupt her son.

As a child, he murdered the "deputy head of the orphanage"[43] where he resided, who had been using the orphans as "his personal harem of scabby kneed love slaves."[44] Enlisted in the services of the powerful Mr. Alice, the narrator displayed his own brand of appetite by hunting down his mother's rapists—his potential progenitors. Mr. Alice in turn is appetite incarnate. Mr. Alice's sexuality is linked to consumption, indulgence, and could even be seen as a commentary of Aristotle's views about the spiritual perfection seen in the male form, and in male love.[45] Yet, the entire story revolves around sexual appetite—marginalized, feminized, and socially destructive. Even Gaiman's description of Earls Court reflects this:

> Sometimes Earls Court reminds me of one of those old women you meet from time to time who's painfully proper and prissy and prim until she's got a few drinks into her, when she starts dancing on the tables and telling everybody within earshot about her days as a pretty young thing, sucking cock for money in Australia or Kenya or somewhere.[46]

Mr. Alice's appetite for sex, not love, leads him to the house of the Shahinai women in Earls Court. The women take on a grotesque decidedly misogynistic form, with the exception that they are an inversion of Mr. Alice. His appetites are described in a positive way by his lackey. Mr. Alice is called a "proper man,"[47] one the narrator identifies with, particularly since his own appetites tend toward prepubescent girls.[48] The Shahinai women, in contrast, are a "repulsive aspect."[49] Gaiman describes them as "shadowy crones,"[50] old witches, animalistic, and decidedly not English. They sell the "Treasure of the Shahinai"[51] for the good of their tribe. They are representations of gender transgression perhaps in a way more severe—more damning—than Mr. Alice's proclivity for young, beautiful men because the "Treasure of the Shahinai" *are* men:

> It's the men... Apparently there aren't many of them. One or two in a generation. The Treasure of the Shahinai. The women are the guardians of the men. They nurture them and keep them safe. Alexander the Great is said to have bought a lover from the Shahinai...Catherine the Great was rumored to have had one, but I think it's just a rumor.... A race of people whose only asset is the beauty of their men. So every century they sell one of their men for enough money to keep the tribe going for another hundred years.[52]

These "banshees"[53] living at the heart of their run-down labyrinth are Gimbutas' earth goddesses, the Regeneratrix-death goddesses, as well as the vulture like images from Neolithic sites like Çatal Hüyük.[54] They haunt the narrator's dreams, and their ultimate goal isn't sexual appetite, but, like Luther's "bad wife," these Shahinai women want the success of their family—their tribe:

> Sometimes, at night, I'd have dreams about the Shahinai women—these ghastly, batlike, hag things fluttering and roosting through this huge rotting old house, which was, at the same time, both human history and St. Andrews Asylum. Some of them were carrying men between them, as they flapped and flew. The men shone like the sun, and their faces were too beautiful to look upon.[55]

The story ends with the death of Mr. Alice's treasure and the disappearance of the Shahinai women. The final image is of the appetite-driven woman. In seeking the Shahinai women, the narrator finds himself back in Earls Court, but in the company of junkies and smack-whores. Etched into his memory is the picture of a girl, "stoned and oblivious"[56]—but not even of *her*, of her breast, "a full, black-nippled breast, which curved disturbingly...."[57] It is eye-like, glaring, accusatory, and represents the objectification and fertility of this young woman—and all women, even the narrator's own mother.

Another complex image of the witch rests in *American Gods*.

Shadow's wife, Laura, considered Luther's "bad wife" because of her extramarital affair, is also witch-like from the simple fact that she returns from the dead. She protects Shadow at several points in his journey, even killing his kidnappers,[58] but she doesn't resort to charms or spells. Despite the fact that she's undead, she isn't properly a witch or a goddess, but she is a woman in-between. She, herself, is the victim of a spell, of a kind, Shadow being the cause of her liminal state—her undeath—because of the coin he placed in her grave.[59]

While alive, Laura's appetite lies in her affair with Robbie. She died because of her drunken desire to fellate her lover while he drove, as a means of farewell to their affair while preparing her husband's welcome home party.[60] During her death, Laura still exhibits appetite, but it's not entirely unreasonable or unnatural. She wants to be alive again, and expects Shadow to oblige.[61] In a very real sense, Laura is similar to the spirits called forth by necromancers. However, Shadow didn't create her in order to receive some wish or ability. It was pure accident and after protecting him, she asks him for the favor.

While they don't grant favors, aren't human witches, but are magical females nonetheless, Gaiman's Zoryi are the Triple Goddess and the Fates. Zorya Vechernyaya, oldest of the sisters, is the Dawn. The practical, controlling, mistress of the house, the Crone, she asks for money to pay for groceries, and her hospitality doesn't come freely.[62] Her middle sister, Zorya Utrennyaya, the Dusk, is the Mother who brings food and provides compassion.[63] Zorya Polunochnaya, the Midnight Sister, is the Maiden who provides Shadow with mystical knowledge and a talisman in the form of the moon, shaped like a Liberty-head silver dollar.[64] The Zoryas are a representation of Gimbutas' "formidable Goddess on earth."[65] While not witches, they serve, protect, and are gatekeepers for Shadow's journey.

Gaiman represents other magical female figures in *American Gods*, Kalī, seen as Mama-ji,[66] and fertility Goddess Easter.[67] There are other, oft-forgotten witches in the text, most complex being Bilquis: "The Queen of Sheba, half-demon... on her father's side, witch woman, wise woman, and queen...."[68] It's tempting to dismiss Bilquis as a literal 'maneater' but she isn't demonized. She isn't grouped in with the stereotypical "witches shriek[ing] overhead in the night" that Wednesday's own magic can confound,[69] nor is she like the old woman in "Feeders and Eaters." Bilquis is infinitely tangible from her dislike of the rain, to her obligation to use personal ads, to her impulse to shave her legs.[70] Bilquis represents a motif that Gaiman uses repeatedly throughout his work—twice in this text alone—the *vagina dentata*, the ultimate female appetite.

Briefly it is seen in the story of the African slave girl, Wututu, who later teaches magic to the infamous Marie Laveau. When threatened with rape on the Dutch slave-ship, Wututu tells her aggressor:

> If you put it in me down there I will bite it off with my teeth down there. I am a witch-girl and I have very sharp teeth down there.[71]

Wututu—also called Mama Zouzou—knew "more secrets" than any of the "voodoo queens" and witch women of the New World. Mama Zouzou is not unlike Laura because waking in the night, feeling "the cold steel between her ribs" as her twin brother was killed, "that was when Mama Zouzou's life had ended. Now she was someone who did not live..."[72] Unlike Bilquis, Mama Zouzou wasn't a free woman. She ended her life in a liminal state not controlled by her own appetites, but the intention of others. She is forced into a life of slavery, forced to bear children, but perhaps her only measure of independence was in magic, in providing "charms and little fetishes" to the folk who came to her, and in being "feared and respected."[73]

When we first see Bilquis, it's a scene often referenced in Gaiman's work, as it ends with the prostitute Bilquis vaginally consuming her client as he "worships" her.[74] Moments before her four thousand years on earth come to a gruesome end under the tires of Technical Boy's stretch limousine, Bilquis observes "that she has a habit as bad as that of the smack whores and the crack whores, and this distresses her...."[75] As a means of staving off the fierce desire to consume, she whispers her own mantra, lines from "The Song of Solomon." Bilquis is another liminal figure in Gaiman's work because she isn't human, but like Laura, she was once human. Being the historical Queen of Sheba, she was "the first 'non-Western woman' who negotiated secular and religious affairs with the West, rehabilitating the role of women."[76]

> In a Jungian sense the Queen of Sheba was the transcendent queen of the sunrise (the Queen of Alchemy, a prototype of the antithesis and synthesis of opposites –feminine on the outside and masculine on the inside). She is also the key (*clavicula*) of power which in general symbolizes the combinations of opposites; she is the 'Father-Mother,' the 'white-black,' the quintessence of all things.[77]

By this association, Bilquis transgresses gender, being allied with Lilith "the quintessential dangerous female...."[78] "[H]alf-demon" and "witch woman," Bilquis is related to the first witches who mated with the Grigori:[79]

> ...the angels, the children of the heaven....took unto themselves wives, and .... they began to go in unto them and ... taught them

charms and enchantments, and the cutting of roots, and made them acquainted with plants. And they became pregnant, and they bare great giants... Who consumed all the acquisitions of men. And when men could no longer sustain them, the giants turned against them and devoured mankind.... and [drank]...blood.[80]

These children of Angels and witch-women are connected to Cain's kin, the cannibalistic "eotenas" from *Beowulf*,[81] and the first vampires.[82] Some believe that Lilith was the possible progenitor of Cain's line, being the first of these witch-women.[83] But, the vagina dentata is a theme harkening back to the medieval concept of women as vampire—examined in both medieval gynaecological treaties[84] and in the *Malleus*.

According to Bildhauer, "early...vampires...are all explicitly or implicitly gendered female; more precisely, they can be seen as embodiments of female sexual appetites."[85] Aristotle and early medieval scientific manuscripts granted women the ability to "suck out men's 'lifeblood' (semen) during intercourse...."[86] The proclivity for cannibalistic absorption—via the vagina—of either her male partner during intercourse or of her unborn child during pregnancy,[87] made women naturally *unnatural*. Women were the antithesis to normative *male* society. They were monstrous wives and bad mothers. Bildhauer asserts that the "feminine is thus constructed as the 'other,' which is then established as the object of fear" and that:

> ...the notions of [female] bloodsuckers... combined with similar ideas of bloodthirsty, child-eating and man-eating women helped to lay the foundations for the persecution of millions of women as witches.... Even modern vampires, if female, often still show striking parallels to these medieval bloodsuckers...in their sexual thirst, their draining of energy, their choice of children as victims and their connections to menstruation, disease, and witchcraft.[88]

Because of the desire to "dominate men" and "usurp power," according to *Malleus* witches would steal a man's penis, often while he slept.[89] On one very obvious level, the idea of female sexual organs with the ability to consume men, is a continuation of the fear rooted in traditions of the succubus, the lamia, the first witch-women, Bilquis and Lilith.

Beginning as the first wife of Adam, Lilith was created "not from Adam's rib, but from the earth, the way Adam himself was made."[90] As tradition goes, a fight ensued when Lilith wanted to be in the dominant position during intercourse.[91] In *Fables and Reflections*, Gaiman tells the story of Adam's wives.[92] While Lilith doesn't consume with her vagina, she is cast out and her womb becomes the source for demons.[93] Gaiman tells us that:

> Lilith was expelled from Eden. And she planted her own Garden. They say she copulated with Demons, or with the Sons of God. She had many children....And Lilith gave birth to the Lilim, the children of Lilith, who have haunted the nights of the Sons of Adam ever since. Mother to so many, then and now....[94]

According to Gaiman, Lilith was perhaps the first witch since she copulated with the Sons of God—the angels—and the offspring, while not demons in the form of cloven-hoofed creatures with forked tongues and tails, were Fallen, semi-angelic creatures. Her female children we meet later in another of Gaiman's tales, *Stardust,* in the form of the Lilim, cannibalistic witches preying on the hearts of fallen stars.

Gaiman's portrayal of the vagina dentata with Bilquis is grotesque but non-violent. Her clients are not torn to pieces. The act of consumption, for the consumed, is "blissful."[95] Far from the castrating witch from *Malleus* or the vampire from medieval scientific texts, this image links to the hero-journey, the symbolic death-life return. Eliade notes "all heroic adventures in which triumph over tribulation is signified by penetration involve the symbolism of the menacing female/mother, the destructive womb, [and]... the castrating vagina."[96] The male hero is literally transformed by the experience and is allowed "access to a transcendental state."[97] Bilquis is "the quintessence of all things."[98] The consuming vagina is a continuation of the "monstrous hell-mouth" which:

> ...conveys the relentlessness of change, and dissolution, the devastating power of time, the inevitability of death....But the absorption of the body by another suggests a grotesque and perverse postmortem continuation of the self within as a part of another, a monstrosity, not of mixed natures, but of confused existences. Without autonomy, without identity or even consciousness, the formless self continues as an imprisoned particle of the other.[99]

Because Bilquis runs contrary to what the new order of gods desires, because she straddles the division between god and human, and because she "represents a woman of intellect and will who demonstrated to cope with any patriarchal and hegemonic societies..."[100] she cannot survive to fight the war between the gods.[101]

Witches, women who transgress gender, and the vagina dentata are central to "Snow, Glass, Apples," which reverses the traditional female roles in "Snow White." The Queen is set up as "Wise, and a witch" while Snow White is a vampiric "thing."[102] The Queen's only appetite stems from her sexuality and her intent for revenge. She foretells the future in "dreams and in reflections"[103] and while it can be argued that she succumbed to the King out of a lust for power, it is more in tune with her character that she fell in love with him during her "sixteen years of dreaming of him..."[104] Despite being a fairy tale creation, the Queen is unlike the stereotype of women in that she enjoys sex with her husband and uses magic only to help others and for the security of her people. The Queen represents Luther's "bad wife" because she uses magic for protection, but as noted earlier—Luther's definition of witch encompasses all of Gaiman's female characters, and indeed most women.

The detrimental female image in "Snow, Glass, Apples" is undoubtedly the Princess. Aside from being a vampire, she commits matricide and ultimately patricide. Killing her mother at birth can be perhaps forgiven as it was a commonality, however, the same cannot be said for the manner in which she murders her father. She doesn't merely feed from him, as would most vampires since close family were, in all practicality, the first victims. She—like the vampiric, cannibalistic women discussed in *Malleus* and medieval scientific texts—takes his manhood, his ability as leader, and asserts herself sexually, raping him.[105] The Queen's intent is toward vengeance, because Snow White, like the witches of *Malleus*, virtually castrated her own father and denied the Queen sexual privilege with her own husband:

> My husband, my love, my king sent for me less and less, and when I came to him he was dizzy, listless, confused. He could no longer make love as a man makes love.... Soon he was a shadow of the man I had met...[106]

Unlike the propaganda and lies about the Queen spread by the Princess—the familiar "Snow White"—the Queen was not fooled by the heart of an animal, nor did she eat the Princess' heart. This we know because we know the Queen in Gaiman's tale—not Snow White. The Queen is the familiar; she is both witch and every woman—in her desire for her husband, her ability to make mistakes, and her skill at caring for her community. The Princess is the demonic, unknowable Other with truly monstrous, socially destructive appetites. She barely speaks and after her exile to the forest, she exists "like an animal: a bat or a wolf."[107]

Unlike Bilquis or even Wututu, the Princess' appetite—represented by her vagina dentata—is violent, destructive, and perhaps a primary means by which she feeds. As the Queen seeks answer to the plea for help from the Lord of the Fair, she observes the Princess in the infamous mirror and we are witness to the Princess feeding on a wandering monk. Not only does she prostitute herself, accepting his tossed coin, she drinks his blood orally, and vaginally.[108] We know the source of the scars on her father's genitals could have been from either orifice.

As the Queen resolves to make the forest and her kingdom "safe once more,"[109] Gaiman shows us the Queen's magic. Rather than merely telling us she enchants the notorious apples, he reveals her glory as a witch in the spell she casts with her body and her own blood.[110] When the Princess takes the apples, she is naked and the "insides of her thighs [are] stained with wet black filth."[111] That is the same animalistic image of the Princess as she lies "naked beneath the glass" of her coffin.[112] Displaying her normal sexual appetites, the Queen cannot take part in the Prince's necrophilia and yet she describes the bizarre union between Princess and Prince 'Charming' as "fancy."[113] The Prince and Princess take both the kingdom and the Queen by force, storming into her room, declaring she would "be with them on their wedding day."[114] The Princess' appetite as vampire isn't contained. Her husband, the Prince, has most likely been made into a vampire. Alluding to the tradition of cannibalizing accused witches in the Pacific Islands,[115] the tale ends with the Queen's own people—having been fed a diet of propaganda against her—"singing, jeering, and banging on the sides of the kiln"[116] as the Queen roasts, seasoned with "goose grease" and possibly fattened through the autumn on apples.

The sorceress Lady Indigo from *InterWorld* stands apart as she is more vampire than witch, picking up where Gaiman's vampiric Snow White, left off. Of all Gaiman's female characters, Lady Indigo is both the most distant and the most evil. Even the Furies in *The Kindly Ones* have more compassion. They destroy because Dream was a kinslayer. They are the penultimate witch in the eyes of Martin Luther because they are fierce protectors of family.[117] Lady Indigo has nothing but Ego and the glory of providing energy to power the trans-dimensional ships of Hex. She isn't a patriot, rivaling Lord Dogknife for control of Hex. She is reminiscent of Tolkien's dark, witch-like Queen Berúthiel—with a little of Lord Sauron thrown in for good measure:

> And there were eyes in the middle of the darkness. The darkness formed itself into a shape. It was a woman. Her hair was long and black. She had big lips….she was small and kind of thin, and her eyes were so green…They looked like a cat's eyes.[118]

The Lady Indigo functions as a solitary agent, taking pleasure in hunting and capturing the Harkers. Tolkien's Queen Berúthiel, merely a footnote in *The Unfinished Tales*[119] was controlled by her own appetite for knowing everything "that men wish most to keep hidden."[120] She uses spellcraft, her cats, and her ability to read the minds of men—and her slaves—to feed her hunger. One could imagine, had Tolkien written more of Queen Berúthiel, she wouldn't have been so different from the Lady Indigo, perhaps minus the fluffy pink bath towels. Both women are last seen disappearing adrift at sea. Queen Berúthiel is literally on an ocean-voyaging ship, with her cats on the prow, set to wander the seas under the light of a "sickle moon."[121] While the Lady Indigo, snared by her own spells used against her by Joey Harker, is trapped within a "crimson whirlwind"[122] moments before her ship, the space-time traveling *Malefic*, explodes. Joey's observation as the Lady Indigo apprehends him, that her perfume was "a sort of mixture of roses and rot"[123] blends images of the living, the dead, the seductress and the vampire. Lady Indigo, like Gaiman's Snow White, is a 'wicked witch' because of her uncontrolled appetite literally for the life energy of Joey and the other Harkers. She is betrayed by her appetite—but at no time is she presented as a compassionate, humane entity. She gives a glimpse into a kind of witch presented in Gaiman's worlds—a vampiric witch grounded in the *Malleus*—the *strigoi vii*.

Other malevolent, evil witches in Gaiman's worlds can be seen in the Lilim and the Other Mother. However, unlike the Lady Indigo, they are not wholly unredemptive. The Other Mother and the Lilim are Luther's extreme, similar in kind to The Kindly Ones, with an inappropriate love of family—and in this familial bond, no matter how perverse, we can find shards of redemption.

Coraline's Other Mother isn't a stereotypical witch and she certainly isn't human. Like the *strigoi vii*—living witches—of Eastern European folklore,[124] the Other Mother is cursed to live between the worlds.

> ...the source of the "curse" is an incomplete transition from one world to the next. ...They are restless spirits, unwilling or unable to cross completely from one world to the next. Caught in a state between the living and the dead, they exist outside of nature, and therefore exist beyond the bounds of natural laws. Bereft of a life of their own to sustain them, they must naturally seek out the life force contained in blood or milk or even fertile fields.[125]

As Gaiman warned us in "Instructions," the Other Mother is betrayed by her appetite. Yet, she serves as a counterpoint to the magical females seen in Coraline and Misses Spink and Forcible.

Coraline, the journeying female hero, is witch-like in that she has a cat as familiar, helps to save her parents' lives and souls, and frees the souls of the trapped children, helping them to cross over into the afterlife. Coraline sets her world right by ending the Other Mother's world. Miss Spink and Miss Forcible are clueless, frivolous, men-less women who provide Coraline with the magical tool to help in the girl's quest—"a stone with a hole in it."[126] More hero than witch, Coraline travels through Campbell's hero's journey—and the has-been actresses are an integral part of Coraline's success. They are to her as the Zoryas are to Shadow. Without the stone, Coraline would not have found the stolen souls. While Miss Spink and Miss Forcible do foresee doom in the tea leaves, they dismiss their warning as "unreliable." The evil witch in the story is the Other Mother.

The ghosts of the children behind the mirror call the Other Mother the Beldam.[127] An antiquated term, meaning grandmother or ancestress, it reflected the time beyond memory that these ghost children have been kept in their bleak prison. However, in Middle English, the term meant specifically a "loathsome old woman...a furious raging woman"[128]—or, a witch. When we first meet her, it's through Coraline's perception—and is Bildhauer's construction of 'other' as object of fear[129]:

> It sounded like her mother. Coraline went into the kitchen, where the voice had come from. A woman stood...with her back to Coraline. She looked a little like Coraline's mother. Only...her skin was white as paper. Only she was taller and thinner. Only her fingers were too long, and they never stopped moving, and her dark red fingernails were curved and sharp....And then she turned around. Her eyes were big black buttons.[130]

As opposed to the *strigoi vii* or even Queen Berúthiel, the Other Mother does not use cats as her familiar spies; she detests them. In Gaiman's worlds cats, like crows and ravens, are the shamanic link to magic, to humanity, to creativity, and to the Goddess.[131] Instead, the Other Mother uses the rats, converse to the life-affirming white mice of the Mouse Circus.[132] But, true to her function as a *strigoi vii*, the Other Mother operates outside our normative reality. Her reach, however, extends into Coraline's world—to kidnap her parents, and, like the reputed cannibalistic child-eating witches from *Malleus*, to steal lives from children. As Coraline learns from the ghost children trapped behind the mirror:

> She left us here...She stole our hearts, and she stole our souls, and she took our lives away.... she forgot about us in the dark.... we could not leave here, when we died. She kept us, and she fed on us, until now we've nothing left of ourselves, only snakeskins and spider husks. ...She will take your life and all you are and all you

care'st for, and she will leave you with nothing but mist and fog. She'll take your joy. And one day you'll awake and your heart and your soul will have gone. A husk you'll be, a wisp you'll be, and a thing no more than a dream on waking, or a memory of something forgotten.[133]

Not unlike the serpentine Duessa from Spenser's *Faerie Queene* or Grendel's mother, the Other Mother is the monster the hero must best. As the story climaxes, the Other Mother is more grotesque—her hands more spider-like, her hair more Gorgon-like, "her mouth full of black beetles."[134] The Other Mother does attempt creation—of a kind. She is outside our world, but creates her own—to possess and to destroy. The Other crazy old man articulates the Other Mother's plans:

"Nothing's changed. You'll go home. You'll be bored. You'll be ignored. No one will listen to you… They don't even get your name right. Stay here with us…We will listen to you and play with you and laugh with you. Your other mother will build whole worlds for you to explore, and tear them down every night when you are done. Every day will be better and brighter than the one that went before.… whatever you desire. The world will be built new for you every morning. If you stay here, you can have whatever you want."

Coraline sighed. "You really don't understand, do you?" she said. "I don't *want* whatever I want. Nobody does. Not really. What kind of fun would it be if I just got everything I ever wanted? Just like that, and it didn't *mean* anything. What then?"[135]

The Other Mother is linked in this fashion to another witch-like image, from *Good Omens*—the Antichrist—and as Aziraphale tells us, "the Antichrist is more than just a witch. He's…THE witch. He's about as witchy as you can get."[136] The Antichrist Adam explains his own views on the creation of a world for himself—and his friends, of course—that would be full of "other" versions of their mothers and fathers, and "new cowboys an' Indians an' policemen an' gangsters an' cartoons an' spacemen an' stuff…"[137] But, like the Other Mother and the Other crazy old Mr. Bobo—Adam fails to understand that when play was complete, when the heroic journey was done, "you could stop…and go home."[138]

Another form of the *strigoi vii* and a reverse Triple Goddess, *Stardust*'s Lilim are individuals, but they're also a singular being with a tripartite function. We first meet them in the fairy tale witch's cottage:

In the middle of a wood … was a small house, built of thatch…

which had a most foreboding aspect. ... The only thing in the house that was clean was a mirror of black glass, as high as a tall man, as wide as a church door. ... The house belonged to three aged women. ... the Lilim—the witch queen—all alone in the woods.[139]

Like Coraline's Other Mother, there are "three other women in the little house. ...in the black mirror."[140] As the last of the previous star's heart is consumed by the eldest of the Lilim, the ancient woman in the cottage is replaced by her younger self from the mirror.[141] After failing to capture Yvaine's heart, the Witch Queen communes with her sisters in a mirrored pool of unicorn's blood spilled into "a rock hollow" on the roadside[142] —a perverse version of Galadriel and her mirrored pool.

The Lilim are the head of their Sisterhood and little is known of their origin. As noted earlier, according to Gaiman's rendition of the tale of Lilith, the Lilim are the daughters of Adam's first wife. Yet, when the eldest sister—Morwanneg—shares a meal with Ditchwater Sal, the Witch Queen reveals "When you knew me last... I ruled with my sisters in Carnadine, before it was lost."[143] Gaiman doesn't explain the reference, yet in Tolkienian fashion, this gives the Lilim deeper history than Faerie—or even than Lilith.

Carnadine, an antiquated term meaning red or fleshly,[144] related to carnāle or carnārius[145]—belonging to the flesh—is associated with another similar term: charnel. Charnel may be related to Charn, the point of origin for Lewis' own Witch Queen, Jadis. Charn is a planet orbiting around a red giant sun and as Jadis explains to Polly and Digory, after the last battle, before Jadis herself destroyed her planet, her people, and all form of life with the "Deplorable Word," Charn "ran red."[146] Jadis ravaged Charn simply to oppose her own sister. She claims to have done to Charn what she did to other worlds,[147] and it's a wonder if she had other sisters to oppose as well.

Connections between the Lilim and Jadis don't end there. After looting parts of London, Jadis commandeered a hansom cab,[148] riding it like Boadicea. When Tristan travels by candlelight, he sees Morwanneg traveling by cart, with her mismatched billy goats looking "the way Boadicea was drawn in history books."[149] Jadis is more animal than Morwanneg or her sisters, and—like The Kindly Ones—the Lilim are all about family. Even though Morwanneg says her sisters will be cruel at her loss of the Star's heart, even though they chastise her for not seizing it at the first opportunity, at no point in the tale do we see them warring against each other. Despite the Lilim's dominant nature, they use life and have a bizarre esteem for it. They don't value human life—or that of a unicorn—but the simple life of a snake, Morwanneg calls friend.[150] It's hard to believe the Lilim would use their magic to destroy all life in Faerie, or indeed on Earth. When Madam

Semele poisons Morwanneg with truth-telling lembas grass, the Witch Queen doesn't kill the "harridan" on the spot: "I swore by the compact of the Sisterhood, that I would do you no harm."[151] Her sisters—even those by oath—are important, if in name only. Later, before her encounter with the Star, the Witch Queen waxes maudlin on her spent youth when her chariot doesn't immediately transform into an Inn at her spell:

> I am getting old… Things inanimate have always been more difficult to change than things animate. Their souls are older and stupider and harder to persuade. If I but had my true youth again…why, in the dawn of the world I could transform mountains into seas and clouds into palaces. I could populate cities with the pebbles on the shingle. If I were young again…. [152]

She gives a strange compliment to living—"animate" things as younger and less stupid—but easier to persuade than mountains and pebbles. Her magic lies in persuasion and in that, the Lilim—unlike Jadis—have some twisted respect for life. This reference to her "true youth" and creating seas, palaces, and populations, gives the Lilim yet another connection to yet another mythology—Tolkien's Silmarillion. The reference is two-fold. In the "Ainulindalë" with the first battle between the Valar and Melkor, it was Melkor who destroyed the building of Middle-earth: mountains were razed, seas emptied, valleys lifted.[153] Morwanneg doesn't say she blasted the mountains—but turned them into seas—nor did she ruin the clouds. She transforms matter in much the same fashion that the Valar do when "Valinor was full-wrought."[154] However, the Valar create truly, while Melkor does not. Rather, he distorts, confounds, manipulates, and corrupts. Morwanneg and her Sisterhood may fall into a space between. Her people were pebbles and her palaces, clouds. As Lewis says of Jadis, "witches… are not interested in things or people unless they can use them; they are terribly practical."[155] Yet, in the end, when we last see her, the image is a compassionate one. If Yvaine can pity Morwanneg and even give the old woman a parting kiss, then we the readers must also empathize with the Witch Queen's fate.[156]

Madame Semele, part of Morwanneg's Sisterhood, is the classical witch from *Malleus* and fairy tale. She's also a con artist and everyone she encounters is a potential mark. Gaiman refers to her in debased tones, much like the Shahinai women—a cackling, gap-toothed, old harridan with wild iron-grey hair, and bony hands.[157] Yet, in her wickedness, she's a vital piece in the story. If she hadn't captured the Lady Una, holding "the first-born and only daughter of the eighty-first Lord of Stormhold"[158] captive, then Una wouldn't have met Dunstan and Tristan wouldn't have been born. If

Madame Semele didn't give Morwanneg the lembas grass, then the Witch Queen wouldn't have laid her curse:

> ...you have stolen knowledge you did not earn, but it shall not profit you. For you shall be unable to see the star, unable to perceive it, unable to touch it, to taste it, to find it, to kill it. Even if another were to cut out its heart and give it to you, you would not know it....[159]

Madame Semele's function as the stereotypical cackling crone is vital to the outcome of the story, despite her turning Tristan into a Doormouse. Had Morwanneg not placed the curse on Semele, Yvaine could've been killed by old Ditchwater Sal—or been revealed to the Witch Queen in Diggory's Dyke.[160]

Certainly, not all witches in Gaiman's world are negative, or consumed by detrimental appetites. In *The Graveyard Book*, Liza Hempstock is subtle, a satirical commentary on witches. Born when Queen Elizabeth I died, Liza candidly describes her death when Bod asks if she was a suicide, since she was buried in unconsecrated ground, without even a tombstone. Her appetites aren't entirely unconventional and her desire comes in the form of a favor Bod wishes to repay for her help with his sprained ankle. She doesn't ask him for a headstone, but he decides to repay her kindness—and to help alleviate her sadness because he finds her sad yet oddly alluring. Liza is "not even a little bit beautiful..."[161] even resembling a "pretty goblin...."[162] The young man who could be blamed for her death, however, didn't need witchcraft to go "mooning"[163] around her cottage, a point she admits readily to Bod which he already noted.[164] The satire comes in the description of her death and her vengeance on the town:

> 'You're a witch!' they shouts, fat and fresh-scrubbed all pink in the morning, like so many pigwiggins scrubbed clean for market day. One by one they gets up beneath the sky and tells of milk gone sour and horses gone lame, ... So they strap me to the cucking stool and forces me under the water...saying if I'm a witch I'll neither drown nor care, but if I'm not a witch I'll feel it. .... I cursed each and every one of them there on the village Green that morning. ... I was surprised as how easily it came, the cursing. Like dancing it was....I cursed them, with my last gurgling pond-watery breath. And then I expired. They burned my body on the Green until I was nothing but blackened charcoal, and they popped me in a hole in the Potter's Field without so much as a headstone to mark my name.[165]

Liza represents the nameless women killed during the Burning Times. Many of the women accused and killed weren't witches; however, confessing the crime of witchcraft did one of two things. It promised them forgiveness, salvation, and a quicker death—or, in the rarest cases, release. Or, it promised an end to their torture. In death Liza fully claims her status as witch by cursing her murderers with her dying breath.

Liza is also an aid to Bod through his journey. When he meets her, he's having difficulty in his lessons, being unable to Fade properly.[166] Already, he has been rescued by magical female forces at various points in his story. First, Mrs. Owens being the only member of the graveyard to speak up for Bod and the one to listen to the lamentation of his own mother's spirit; then Miss Lupescu, not merely teaching him some of the most important lessons of his life—both in and out of 'school'—but as a Hound of God, she rescues him physically from Ghûlheim, and later lays her life down when she, Silas, and the other guardians battle the Jacks. Liza serves as a warning, literally warning Bod of impending doom at various points in the tale. She is truly a guardian spirit, helping him to evade physical harm. The snapshot of history surrounding Liza's death as a witch is a truncated, starker version of another witch-killing in Gaiman's work—that of Agnes Nutter from *Good Omens*.

While many of Gaiman's witches can be seen as his commentary on the stereotypes surrounding witches and women, *Good Omens* goes further than that. It's satire and social commentary on all things from the steady march of capitalism, to unbending zealotry, to the affect of the apocalypse on the humdrum of everyday life—all very much in an Adamsian mode. Despite being written in tandem with Terry Pratchett, *Good Omens* is still Gaiman's own—with a humor crafted from *Hitchhiker's Guide to the Galaxy*. Throughout the text are historical facts regarding the Inquisition and witch hunts—along with satire about the period known as the Burning Times:

> There's no witches any more, actually. People invented medicines and that and told 'em they didn't need 'em any more and started burning 'em.[167]

It's not so much that the witches in *Good Omens* are realistic, as the information surrounding them paints an accurate picture of the attitudes about witches.

While there may not have been a Witchfinder Army, England did have a self-styled Witchfinder General, Matthew Hopkins.[168] Far from fictitious, Hopkins gave rise to "the most notorious and deadly witch hunt in England" in barely a 14-month period, from 1645–1646.[169] More than 250 women were accused of witchcraft and identified via torture, while over 100 were executed.[170] Unlike the account presented by Gaiman and Pratchett, Hopkins was not "hanged as a witch by an East Anglian village" intent on "eliminating the middleman."[171] Shortly after his trade in witch location and eradication began, Hopkins died of tuberculosis.[172] Prior to his death, Hopkins did make enemies in Norfolk because of his enhanced interrogation techniques used on the accused.[173]

One such technique Hopkins used was the "pricker." The job of the "pricker" was to find the "devil's mark" or "witch's teat" and literally jab a special needle into it.[174] Shadwell reflects this in the question he poses to any would-be acquaintance: "How many nipples hae ye got?"[175] Often the needle was retractable—as noted by Gaiman and Pratchett[176]— or the woman was in such a state of shock, not noticing she was being pricked, she didn't react. Favorite torture techniques advocated by witch hunters like Hopkins were sleep deprivation, denying the accused means of warmth including clothes, removing all the hair (so as to better see the "witch's mark"), starvation, rape, and physical abuse. With all that, who would notice a little prick?

When we first meet Anathema Device as a woman, the authors describe her as wearing a "sensibly waterproof" cloak with a warm lining."[177] Pointing specifically at Gardnerian forms of Wicca and to past views on witchcraft from texts like *Malleus*, the authors note:

> Most books on witchcraft will tell you that witches work naked. This is because most books on witchcraft are written by men.[178]

While this text, like those, is written by men, they are practical. Anathema, like Liza Hempstock, is "not astonishingly beautiful"[179]—but she is pragmatic:

> Young women should not go alone on dark nights…But any prowling maniac would have had more than his work cut out if he accosted Anathema Device. She was a witch…And precisely because she was a witch, and therefore sensible, she put little faith in protective amulets and spells; she saved it all for a foot-long bread knife she kept in her belt.[180]

Yet, Anathema lives her life according to the prophecies of Agnes Nutter, her ancestress. It's not until after the ending of the Apocalypse that Anathema, with the aid of Newt Pulsifer, moves beyond the prophecies of Agnes. Anathema is the classical witch, living in Jasmine Cottage. She unknowingly passes wisdom about the occult and the environment on to Adam, the Antichrist, and through the imparting of knowledge, plants the seed that both causes the Apocalypse and ultimately prevents it from happening. Through the knowledge shared with Adam, Anathema in some respects is more influential in the Apocalypse than the seer Agnes Nutter.

Before describing the demise of the undervalued prophetess, Agnes Nutter, Gaiman and Pratchett show a satire of how witches—like Liza Hempstock—were murdered. Adam and his gang of Them decide to combat the ensuing witch plague in Oxfordshire by starting their own Spanish Inquisition, complete with the 'torture' of Pepper's six-year-old sister. Since the "British Inquisition was...not ready for the reintroduction of the Iron Maiden and the choke-pear..." the Them decided on a homemade version of the ducking stool, which turned out "just like a seesaw."[181] Since the accused was "too soggy to burn"[182] Adam and the Them take their own turns on the ducking stool before going home to face the "questions asked about muddy shoes and duckweed-encrusted pink dresses."[183]

While Agnes' own execution is more serious, it, too, has a satirical tone since in burning her, the town unwittingly kills half its population. The reason for her execution wasn't so much about her being a witch, but because the town became: "A howling mob, reduced to utter fury by her habit of going around being intelligent and curing people...."[184] As with Liza, with Agnes' last breath, before being gagged and set alight, she utters her curse—but she doesn't doom them to die: "*mark well the fate of alle who meddle with such as they do notte understande.*"[185] The village explodes as Agnes burns, since she "concealed eighty pounds of gunpowder and forty pounds of roofing nails" in her petticoats.[186]

The witches in *Good Omens* are a satire of witches, rather than proper witch figures with revealing appetites. Agnes, like Luther's bad wife, creates her prophecies *not* for the good of mankind, necessarily.

> Agnes was the worst prophet that ever existed. Because she was always right. ...It was obvious that Agnes had a line to the Future, but it was an unusually narrow and specific line. In other words, almost totally useless.[187]

Agnes' bizarre prophecies, curing sickness with mold and not buying Beta-Max, turn out marginally important to humanity, but do give aid to her descendents. Anathema's intent isn't for personal gain, but, as with the rest of her family before her, to decipher the prophecies of Agnes Nutter and to recognize the events leading up to the Apocalypse.

A witch that exists somewhere among the Lilim, Liza Hempstock, and the Queen from "Snow, Glass, Apples" is Thessaly from *The Sandman*.

Thessaly's name comes from Thessaly—a Greek province. Thessaly was linked to negativity and barbarism when they conspired against Athens.[188] Preempting the *Malleus* by over a thousand years, the Thessalian witch was a fearsome image, epitomized in Erictho—a compilation of all witch women, from Circe to Medea to Hecate, the Witch Goddess herself.[189] Robert Graves claims that Thessaly was a "semi-matriarchal Bronze Age civilization" found in central Greece by invading "Achaeans...patriarchal herdsmen."[190] A site for the revelries of the Bacchantes, Thessaly was also home to the Moon Goddess Artemis' primary temple, regulated by priestesses who were overseen by a high priestess representing the Goddess herself.[191] In addition to rites, later in Neo-Paganism called Drawing Down the Moon, Thessalian witches used menstrual blood as a powerful magical connection to the Goddess.[192]

First seen in *A Game of You*, Thessaly is calm, yet is anything but timid or beautiful. Portrayed as plain-faced, dull-haired, and without curves, Thessaly's most remarkable features are her sharp tongue and a pair of enormous, moon-like glasses. Thessaly seeks out Foxglove, Hazel, and Wanda not to help Barbie, but because the Cuckoo tried harming her and she doesn't "take things like that lightly."[193] Thessaly has been called cold and callous, but she doesn't wantonly kill. Unlike Lady Indigo or the Other Mother, Thessaly uses violence as a means of self-defense, not as a psychotic. She kills George because he "gave himself to the Cuckoo."[194] She later threatens Lyta Hall with death, after protecting Lyta from both Dream and the Furies inside a witch's circle, because Lyta was responsible for not only the destruction of many in the Dreaming, but of Dream himself.[195] Thessaly has both redemptive and unredemptive qualities. Not necessarily a goddess, she is linked to Hecate through ritual, connection to the moon, and to association with Thessaly itself. In *The Kindly Ones*, she alters her name from the province Thessaly to Larissa—its capital city.

To gain information, Thessaly reanimates George in exactly the same fashion that Morwanneg reanimates the unicorn: blood transmitted into the mouth of the deceased by the tongue of the witch. Thessaly kisses George, taking his tongue into her mouth, biting it off, and inserting it into his skinned face[196]—after the face is pinned to Wanda's wall by iron nails, itself a protection against *maleficia*. Morwanneg bit on her own tongue, mixed her saliva with her blood and spat that into the unicorn's mouth.[197] The connection serves to remind us that Thessaly—like Morwanneg— has no proper name, an unknown history, and similar magical capability. Thessaly is ancient, as she tells Dream when he arrives for Lyta Hall, "maybe a couple of thousand years."[198]

Thessaly calls down the Goddess Hecate—and yet, she is Hecate, just as the Lilim are one and three together. For her spell, Thessaly requires menstrual blood from Hazel and Foxglove. Wanda is excluded, being a transsexual. Hazel remarks that she did "some witchy stuff,"[199] but it was more for empowerment. Casting her spell, Thessaly reveals she is even more powerful than previously thought, since she has the ability to call down, bind, and dictate to the Witch Goddess Hecate, calling her by her three names:

> Gorgo, Mormo, Ereshgal: Three-faced woman. I fetch you, tie you, bind you. There are none left to save you in this old world. None to beat cymbals, and distract you with sharp cries. We have walked together in the past, you and I. I have bound you as a hare, as an owl, as a lantern: I have bound you in your House in the Heavens, now I call you down to me. We are old friends, you and I. She who dies and lives and never dies, be here for me.[200]

The power of this statement reveals that Thessaly is perhaps older than Hecate since Thessaly "bound" this Goddess into her "House"—or the moon itself. Thessaly tells us that she "was born in the day of greatest Darkness, in the year the Bear Totem was shattered."[201] When entering the Dreaming, Thessaly displays her power over the dead—like Erichtho, Hecate, and other Killer-Regeneratrixes—by reanimating Wilkinson for information.[202] Gaiman gave the Lilim connections to the Bible and Enochian texts, to Narnia and to the Silmarillion. Thessaly is linked to the Lilim, but she is also perhaps the creator of the moon. In Tolkien's mythology, Yavanna formed the moon out of the fruit of the dying Telperion, with the aide of Aulë and Manwë.[203] In the panels depicting Thessaly Drawing Down the Moon, her glasses reflect the Moon's face—and her own make the Three. The Witch Goddess chafes under Thessaly's command, but still obeys.[204] When Thessaly travels with the weird sisters Foxglove and Hazel, "Identity blurs on the Moon's road."[205] In this sense Thessaly can be Hecate and the Lilim and even Yavanna; Thessaly is every woman, and especially every witch.

The final witch image isn't satirical, as with Agnes Nutter or even Anathema Device, but shows appetite, intent, and realism, to the point of humor. In *Anansi Boys*, Fat Charlie appeals to Mrs. Dunwiddy and Mrs. Higgler for help in ridding him of his brother Spider:

> It was sort of like *Macbeth*, thought Fat Charlie...if the witches in *Macbeth* had been four little old ladies and if, instead of stirring cauldrons and intoning dread incantations, they had just welcomed Macbeth in and fed him turkey and rice and peas....[206]

Usually, when we see any of these old women, they're eating, smoking, or drinking massive cups of coffee. Their appetites are human appetites for food, calm, and even love. Mrs. Higgler tells Fat Charlie how she was smitten with his father—until he disappeared and she married another man. Mrs. Higgler is the first to tell Fat Charlie his father was a god, and that Fat Charlie did have a brother—a brother banished by Mrs. Dunwiddy.[207] We learn later, Mrs. Dunwiddy didn't simply send Spider away—she removed him from inside Fat Charlie, essentially splitting the boy into light and dark for breaking the shiny ball in her garden and to teach Fat Charlie a lesson.[208] In her is a desire to teach, and in teaching, protect since the broken garden ornament—also called a 'witch's ball,' used against *maleficia* —was a broken protection.

When Fat Charlie visits the old ladies, each time they cast a circle to help him cross into the in-between dream-world of the gods. Yet their spell isn't like any other—not like the Stepmother's in "Snow, Glass, Apples" with her sky-clad passion for the safety of her kingdom, nor like Thessaly's Drawing Down the Moon. The first time Fat Charlie visits them, Miss Noles laments that she could only find one true black candle. The others were black penguins. "And I had to go to three stores before I found anything."[209] Instead of the magical herbs necessary, Mrs. Bustamonte provides "mixed herbs" because "You ask me, it's all mixed herbs."[210] A similar tale is told with the next spell—multi-colored sand from the gift shop, small white candles from the pool-side, and a borrowed bouquet-garni from the hotel kitchen. The lack of attention to so-called ritualistic detail is intriguing because of its realism. While most Neo-Pagans and most modern witches like to imagine their apothecaries are well-stocked with "devils grass, ...St. John the Conqueror root, and ...love-lies-bleeding..."[211] more often than not, they make do with mixed herbs and novelty candles from the local discount shop. As Fat Charlie notes:

> I think it's all a matter of confidence. ... The most important thing isn't the details. It's the magical atmosphere.[212]

The same can be said for Gaiman's witches and for women's magic—it's not in the details, but in the intent or the atmosphere. Magic is, like women are, myriad, unique, and integral to what a woman is. Likewise, the witch is an image close to women—and yet held distant because of the negative stereotypes. Neil Gaiman's role in portraying the witch can't be easily categorized as feminist or misogynist. His work is neither, and yet he portrays a realistic view of witches, of the culture surrounding them, perhaps more so than any other.

1 Shlain, *The Alphabet versus the Goddess*, 363.
2 Gaiman and Pratchett, *Good Omens*, 185.
3 For the sake of brevity, future references to *The Malleus Maleficarum*, save for its use in titles, will appear as *Malleus*.
4 Gaiman, "Instructions," ll, 46-47.
5 McAvoy and Walters, *Consuming Narratives*, 3.
6 Roderick, *Dark Moon Mysteries,* 9.
7 Brauner, *Fearless Wives & Frightened Shrews*, 21.
8 Adler, *Drawing Down the Moon*, 45-47.
9 Bailey, Michael D. "The Malleus Maleficarum and the Construction of Witchcraft," 125.
10 Bailey, Michael D. "The Feminization of Magic and the Emerging Idea of the Female Witch in the Late Middle Ages," 120-126.
11 Broedel, *The Malleus Maleficarum and the Construction of Witchcraft*, 3.
12 Gardner, Gerald. *Witchcraft Today*, 102.
13 *Oxford English Dictionary* (OED) online "Witch, n1." <http://www.oed.com/view/Entry/229574>
14 Thanks to Jason Fisher for the translation.
15 Exodus 22:18. KJV
16 Damico, *Beowulf's Wealhtheow and the Valkyrie Tradition*, 44.
17 Clark Hall, *A Concise Anglo-Saxon Dictionary*, 393.
18 Gimbutas, *The Language of the Goddess,* 189.
19 Gimbutas, 209-210.
20 Ibid.
21 Gimbutas, 210.
22 Brauner, 15.
23 Thurston, *Witch, Wicce, Mother Goose*, 22-33.
24 Thurston, 17.
25 Thurston, 34.
26 Thurston, 31.
27 Thurston, 42.
28 Brauner, 16-17.
29 Ibid.
30 Thurston, 45.
31 Brauner, 36.
32 Ibid.
33 Brauner, 62.
34 Ibid.
35 Gaiman, *Fragile*, 223.
36 Gaiman, *Fragile*, 226-227.
37 Gaiman, *Fragile*, 228.
38 Brauner, 42-44.
39 Gaiman, *Fragile*, 117.
40 Gaiman, *Fragile*, 113.
41 Ibid.
42 Gaiman, *Fragile*, 114.
43 Gaiman, *Fragile*, 115.
44 Ibid.
45 Brauner, 36.
46 Gaiman, *Fragile*, 121.
47 Gaiman, *Fragile*, 119.
48 Gaiman, *Fragile*, 129.

49 Gaiman, *Fragile*, 122.
50 Gaiman, *Fragile*, 123.
51 Gaiman, *Fragile*, 128.
52 Ibid.
53 Gaiman, *Fragile*, 125.
54 Gimbutas, 189.
55 Gaiman, *Fragile*, 129.
56 Gaiman, *Fragile*, 131.
57 Ibid.
58 Gaiman, *Gods*, 150-153.
59 Gaiman, *Gods*, 39-44; 50; 289-290.
60 Gaiman, *Gods*, 62.
61 Gaiman, *Gods*, 153.
62 Gaiman, *Gods*, 73-74; 85.
63 Gaiman, *Gods*, 76-78.
64 Gaiman, *Gods*, 87-91.
65 Gimbutas, 210.
66 Gaiman, *Gods*, 138-139.
67 Gaiman, *Gods*, 305-313.
68 Gaiman, *Gods*, 373.
69 Gaiman, *Gods*, 288-289.
70 Gaiman, *Gods*, 374-375.
71 Gaiman, *Gods* 328.
72 Gaiman, *Gods*, 337.
73 Gaiman, *Gods*, 333.
74 Gaiman, *Gods*, 27-31.
75 Gaiman, *Gods*, 374.
76 Coltri, 1.
77 Coltri, 8.
78 Ibid.
79 I Enoch, VII: 1-6.
80 I Enoch, VI: 2; VII: 1-6.
81 Orchard, *Pride and Prodigies*, 58-58.
82 Belanger, *Sacred Hunger*, 127-128.
83 Belanger, 124-125.
84 Bildhauer, "Bloodsuckers: The Construction of Female Sexuality in Medieval Science and Fiction," 104-105.
85 Ibid.
86 Bildhauer, 105.
87 Bildhauer, 106.
88 Bildhauer, 112.
89 Brauner, 42-44.
90 Thurston, 58-59.
91 Ibid.
92 Gaiman, *Fables*, "Parliament of Rooks," 13-17.
93 Ibid.
94 Gaiman, *Fables*, "Parliament of Rooks," 14-16.
95 Gaiman, *Gods*, 29-30.
96 Williams, *Deformed Discourse*, 165-166.
97 Ibid.
98 Coltri, "The Challenge of the Queen of Sheba," 8.
99 Williams, 143-146.
100 Coltri, 7.
101 Gaiman, *Gods*, 377-379.
102 Gaiman, *Mirrors*, 331.

103 Ibid.
104 Ibid.
105 Gaiman, *Mirrors*, 333-334.
106 Ibid.
107 Gaiman, *Mirrors*, 337.
108 Gaiman, *Mirrors*, 338.
109 Ibid.
110 Gaiman, *Mirrors*, 339.
111 Gaiman, *Mirrors*, 340.
112 Gaiman, *Mirrors*, 341.
113 Ibid.
114 Gaiman, *Mirrors*, 344-345.
115 Raffaele, "Sleeping with Cannibals," 2-5.
116 Gaiman, *Mirrors*, 345-346.
117 Brauner, 62.
118 Gaiman and Reaves, 31.
119 Tolkien, *The Unfinished Tales of Númenor and Middle-Earth*, 401-402.
120 Ibid.
121 Ibid.
122 Gaiman and Reaves, 230-231.
123 Gaiman and Reaves, 136.
124 Belanger, 22.
125 Ibid.
126 Gaiman, *Coraline*, 21.
127 Gaiman, *Coraline*, 81.
128 OED online "beldam" <http://www.oed.com/view/Entry/17334>
129 Bildhauer, 112.
130 Gaiman, *Coraline*, 27-28.
131 As discussed in Melody Green's article in this present volume, and throughout Goddess Studies, cats, and crows, are representations of creation, as seen in their links to the Goddesses Bast and the Morrígan—both of whom make appearances in *The Sandman* series. Gaiman eschews negative stereotypes of these creatures—even seen in his beloved inspiration Tolkien.
132 Gaiman's mice, paying homage to the pan-dimensional beings controlling our sector of space-time, are the only creatures to know Coraline's name—and are the only to properly warn her (Gaiman, Coraline, 16). For more about white mice, space time, and Gaiman's inspirations, see Anthony Burdge's discussion of Gaiman and Douglas Adams in this present volume.
133 Gaiman, *Coraline*, 84-86.
134 Gaiman, *Coraline*, 78.
135 Gaiman, *Coraline*, 118-120.
136 Gaiman, *Omens*, 271-272.
137 Gaiman, *Omens*, 208-209.
138 Ibid.
139 Gaiman, *Stardust*, 63-64.
140 Ibid.
141 Gaiman, *Stardust*, 67.
142 Gaiman, *Stardust*, 175-177.
143 Gaiman, *Stardust*, 122.
144 OED, online "carnadine" <http://www.oed.com/view/Entry/28058>
145 OED, online "charnel, n1. and adj.1." <http://www.oed.com/view/Entry/30785>
146 Lewis, *The Magician's Nephew*, 65-66.
147 Lewis, 101-102.
148 Lewis, 93.
149 Gaiman, *Stardust*, 101.
150 Gaiman, *Stardust*, 202-203.
151 Gaiman, *Stardust*, 122.

152 Gaiman, *Stardust*, 147.
153 Tolkien, *The Silmarillion*, 12-13.
154 Tolkien 1977, 33.
155 Lewis, 79.
156 Gaiman, *Stardust*, 239-241.
157 Gaiman, *Stardust*, 187-196.
158 Gaiman, *Stardust*, 235.
159 Gaiman, *Stardust*, 122.
160 Gaiman, *Stardust*, 204-205.
161 Gaiman, *Graveyard*, 109.
162 Gaiman, *Graveyard*, 111.
163 Gaiman, *Graveyard*, 112.
164 Gaiman, *Graveyard*, 111.
165 Gaiman, *Graveyard*, 110-111.
166 Gaiman, *Graveyard*, 105.
167 Gaiman, *Omens*, 114.
168 Gaiman, *Omens*,153.
169 Thurston, 153-155.
170 Ibid.
171 Gaiman, *Omens,* 153.
172 Thurston, 155.
173 Ibid.
174 Shlain, 367.
175 Gaiman, *Omens*, 156.
176 Gaiman, *Omens*, 179.
177 Gaiman, *Omens*, 74.
178 Ibid.
179 Ibid.
180 Ibid.
181 Gaiman, *Omens*, 122.
180 Gaiman, *Omens,* 123.
181 Ibid.
182 Gaiman, *Omens*, 181.
183 Ibid.
184 Ibid.
185 Gaiman, *Omens*, 195.
186 Clark, "The Witches of Thessaly," 3.
187 Tully, "Witches of Ancient Greece & Rome," 1.
188 Graves, *The White Goddess*, 62.
189 Graves, 128.
190 Graves, 166.
191 Gaiman, *Game*, 85.
192 Gaiman, *Game*, 84.
193 Gaiman, *Kindly Ones*, "Part Thirteen," 20.
194 Gaiman, *Game*, 81-82.
195 Gaiman, *Stardust*, 175.
196 Gaiman, *Kindly Ones*, "Part Nine," 20.
197 Gaiman, *Game*, 84.
198 Gaiman, *Game*, 86.
199 Gaiman, *Game*, 171.
200 Gaiman, *Game*, 133
201 Gaiman, *Game*, 133
202 Gaiman, *Game*, 87.
203 Tolkien, *The Silmarillion*, 1977, 113.
204 Gaiman, *Anansi*, 135-136.
205 Gaiman, *Anansi*, 31-33.

206 Gaiman, *Anansi*, 216; 234.
207 Gaiman, *Anansi*, 139.
208 Ibid.
209 Ibid.
210 Gaiman, *Anansi*, 290-91.

Fables and Reflections:
Doubles, Duality, and Mirrors in the Fiction of Neil Gaiman

Samuel Brooker

Doubles pervade literature. They haunt the Gothic as doppelgängers, where movement behind mirrors and manifestations of the twisted unconscious provide fodder for psychoanalysis. They lend shape and structure to superhero and fantasy fictions, acting as conceptual bedrock for titanic struggles between diametrically opposed factions,[1] not to mention perfectly matched nemeses, polarized alien species, and shadowy organizations who parallel their real-world counterparts. Borrowing as he does from each of these traditions, Gaiman's work inevitably reflects these ideas, which we will explore through deities with many faces, the nature of twins and dual identities, Gothic ideas of nemesis and shadow, and the question of mirrors.

Myths with a Thousand Faces: Three-In-One

Works of mythological reduction like Joseph Campbell's *The Hero with a Thousand Faces* suggest that certain archetypal figures will emerge in any mythological system, though they will be dressed in the culturally appropriate trappings of the community from which they stem and is an idea sharing much with the psychoanalytic theory of Jungian Archetypes. To better understand Campbell's hypothesis, let us first look at The Endless from Gaiman's comic series *The Sandman*. They are seven 'anthropomorphic personifications' who sit at a level beyond gods. In the language of taxonomy, we can think of them as super-types, comparable to a Kingdom in biology — they have no parent. Beneath each, like the branches of a family tree, are its subtypes, figures that human (and alien) imaginations created as representation of the super-type. So Anubis, Thanatos, Yana, and Charon can each be thought of as a subtype of Death, the super-type. One way of understanding this system is through the Mesopotamian god and patron of Babylon, Marduk.

In "The Fifty Names of Marduk,"[2] Andrea Seri quotes numerous earlier works that detail the fifty names by which the god Marduk was known: Barashakushu, who works miracles; Tutu, who silences weeping, etc. These are not nicknames for the same individual: when Marduk works a miracle you are served by Barashakushu; when Marduk comforts you, you are comforted by Tutu. So it is with The Endless. In *Preludes and Nocturnes,* Dream appears in an entirely different aspect (and under the name L'Zorill) when he meets Martian Manhunter. Similarly in *Death: The High Cost of Living,* when Death takes the form of Didi —on the one day a century she spends in human form — her own Death is there to destroy her. As Gaiman puts it, "we perceive but aspects of the Endless, as we see the light glinting from one tiny facet of some huge and flawlessly cut precious stone."[3]

Each subtype often has its own set of subtypes. Odin, whom Shadow meets at the end of *American Gods,* is not the Wednesday with whom he traveled through the rest of the book, though they are the same god. In *Anansi Boys* a young boy, divided in two after breaking a neighbor's orb, grows up as two separate people—one a playful demigod, the other a retiring, stoic businessman. Only upon the death of their father do they meet again, each influencing and changing the other until eventually their personalities converge (or swap), creating two more 'balanced' individuals. As aspects of a whole, they are not complete: the demigod too capricious and destructive, the banker too timid and retiring. Charles Nancy and Spider are thus facets of one being, facets that together embody the super-type. In some cases, the subtypes seem to be interchangeable, as in the case of the Fates, Furies or — as they are known in *Preludes and Nocturnes* — Three-In-One. Never seen apart, these three figures are interchangeable, but when they wear a particular aspect — Maiden, Mother, Crone—they seem to embody that character; witness how their speech patterns change to suit the character which they are playing (maternal, playful) when they come to comfort/coerce Lyta Hall into invoking them in their guise as The Kindly Ones. So we have a super-type — the Three-In-One — whose subtypes include Fates (prophetic), Furies (vengeful), and others, each subtype containing three interchangeable characters: Maiden, Mother, Crone.

An additional layer of complexity emerges in Eve, who lives in a cave in the Dreaming. In "A Parliament of Rooks" she tells the story of the Lilim, Adam's three wives, of whom she is a personification. These clearly mirror the Fates in the model of Maiden-Mother-Crone. One-Who-Is-Three-Who-Mirrors-Three. Eve's contention that all men have, after a fashion, only married once not only returns us to the idea of an archetypal marriage, but also creates the One-Who-Is-Many-And-Three-Who-Mirrors-Three: an impressive edifice of mirroring. These kinds of inter-mythological parallels are a staple of Gaiman's work. Lord Susano-o-no-Mikoto, for example, becomes Loki's target because Loki doesn't like Storm gods, despite the source of his dislike — Thor – belonging to a different pantheon. Later, in *The Kindly Ones,* Loki himself befriends Puck because they are both tricksters. This hints at super-types (Storm god, Trickster), which exist outside the usual fraternity of common origins; despite being from Japan and Scandinavia respectively, the nature of a storm-god unites Lord Susano-o-no-Mikoto and Thor.

To explore this idea in more depth, let us explore Death as double, metonym, and archetype.

Myths with a Thousand Faces: Death as Metonym

The *fetch,* sometimes conflated with the psychopomp, is a double seen as a sign of impending death.[4] Psychopomp, in turn, comes from the Greek *psychopompus* meaning 'guide of souls,' which describes persons or beings responsible for escorting newly deceased souls to the afterlife. Psychopomps make several appearances in Gaiman's fiction — the gigantic Jackal god Anubis who weighs Shadow's heart in *American Gods*, for instance, or *The Sandman*'s Charon, the boatman who carries Orpheus across the Styx and Acheron. There is even a city of Psychopomps, the necropolis Litharge. Gaiman suggests that they emerge from a central, universal constant called simply Death. In this respect, mythic characters may be seen as functioning at the level of metonym.

A metonym is a part standing in for the whole. For example, the phrase *sword and sorcery* is a metonym, representing the entire fantasy genre. Metonyms are often unfair and irrelevant, as they define something in a narrow way. In the same way, the aspects and images of Death as portrayed in Gaiman's fiction are not to be considered Death per se, but as parts of a totality. This metonymic strategy has a more specific name – synecdoche – by which something is understood by perceiving facets of it.

An interesting exploration of this comes in *Death: The High Cost of Living*, in which Death has temporarily taken on the guise of Didi, a girl created to allow her to experience being alive. In the book Didi is pursued (and captured) by The Eremite, who steals her symbol and traps her in a basement. It is here that we see Death experiencing both remorse and anger, emotions at odds with her normally upbeat disposition.

With rescue her *joie de vivre* returns, though The Eremite still holds her symbol. Unperturbed, Didi/Death finds a cheap facsimile of her Ankh at a market stall. As soon as she wears it the object becomes the symbol of Death, rather than the cheap copy that it was previously. Here the symbol does not have implicit power, but by association with the larger concept it gains meaning and power. Dream's stone, too, is explicitly stated to be not the source, but a means of focusing his power. Dream is Dream, no other symbol being capable of embodying his nature.

Twins and Dual Identities

There is a clear relationship between subtype Didi and super-type Death, which compels us to compare and contrast them. Such contrasting pairs — and especially twins – appear regularly in Gaiman's work, often in the sense that de Nooy understands them: as "sites of contestation in the struggle to claim legitimacy for particular perspectives,"[5] representatives of contrasting or conflicting points of view. In this sense we are returned to the earlier idea of multiple facets of the same super-type.

We can see this in the most prevalent and intriguing pair in *The Sandman*: Despair and Desire. Though referred to as twins, on the surface they could not appear more different: Desire is tall and thin, for instance, where Despair is squat and fat. Desire is meddling and hectoring, Despair depressed and solitary. In what respect, then, are they twins? The link is perhaps best explained through Zizik, who suggests that the function of desire "is not to realize its goal, to find full satisfaction, but to reproduce itself as desire."[6] So it is at the level of metaphor that they are twins; emotional desire wants only to replicate itself over and again, meaning it can never be satisfied; the inevitable outcome, then, must be emotional despair, mirrored in Desire's twin shadows: "one black and sharp-edged, the other translucent and forever wavering, like heat haze."[7] We know what we want, but that want cannot be satisfied. Psychoanalyst Jacques Lacan calls this 'object petit-a'[8] (object little-a), something outside the body that is craved but cannot be possessed. So here we have Despair and Desire inextricably linked, twinned at the level of metaphor.

Abandoning Despair for now, we can also think of Desire as embodying two natures: that of woman and man. Karl Jung, founder of analytic psychology, believed that there were certain universal ways of thinking that manifested differently in different cultures, but which share an affinity, an idea later developed by Campbell. Among these universal ideas, Jung suggested, is the concept of Anima and Animus. Jung believed that every culture would have an idea about what it was to be female and male, and that characteristics you shared with the opposite sex would find psychological outlet. This is the Anima and Animus; the totality of femininity in the male psyche and the totality of masculinity in the female psyche, respectively. This is equally explored in the characters of Wanda (a transsexual woman) and Hal (who performs in drag); both give play to the Anima whilst being biologically male. Gaiman posits gender as biological accident, while identity is a matter of choice. Desire's androgyny represents this *in extremis*, since s/he is simultaneously both and neither, the Anima and Animus perfectly present or perfectly absent.

Pursuing this idea of a divided self leads us to consider another pair of metaphorical twins: Delirium and Delight. Following the same logic, we can look at Delight (precursor to Delirium) not as precedent, but as twin. Delirium can be defined as both an acute disturbance of mind and a state of wild ecstasy and excitement, alluded to when Delirium is accused of being "E'd off her bonce."[9] Thus Delirium and Delight are two sides of the same idea, a dualistic nature hinted at by their heterochromatic (two-colored) eyes. Destruction later extends this idea of embodying opposites: "Our sister defines life, just as despair defines hope, or desire defines hatred, or as destiny defines freedom."[10] He is Destruction, yes, but he is also Creation, evidenced by his keen interest in (if not concomitant skill with) cooking, sculpture, and painting. When Dream subsequently asks what he then defines, Destruction suggests reality. Prosaic? By no means; Dream is shown repeatedly to be the Endless most wedded to his function (save, perhaps, Destiny), the entirety of *The Sandman* arguably being about his voluntary abdication of responsibilities. Death seems to concur, stating elsewhere that without limits, life has no meaning;[11] she is later seen granting the gift of life to the golem Eblis O'Shaughnessy. We can explore these ideas in more depth through the theory of binary oppositions.

Mirrors: Binary Opposition

The theory of binary opposition arose from the Structuralist movement, which sought to understand the world as a system of signs.[12] A sign, in this context, is made up of two parts: a signifier (what we perceive) and a signified (what we understand by it); for example, the name Dream, despite being five arbitrary shapes we call letters, conjures in our mind the image of a tall, thin man with pale skin and strange eyes. The word Dream here is a signifier, the 'anthropomorphic manifestation' it makes you think of is the signified.

Binary opposition, "the generation of meaning in one term or sign by reference to another mutually exclusive term,"[13] refers to two signs which, by virtue of being opposites, define one another. Recall Destruction's speech: can something be simultaneously alive and dead? No; they are opposites, the limits of death defined by life.

Many mythologies are underpinned by such oppositions — in Western Christianity, for example, God and the Devil represent good and evil, Adam and Eve masculinity and femininity, respectively. Around these opposites cluster other, related ideas: cruelty is an 'evil' trait, so the Devil is cruel; kindness is a 'good' trait, so God must be kind. The angels in *Good Omens* emerge from this tradition, their comic efforts to aid and hinder humanity respectively representative of their good/evil natures. It is worth noting here that, as with other Gaiman works, neither character is wholly good or evil, though the comedy comes from our polarized understanding of these archetypal characters.

Claude Lévi-Strauss thought such binary opposition intrinsic to myth, calling it "an inherent feature of the means invented by nature to make possible the functioning of language and thought."[14] He believed that we use opposites (good/evil, friend/foe, night/day) to make sense of and define the world. By way of illustration, let us look at two indicative pairings from *The Sandman*: Chaos and Order, Brute and Glob.

Chaos is defined as an absence of Order, making them classic opposites. When they are introduced in *Season of Mists,* their responses to the availability of Hell are placed alongside one another on the page, allowing us to contrast the clipped speech of Order, which omits unnecessary terms and is illustrated almost as a Mondrian painting, with the semi-intelligible, fractured world of Chaos. What is important is that Chaos, despite being fragmentary, does still resemble Order, if a distorted version thereof, emphasized by their mirrored panels.

There are other explorations of these binary oppositions. Tall, thin Cain is associated with murder and secrets while his short, rotund brother Abel, the victim, is associated with truth. Daniel's white robes when he becomes the Dream King directly contrast with the darker robes of his predecessor. Even landscapes can mirror this model: in *MirrorMask* it is shadows that consume the city of light; many of the stories in *The Sandman* take place in run-down tenements and motels, in stark contrast to the dramatic castles and spectacular environs that make up the mythic landscapes.

In *A Doll's House,* Brute and Glob are nightmares who, having kidnapped Hector Hall, plan to install him as ruler of the Dreaming. Brute is physically strong and slow-witted while Glob, essentially a brain with stick-like legs, is shown to be conniving and cunning. We see this correlation again in other Gaiman characters, such as Croup and Vandemar in *Neverwhere*. Here we see two cultural oppositions — weakness and strength, naivety and cunning — intertwined, as they often are. But why are they intertwined? What is this correlation between physical weakness and mental acuity, strength and naivety?

This hints at one of the intriguing questions raised by Jacques Derrida. A member of the Poststructuralist movement, which sought to question and critique its predecessor, Derrida queried the reality of these intertwined opposites. Firstly, he suggested that in any pairing there will be a 'dominant' member. In the West, for example, he suggests that in the male/female dynamic there existed a "violent hierarchy... [in which] one of the two terms govern(s) the other,"[15] with women defined by what they were not (men). Secondly, he suggested that such terms were so value-laden that they automatically carried cultural assumptions with them. In the example above, strong/naïve and weak/clever are bound together, despite there being no implicit reason to connect the two.

We can explore this idea through Ken and Barbie, first introduced in *A Doll's House*. On the surface gender seems to be the only thing that differentiates them, emphasized by the identical clothes and the manner in which they complete one another's sentences. Their contrasting dreams—one pornographically capitalist and lustful, the other a whimsical fairy tale—show them to be very different behind the superficial similarities. Similarly, in *American Gods* we have Czernobog and Bielebog, the black and white god (respectively) of Slavic mythology. Winter god Czernobog is cantankerous, moody and aggressive, while springtime Bielebog is playful and friendly. Even landscapes can mirror, in this description of hell as "Heaven's dark reflection. Like a landscape inverted in water."[16]

It is often from such cultural expectations that Gaiman derives his most surprising characters. Death, in his mythology, is compassionate rather than something to be feared, while life is often shown to be complex and cruel. In "Snow, Glass, Apples" the villain becomes the heroine. In *The Graveyard Book* a place of traditional fear and threat becomes a place of security and safety. By inverting our expectations—caring ghosts, innocent heroines as creepy, supernatural figures—our understanding of what can appear to be two dimensional archetypes is deepened.

In his *Morphology of the Folk Tale*, structuralist Vladimir Propp took one hundred Russian folk tales and dissolved them down to eight constituent characters,[17] suggesting that the interaction between these kinds of characters was what drove folk tales, which could then be clad in whatever way the storyteller chose—rather like a range of different colored cars may share the same engine and basic components. Certainly there is a correlation between this idea and the super-type/subtype relationship, with the Hero—one of Propp's own categories—well represented in characters as diverse as Odysseus and Major Alan 'Dutch' Schaeffer in *Predator*.

Again, where Gaiman differs is in his tendency to subvert rather than mirror these traditions. He is playful, subverting our expectations for narrative effect. In *Good Omens* he gives us friendly demons. In *American Gods* we meet a fatherly god compromised by fear. *A Game of You* offers us sympathetic witches. These are recognizable archetypes, but by changing heroes for villains (whilst still crucially retaining those characteristics that first made them heroes) he forces us to question the archetypes on which we generally rely. Witness this most spectacularly in "Snow, Glass, Apples," where a mirror is held to our expectations of wicked stepmothers and naïve, lovely daughters. In *Smoke and Mirrors*, Gaiman cites as a significant influence Ray Bradbury's "Homecoming," a short story in which a human boy born to a pantheon of supernatural creatures gathers his family to mourn his inevitable death. Here the polarities of aberration and normalcy are revered. The supernatural becomes commonplace, monsters friends. Our expectations are subverted.

Mirrors: Analogues and Real World Counterparts

The Sandman offers an opportunity to explore in more depth how Gaiman's work sets up comparisons between our collective understanding of a character and his own, unique reading. Eschewing the option to rehabilitate a retired DC character – to create a new subtype — Gaiman instead positioned his *Sandman* as progenitor — super-type — to the original Wesley Dodds. In *A Midsummer Night's Dream*, the characters of our common cultural inheritance — the royal court of Faerie — come to see a play in which they are mimicked by actors, with some characters even objecting to the manner in which they are portrayed. Rather than parody or mimicry, Gaiman is engaged in a kind of cultural retcon (retroactive continuity), altering the histories of extant characters to fit with his own burgeoning mythology. Likewise his Cain, Abel, and Eve, also existing DC characters drawn from the common pool of myth, have now become the canonical originals.

Another example of this intercession occurs in *Fables and Reflections*. At the opening of "Orpheus," Eurydice is bitten on the ankle by a snake on the day of her wedding to Orpheus. From here the tale continues largely as originally written until, having washed up on a beach, Orpheus is almost bitten by a snake. This would be a perfect and poetically circular end to his tale, but Dream intercedes, kicking aside the snake and forcing his son to live on. In this Gaiman interrupts the myth, taking ownership of it. Doctor Destiny — referred to in the comic as D — is also an older character resurrected and complicated by his presence in *The Sandman*, his back story and history filled out in the comic. This material came to represent canon, an example of further 'retconning'.

In this way, Gaiman's characters can be seen as analogs of existing ones, sharing a family resemblance. We see this in Urania Blackwell,[18] whose complex, agoraphobic personality expands greatly on her original comics' persona. It is present too in Prez,[19] originally conceived as a one-off parody of 60s student politics, now retrospectively recontextualized as a Christ allegory. In a way Prez's frame story illustrates Gaiman's process of appropriation and adaptation, the scribe whose stories carry amend figures from our pool of common myth.

A real-world consequence of this is the question of copyright. While the mythological figures may appear under their own name, issues with ownership mean that characters like *Spiderman's* Peter Parker appear as Perry Porter. The analog in these cases is concealed by an adapted name, but we know who they are because of a shared cultural context, the aforementioned pool of common myth. Gaiman himself spoke of his frustration that the Bizarros' from *Superman* could not be used, necessitating the analogous creation of the Weirdzos (for all intents and purposes the same characters).

There is something appropriate about this change, however. Wanda, in whose dream these characters appear, has dim recollections of these figures, and their behavior — darker, more adult when compared to their more playful actions in *Superman* — seems more appropriate rather than the real thing, under these specific circumstances. Subtypes of the same idea, Weirdzos are the Bizarros as seen through a distorting mirror: simultaneously familiar, yet creepily different.

Distorting Mirrors: Nemesis and Shadow

The Freudian concept of the *Unheimlic*, or "unhomely" refers to the feeling of unease generated by precisely this contrast between familiarity and difference. More specifically, it is the dread caused by "a peculiar commingling of the familiar and unfamiliar."[20] Gaiman-esque tropes like the rendering of juvenile characters in an adult way, children stumbling onto dark mirrors of their own world or the idea of our own familiar body suddenly behaving abnormally ("...but then the reflection slowly raised one hand, while your own hand stayed still...")[21] seem to invite such parallels. An aspect of the *unheimlich* particularly worthy of more careful study is the *doppelgänger* (German: 'double walker'), an uncannily similar or identical person whose appearance is seen as a symbol of impending doom. Sometimes the connection is more coincidental — a shared birthday, for example — but more often the similarities are starker and less ambiguous.

In *MirrorMask* for example, Helena, peering through a paper window from the mirror world to her own, sees her doppelgänger in her bedroom, arguing with her father. When she spies Helena, the double begins to tear the paper world apart, in turn dismantling the mirror world in which the real Helena is trapped. In *Coraline*, too, the eponymous protagonist passes through a doorway to an idealised version of her own world where all is perfection—save that everybody has buttons for eyes. During the most hallucinatory and paranoid sequence in *Neverwhere*, Richard believes he is speaking to his friends until they ask him to touch their faces, at which point they distort "like warm bubblegum."[22]

In each case, there is a paranoia associated with the double, and consequences for questioning their reality. When doppelgänger Helena spies her progenitor, for example, she begins to tear the world apart. Equally when in *Coraline* the eponymous heroine refuses to become part of the Other Mother's family — to make it her home — she starts a train of events that lead to the world's destruction. In *Neverwhere* Richard's discovery that he is indeed hallucinating almost destroys his sanity. The idea that an enemy might conceal themselves perfectly arises again in the almost Capgrasian perfection of *Black Orchid's* disguise, allowing her to precisely mimic the behaviours of those close to her quarry. Perfect disguise is equally deployed by Loki in *American Gods* and *The Sandman*, as Low Key Lyesmith and when disguising himself as Susano-o-no-Mikoto, respectively. In the latter case Morpheus creates a duplicate made of 'dreamstuff' to take Loki's place, in return for a (then) unspecified favour.

The doppelgänger makes another, similarly threatening appearance in the form of the nemesis. In current usage nemesis means a perfectly matched archenemy, but in classical literature it is a spectre of divine vengeance and restorer of balance. It is as vengeful restorer of balance that the term is used in *The Sandman*, when Lyta Hall summons The Kindly Ones to punish Dream for killing her son — though it is for the death of his other son, Orpheus, that he is truly punished. It is in this sense that Freud, after Rank, suggests that the double, created in childhood as an "energetic denial of the power of death," becomes the opposite as we grow older — a harbinger of our future demise.[23]

According to G.R. Thompson, Gothic literature is characterized by just such "irreconcilable dualities,"[24] by which token Dream is very much in the mould of a Gothic protagonist. Thompson suggests that Gothic literature presents conflicting ideas which the protagonist often cannot resolve. Dream is unable to directly abandon his role, as Destruction did. Instead he may be relying on the Furies (who appear as nemesis-like shadows as they set about dismantling the Dreaming) to facilitate his own desire for death by proxy. This would make sense given that, as Gaiman summarizes the plot of *The Sandman* in the foreword to *Endless Nights*, "The Lord of Dreams learns that one must change or die, and makes his decision." One so dedicated to his duty would need an equal nemesis to make him abandon it, a harbinger fit to restore the balance.

The nemesis as symbol of our own wild and untamed desires — what Freud would call the Id — is another common trope. Witness Alan Moore's reading of Hyde in *The League of Extraordinary Gentlemen*, for example. The double allows us not only to "confront and recognize the dark aspect of one's personality," as Ozolins suggests,[25] but also to show another facet of our personality. At the House on the Rock, Shadow simultaneously sees gods in their human and divine aspects: irreconcilable dualities indeed. In *Anansi Boys* Graham Coats — a weasel in the metaphorical sense — becomes a stoat. In *Odd and the Frost Giants*, Odd meets the gods of the Norse pantheon in the guise of animals appropriate to their natures (Loki the cunning fox, for example). A double as a facet of our personality can also be seen in two sets of warring brothers: the *Anansi Boys*, with Charles Nancy forced to endure what to him feel like mortifications (Karaoke, among other things) but which his twin would have seen as deep pleasures, and Cain and Abel, whose relationship also echoes binary opposition (secrets/truth, victim/perpetrator, brave/coward). It is perhaps for this reason that Cluracan's nemesis —released from a mirror — is identical to his creator, the fairy being mostly Id anyway.

Familiarity with one's reflection is used also to show self-knowledge or self-delusion. In *A Game of You,* Barbie looks in a mirror and doesn't recognize herself, foreshadowing the conflict of identity that will form the basis for the remaining book; in *"Façade,"* Urania Blackwell attempts to hide her face, achieving release only when she presents it to her creator. In "Troll Bridge" a man volunteers to take over the job of bridge troll,[26] in doing so allowing another to take over his human body; in *Brief Lives,* the Alder Man becomes a bear, literally shedding his skin. In the latter cases the protagonists, knowing themselves, become their doubles by choice.

In the above cases we see the idea of the shadow, the Id, as our true self, unmediated by social niceties and honest about our natures. Surrealism sought this liberty, to express ideas "in the absence of any control exercised by reason, exempt from any aesthetic or moral concern."[27] Rather than be limited by our mere physical nature, Gaiman's characters are able to shape themselves to represent themselves truthfully (as possessing multiple aspects) rather than as a single entity; or, as Morpheus puts it: "Dream the world. Not this pallid shadow of reality. Dream the world the way it truly is."[28] It is interesting that Dream himself casts a shadow "when it occurs to him to do so,"[29] uniting the *Unheimlich* and the surreal; he may appear human but he is not. So sometimes the double is welcome, as in "The Wedding Present" (where a woman chooses a troubled life with a living husband over her own) or the voluntary transformation of "Troll Bridge" or Morpheus' voluntary abdication/reinstatement. More often they are villainous mirrors of those we know, as in the case of Coraline's other mother, Mr. Punch (the suppressed Id of *Violent Cases*), or the zoomorphism of Graham Coats.

Mirrors: Both Sides of the Curtain

In *American Gods,* Shadow and Wednesday are on the run, driving a Winnebago on the interstate, when they spy a roadblock ahead. Ignorant of any alternative routes, Wednesday has Shadow continue driving, as he traces complex shapes on the dashboard, "making marks as if he were solving an algebraic puzzle."[30] At the last minute he has Shadow turn right, taking him beyond our world into a place he later calls 'backstage' or, at another point, 'behind the curtain.'

Fantasy and science fiction imply two worlds: our own, the one in which we are reading, and the other — the world of aliens, myths, fairies and gods. Whatever its function —whether as metaphor, to mirror the conflicts, triumphs and disasters, or to offer polarized versions of our own (echoing the idea of binary opposition) —it remains inaccessible; the world of the fantastic separated from our own. This is not the case in Gaiman's fiction, which cuts through that barrier, breaking a hole in the wall between our worlds (or the wall in Wall, if we recall *Stardust*).

He is not unique in this — the idea of a rift between the worlds, a means by which creatures can pass from one to the other, is a common trope — but Gaiman is different. He rarely follows the conventional logic of an alien invasion or demonic incursion, relying on pat villainous plan or shadowy corporation bent on "closing the rift"; he explores what might pass through that barrier, how the idiosyncratic creatures of our collective unconscious — every supernatural being, god, nightmare—might cope if they found themselves in our world. This interzone, where gods and mortals walk together, can be explored through the idea of liminality.

Liminality literally refers to a threshold, where two planes intersect. In *Stardust*, for example, the hole in the wall is a liminal space, through which mythological creatures and Victorian mortals may pass. The same logic applies to *Wolves in the Walls*. This threshold need not be literal: in *The Graveyard Book,* Nobody Owens is granted the freedom of the graveyard, which removes him from our world and makes him invisible to Jack.

Mirrors perform this function for Despair: despite her realm being one location she is able to look through any mirror, just as Door's *(Neverwhere)* family home has doors that open into every location in London Below. In "Dream of a Thousand Cats" it is a critical mass of cat dreamers who are required to transform our world into one in which we are playthings for feline overlords. For Richard Mayhew *(Neverwhere)* it is merely laying hands upon Door that precipitates his transfer from a denizen of London Above to London Below. In *Coraline*, the reference is more explicitly Carollian, with a small door leading to a mirror world that recalls the miniature doors, rabbit holes, and mirrors that allow Alice access to Wonderland.

There are some worlds, however, which exist as models or inaccessible archetypes. In "Ramadan" we see Baghdad at its height, a city which the Caliph believes can grow no better. Desperate to keep it perfect forever, he gives it to Dream, who takes it into the realm of stories, to inspire dreamers forever. A similar sentiment is expressed in *Books of Magic:*

> The true Atlantis is inside you, just as it's inside all of us. The

sunken land is lost beneath the dark sea, lost beneath the waves of wet, black stories and myths that break upon the shores of our minds. Atlantis is the shadow-land, the birth-place of civilization. The fair land in the west that is lost to us, but remains forever, true birthplace and true goal.[31]

Like the Endless, these cities exist as archetypes of which we see mere facets. In Plato's famous allegory, we are asked to imagine prisoners chained in a cave who have spent their entire lives watching shadows pass across the wall. When one of their number frees himself, he sees the true things that created those shadows and is irrevocably changed. There are the real things that cast the shadows, which we cannot change; then there are the shadows themselves, which we can interpret in the same way we turn vapour in the sky into rabbits and sheep and faces.

---

1 Clute and Grant. *The Encyclopedia of Fantasy*, 422.
2 Andrea, "The Fifty Names of Marduk in Enma eliš," 507-519.
3 Gaiman, *Mists*, 12.
4 Neville, 107.
5 Nooy, 164-5.
6 Zizek, 39.
7 Gaiman, *Mists*, 11.
8 Lacan, 1998, 62.
9 Gaiman, *Brief Lives*, 7.
10 Gaiman, *Brief Lives*, 16.
11 Gaiman, *High Cost*, 19.
12 Broekman, 23.
13 Edgar and Sedgwick, 1997, 28.
14 Levi-Strauss, *The Naked Man*, Volume 4, 559.
15 Derrida, 1981, 41.
16 Gaiman, *Mists*, 10.
17 Propp, *Morphology of the Folk Tale*, 79-80.
18 Gaiman, *Sandman* #20.
19 Gaiman, *Sandman* #54.
20 Royle, The uncanny: an introduction, 1.
21 Gaiman, *Kindly Ones*, 14.
22 Gaiman, *Neverwhere*, 247.
23 Freud, "The Uncanny," 235.
24 G.R. Thompson, *Gothic Imaginations: Essays in Dark Romanticism*, 34.
25 Ozolins, 103-110.
26 Gaiman, Introduction 1999, 59.
27 Breton, 26.
28 Gaiman, *Mists*, 17.
29 Gaiman, *Mists*, 12.
30 Gaiman, *Gods*, 343.
31 Gaiman, *Books of Magic* 1, 26.

Through a Telescope Backwards: Tripping the Light Fantastic in the Gaiman Universe

Kristine Larsen

Like J.R.R. Tolkien, an author to whom he is often compared, Neil Gaiman is a master myth-maker. He takes age-old motifs and breathes new life into them, giving them a fresh face and a modern voice. He creates new fantastical worlds—what Tolkien called Secondary worlds—into which the reader can immerse themselves while willingly suspending all disbelief. The reader loses him or herself within this Secondary world, and at the conclusion of the experience, the reader finds him or herself reemerging into our primary existence with a keener understanding of both human nature and human interactions with the natural world. Like all great literature, Gaiman's works seamlessly combine reality with fiction, and in his able hands, even the most mundane and obvious aspects of the world become shiny and new when viewed through his personal lens. Light is an example of such an everyday occurrence that becomes sculpted into something novel and unexpected within Gaiman's worlds.

In a 1951 letter, J.R.R. Tolkien explained that "Light is such a primeval symbol in the nature of the Universe, that it can hardly be analysed."[1] Central to the creation of the universe in the Judeo-Christian *Book of Genesis* is the deity's utterance "Let there be light!" and the subsequent separation of the light from the darkness.[2] According to the Icelandic creation myth recounted in the *Prose Edda* of Snorri Sturleson, there was once a southern land of fire and light separated from the northern land of ice and darkness by the Guinnungagap, the primordial void. In the mixing of these two primeval opposites, life first took form as the frost giant Ymir.[3] In Gaiman's modern creation myth *MirrorMask* a troubled young girl, Helena Campbell, separates herself (and reality) into light and dark within the dream world of her drawings. This bifurcation mirrors her feelings of being torn between her everyday life in the circus and the larger society beyond which she dreams of escaping to. Each of these lands has a queen, and the "land of shadows"[4] has a copy of Helena, a princess who, like Helena, is desperate to escape from her life (from her universe) into another existence —a parallel or mirror world—which happens to be the world that Helena herself inhabits.

Darkness is not merely the lack of light, or its simple opposite, but is instead a powerful thing on its own. Gaiman explains in *Neverwhere* that darkness can be "something solid and real, so much more than a simple absence of light....It felt not so much as if the lights were being turned down but as if the darkness were being turned up."[5] The Other Mother of *Coraline* and the Dark Queen of *MirrorMask* have black button eyes, symbolic of the power of darkness in their souls. Likewise the Four Horsemen of *Good Omens* have negative auras "like black holes,"[6] and Joey Harker of *InterWorld* experiences a darkness "like something you could touch, something solid and tangible and cold."[7] Gaiman and Terry Pratchett jokingly describe "dark light" or "infra-black" as being the color that one experiences when running headfirst into a brick wall,[8] but there is nothing funny about the black light "like rays of obsidian"[9] that Lord Dogknife uses to trap the mudluff Hue, who is himself the living embodiment of light. These examples remind this author of Tolkien's description of the ghastly spider Ungoliant: "she sucked up all light that she could find, and spun it forth again in dark nets of strangling doom."[10] After Ungoliant and the satanic figure Melkor destroy the light-giving Two Trees of Valinor, "the Darkness that followed was more than loss of light. In that hour was made a Darkness that seemed not lack but a thing with being of its own...."[11]

Darkness has the power to seduce one, to corrupt one utterly beyond redemption, with the archetypal example being Lucifer and all other fallen angels (and by extension fallen humans). In Tolkien's universe, Melkor seeks the Light Imperishable throughout the cosmos so that he can become as powerful as Ilúvatar the Creator. He finds it not, and his mind and soul turn to darkness and destruction. Not merely the absence of light, Melkor embodies the very power of darkness. It cannot create, but it can certainly destroy and corrupt. When the first humans awake in Middle-earth, Melkor also corrupts some of them, appearing as a great voice in the darkness. "Greatest of all is the Dark," boasts Melkor, "for it has no bounds. I came out of the Dark, but I am Its master.... I will protect you from the Dark, which else will devour you."[12] Melkor promises humans knowledge and power, but in the end, can only lead them into evil behavior and regret. In Gaiman's short story "Murder Mysteries" Lucifer is likewise set on his downward spiral by being seduced by voices in the darkness. "They promise me things," he explains, "ask me questions, whisper and plead."[13] He claims that he alone among all angels is strong enough to resist the darkness. But as we all know, Lucifer is mistaken, for the darkness is powerful. As anyone with young children knows from firsthand experience, the fear of the dark is a potent motivator. It can overwhelm someone, and even after one is shown that there is no monster under the bed or in the closet, somehow the fear remains. Like Tolkien before him, Gaiman reminds us that sometimes this fear is well-warranted.

If both the darkness and the light are sources of power, what are we to make of their balance—the various shades of gray that one finds populating a moonlit night? In Gaiman's worlds, gray often represents the dynamic tension between worlds, whose balance is easily disrupted. Examples are the gray winding sheet of Bod, the living boy who inhabits a cemetery in *The Graveyard Book*, and the gray suits worn by Walkers in *InterWorld* to protect themselves against the harsh conditions of the space between realities—the so-called In-Between. Shadow, the main character of *American Gods*, also inhabits a space between realities, as he uneasily navigates between the world of humans and the world of the gods (referred to as the world behind the scenes). Gray can also denote uncertainty, uncertainty as to the state one is in, or whether one's motives are good or evil. For example, the normally colorful Hue turns a "terrified shade of translucent gray" when he and the Walkers are captured by Lady Indigo. The Angel Islington, whose true motives are not revealed until the end of *Neverwhere*, has gray eyes "as old as the universe."[14] Like Lucifer (whom he bristles at comparisons to), Islington is a fallen angel, and has not only fallen from heaven to an underground world, but from lightness to the dark. It is as Gaiman and Pratchett offer in *Good Omens*: "most of the great triumphs and tragedies of history are caused, not by people being fundamentally good, or fundamentally bad, but by people being fundamentally people."[15] In Gaiman's works, angels—and demons—show themselves to be people as well, in terms of their equal potential for good or ill. The most interesting characters are therefore those who are an uncomfortable shade of gray, those whose motives are far from obvious and are capable of both acts of good and evil, depending on the situation.

But to merely describe Gaiman's universe in terms of black, white, and gray is to be superficial in one's analysis. For light is not only primeval, but like Gaiman's works, it is complex. One might say it is legion—composed of an infinite number of wavelengths that we mere mortals simplify into the seven colors of the rainbow or the sixty-four colors of a crayon box. Gaiman's works are populated by a series of 'colorful' characters, including Miss Violet and Scarlet of *The Graveyard Book*, Miss Indigo of *InterWorld*, and Mrs. Cherry of *Stardust*. The tattooed men Scarabus (*InterWorld*) and the Indigo Man (*The Graveyard Book*) wear their colors on their skin for all the world to see. How does one describe the indescribable, what physicists would term the hyperspace between parallel universes? The In-Between traveled between realities in *InterWorld* is represented as a dizzying geometrical cacophony of shapes and colors that leaves Joey in awe. A specific geometrical shape that continually changes its number of sides is tentatively described as yellow "because that's the color it was saturated with." Shapes throb, colors pulse, and the view is "like a 3-D collaboration between Salvador Dali, Picasso and Jackson Pollack."[16] In such a space words fail, and only colors can hope to convey meaning. Hence we are introduced to the little alien mudluff dubbed Hue by Joey Harker, a bubble-shaped creature who speaks in colors. Although Joey initially laments that he doesn't "speak colors," he and Hue grow to understand each other, and Joey is able to discern between "a rather miserable shade of purple" and gold as a sign of agreement.[17] Where words fail, colors, music, and even body-movements allow communication, as vividly seen in the 1977 film *Close Encounters of the Third Kind*. The soul lights of *InterWorld*—the boiled-down remains of Walkers—pulse in firefly colors, and certainly make their intentions known as they threaten Lord Dogknife, their nemesis. Joey uses the stone necklace given to him by his mother to converse with the soul lights in their tongue, and notes that watching the pulsations of color is like "hearing two contrapuntal melodies that are slowly merging."[18] A similar use of non-spoken communication occurs in Philip Pullman's *His Dark Materials* trilogy when Lyra uses physicist Mary Malone's computer to speak with the angels. The ethereal beings answer her via "A stream of dancing lights, for all the world looking like the shimmering curtains of the aurora.... They took up patterns that were held for a moment only to break apart and form again, in different shapes, or different colors."[19]

Colors can not only speak, they can also form a bridge between realities, in the In-Between, and in the Underground of *Neverwhere*, when Door opens a doorway for the Angel Islington. He expects to find a passageway to heaven, but instead is faced with "a swirling maelstrom of color and light... all vicious orange and retinal purple." Rather than heaven, or the hell of theology, Door has opened a passageway to a Hades of modern physics, "the surface of a star, perhaps, or the event horizon of a black hole...."[20] The most vivid example of colors denoting a pathway between realities is the rainbow bridge of *Odd and the Frost Giants*. Odd forms a prism out of ice, because when "water freezes, the rainbows are trapped in it, like fish in a shallow pool. And the sunlight sets them free."[21] Odd and his companions, Norse gods transformed into animals, plunge through the resulting puddle, vividly described not in terms of staid red, blue, and purple, but rather in the delicate hues of wine, blueberry, leaf, raspberry, and gold. The travelers are "swept up in the colors" and are carried along by them, across this rainbow bridge to Asgard.[22]

Colors are a natural part of our experience, but what happens when the colors are obviously wrong? When the colors are at odds with our expectations, they act as an important clue that we are passing from our normal realm of experience into another world, one that is not only foreign but (in the Gaiman universe) most probably perilous. After the goddess

Bast recommends that he takes the middle path in his journey through the afterlife, Shadow notes the moon begins "pinking and going into eclipse."[23] In the same novel, the people of Kaluna travel across the Bering Land Bridge to North America in 14,000 BCE under the frightening veil of the most vivid auroral display they had ever seen, a sky that was "alive with lights, knotting and flickering and winding, flux and pulse, white and green and violet and red."[24]

When Bod passes through the ghoul gate, he notices that the "sky was red, but not the warm red of a sunset. This was an angry, glowering red, the color of an infected wound." The moons in this ghoul land are also abnormal in appearance, one "huge and pitted and white" and the other "the bluish-green color of the veins of mold in a cheese...."[25] Joey Harker first notices that he has passed from his universe into a parallel reality through his observation of colors being out of place. In this reality, McDonald's golden arches are green tartan, police siren lights are green and yellow, and the usual silver and black of the standard sedan are replaced with "bright colors — all orange and leaf greens and cheerful yellows."[26]

Gaiman muses in "Pages From a Journal Found in a Shoebox Left in a Greyhound Bus Somewhere Between Tulsa, Oklahoma, and Louisville, Kentucky" that "the world will end in black-and-white.... Maybe as long as we have colors we can keep going."[27] But as Gaiman also notes, in our modern technological world colors are often hidden from sight, and the world is artificially presented in a binary mode, not of black and white, but black and yellow. In at least five short stories and three novels, Gaiman bemoans the effect of the ubiquitous low pressure sodium street light (LPS) on our perception of the night. For the last quarter of the twentieth century LPS was the most common form of lighting in the United Kingdom (and likewise found in many U.S. cities). Although highly efficient, because the low pressure sodium lamp only gives off yellow-orange light, it robs one of the ability to distinguish colors. In "The Flints of Memory Lane," the narrator explains that a sodium lamppost "washed out all other colors, turning everything yellow and black."[28] The LPS lamp deceives us by distorting our view of reality, especially in the night, when the power of the darkness already plays tricks on our minds. *Anansi Boy*'s Fat Charlie sees a brown garden spider as black in the sodium lights, and Shadow is unable to discern the color of Tessie the old roadster for the same reason.[29] Human faces are also transformed by the monochromatic LPS lamp. While two teenagers find their "black lips and pale yellow faces" humorous in "Troll Bridge,"[30] the narrator of "The Flints of Memory Lane" — Gaiman himself — is haunted by the vision of a woman standing outside his house, remembering "the yellow-black of her smile, and a shadow of the fear that followed."[31] Likewise, the narrator of "Keepsakes and Treasures" has indelibly painted in his memory the sight of a naked woman, "a full black-nippled breast which curved disturbingly in the sodium yellow light of the street."[32] In "The Facts in the Case of the Departure of Miss Finch" Gaiman twists the metaphor, using the eerie yellow sodium light as a sign of normalcy and sanity. Here the narrator and his companions are only certain that they have safely escaped from the nightmarish events of the sideshow when they reach an unoccupied room filled with souvenirs, a room illuminated by reassuring normalcy of the sodium lights from the outside world.

While it appears that Gaiman may have an unhealthy fixation with LPS lighting, as an Englishman of a certain age the effects of sodium lighting would have been part of his entire life. In *Neverwhere* Gaiman differentiates between the parts of the London Below that are "gaslit streets, and sodium-lit streets, and streets lit with burning rushes."[33] From the 1930s through the 1950s LPS lamps were increasingly installed in the British Isles not only due to their efficiency but because their yellow light could better pierce through the ubiquitous English fog than other light beams. However, because of its monochromatic nature (and thus inability to discern color) it was more widely used on roadways than in residential areas and hence became known as the "drivers' lamp."[34] With the energy crisis of the 1970s energy efficiency overruled aesthetics, and by the end of the 1980s LPS became the dominant form of outdoor lighting in the U.K.[35] It is no wonder, then, that the sickly yellowish glare of the LPS lamp became a fixture in Gaiman's writings. Perhaps he would be heartened to know that in recent decades there has been a movement in his country of birth to replace some of these lamps with High Pressure Sodium (HPS) lamps, which have greater ability to show realistic colors at night. The ratio of HPS to LPS in roadway lighting in the U.K. is now approximately 1:1.[36] Perhaps if Gaiman had remained in England his more recent stories might feature nighttime tableaus draped in hues of salmon-pink.

Low pressure sodium lights are recommended by astronomers for the simple reason that because they only emit yellow light, their effects on telescopic views can be largely filtered out. But there are no LPS filter contact lenses available to the general public, and the cumulative effect of all outdoor lighting, whether LPS or not, continues to take its toll on our view of the night sky. The U.K. and the U.S. have been central battlegrounds in the fight against this light pollution, the wasteful upward direction of outdoor lighting which is estimated to burn up 22,000 gigawatt-hours of electricity world-wide per year.[37] While the problem has accelerated in past decades, the first warning signs were clearly evident in the mid 1950s, when the British Royal Observatory was moved from Greenwich to Sussex in a vain attempt to seek dark skies. Today there are no world-class visible light astronomical telescopes in the United Kingdom, following the Isaac Newton Telescope's relocation to the Canary Islands in 1984. Four decades ago the Milky Way was still visible from Liverpool, and three decades ago residents of Finchley, Bexleyheath, and Bristol could still view the magnificent plane of our galaxy. Sadly, this is no longer the case.[38] And the problem is accelerating. The same is true in far too many locations in the U.S., as Gaiman is well aware from personal experience. As a result, both American and British citizens have mobilized to begin taking back their view of the stars, and have been mildly successful in passing legislation to protect against light pollution. Amateur and professional astronomers have likewise fought against light pollution during the last few decades, with mixed results.[39]

In the 1980s the 100-inch telescope at Mount Wilson, housed in the mountains overlooking Los Angeles, was mothballed for six years due to the deteriorated sky conditions. One might think it absurd to build a telescope in such a light polluted location, but the observatory was built at that local because of its stable air (and hence stable images as seen through the telescope) in 1904, long before light pollution was even a possibility, let alone a reality. Gaiman brings attention to the plight of L.A. stargazers in "The Goldfish Pool and Other Stories," where the narrator laments that he

> wanted to see the stars, but the lights of the city were too bright, the air too dirty. The sky was a dirty, starless yellow, and I thought of all the constellations I could see from the English countryside, and I felt, for the first time, deeply, stupidly homesick. I missed the stars.[40]

It is certainly not a stretch to call this passage autobiographical in nature. Without a doubt, the skies of L.A. are a foreign landscape when compared with the English countryside (or that of Gaiman's reported Upper Midwest American homestead), and there is no doubt that the author loves the stars. These primeval lights of the heavens—and their commonly recognized shapes—turn up as welcome reoccurring characters in the constellation of Gaiman's works. In *American Gods* Zorya Polunochnaya points out the Big Dipper to Shadow, and explains the celestial myths of her people (including her place in the myths). Miss Lupescu teaches Bod the constellations in *The Graveyard Book*, including Orion and Taurus, and in *Stardust* Tristran and Victoria also view Orion, and the Orionid meteor shower that radiates from it each October. Gaiman also invents his own celestial myth (an interstellar creation myth) in the short vignette "The Star." Here extraterrestrial vampires create a tradition of pointing out the constellation Draco the Dragon to the next generation, explaining that "We come from there. One day we shall return."[41] The younger ones brush off the stories as merely that, until homesickness awakens in their hearts, and they are drawn to live in the Northern Hemisphere where this circumpolar constellation is visible (and from most locales, visible all night long).

Yes, as Gaiman well understands, the stars draw us to them, as they ever have since the dawn of our species. Today we have the technology to reach outward to them, through our telescopes, both earth-bound and earth-orbiting, and humanity has taken its first tentative steps out of its earthly cradle towards the stars from which our very atoms originated. The very title of the novel in which Tristran and Victoria appear reminds us of our unique relationship with the stars. As Carl Sagan often said, "We are star stuff" —we are stardust come alive and self-aware, and within the past hundred years cognizant of the depth of that special relationship which our ancient ancestors felt with the universe above their heads. Like astronomers, Gaiman understands the power of viewing the stars, and both he and his characters express a longing for, and appreciation of, the simple yet powerful view of the celestial host. Unfortunately, due to light pollution, this human birthright is increasingly relegated to history, memory, and fiction. In "It's Only the End of the World Again" the narrator is awed by the view of the stars as seen from the seashore as compared to that of the city, describing them as "sprinkled like diamond dust and crushed sapphires across the sky."[42] When Bod stands at the boundary of the ghoul gate in the space between his world and that below, he sees the Milky Way above his head "as he had never seen it before, a glimmering shroud across the arch of the sky."[43] Likewise Joey Harker sees more stars than he "had even imagined existed" when traveling in the Static or Nowhere-at-All (the boundary of the In-Between).[44]

The village of Wall also stands at a boundary between worlds, and the stars are similarly a sight to behold. The narrator of *Stardust* reminds us of several differences between our modern world and that of Tristran's time, including the important fact that

> Few of us now have seen the stars as folk saw them then – our cities and towns cast too much light into the world – but, for the village of Wall, the stars were laid out like worlds or like ideas, uncountable as the trees in the forest or the leaves on a tree.[45]

Indeed, it is ironic that in our light-polluted times the only "stars" that most people are likely to see are brilliant fireballs that rival the magnitude of the planet Venus (the "Evening star"). These brightest of meteors (or falling/shooting stars in the common vernacular) are burning bits of stardust that were once assembled into the form of a comet. Once shed from that dirty snowball in its race sunward in its orbit, these primeval dust bunnies float through interplanetary space until our home planet plows into them and the heat produced by friction with our atmosphere destroys them in a blaze of glory. It is no wonder that the ancients had varied and beautiful mythologies surrounding these temporary celestial visitors. Gaiman's tale of a star fallen to earth in the form of a beautiful woman is a modern echo of these myths. The stars are also destined to fall in the Norse myth of Ragnarök, the Twilight of the Gods, as referenced in *American Gods*. As Shadow wonders at the unworldly brightness and vividness of the stars as seen from "behind the scenes," Buffalo Man explains that the stars will soon fall, heralding the transition of gods to heroes in this modern world. "This is a poor place for gods," he reminds Shadow.[46]

It is a poor place for gods, and perhaps a poorer place for stars. Just as modern society creates new gods in *American Gods*, so too do we create new stars, ironically out of the very streetlights that have obscured our view of the sky. In the novel the lights of L.A. are described as "a twinkling electrical map of an imaginary kingdom, the heavens laid out right here on earth."[47] In *Neverwhere* "a riot of crisp and glittering autumn stars" is seen at the same time as streetlights and building lights "which looked like earthbound stars," the entire scene reminding Richard of a "fairyland."[48] But the most deliberate attempt to replace the stars with their modern simulacrum appears in "The Goldfish Pool and Other Stories." The very same narrator who bemoans the lack of stars in the sky in the beginning of the story is lead by June Lincoln to see in the valley of Hollywood "constellations in the streetlights and the cars."[49] But it is only a trick of the mind, wishful thinking on our part. Less than falling stars, the streetlights are *fallen* stars, perhaps in multiple senses of the term.

Streetlights trick us, obstruct our view of the heavens, and show us false colors; mirrors also trick us, while pretending to be a simple reflection of reality. Sometimes the trick brings us hope or happiness, as in the case of Odd. When drinking from a spring he sees a vision of his father playing with him and his mother, as well as other memorable moments such as how his parents met. Some visions seen in a mirror are startling and unnerving for a time, before we regain our bearings. *InterWorld*'s Joey Harker is surprised to see his own features distortedly reflected back at him in the mirror-like mask of his parallel world self, and *MirrorMask*'s Helena is initially shocked to find that a looking glass in the bedroom of the Dark World's princess has eyeholes cut into it. But the realization that the Dark Queen uses it to watch over her daughter pleased her: "It made me feel loved."[50] Gaiman explains in his introduction to *Smoke and Mirrors* that mirrors "appear to tell the truth.... But set a mirror correctly and it will lie so convincingly you'll believe that something has vanished into thin air." Mirrors, he further explains, can "show you anything you can imagine and maybe a few things you can't."[51] Mirrors, therefore, have a sinister character, as discovered by numerous other literary and cinematic characters. Alice travels *Through the Looking Glass* and enters a world fraught with peril. Galadriel's mirror in Tolkien's *The Fellowship of the Ring* is also an unreliable reflector of reality. In *The Matrix*, the metaphor of the mirror as an unreliable reflector of reality appears throughout the film.[52] Perhaps the most visually vivid is the scene in which Neo is literally consumed by the mirror as he passes from the fantasy world of the Matrix into the real post-apocalyptic world. A less widely known example can be found in the John Carpenter film *The Prince of Darkness* (1987), in which physics students, their professor, and a priest do battle with Satan and his father, who has been trapped (via the combined efforts of science and religion) on the other side of a mirror (in a parallel universe). At the end of the film, a female student sacrifices herself to save the world when she throws herself and a fellow student whose body had been co-opted by Satan into the mirror in a vain attempt to permanently trap the evil within the mirror universe.

In Gaiman's world, various characters use mirrors and the worlds within/beyond them for their nefarious purposes. The Other Mother of *Coraline* traps the young girl's parents within the hallway mirror, while Coraline and the ethereal remains of other children she has likewise kidnapped over the centuries find themselves trapped in a dark space behind a mirror. In *The Graveyard Book* Haroun, an Ifrit (djinn), is trapped in an array of mirrors and burned in its light. The three witches, the Lilim, of *Stardust,* appear to exist in both the world behind the Wall as well as within the world of their mirror simultaneously. However, their mirror-selves appear significantly younger than their "real world" selves, and one of the younger versions leaves the mirror world in order to hunt for the fallen star (and hence regain years of youth for herself and her sisters). The Dark Princess of *MirrorMask* uses the device of the novella's title to trade universes with Helena, and Helena must find the illusive mask in order to return to her original life. She finds it hiding in plain sight, and as she presses her face into the looking glass the Mirrormask forms on her face. Helena's description of the experience demonstrates the power of mirrors to seduce us, confuse us, and sometimes give us an inflated sense of self:

> It was like being in the eye of the hurricane: the world swirled and shook around me, but I was fine..... For a moment I couldn't remember which one I was. It's a lot like being some kind of god, when you wear the Mirrormask. Or it's like writing a book. You can fix things, or you can sort of do something in your head and let them fix themselves. It's not hard. With the Mirrormask on, I

could see everything.[53]

A normal mirror allows one to fix one's hair or make-up; the Mirrormask allows one to fix entire worlds. Like a mirror itself, the word *fix* has subtleties. For example, the Dark Princess certainly thought she was "fixing" things (from her perspective) when she stole Helena's life. Mirrors not only have the power to reflect and distort light, but our perceptions and beliefs in the process.

Light can also be distorted, for good or ill, by looking through a lens. For example, in *Coraline* the titular character gains a different view of reality when viewed through a stone with a hole in its center. The stone allows her to identify the hidden souls of the captured children. Gaiman sets the tone for *Stardust* by situating Tristran's era within its scientific context. One of the milestones he mentions is John William Draper's taking of the first photograph of the moon (in December 1839), "freezing her pale face on cold paper."[54] The view through the camera lens is clearly not that seen by the eye. In *InterWorld* Joey and his friends are tricked by HEX into thinking a magical world to be a technological one, leading to the capture of Joey's team. By looking through the lens of Hue's transparent form, Joey can see this world as it really is. However, in the In-Between Joey is not certain whether he is observing a normal Hue beside him "or maybe a Hue the size of Vermont was a thousand miles away from me...."[55] Similarly, when he dons Jay's travel suit and views the universe through its "Mirrormask" helmet, he finds it is "like looking at something huge through binoculars held the wrong way." Although Hue is in reality the size of a cat, Joey can't "shake the idea that it was truly the size of a skyscraper, only it was ten miles away."[56] Likewise, in the Dark Queen's palace, Helena feels as if she is "watching the world through the wrong end of a telescope," and in the spirit world of *Anansi Boys* Spider sees the world receding from him "as if he were looking at it through the wrong end of a telescope."[57] The fallen Angel Islington of *Neverwhere* is said by his henchman Mr. Croup to have "traveled so far beyond right and wrong that he couldn't see them with a telescope on a nice clear night."[58] While the world does seem more distant when viewed through binoculars backwards (one barrel at a time, unless the binoculars are very small or one's head is very large), the view through the wrong end of a telescope is more complex. When one looks down the tube of a common backyard telescope, one is more often than not greeted with a distorted view of one's own face, not dissimilar to what Joey initially views as his own reflection seen in the mirrored mask of Jay's helmet.

Light interacts with our world in myriad ways. It can be diffracted around a barrier, bent through a lens, or bounced off a mirror. In each of these cases the visible image is not an exact copy of the original, but a distortion that may appear more or less pleasing than the original. Even the simple act of light illuminating the book you hold in your hand is only successful insofar as the light reflects off the page and then refracts through the lenses in your eyes (and in some cases after passing through reading glasses or contact lenses as well). Does light tell the truth? Can sight ever capture the true essence of reality? In the Gaiman universe, the possibilities for distortions and enhancements are often central to the story. In the introduction to *Smoke and Mirrors* Gaiman explains that fantasy (meaning all fiction) is "A distorting mirror, to be sure, and a concealing mirror set at forty-five degrees to reality." He continues to warn us that this mirror can be used "to tell ourselves things we might not otherwise see" (or might not *want* to see).[59] When one reads one of Gaiman's works, one often sees one's own self reflected within its pages, and if the interplay of words and light reflects back a potentially grotesque image of human nature, perhaps in this case the mirror does not lie.

1 Tolkien, *Letters*, 148.
2 Genesis 1: 1-4, KJV.
3 Leeming and Leeming, *A Dictionary of Creation Myths*, 133.
4 Gaiman and McKean, *MirrorMask*, 22.
5 Gaiman, *Neverwhere*, 102-3.
6 Gaiman and Pratchett, *Omens*, 351.
7 Gaiman and Reaves, *InterWorld*, 31.
8 Gaiman and Pratchett, *Omens*, 308.
9 Gaiman and Reaves, *InterWorld*, 184.
10 Tolkien, *The Silmarillion*, 73.
11 Tolkien, *The Silmarillion*, 76.
12 Tolkien, *Morgoth's Ring*, 346.
13 Gaiman, *Mirrors*, 321.
14 Gaiman, *InterWorld*, 135; Gaiman, *Neverwhere*, 202.
15 Gaiman and Pratchett, *Omens*, 30.
16 Gaiman and Reaves, *InterWorld*, 59-60.
17 Gaiman and Reaves, *InterWorld*, 85-88.
18 Gaiman and Reaves, *InterWorld*, 218.
19 Pullman, *His Dark Materials*, 367-8.
20 Gaiman, *Neverwhere*, 328-9.
21 Gaiman, *Odd,* 50.
22 Gaiman, *Odd*, 54-5.
23 Gaiman, *American Gods*, 477.
24 Gaiman, *Gods*, 416.
25 Gaiman, *The Graveyard Book*, 78-9; 83.
26 Gaiman and Reaves, *InterWorld*, 11; 15.
27 Gaiman, *Fragile Things*, 237.
28 Gaiman, *Fragile*, 64-5.
29 Gaiman, *Anansi Boys*, 57; Gaiman, *Gods*, 251.
30 Gaiman, *Mirrors*, 65.
31 Gaiman, *Fragile*, 66.
32 Gaiman, *Fragile*, 126.
33 Gaiman, *Neverwhere*, 305.

34 Cornwell, "Thorn Beta 5."
35 Ibid.
36 The Royal Commission on Environmental Pollution, 24.
37 International Darksky Association, "Light Pollution and Energy."
38 House of Commons Science and Technology Committee, 23.
39 Interested readers are encouraged to view the NASA composite image of the Earth at night (taken in 2000) (http://apod.nasa.gov/apod/image/0011/earthlights2_dmsp_big.jpg). The bright spots visible in this picture represent light (and therefore electricity, money, and in many cases fossil fuels) being wasted in upward-directed lighting.
40 Gaiman, *Mirrors*, 92.
41 Gaiman, *Fragile*, 201.
42 Gaiman, *Mirrors*, 188.
43 Gaiman, *Graveyard*, 95.
44 Gaiman and Reaves, *InterWorld*, 42.
45 Gaiman, *Stardust*, 41.
46 Gaiman, *Gods*, 247-8.
47 Gaiman, *Gods*, 378.
48 Gaiman, *Neverwhere*, 85.
49 Gaiman, *Mirrors*, 107.
50 Gaiman and McKean, *MirrorMask*, 52.
51 Gaiman, *Mirrors*, 1.
52 Neil Gaiman was asked to write a short story for a collection celebrating the release of the first *Matrix* film. The result was "Goliath" (published on the film website and in the anthology *Fragile Things*).
53 Gaiman and McKean, *MirrorMask*, 73.
54 Gaiman, *Stardust*, 5.
55 Gaiman and Reaves, *InterWorld*, 138.
56 Gaiman and Reaves, *InterWorld*, 88.
57 Gaiman and McKean, *MirrorMask*, 51; Gaiman, *Gods*, 293.
58 Gaiman, *Neverwhere*, 320.
59 Gaiman, *Mirrors*, 2.

The Eternal Carnival of the Myth:
Or How to Kill Myths and Live Happy

Camillo A. Formigatti

> One thing that puzzles me (and I use puzzle here in the technical sense of really, really irritates me) is reading, as from time to time I have, learned academic books on folk tales and fairy stories that explain why nobody wrote them and which go on to point out that looking for authorship of folk tales is in itself a fallacy; the kind of books or articles that give the impression that all stories were stumbled upon or, at best, reshaped, and I think, yes, but they all started somewhere, in someone's head. Because stories start in minds—they aren't artifacts or natural phenomena.
>
> —Neil Gaiman, *Fragile Things*[1]

In a paper supposed to deal with mythological dimensions it seems suitable to start with definitions of myth and mythology as clear cut as possible. Unfortunately, this would prove to be quite an impossible task, at least within the scope of this short essay. The scientific and critical literature on this topic is broad and manifold, ranging from works with a historical or anthropological approach to others with a psychological or philosophical one, to include all nuances in between these two extremes. The risk of losing one's own path in such a wide and thick forest is very high. Nevertheless, a minimal "working definition" should be provided, at least in order to help the reader understand better from which point of view Neil Gaiman's personal and original (re)interpretation of myths and mythology is analyzed in the present paper.

The starting point is the admittedly partial and one-sided scholarly definition of myth as provided in the New Pauly Wissowa:

> [Myth is] a "traditional narrative of collective significance"... The term "traditional" implies a transmission that is not tied to a first original narrator known by name, and describes, in the context of oral narrative, not a transmission of fixed stories but of narrative structures (plots) that are tied to certain protagonists."[2]

These narrative structures need to be filled with substance, in other words with the myths themselves. And it is exactly by this process of filling that we come to the mythology, intended as the " 'account' (*logos*) of the deeds of gods and heroes" in the sense of "the total store of traditional narratives ('myths') of an ethnic group."[3]

After having more or less described the "playground," one may think that there is still a fundamental question to answer, namely *from where* does Neil Gaiman take the "traditional narratives," *i.e.*, the myths he (re)tells. However, the answer to this question will not be the central focus of this paper. As pointed out by Harley J. Sims in his contribution to this collection, Gaiman creates a pan-pantheon consisting of "deities and spirits of all cultures and historical periods."[4] The focus of the present paper will be rather shifted to an analysis of *how Gaiman* deals with these deities, their stories, and their lives and *how the reader* perceives them. This approach has its roots in the simple and yet insightful question which is the starting point of many of Gaiman's stories, namely, "What do Gods do when they are not worshipped anymore?" In *The Sandman* comic book series, and above all in the novels *American Gods* and *Anansi Boys*, Gaiman provides very accurate and amusing descriptions of the daily life, the troubles, and the occupations of the mythical protagonists. There are indeed many passages in Gaiman's works that one could take as examples here, but on account of the limited space available I will examine in detail only some of them from *American Gods* and from selected short stories.

With the first appearance of Czernobog and the three Zoryas in *American Gods*, the reader does not enter the magical and mysterious world of the Slavic deities, but rather is catapulted into the world of East European immigrants in today's Chicago. If we take a closer look at how Gaiman constructs this first encounter between Shadow and one of his future travel companions, we may think for a moment that we are reading a realistic novel inspired by nineteenth-century French Naturalism, rather than a fantasy story ending with a battle between old and new Gods. It began with Shadow and Wednesday slowly approaching the city of Chicago, "driving through countryside" until "imperceptibly, the occasional town became a low suburban sprawl, and the sprawl became a city."[5] They do not reach a holy place or an ancient and sacred temple, instead they park "outside a squat black brownstone."[6] When the two press the top button of the intercom box (no abracadabra, no magic formula or oath to open the door), it simply does not work. And that's not the only thing that does not work in the building. We get to know that also the heating is out of order, and even if the tenants have already informed the superintendent, he did not fix the problem, because "he does not care, goes to Arizona for the winter for his chest."[7] Who has not yet experienced similar problems and shortcomings? And that's not all, apparently there is no elevator (or maybe it is not working) and unfortunately Shadow and Wednesday have to climb all their way up to the last floor (remember, they pressed the top button). But this it is not a marvelous journey through lands of wonder with pastel landscapes from which the sweet fragrance of blossoming flowers arise, for "the landing two stories up was half filled with black plastic garbage bags and it smelled of rotting vegetables."[8]

When they finally reach the top floor, Wednesday is panting— after all, he is an old man out of shape. They are welcomed by Czernobog in a rough way—who does not have among his neighbors a gruff old man? As soon as he lets them in, the reader gets a first impression of him, an old retired man wearing "pinstripe pants, shiny from age, and slippers."[9] He shakes Shadow's left hand with his rough and callused one, and Shadow notices immediately that the tips of his fingers are yellow from too much smoking. The reader then gets directly an idea of the smells in the apartment: over-boiled cabbage, a cat box, and unfiltered cigarettes. Zorya Utrennyaya offers the two guests a coffee, and then they begin to chatter with Czernobog. He tells them that like all immigrants, they firstly came to New York and only afterwards they moved to Chicago; he worked in the meat business, but now he is retired. Like many other retired persons, he likes to play checkers, and offers Shadow to play with him, to kill time while they are waiting for dinner. At last dinner is ready, but they have to free the table from the game, because there is no extra table in the small apartment. They finally start to eat a typical Russian meal, whose detailed description leaves little space for imagination. It sounds not very appetizing, starting from the "ferociously crimson borscht ... with a spoonful of white sour cream,"[10] through the "leathery pot roast, accompanied by greens of some description—although they had been boiled so long and so thoroughly that they were no longer ... greens, and were well on their way to becoming browns."[11] The last course is even worse, "cabbage leaves stuffed with ground meat and rice, leaves of such toughness that they were almost impossible to cut without spattering meat and rice all over the carpet."[12] At least the apple pie is good (no wonder, Zorya Vechernyaya did not bake it herself, she bought it in a store and oven-warmed it). By this time, the point of view of the reader has changed and he or she does not know anymore of whom the author is speaking, old Slavic gods or old Russian immigrants. Gaiman reaches this goal through a masterly description of the characters and their surroundings, and doing so he challenges almost all five senses of the reader, who, like Shadow, smells unpleasant odors, touches rough and callused hands, and eats food that tastes even worse than prison food.

In a series of short stories ("Shoggoth's Old Peculiar," "It's Only the End of the World Again," "A Study in Emerald," "I Cthulhu") Gaiman applies this technique of the changing and inversion of the point of view even to the literary pantheon of cosmic deities created by H.P. Lovecraft. In "Shoggoth's Old Peculiar,"[13] while on a walking tour of the British coastline, the young American tourist Benjamin Lassiter reaches the small and out-of-the-way village of Innsmouth. After having spent five days wandering from village to village under the rain, he needs some rest and so decides to eat something at a local pub. Among the three pubs of the village—*The Book of Dead Names*, *The Public Bar*, and the *Saloon Bar*—he chooses the last one. He enters the bar and the reader finds himself again in a description very similar to the one of Czernobog's apartment. First comes what the sense of smell perceives, "it smelled like last week's beer and the day-before-yesterday's cigarette smoke."[14] Ben orders his meal, a "ploughman's," and so now we turn to the sense of taste—which is not pleased, for the food is awful, since "a ploughman's turned out to be a rectangular slab of sharp-tasting cheese, a lettuce leaf, an undersized tomato with a thumb-print in it, a mound of something wet and brown that tasted like sour jam and a small, hard, stale roll."[15]

Meanwhile, two other guests, inhabitants of Innsmouth, come and sit beside him. They order for him a pint of local beer, the renowned Shoggoth's Old Peculiar, and suddenly Ben finds himself involved in a lively discussion on H.P. Lovecraft's literary style. After some time, Ben says that he is a student and asks his drinking partners what they do. They answer innocently that they are acolytes of Great Cthulhu. This is light work, they add, since it consists mostly of praying and waiting until their boss Cthulhu wakes up "in his undersea living-sort-of quarters" where he will "... stretch, and yawn and get dressed... probably go to the toilet... maybe read the papers" and after all this morning activities, "come out of the ocean depths and consume the world utterly."[16]

Life does not seem to be very different in the American Innsmouth, at least as we are told in another short story, "It's Only the End of the World Again."[17] The main character is Lawrence Talbot, a werewolf who works as an "adjuster," as he defines himself. Actually he is very similar to a private eye from a hard-boiled novel,[18] but his rivals are not petty criminals or mafia bosses, they are evil Cthulhoid entities and their acolytes. Already the title of the story betrays one of the main stylistic aspects of the narration: the end of the world is nothing special; it occurs from time to time. The story begins in *medias res*, with Talbot waking up naked one afternoon in his room. As every self-respecting fictional private-eye, he has the symptoms of a bad hang-over and has to run to the toilet to throw up. However, among common things like a tomato peel, diced carrots and sweet corn, in the content of the vomit there are also two items that the reader does not expect to be there: a dog's paw (possibly a Doberman's) and a small child's fingers. At this point, it is already clear to the reader that Talbot is a werewolf. Unfortunately for him, this condition does not help him very much in his everyday life. As a matter of fact, he finds under the door an unpleasant message from his landlady, in which she reminds him that he still owes her two week's rent, and that all the answers are in the *Book of Revelations*. Moreover, in the future he should be quieter and not make too much noise when he comes home early in the morning, and just in the case that he has already forgotten it, she kindly reminds him that "when the Elder Gods rose up from the ocean, all the scum of the Earth, all the nonbelievers, all the human garbage and the wastrels and deadbeats would be swept away, and the world would be cleansed by ice and deep water."[19] And last but not least Talbot notes, "she felt she ought to remind me that she has assigned me a shelf in the refrigerator when I arrived and she'd thank me if in the future I'd keep to it."[20]

Towards the end of the story, Talbot even has time to drink a Jack Daniel's in his favorite haunt, where he has the opportunity to listen to the barman reciting a poem by Tennyson. After all, the end of the world is not such an uncommon or thrilling event for which the pub should close in advance. Talbot's last stop at the pub reveals to us an interesting common feature of the Innsmouthians of both sides of the Atlantic: they are fond of literature and literary critique (the Innsmouthians in England criticize Lovecraft's literary language, while the barman in the American Innsmouth loves English poetry).

The peak of the inversion of roles is reached in the story "A Study in Emerald,"[21] in which Gaiman pays homage to both H. P. Lovecraft and Arthur Conan Doyle by inverting the point of view in a twofold way: the world is dominated by Lovecraft's Great Old Ones and their cultists, and accordingly the hero becomes Moriarty, while Holmes is the antagonist. The unusual setting of this story presupposes that the reader signs a sort of agreement with the author in the form of the suspension of disbelief. One should regard the combination of the fictional worlds of A. Conan Doyle's Sherlock Holmes and H. P. Lovecraft's extra-terrestrial monstrous deities as being one coherent and real world. Much in the same way as Wednesday, Czernobog, Mr. Nancy, and all other deities living in the America of *American Gods*, Lovecraft's Great Old Ones are a firm part of the world in which this short story is set; even more, they rule it. In such a fictional world, the feeling of familiarity for the reader is achieved through a different means. Winking to Alan Moore's *The League of Extraordinary Gentlemen* graphic novels and to Kim Newman's *Anno Dracula*, Gaiman introduces in the story other characters and elements taken from other works of fiction (Jekyll, Hyde, or Victor von Frankenstein). However, these characters are not part of the main plot, they are just mentioned in the epigraphs put at the beginning of each section.

According to G. Genette, the epigraphs belong to the category of paratexts, and are at the threshold of the text: "they surround it and extend it, precisely in order to *present* it, in the usual sense of this verb but also in the strongest sense: to *make present*, to ensure the text's presence in the world..."[22] and in our case, to ensure their presence in *a fictional world*. In the version of this story available on Neil Gaiman's website, an ever stronger effect of "presence in the world" is granted by yet another means, which however does not belong directly to the content of text: the page layout. Online we have as faithful as possible an imitation of the page layout of a newspaper from the second decade of the twentieth century, and even an exact date is provided, Sunday, June 28, 1914.

As I have tried to outline in the preceding paragraphs, in his "Lovecraft" stories, Gaiman tries to portray all the situations as if belonging to the normal world and the daily routine of life-as-it-is. The notion of "normality" is of course subjective and has to be applied within the framework of each single world. Therefore, in an imaginary and fantasy world (like the one portrayed in "A Study in Emerald") normality has fantastic features, but the reader should nevertheless regard them as normal. This process of "normalization of the uncanny" is central in the short story "Forbidden Brides of the Faceless Slaves in the Secret House of the Night of Dread Desire."[23] The protagonist is a writer who lives in a fantasy and horror world, but writes fantasy stories settled in our common world, for instance, a story about a couple with a marriage crisis. Normality becomes thus myth and fantasy, and vice-versa.

Gaiman's approach of turning the weird and unknown into the common and well-known may be considered to be an implicit manifesto, a sort of counterpart to the explicit and programmatic statements made by Lovecraft in two short essays in which he expounds his literary aesthetics. First in "Supernatural Horror in Literature:"

> The oldest and strongest emotion of mankind is fear, and the oldest and strongest kind of fear is fear of the unknown . . . The appeal of the spectrally macabre is generally narrow because it demands from the reader a certain degree of imagination and a capacity for detachment from every-day life.[24]

Followed by "Notes on Writing Weird Fiction":

> I choose weird stories because they suit my inclination best . . . These stories frequently emphasize the element of horror because fear is our deepest and strongest emotion, and the one which best

lends itself to the creation of nature-defying illusions. Horror and the unknown or the strange are always closely connected, so that it is hard to create a convincing picture of shattered natural law or cosmic alienage or "outsideness" without laying stress on the emotion of fear.[25]

Reading Lovecraft's stories, one should abandon his or her everyday life and emotions to "feel a burning curiosity about unknown outer space, and a burning desire to escape from the prison-house of the known and the real into those enchanted lands of incredible adventure and infinite possibilities."[26] In order to achieve this goal, in his works Lovecraft often plays with the notion of time and its infinity, as opposed to the limits of human life.[27] For instance, in the short novel "At the Mountains of Madness," a scientific expedition to Antarctica discovers that millions of years ago an alien race colonized Earth and developed a technologically advanced civilization that lasted for a time-span unthinkable for humanity. The scientists involved in the expedition thus acquire the knowledge of the real history of the planet and of the very marginal role that mankind plays in it.

An even deeper confrontation with the abysses of time and space is experienced by the protagonist of the short story "The Shadow Out of Time," Nathaniel Wingate Peaslee, a normal person with a normal job. Professor of political economy at Miskatonic University, his mind is switched with the mind of an extraterrestrial creature from the planet of Yith. Suddenly, he is no more in twentieth-century New England in a human body, but finds himself to be in an alien city in Australia during the Mesozoic era, trapped in the body of a cone-shaped cephalopod creature. When reading these two stories, much like their protagonists the reader too should sense the inanity of his own life and efforts in comparison with the immensity of the universe. He or she is removed from a familiar home place and transported to totally alien and uncanny places.

On the other hand, when we read Gaiman's stories, we feel like Timothy Hunter on his journey through the realms of magic, having John Constantine as mentor. In *The Books of Magic*, the unknown and irrational lurking behind our common world becomes a matter of everyday life. When Timothy is guest of the witch Zatanna in her house in San Francisco, he calls his father to let him know he is safe, and his father asks him how he is doing in Brighton with his aunt Blodwyn. Timothy is understandably surprised, and when Zatanna asks him how is father is, he answers that his father thinks he is in Brighton.

"I *told* him I wasn't," he adds, "and he didn't hear me. This is really weird, you know that? I mean, it's okay when I'm with John. When you're with him the weird stuff seems almost *normal.*"[28]

This is the feeling Gaiman's narrative technique conveys to the reader. It is the normality of the actual lives of the gods and mythical beings that strikes us and brings us near to them. It is the *removal of their mythological dimension*, their descent in our world to live with us, to grow older and die like we do, that changes their status and our perception of them.

After having seen that the Gods too have to earn their living just like we have to, we feel that they are not all too different from us. In a more or less explicit way, the key to this interpretation is provided by Gaiman himself in the epigraph[29] to chapter seven of *American Gods*, where he quotes a passage from W.D. O'Flaherty's book *Hindu Myths*:

> As the Hindu Gods are "immortal" in a very particular sense—for they are born and die—they experience most of the great human dilemmas and often seem to differ from mortals in a few trivial details… They are actors playing parts that are real only for us; they are the masks behind which we see our own faces.[30]

In Gaiman's worlds, these masks allow the Gods to live among us undisturbed. There are no boundaries anymore between them and us, and with some effort it is even possible to travel to their worlds—or if you prefer, to the backstage—and come back. The masking, the inversion of roles and the trespassing of boundaries, are characteristics of the spirit of carnival. However, they draw their power precisely from the fact that after the end of the celebrations, the natural order and roles are restored. In some Italian folk traditions, the personified Carnival even *dies* at the end of the celebrations.[31] On the other hand, in Neil Gaiman's stories the original roles are never restored, and the Gods go on wearing their masks: the myth abides in our world.

---

1 Gaiman, *Fragile*.
2 Brill's New Pauly Online, s.v. "Myth (Antiquity) I. Theory of Myth," by Fritz Graf, accessed February 21, 2012, http://brillonline.nl/subscriber/entry?entry=bnp_e815160.
3 Brill's New Pauly Online, s.v. "Myth (Classical Tradition) I. Concept," by Robert Matthias Erdbeer, accessed February, 21, 2012, http://brillonline.nl/subscriber/entry?entry=bnp_e1505640
4 See Sims' essay in this present volume.
5 Gaiman, *Gods*, 72-3.
6 Gaiman, *Gods*, 73.
7 See note 5.
8 Gaiman, *Gods*, 74.
9 Gaiman, *Gods*, 75.
10 Gaiman, *Gods*, 84.

11 See note 9.
12 See note 9.
13 Gaiman, *Smoke and Mirrors,* 173-184.
14 Gaiman, *Mirrors*, 175.
15 Gaiman, *Mirrors*, 176.
16 Gaiman, *Mirrors*, 181-2.
17 Gaiman, *Mirrors*, 201-18.
18 His hard-boiled characteristics are more marked in another short story in *Smoke and Mirrors,* "Bay Wolf," a retelling of "Beowulf as a futuristic episode of Baywatch," as Gaiman describes it in the introduction to volume (Gaiman, *Mirrors*, 26).
19 Gaiman, *Mirrors*, 202.
20 See note 18.
21 Gaiman, *Fragile*, 27-56.
22 Genette 1997, 1.
23 Gaiman, *Fragile*, 89-106.
24 Lovecraft 1927, text retrieved on http://www.hplovecraft.com/writings/texts/essays/shil.asp
25 Lovecraft 1937, text retrieved on http://www.hplovecraft.com/writings/texts/essays/nwwf.asp
26 Lovecraft 1927.
27 "The reason why time plays a great part in so many of my tales is that this element looms up in my mind as the most profoundly dramatic and grimly terrible thing in the universe. Conflict with time seems to me the most potent and fruitful theme in all human expression." (Lovecraft 1937).
28 Gaiman, *The Books of Magic*, chapter II: The Shadow World.
29 Again, by means of a paratext, like in "A Study in Emerald."
30 Gaiman, *Gods*, 155.
31 Sordi, 1982, *passim*.

"It Starts With Doors:"
Blurred Boundaries and Portals in the Worlds of Neil Gaiman

Tanya Carinae Pell Jones

Lucy has gone through the wardrobe and into the cold, Narnian landscape thousands of times with countless readers trailing after her. So too has Alice tumbled headlong down her rabbit-hole and into Wonderland while wide eyes and fingers (both big and small) track her movements across the page. And somewhere, even now, a book is being cracked so a portal can be opened and a reader can cross a boundary between worlds.

Neil Gaiman is not the first author to toy with the notion of worlds within worlds. The idea that there are worlds just beyond our line of sight has been a part of literature for hundreds of years as has the necessity of a point of entry. The portal between the reality and fantasy worlds is usually an everyday object:

> [T]here is an object, at first not much noticed...as being of great importance...until it becomes plain that these objects are, in a way, touchstones: visible, physical concentrations of time magic.[1]

Mirrors, wardrobes, tollbooths, rabbit-holes, books—all have been portals into other worlds. The entry point may vary from story to story by growing larger or smaller, changing shape or changing color. The world beyond the gate may be upside down, from a different time, or on a different planet. But stories have shown us the portal is there and so is the world beyond.

Traditionally in fantasy literature, a portal is a passage between worlds. Specifically, the portal is employed "to move a character from the Primary to the Secondary space" or, rather, to move them from their (and generally the reader's) *known/reality* to the *unknown/fantasy*.[2] It should be noted that I will be using Tolkien's definitions from his essay "On Fairy Stories," referring to conventional reality as the Primary world and the fantasy beyond the portal as the Secondary world. The crossing of the threshold means passing beyond the established bounds of reality and into a neighboring world, one that is, quite often, a distorted mirror image of what we think of as reality. This movement symbolizes a character's desire for more than they have been allotted in their Primary world and inevitably results in a change for that character. By making the movement between the known and the unknown, the characters are, consciously or not, putting themselves in a position where they will forever be altered.

The change in the character is mandatory, for every journey or adventure has its costs/rewards. In his work *The Hero with a Thousand Faces,* Joseph Campbell said as much when he outlined the hero's journey:

> The hero adventures out of the land we know into darkness; there he accomplishes his adventure, or again is simply lost to us, imprisoned, or in danger; and his return is described as a coming back out of yonder zone.[3]

Thus, regardless of the specifics of the journey, there are three possible outcomes: the character will return to their world changed for the better, changed for the worse, or they will not return at all.

In 2002, Neil Gaiman introduced us to the titular character in his novella *Coraline.* Early in the book, it is clear that Coraline Jones is a very average, unextraordinary little girl with ordinary parents and a peculiar name that her neighbors seem unwilling to pronounce properly. Though Gaiman's heroine seems to have a penchant for exploring, it is only in a moment of boredom when she is wandering around her flat that she ultimately discovers the doorway through which her adventures will begin. There originally seems to be nothing remarkable about the door and the only reason it catches Coraline's attention is because it is the only door in the house that appears to be locked. As Tolkien pointed out in his essay "On Fairy Stories," a "Locked Door stands as Eternal Temptation," and Coraline immediately entreats her mother to open it.[4] Her mother assures her it leads nowhere and, indeed, only a brick wall is revealed upon opening, so the door is quickly dismissed as nothing special. But the savvy reader knows otherwise.

Soon, just as Tolkien predicted, the locked door is too great of an enticement for Coraline to resist despite the initial encounter of the brick wall beyond the threshold. She knows, as all children do, that there must be more to the door than appearance would have her believe. So, at the first opportunity, Coraline retrieves the key and fits it in the lock. This time when the door swings open, the bricks are gone and a hallway is in its place. Now, Coraline must decide if she is willing to move beyond the safe boundary of her home and through the portal without knowing what is on the other side. She has speculations, of course. Her first thought is that it is simply the empty flat next door. But that doesn't explain the now missing brick wall. This little detail does not deter our heroine and, like countless characters before her, Coraline makes a choice to move beyond the veil and into her adventure, eager to put an end to her boredom and become the explorer she imagines herself to be.

When Coraline takes that first, deliberate step into the corridor, she is crossing the threshold into another world—an oddly distorted, incomplete version of her own world populated by "bad copies" of her neighbors and, more importantly, her "Other Mother" and "Other Father." Like the world beyond the door, these parent doppelgängers are imperfect representations of her real parents; dirty mirror images of Mr. and Mrs. Jones. The same holds true for the faultily cloned neighbors. But, like Carroll's Alice could have told us and as the Other Mother says, "Mirrors... are never to be trusted."[5] For just like a mirror shows only a limited amount of the space it reflects, so too does the "Other Mother's World" only branch out so far. As Coraline ventures away from the Other Mother's House only to immediately return to it, she finds that the scope of the world is rather small and that her Other Mother stopped creating when she had enough of a copy of the Primary world to please Coraline:

> "But how can you walk away from something and still come back to it?"
> "Easy," said the cat. "Think of somebody walking around the world. You start walking away from something and end up coming back to it."
> "Small world," said Coraline.
> "It's big enough for her," said the cat. "Spiders' webs only have to be large enough to catch flies."[6]

The world Coraline has crossed into is one of very narrow boundaries. She may have entered another world when she crossed through the portal, but it is a small world indeed, constructed with great care by the Other Mother to entice and deceive. However, as the cat pointed out, a trap only has to be big enough to ensnare.

Temptation is how this Other Mother, with her black button eyes and twisted version of love, truly entangles her victims. She simply baits her trap (in this case, the Secondary world) with everything her prey could desire. It is here, possibly, that we see the reason for Coraline's adventure. On a rainy day with nothing to do, she craves the exploration of an adventure, to prove her independence, and to even be a little disobedient. She had been denied her desires by her real parents (the Day-Glo gloves and the opportunity to do as she pleased) and is susceptible to enticement, especially when promised whatever her heart desired. In her Primary world, Coraline has been made to want. But in the Other Mother's World (the Secondary world), Coraline finds that she will never be bored and, most certainly, "never be allowed to want."[7] Nothing is denied her in the Other Mother's World because it is a world created for the sole purpose of pleasing Coraline in the hopes of trapping her forever. But the most gilded cage is still a cage, and Coraline soon realizes that having everything you could ever want means that you will simply never have the opportunity *to want*:

> I don't *want* whatever I want. Nobody does. Not really. What kind of fun would it be if I just got everything I ever wanted? Just like that, and it didn't mean anything. What then?[8]

Coraline *needed* the adventure beyond the portal in order to take a step into maturity. She is growing up and this is evident in her recognition of the fact that life does not mean getting everything you desire. The wanting is part of the process. Her adventures and trials in the Other Mother's World are milestones of maturity that require her to turn her back on the twisted Eden and, instead, fight for the return of her real parents. Coraline wins, but it takes being unselfish, a true indicator of maturity, and channeling reserves of will she was unaware she possessed to return to her Primary world more "grown up" and appreciative of a life that will be ripe with both days of boredom and gray clouds as well as countless joys.

Coraline is not Neil Gaiman's only child hero to move through the portal. In his short story-within-a-story, "October in the Chair," we meet ten-year-old Donald "Runt" Covay. Runt, dissatisfied with the way he is treated by his teachers, his parents, and especially his twin brothers, decides to run away from home. With his backpack full of candy, comics, and thirty-seven dollars in quarters, Runt purchases a bus ticket "west." When he climbs off the bus, he walks along a dirty stream with the intention of following it to the seaside. However, fate has other plans.

Unlike Coraline, who has to open the portal and cross into another world to interact with the fantastic, the fantastic comes out to meet Runt in a moonlit pasture in the form of a little ghost boy. The ghost child, who introduces himself as "Dearly," though he "used to have another name, but can't read it anymore," invites Runt to play with him in the abandoned houses near his little graveyard and to climb trees in the moonlight.[9] In Dearly, Runt has found a kindred spirit, a boy just as lonely and desperate for a friend.

In this instance, the two worlds have become one. Runt is able to experience the fantasy of a Secondary world while still keeping himself in the boundaries of his Primary world. He has not accidentally fallen into "Faërie" (at least not that we know), but he is still experiencing the fantastic and supernatural elements that are generally reserved for the Secondary worlds. No portal has been crossed and no physical boundary has been breached. Yet.

The confrontation of the portal comes near dawn, when Dearly must—as his tombstone implies—"depart." But, Runt is reluctant to surrender the only friend he has ever had and he realizes that if he continues with his original scheme to run away to the sea, he will be found and forced back home. In a moment of desperation, he suggests that he might stay in the little graveyard with his new friend. But, in order to do that, he would have to be as dead as his new friend. Dearly suggests that Runt consider looking for "help" in the abandoned farmhouse that borders the pasture:

> "I can't do it," said Dearly, eventually. "But they might."
> "Who?"
> "The ones in there." The fair boy pointed up the slope to the tumbledown farmhouse with the jagged, broken windows, silhouetted against the dawn. The gray light had not changed it. The runt shivered. "There's people in there?" he said. "I thought you said it was empty."
> "It ain't empty," said Dearly. "I said nobody lives there. Different things." [10]

Once again, Gaiman's portal is an actual door. This time, however, the doorway is not as tempting as Coraline's. Runt knows full well that nothing good lies beyond this threshold whereas Coraline had to venture beyond hers before she could learn that fact. Runt's doorway is an almost literal separation between light, the known, and dark, the unknown: "It was darker inside there. Darker than anything."[11] Gaiman paints for us a vivid picture of a child caught between worlds and, once again, an issue of growing up is at stake. Does Runt wait to be caught, go home, and grow up as an inconsequential shadow fading in and out of rooms? Or does he cross the barrier in an attempt to ensure he never grows up at all?

Just like Coraline, Runt has to make a choice: stay in his Primary world where he knows the rules and can guess at the outcomes, or venture beyond the veil and into the unknown. After eating his last candy bar and weighing his options, a terrified Runt walks up the farmhouse steps: "He stopped at the doorway, hesitantly, wondering if this was wise. He could smell damp, and rot, and something else underneath...Eventually, he went inside."[12] Here, very *unlike* Coraline, Runt has decided growing up is just too hard.

Runt's desire for a life different from the one he had been dealt is stronger than his instinct for self-preservation. He does what all children have dreamed of doing at one time or another: run away. However, by making the choice to enter the portal and cross into the farmhouse where danger—and perhaps death—almost certainly awaits, he has willingly thrown away his ties to reality, choosing instead the fantasy. Though it is possible that Runt will be granted his rather unusual wish to remain in the graveyard, he may find it more costly than he anticipated. Oddly enough, the average reader is quite likely rooting for Runt's wish to be granted because we have been privy to the sad (though certainly not abusive) circumstances of his home life. We end up wanting Runt to be able to play with Dearly for eternity, even though we are consciously aware of the probable danger lurking in the darkness beyond the farmhouse door. Gaiman leaves us guessing as to what happens to Runt, but the reader is certain of one thing: Runt will not emerge from the house unchanged (if he comes out at all).

Often, portal-quests feature a character who intentionally moves through the portal; crossing the boundaries between worlds in pursuit of an adventure. Yet, many characters are drawn through the gates and into the unknown without their knowledge or consent. These unwilling heroes may not realize what is happening to them until it is too late since an "adventure may begin as a mere blunder...or still again, one may be only casually strolling, when some passing phenomenon catches the wandering eye and lures one away from the frequented paths of man."[13] This is what happened to one of Gaiman's most memorable characters, Richard Mayhew, in his urban-fantasy, *Neverwhere*.

As the hero of his own portal-quest, Richard manages to move— though unwillingly—from his safe, urban life in "London Above" to the "sewers and the magic and the dark" of "London Below."[14] London Below, a nonsensical mirror image of the city of London, is a labyrinthine world of tunnels and sewers and subways that operates under fantasy rules. In the Secondary world of London Below, those people that "fell through the cracks of the world" have created a realm where rats are to be respected, one's life can be kept in a trinket box as insurance against death, and succubae prey on the warmth of others. It is this world that Richard Mayhew has fallen helplessly into through a simple act of kindness.

Walking to dinner one night with his overbearing fiancée, Richard, a rather dull and absent minded individual, finds a "homeless" girl bleeding in the street. He treats her wounds, lies for her when questioned, and even relays a message to a man known as the Marquis de Carabas, a mysterious figure who deals in favors. However, after helping the girl (an inhabitant of London Below), Richard has somehow become disassociated within his own reality. His employers no longer recognize him, his fiancée has no recollection of him, and his landlord cannot see him. For all intents and purposes, Richard no longer exists in his own world. So, he does the only thing he can think to do: find the "homeless" girl in hopes that she can undo the damage.

The portal "through which" Richard will traverse into the fantasy realm of London Below is rather unconventional. The girl Richard found in the streets that he cared for is actually the Lady Door, daughter of the late Lord Portico. Door—"Like something you walk through to go places"—is an "opener."[15] Door's family has been gifted with the ability to "open doors. They can create doors where there were no doors. They can unlock doors that are locked. Open doors that were never meant to be opened."[16] In a sense, they *are* doors. It is his first encounter with Door that puts Richard at odds with his known reality; he has broken through the invisible barrier between worlds and into the unknown. His portal *is* a "door," but not in the traditional sense. In *Neverwhere*, Gaiman has created not just a separation of worlds by an invisible boundary, but he has also utilized a device known as a *porter*.

A porter, much like a portal, is a means of conveyance from "here to there." However, unlike the traditional doorway, porters are "all those living beings...that act as agents for the hero(ine) to travel between worlds."[17] Here, Gaiman has introduced a porter by the name of Door to *act* as Richard's doorway between worlds. (Obviously, Gaiman used a lighthearted touch when naming the family of "openers" after the very symbols they represent: Door, Portico, Portia, Ingress, and Arch.) Richard will use the subterranean passages in the underworld to travel through the physical spaces of the two worlds, but it is Door herself who is the true portal in the story: "The action of helping her had tumbled him from his world into hers."[18]

Yet, the "tumbling" Richard does from one world to another is both linear and "multi-dimensional." Richard is able to physically move from his Primary world of London Above, into the sewers of London Below and back again following a linear course, but by interacting with Door (a living portal), he is no longer truly "there" in his Primary world. He has become an interloper. He may physically be occupying space, but he is no longer perceived in that space (just as Alice's Looking-Glass House reflects what is not there as well as what is). Richard struggles with this very notion when he and Anaesthesia, a rat-speaker, are trying to locate the floating market. Anaesthesia tries to explain to Richard that even though the market is held in a physical space that they could reach easily from London Above, the market would not be "there" should they try to reach it using any passage from that world:

> "We can get to the place it's in," she said. "But the market wouldn't be there."
> "Huh? But that's ridiculous. I mean, something's either there or it's not. Isn't it?"

She shook her head.[19]

A similar conversation about object permanence was held between Peter, Susan, and the Professor in C.S. Lewis' *The Lion, the Witch, and the Wardrobe*. Peter insisted that Lucy's account of Narnia through the wardrobe was fabrication if for no other reason than Narnia had not been there when they had opened the wardrobe themselves:

> "There was nothing there when we looked; even Lucy didn't pretend there was."
> "What has that to do with it?" said the Professor.
> "Well, sir, if things are real, they're there all the time."
> "Are they?" said the Professor; and Peter didn't know quite what to say.[20]

Richard, like Peter Pevensie, cannot immediately rationalize a world where things can be there and not at the same time. For him, space and time have always been linear, but in London Below the rules seem to have distorted. These "new rules" explain Door's associative home where the rooms are located miles apart from each other and how there are creatures and people in the tunnels that time cannot seem to touch. So, though he can physically move beyond the barrier from one place to another in a linear fashion, circumstances and characteristics *of* the space may change based on his orientation in the Primary or Secondary world and the road he chooses to travel. This paradox that Gaiman has created in *Neverwhere* makes the boundaries between the two worlds both visible (linear) *and* invisible (multi-dimensional).

And yet, the idea of invisible barriers is not as strange as we would immediately believe. We consciously create boundaries and imaginary lines and borders to keep us safe and grounded in reality, especially globally and socially. In *Neverwhere*, Gaiman is merely illustrating that the world is boundless, yet we imagine boundaries everywhere: between nations, between social classes, and even between races. Gaiman, in an interview, addressed this very issue and has insisted on boundaries being "completely notional. They don't tend to exist…They're just imaginary lines we draw on maps."[21] By using both visible physical boundaries (London in relation to the underworld of the sewers) and invisible social boundaries (those from London Above in relation to the homeless/forgotten), Gaiman is challenging the reader to step outside the safety of preconceived notions and look at things from a different perspective, even if that means challenging norms and social values. Joseph Campbell argued a similar point about value systems in the two worlds in *The Hero with a Thousand Faces*:

> [T]he exploration of that dimension, either willingly or unwillingly, is the whole sense of the deed of the hero. The values and distinctions that in normal life seem important disappear with the terrifying assimilation of the self into what was formally only otherness.[22]

In London Below, the things Richard previously thought were important have little meaning, forcing him to turn inward to see what truly matters. Gaiman's hero does challenge social norms and Richard is perfect as an ambassador between worlds because he is heroic enough—and possibly simple enough—to see past outward appearances.

Though it is his selfless act of compassion for a stranger that forces Richard into the Secondary world, it is his desire to return to the normalcy of his Primary world that originally guides his feet throughout his adventures with Door and her companions. Richard's quest is ripe with peril in the forms of Mr. Croup and Mr. Vandemar, two masochistic figures who stalk his and Door's every step, a fallen angel, and the horrors and nightmares found below the surface. But, Richard is desperate to return to his previous life and he is willing to assist Door on her quest if it means getting back to where he feels he belongs.

To his dismay, however, Richard is told by his new associates that he cannot return to his Primary world of London Above. They insist he is suddenly and irrevocably one of society's forgotten:

> "You can't go back to London Above. A few individuals manage a kind of half life…But that's the best you could hope for, and it isn't a good life."[23]

Time and again, Richard rejects this notion by claiming he does not belong in the Secondary world. He feels cheated out of his life and maintains there must be something that can be done to give him back the life he lost. His determination is not admired by his companions below. Instead, they look upon him with pity and frustration for his inability to understand that the place he considers "the real world" is closed to him and there is no going home again: "You can't. It's one or the other. Nobody ever gets both."[24]

And yet, all is not lost for Richard Mayhew. Through a twist of fate, it seems that Richard does have the power to go home. Since he is the one who conquered the ordeal of the Black Friars to win "the key to all reality," he has become its master.[25] By using the key and Door as his opener, Richard returns to London Above where he is recognized and accepted back into the Primary world as if he had only been on vacation.

So, Richard goes home, like many characters before him, to the Primary world changed for the better after having assisted Door, defeating the great Beast of London, and saving the world(s) from a fallen angel who would overtake Heaven. The hero, as Joseph Campbell predicted, has returned.

The problem with his return, however, is Richard cannot forget his time in London Below. Suddenly, the predictable Primary world with its work, pubs, and warm home is no longer enough (if it ever was in the first place). Though he was previously sure it was exactly what he wanted, Richard feels that his life is lacking substance after his return: "Have you ever got everything you ever wanted? And then realized it wasn't what you wanted at all?"[26] Richard, a mere observer in his own life prior to the crossing of the threshold, is no longer satisfied with the role he plays in his Primary reality because the void he now feels was once filled by adventure in the Secondary world. Richard *has been* changed by his adventures in London Below, and many of those changes were for the better, but now the safe life of mediocrity is too difficult to bear. So, in a moment of inspiration and intense longing, Richard uses Hunter's knife to scratch the outline of a door into a wall. As if waiting for him, the Marquis appears, offering Richard a chance to return once more to the Secondary world. Richard, like Runt, chooses the fantasy and he and the Marquis walk "away together through the hole in the wall, back into the darkness, leaving nothing behind them; not even the doorway."[27]

The portal, however, is not always as tangible as a doorway or a girl. Sometimes, the portal has no physical location, but it is there all the same. Perhaps it exists in that place between sleep and awake where we begin to dream. It is Morpheus, Neil Gaiman's Dream King who rules this realm, guarding the portal as he passes in and out of worlds on a whim, leaping through dreams and nightmares, often dragging the unsuspecting along with him.

In Neil Gaiman's revolutionary comic series *The Sandman*, Gaiman wrote into being The Endless (Dream, Death, Destiny, Desire, Delirium, Despair, and Destruction), seven personifications of traditional mythological archetypes with a twist. Gaiman, a lover of mythology in all its forms, created The Endless to represent and control—or at least manipulate—various aspects of the universe, giving each anthropomorphic personality their own dominion (as their names suggest). As the title implies, *The Sandman* is really a collection that follows the true Sandman, Dream (aka Morpheus, The Dream Lord, The Prince of Stories, *etc.*), as he loses his power, regains it, makes choices and "faces obstacles, tests, and trials before coming to realize his ultimate destiny."[28] In his outline for the original series, Gaiman said Dream's primary functions were "to rule the world of dreams" and "to guard the borders of things, since it is possible for dream things to escape into other places."[29]

The portal between the waking world and the Sandman's "dreamworld" is the thin veil of sleep. Unlike the other portal quests discussed in this chapter, the portal in *The Sandman* series is open to all those who sleep and dream. In most fantasy featuring a portal-quest, the portal will only open for the hero(es) of the story, but each person that dreams becomes the hero of his or her own story. Though some may venture further into the dreamworld than others, the portal, and by consequence the land beyond, is not restricted to a select few: "Each human is connected to the dreaming. They spend a third of their lives in this realm."[30] The consequence of the crossing of the threshold and into the dream is that we do not have control over the dream because dreamers move "into the adventurous realm unconsciously, as we all do every night when we go to sleep."[31] Morpheus controls the "Dreaming," and he manipulates it at will.

Just like the portal between reality and the Dreaming is more conceptual than physical, so are the boundaries that border the Dreaming: "Beyond, outside my dreamworld there is infinite dust, infinite dark. And the dreamworld is infinite, although it is bounded on every side."[32] In Gaiman's *The Sandman*, there seem to be no specific borders to the dreamworld, but references are made to the possibility of kingdom limitations. For example, after Dream's escape from the seventy-year imprisonment that opens the storyline, Dream tries to return to his castle in the center of the Dreaming, "but weakened and exhausted, [he] stumbled through the FRINGES of the DREAMTIME."[33] Though Gaiman does not indicate exactly what the "fringes" of Dream's realm are, one can make the assumption that these areas are on the outskirts of his realm.

In issue #39 "Soft Places," an even more specific allusion to borders is made as a young Marco Polo and Rustichello of Pisa sit alongside the physical incarnation of dreamt place, Fiddler's Green, as "he" tells the men how they have managed to come together and chat outside of time. His claim is they have accidentally stumbled into one of the "soft places" of the world. Fiddler's Green tells the two:

> Time at the edge of the dreaming is softer than elsewhere, and here in the soft places it leaps and whorls on itself. In the soft places where the border between dreams and reality is eroded or not yet formed... Time.
> It's like throwing a stone into a pool. It casts ripples...That's where we are. Here. In the soft places, where the geographies of dream intrude upon the real.[34]

In fact, not only does Fiddler's Green explain what the "soft places" are to the men, but he admonishes them (especially Marco Polo) for the part they played in the loss of such places: "[Soft places] were a sight more common than now...sometimes I think their loss is your fault...the explorers, and the ones who came after you, who froze the world into rigid patterns."[35] This is not the only time Gaiman has used his prose to reproach those who dissect the world into puzzle pieces. In his novel *Stardust*, Gaiman spoke of Faerie (the fantasy) as being composed of "each land that has been forced off the map by explorers and the brave going out and proving it wasn't there."[36] With Gaiman's own feelings about borders being "completely notional," it is no wonder that so many of his stories have characters moving beyond those borders and into new worlds.

    As the portal and the boundaries of the Dreaming are theoretical, so too is the Dreaming itself. When Gaiman outlined his original proposal for *The Sandman*, he explained the setting of the Dreamworld as "the sum total of the part of the human psyche that expresses itself through dreams; and it's a place; and it's the dreams of people who are dreaming at that time; and it's a state of mind."[37] Gaiman did not force himself into a corner by making the Dreaming a territory limited by physical criteria. The world he created *is* infinite because it *has the potential to be* infinite as each character dreams up his or her own land. This means that the world beyond the veil of sleep is a shifting landscape of endless possibilities. With no physical restrictions on the setting, Gaiman could have created each character's version of the Dreamworld to fit his or her storyline.

    Yet, we are not bound to only reality and Dream's realm in *The Sandman*. Though the majority of the stories take place in either the Primary world or the Dreaming, other Secondary worlds make appearances as well. Morpheus travels to the Christian ideal of Hell in multiple issues. We are not told where Hell is located, yet we can infer that it is not anywhere we can travel to by moving in a linear fashion. According to Dream, the road to Hell is "not a place, after all. It is BETWEEN places. [It] is NOWHERE."[38] The realms of other Endless are also visited; we are given glimpses into the homes and kingdoms of Destiny, Desire, and Delirium. Again, the whereabouts of the realms are vague and open to interpretation. They are not necessarily *in* the Primary world, but they are not separate from it either. Without being told the specifics of the kingdoms, we are still able to infer a difference between "here and there" in Gaiman's writings. Here again, these Secondary worlds are just as notional as the Dreaming.

    Like all characters in portal-quests, as they move between worlds, the characters in *The Sandman* are altered permanently, sometimes for good, sometimes for ill, and, sometimes, they never leave the Dreaming at all. Morpheus, as master of the realm, is the least affected by the movement between worlds; rather, he is affected by the characters he meets on his journeys as he moves across the divide. It is these other characters that are truly changed by going through the portal and into the Sandman's realm.

Early in the series, Morpheus escapes from captivity and quests to find his tokens of power: a helm, a pouch, and a ruby. After the Dreamstone ruby is taken, it changes hands, finally falling under the control of John Dee. Dee used the ruby to become Doctor Destiny, controlling the dreams and nightmares of his victims in a corrupted version of Dream's powers. With the ruby in his possession, Dee can actually move into the Dreaming as Morpheus would, forsaking the portal of sleep. It is the ruby that becomes Dee's portal, but it was never intended as such and it ultimately destroys his sanity. In a battle between Dee and Morpheus in the Dreaming, the ruby is destroyed and Dream's powers returned to him. In the end, it is Morpheus who remarks that manipulating the fabric of the Dreaming must have caused irrevocable damage to Dee: "[The ruby] was not made for mortals. The damage to your mind must have been considerable."[39] Dee has been permanently damaged from possession of the ruby and his movement between worlds—drunk with a power he never had the skill to control.

However, it is the women of *The Sandman* series who seem to cause the greatest stirs in both Dream and his realm as they cross the threshold. In several issues, we encounter Nada, a former lover of Morpheus. Nada, though manipulated by Desire, follows Morpheus into his world through the dream portal. When she realizes that it is Dream of the Endless she loves, she flees from the Dreaming and back to reality "because it is not given to mortals to love the Endless. Only disaster can follow from it."[40] Morpheus, intrigued by love, offers to make her his queen. Though she tries to escape him, Nada eventually capitulates to her desires, but the city she ruled is razed to the ground as a result. In a last effort to escape Dream—and to save both of them—Nada throws herself from a mountaintop. Morpheus follows her into Death's realm and asks her again to be his. She refuses and, as punishment for wounding his pride, Dream condemns her to eternal suffering in Hell. Nada, like Dee, crossed a portal and into Secondary worlds. Though Nada *tried* to resist the temptation of the fantasy while Dee sought to immerse himself further *into* it, the outcomes are still the same, leaving both to suffer.

Not all of Gaiman's female characters see their stories "end" with such pain, however. Rose Walker and Barbie are both heroines that undergo severe tribulations and losses by moving through the Dreaming, yet come out better for their pains on the return side of the portal. Rose, her life threatened by Morpheus when he reveals she is a vortex (a destructive dreaming force), is rewarded for her troubles with a reunion with her kidnapped little brother and a new outlook on life. Emotionally scarred Barbie, who must face the wrath of the Cuckoo (a dream entity) when she passes into the Dreaming, learns she is a strong, independent woman after her adventures in Morpheus' realm. While on their quests, both women put others before their own wishes. Though their losses are great, their gains are just as powerful. Rose and Barbie needed to journey through the veil of dreams to help others and find themselves so they could return to reality with new purpose, for "[i]t's the journeys we make for others that give us the power to change ourselves."[41]

The theme of desires comes around again in *The Sandman*. Gaiman, who consistently refers to this theme in his writing, seems to be of the opinion that wants are generally fleeting things and suggests that we tend to take life for granted in the pursuit of momentary pleasures. Morpheus, as Gaiman's creation, is of the same opinion: "[Mortals] only see the prize, their heart's desire, their dream...But the price of getting what you want is getting what you once wanted."[42] When we achieve our heart's desire, there always seems to be something new to take its place. "Mortals" are rarely satisfied. Coraline, Richard Mayhew, and possibly Runt, learned this lesson stepping through their own portals. Getting what you want has to mean something and what you get is sometimes not what you thought it would be. Yet, time and again, the characters Neil Gaiman creates grow and change and learn.

So it would seem that Neil Gaiman's characters tend to step through the portals and into other lands in order to find who they truly are. Sometimes this journey across the threshold is at odds with what they feel they want or even deserve. Sometimes it turns out they are right. Regardless, the movement through the portal and across the boundaries of neighboring worlds is a way for characters to confront desires, chase dreams, and find what they truly need. And we are invited to take that journey with them as they move portals and between worlds.

Gaiman's portal stories resonate with the memories of our own imaginings as children when we passed a wardrobe or a mirror and wondered, "What if?" We are captivated by his words because they so clearly illuminate the spaces where our reality ends and our dreams begin. As heroes of our own stories, Neil Gaiman challenges us to pass through the portals and discover new worlds of our own.

---

1 Tal, "Tony and the Wonderful Door," 133.
2 Campbell, et al., *Portals of Power*, 14.
3 Campbell, *The Hero with a Thousand Faces*, 217.
4 Tolkien, "On Fairy-Stories," 33.
5 Gaiman, *Coraline*, 92.
6 Gaiman, *Coraline*, 89.
7 Coats, "Between Horror, Humour, and Hope," 87.
8 Gaiman, *Coraline*, 145.

9 Gaiman, *Fragile*, 38.
10 Gaiman, *Fragile*, 42.
11 Ibid.
12 Ibid.
13 Campbell, *Hero*, 58.
14 Gaiman, *Neverwhere*, 128.
15 Gaiman, *Neverwhere*, 40.
16 Gaiman, *Neverwhere*, 323.
17 Campbell, et al., *Portals of Power*, 6.
18 Gaiman, *Neverwhere*, 30.
19 Gaiman, *Neverwhere*, 100.
20 Lewis, *The Lion, the Witch, and the Wardrobe*, 45.
21 Crispin, Interview with Neil Gaiman, October 2006.
22 See note 3.
23 Gaiman, *Neverwhere*, 340.
24 Gaiman, *Neverwhere*, 88.
25 Gaiman, *Neverwhere*, 341.
26 Gaiman, *Neverwhere*, 368.
27 Gaiman, *Neverwhere*, 370.
28 Wagner, et al., *Prince of Stories*, 30.
29 Gaiman, *The Absolute Sandman*, Vol. I, 547.
30 Gaiman, *The Absolute Sandman*, Vol. I, 298.
31 Campbell, *Hero*, 220.
32 Gaiman, *The Absolute Sandman*, Vol. I, 63.
33 Gaiman, *The Absolute Sandman*, Vol. I, 56.
34 Gaiman, *The Absolute Sandman*, Vol. II, 496.
35 Ibid.
36 Gaiman, *Stardust*, 84.
37 Gaiman, *The Absolute Sandman*, Vol. I, 450.
38 Gaiman, *The Absolute Sandman*, Vol. II, 61.
39 Gaiman, *The Absolute Sandman*, Vol. I, 200.
40 Gaiman, *The Absolute Sandman*, Vol. I, 243.
41 O'Keefe, *Readers in Wonderland*, 37.
42 Gaiman, *The Absolute Sandman*, Vol. I, 514.

The End of the World as We Know It: Neil Gaiman and the Future of Mythology

Lynn Gelfand

The pre-Socratic Greek philosopher Heraclitus once noted, "Nothing is permanent except for change."[1] While change can be deeply invigorating, it can also be highly disorienting and truly threatening. It should come as no surprise that many myths portray the mental and physical stress that often accompanies significant cultural change as a clash between old and new deities. Neil Gaiman's novel *American Gods* builds upon this rich mythic tradition. *American Gods*, however, depicts not simply a battle between old and new gods in a fight for survival; it suggests that if the pace of technology continues to accelerate, even new and powerful gods can become obsolete within a matter of decades rather than centuries. The theme of world-shaking disruption is also found in the theories of American inventor and author Ray Kurzweil who has argued that at the current rate of technological development, the next fifty years of human achievement will be the equivalent of ten thousand years of progress. How will mythology — one of the most ancient narrative genres in human history— fare under such conditions? Gaiman's body of work suggests some provocative answers.

To understand the role of mythology in Gaiman's stories, we need to first look at the function of culture. Cultures are formal constructions designed to reduce the impact of chaos and random experience. A culture is a set of learned beliefs and behaviors that provide a sense of order and cohesion —qualities that make it more likely for a people to survive the vagaries of nature. Myths are traditional narratives that shape and support the intellectual, emotional, and social features of a culture, making the abstract principles of a society concrete and comprehensible through stories that bind a people together and ensure the continued stability of a culture from generation to generation.

Yet, to survive, myths must be relevant to a culture, and to remain relevant, myths must fit the changing social, economic, and technological requirements of a society. This process is often represented in myth as a conflict or war between competing gods. An example of such a conflict can be found in Hesiod's *Theogony*, an account of the early Greek gods written in the eighth century BCE. Out of Chaos came Gaia ("Earth"), who gave birth to Uranus ("Sky"), with whom she conceived many children. Among them were Rhea ("Stream") and Cronus ("Time"). Uranus refused to let his children see the light of day and forced them to remain in the bowels of the earth. To free her children, Gaia armed her son Cronus with a sickle. While Uranus and Gaia copulated, Cronus castrated his father, destroying Uranus' power and simultaneously separating the earth from the sky. Cronus ascended to his father's position and Rhea replaced Gaia.[2]

Like their parents, Rhea and Cronus produced children: Hestia, Demeter, Hera, Hades, Poseidon, and Zeus. Cronus knew that he was destined to be overthrown by one of his children and devoured each child as it was born. To save her youngest child, Rhea hid Zeus in a cave and gave Cronus a stone swaddled in a blanket to swallow. After Zeus grew to maturity, Rhea tricked Cronus into disgorging her other children, who then joined Zeus in overthrowing their father.[3] Zeus emerged from the battle as the sovereign of the gods, as well as the god of the sky and of thunder. Hera became his spouse and the goddess of marriage. Poseidon took charge of the seas while Hades ruled the underworld. Demeter was established as the goddess of the grain and Hestia became the goddess of the hearth fire.

Each succeeding generation of Greek gods in the *Theogony* reflects a significant social, economic, and technological shift in culture. Gaia and Uranus represent the deities of a gatherer-hunter society, where human life is dominated by the powerful forces of nature above and the churning fecundity of nature below. Rhea and Cronus are also closely connected to the potency of the earth, but while Gaia represents the earth in its totality, Rhea is the earth specifically in relation to time; Rhea and Cronus are the gods of an agricultural society, where crops are periodically planted and harvested and where animals are domesticated as sources of farm labor as well as food.

By the time we come to the generation of Zeus and Hera, we see a more complex model of society, the city-state, which depends upon specialized skills and roles to sustain itself. The compartmentalization of society is echoed in the characteristics of the gods who dominate this increasingly urbane environment. Though Zeus, like his grandfather Uranus, is identified with the sky, he shares power to some extent with his brothers, who reign over different parts of the earth. Hera has strong and deep roots as a mother-goddess, but Hera's connection to fertility in classical Greece is secondary to her role as the wife of Zeus and the queen of the Olympians. Demeter, a goddess who is intimately linked to the cycle of plant life and to motherhood, remains closer to the chthonic operations associated with Rhea and Gaia, but by the classical era she is not strongly identified with sexual love (the realm of Aphrodite), animal young (the world of Artemis), or spring plants (Kore's domain). Like a prism refracting white light into a spectrum of individual colors, the society of classical Greece has reconfigured the earth goddess and her consort into a multitude of related but distinct deities.

A close study of traditional mythologies reveals narratives in a state of continual flux. This process of change is usually not apparent within one's lifetime, but it can be seen incrementally over a span of centuries. The mythical beings depicted in *The Sandman* graphic novels portray the age-old conflict between stability and change as it relates to modern society. Let's look more closely at four mythic characters in *The Sandman* (Odin, Ishtar, Lucifer, and Dream) and see how they recapitulate the often tense relationship between the need for cultural stability and the drive for change.

Odin in *Season of Mists* is a god from an ancient belief system. A clever and somewhat sinister chess master-figure, the Norse ruler of the gods seeks to assume control of the Christian Hell after Lucifer hands it over to Dream. Odin's character in *Season of Mists* does not deviate greatly from the deity found in traditional myth; he is instantly recognizable by his grim demeanor and his goal to avoid the predestined Nordic apocalypse, Ragnarök. The only significant alteration Gaiman has made to Odin has been to place him in a larger mythological context, among gods from diverse cultures. This, however, is highly important. Though still a powerful presence, Odin in *Season of Mists* is now merely one god among a multitude of supernatural beings from all over the world, all attempting to gain dominion of a realm outside their traditional spheres of power, reflecting the growing competition among different cultures in an increasingly global society.

Ishtar in *Brief Lives* is another ancient deity. Yet unlike Odin, who retains the same mythic persona found in traditional Norse mythology, Ishtar struggles to adapt to a contemporary world that no longer values what she represents. A former lover of Dream's absent brother Destruction, Ishtar is a stripper in the modern world. However, she was once the powerful and complex Assyro-Babylonian goddess of fertility, love, and war: a divine being who gave life and took it away, straddling the uncanny crossroads of desire and death. Ishtar describes temple sex in Babylon to her mortal friend and fellow stripper as a ritual that was a "terrifying experience for both the women and the men, where they gave themselves to lust and the unknown."[4]

In the modern world, Ishtar is reduced to living cheaply off of her sexual attributes to achieve the weak form of worship "generated by money given for lust."[5] The small pieces of paper now used to acquire goods and services have little in common with what was once considered wealth: grains, fruits, vegetables, and animals, as well as objects shaped by skilled human hands in exchange for food and other highly valued items. Now, all that exists of this economic fusion of nature and culture is a chain of increasingly abstract symbols: scraps of paper that stand for gold, which is a precious metal that once represented the sun, which is a celestial body that is intimately connected to the cyclical products of chthonic fertility. In our current monetary system, both Ishtar and the urban audience for whom she dances are far removed from the sacred sexual rituals that were once associated with the riches of the earth.

In contrast to the diminished Ishtar, Lucifer in *Season of Mists* is a strong entity from a contemporary belief system who openly challenges his traditional role in myth. A charming but ruthless fallen angel from Christianity, a being whom even Dream fears, Lucifer simply decides one day to abdicate his position as monarch of Hell. "Ten billion years I've spent in this place," Lucifer complains to Dream, "That's a long time...and we've all changed, since the beginning. Even you, Dream Lord. You were very different back then."[6]

Lucifer questions his well-established role as the villain in Christian mythology. "You know," he says of his rebellion against God, "I still wonder how much of it was planned. How much of it He knew in advance."[7] Rejecting his place in what appears to be a cosmic puppet show, Lucifer yearns for a more mundane form of existence: "I could lie on a beach somewhere....Learn how to dance, or to play the piano."[8] Gaiman turns inside out the Miltonian Lucifer of literature who declared that it was "Better to reign in Hell than serve in Heaven." Mocking both the fearsome Satan of Christianity and the grandly tragic anti-hero of Romantic literature, Gaiman's Lucifer craves an almost comically ordinary life, but one that, unlike his traditional role as the deifier of God's will, may truly be open to endless possibilities.

The Lucifer that emerges from the pages of *Season of Mists* reflects a society that embraces both the scientific Big Bang and the Judeo-Christian Genesis. He does not hesitate to put his own mythic status under a microscope, so to speak, coolly dissecting his myth's contradictions and sentimental values with the precision of a scientist. Yet he seems to relish his act of meta-rebellion with the fervor of a true religious believer. He is, ultimately, a postmodern mythic being: a creature of myth who laughs at his own paradoxes and rejects his own mythology.

By the end of the series, the archetypal Dream dies in *The Kindly Ones*, making way for his successor Daniel. The child of two DC Comics superheroes, Daniel gestated in the world of dreams and is therefore a spiritual son to Dream. Though Daniel is as attentive to his responsibilities as his predecessor, we find in *The Wake* that he is kinder and gentler than the grave and often pitiless Dream. Daniel is the embodiment of the compassion that gradually developed in Dream as the series progressed. In a sense, Daniel is the same Dream, but from a newer perspective, just as the Greek Rhea was a different type of earth-mother from her predecessor, Gaia. Throughout *The Sandman*, readers are shown that the mythical beings of various cultures and even the seemingly fixed archetypes that underlie those mythic beings can (and sometimes must) change.

The theme of modern mythic adaptation is central to Gaiman's novel *American Gods*, where the supernatural beings of the Old World must reconfigure themselves to suit the needs of the relatively newer culture of the United States, a country based chiefly on capitalistic principles rather than the agricultural or martial values from which the older gods drew their authority. For example, Anubis, an Egyptian god associated with the world of the dead, survives in the modern world by co-running a funeral parlor that caters to those who have been marginalized by racial discrimination—like the dead, their existence lies outside of the official social and economic system.

In *American Gods*, readers are introduced to Mr. Wednesday, an Americanized incarnation of Odin. (The term for the middle day of the week is derived from the name Wotan, the Germanic version of the Scandinavian Odin.) Acting as an employer and a mentor to our protagonist, Shadow, the Americanized version of Odin excels in the arts of the con man, amplifying the subtler trickster qualities associated with the Norse god who is identified with both wisdom and warfare. Mr. Wednesday has adapted the skills found in traditional myths of Odin to fit the cunning and cutthroat business practices that are often required to succeed in a capital-driven culture.

Quick-witted and fierce, Wednesday is the first to alert the gods of the Old World who have settled in the U.S. about the growing danger they face. They are at risk of being obliterated by "gods" who have little or no connection to traditional mythic systems: "of credit card and freeway, of Internet and telephone, of radio and hospital and television, gods of plastic and of beeper and of neon."[9] The sneering teenage boy who represents the Internet refers to religion as "an operating system"[10] and tells Shadow "we have fucking reprogrammed reality."[11] These new gods are lead by Mr. World, a mysterious figure who appears to represent the growing globalization brought about by recent advances in technology.

Some traditional gods answer Wednesday's call to arms, while others resist. It is not until Wednesday is assassinated by Mr. World on television that the old gods fully realize the threat the new gods pose to them. With the martyred Wednesday as a symbol of their righteous cause, the traditional gods declare war on the new gods and a bloody battle ensues. The battle is brought to a standstill midway when Shadow reveals the truth of what he has discovered to both sides: Mr. World is actually Loki in disguise. Wednesday's death had been a ruse. Fearing their own weakening power, Loki and Wednesday had been working together from the start in order to bring about a massive blood sacrifice of gods that would empower the two of them. Their con slyly made use of the terror of obsolesce that runs deeply through old and new gods in the U.S. — the one thing that unites the two warring sides. "There was arrogance to the new ones," Shadow observes, "But there was also fear. They were afraid that unless they kept pace with a changing world, unless they remade and redrew and rebuilt the world in their image, their time would already be over."[12]

It is no wonder that Loki is able to successfully assume the role of Mr. World in *American Gods*. A trickster god who is strongly associated with chaotic acts is, indeed, a fitting symbol for the clash of cultures and the general cacophony brought about by ever-changing societies in a globalized world. With its host of old gods struggling to remain relevant in the face of radical change, and its portrayal of new "gods" (automobiles, television, the Internet) who tear down tradition because they fear their own looming demise, Gaiman's *American Gods* offers readers a glimpse into a future of mythology that may have already started.

While the bloody war in *American Gods* eventually halted through Shadow's intervention, the over-arching issue of mythologies threatened by rapid cultural change remains unresolved. According to Ray Kurzweil, rapid cultural change will only accelerate in the coming decades. Kurzweil is an American inventor and entrepreneur who first began tracking the relationship between technology and social change when he realized that, to be successful, his inventions needed to make sense in terms of market forces.[13] In *The Singularity is Near*, Kurzweil explores the role of cultural change from the perspective of the development of human-created technologies, which allow people to extend their physical and mental capabilities through tools that are subject to a faster cycle of evolution than either the human body or brain, neither of which has changed drastically over tens of thousands of years.[14] Kurzweil foresees a time in the very near future where the pace of technological change will be so rapid due to the Law of Accelerating Returns (similar to Moore's Law) that human life will be radically altered — and continue to be altered ever after at an exponential rate. Changes that had once taken place over the course of centuries will take place in decades, and changes that once had taken place over decades will be seen in a matter of weeks. Over the next fifty years, we will see technology evolve in manner that will be the equivalent of ten thousand years of progress,[15] which predicts that by the middle of this century, the emerging technologies we have today will be integrated into our brains and bodies, allowing us to:

1. Amplify the cognitive abilities of the human brain by augmenting our relatively slow biochemical neural connections with high-speed electronic implants, resulting in greater pattern-recognition skills, memory storage, and overall thinking.[16]
2. Radically redesign our internal and external body parts, entirely replacing the digestive tract, for example, with nanobots in the bloodstream that can provide the precise nutrients we need.[17]
3. Overcome most forms of death thorough genetics /[18] or nanotechnology,[19] which will prevent or reverse damage to the body caused by illness, injury, or aging.
4. In essence, the distinction between humanity and its technologies will cease to exist as we use our technologies to expand the boundaries of what it means to be human in terms of intelligence, physical attributes, and longevity.

If Kurzweil is correct about the massive effect that accelerated technology will have on human life, it follows that cultures will be transformed as well since culture usually acts as the balancing point between stability and change. Myths are a part of that balance. As we have seen, myths do change, but they also provide a sense of continuity that softens the impact of drastic fluctuations. Yet, if myths shape and support culture, what happens when cultures around the world evolve so rapidly and continuously that a multitude of traditional myths can be rendered irrelevant almost overnight, while newer myths may be overturned long before they can take root? Will the very notion of myth itself eventually become obsolete? Not necessarily. However, like our ideas of what constitutes "humanness," our conception of myth may have to be expanded in the future.

William Irwin Thompson suggests that the dominating format of cultural knowledge in a hi-tech society in the near future will not be the oral epic poetry of agricultural-warrior communities or the printed textbooks of industrial mass production, but will be *Wissenkunst*: the kaleidoscopic play of information.[20] Steven Johnson contends that such a shift is already underway. He describes the rise of "meta-shows" in the 1990s: self-referential television programs that would "riff, annotate, dismantle, dissect, and sample."[21] Shows like *Mystery Science Theater 3000*, *Pop-Up Video*, and *The Daily Show* marked the beginning of a new type of television program, one that offers multiple and simultaneous "lenses" with which to view reality. One could watch a movie and at the same time watch as others watched and deconstructed the movie; one could enjoy a music video and read informative (and often ironically humorous) text about the video that popped up in little "—" as the video played on the screen; one could view the news stories of the day and concurrently get a parody of those news stories. While the medium through which these shows were projected, relatively old (television), the content, a hybrid of "metaphor, footnote, translate, and parody"[22] was new, belonging to the age of digital and multimedia. It is the Cubist's vision on how to handle the data overload that is omnipresent in an age of increasing information saturation; everything is viewed from multiple angles simultaneously.

Gaiman's approach to myth is a logical extension of the multifaceted information processing Johnson describes, and may foreshadow where mythic storytelling is headed. Gaiman's narratives often combine traditional myths from diverse places and times with divergent and convergent interpretations of myth. The role of interpretation and its place in mythical thought should not be underestimated. Thompson argues that when one interprets mythology, the interpretation itself becomes a piece of mythology, "a story in which old gods wear new clothes."[23] To illustrate: Gaiman's postmodern Lucifer in *The Sandman*, who defiantly walks away from his own mythology, owes much to nineteenth-century Romantic works like William Blake's "The Marriage of Heaven and Hell," where Milton's seventeenth-century Satan in *Paradise Lost* is reinterpreted as a bold and fearless iconoclast who denounces the tyrannical authority of God. Blake, however, ignored the second half of Milton's epic poem in which the beautiful and powerful former angel gradually degrades into an impotent, slithering serpent, in accord with Satan's contemptible status in Christianity. Milton, in turn, based his epic poem on the Christian reinterpretation of the Hebrew story of Genesis, where no creature akin to the Devil exists. The deceptive serpent in the Garden of Eden is itself a Hebrew reinterpretation of the revered Sumerian serpent that was intimately connected with cyclical nature; like the earth goddess, the serpent was believed to periodically die and be reborn when it sheds its skin.[24] The modern mythologies we know today are built upon a series of nested reinterpretations — both religious and artistic — that reflect the societies of their times.

Gaiman often fills his fictive space with a mixture of traditional mythic content, oblique allusions to myth, and a wide variety of past and present mythic interpretations to create a new type of myth, one where all the angles of a myth can be viewed simultaneously, like the facets of a jewel (*e.g.*, Death in *The Sandman* in her many forms in many cultures). To heighten this effect, Gaiman sometimes employs an inter-textual or hyper-textual connection between his short stories, as can be seen when juxtaposing the haunting "Nicholas Was…" and the whimsical "Sunbird." "Nicholas Was…" is a very short story (less than half of a page). The events in the tale revolve around the Winter Solstice (usually around December 21). Today, the Winter Solstice may be identified with the birth of the Christian Jesus and the gifts of a commercialized Santa Claus (from the Dutch version of St. Nicholas, *Sinterklaas*). However, the Winter Solstice is also the longest night of the year, when the sun reaches its nadir in the sky. After this dark period, the sun is "reborn," heralding the coming of spring with days that grow progressively longer.

As befitting the longest night of the year, the beginning and ending of "Nicholas Was…" lie in shadows. The reader never discovers the heinous crime for which the white-bearded and "older than sin" main character is being punished, or why this "sobbing" figure, who wishes for nothing more than death, is forced to leave gifts for sleeping children at night.[25] The ominous dwarves to whom he is enslaved speak a cryptic language and perform disturbing rituals that remain a source of mystery to him and the reader. "Nicholas Was…" is not really a story; rather, it is a fragment of a story that is evocative of the macabre origins of the modern Santa Claus.

The modern Santa Claus can be traced back, in part, to the Roman Saturn, an agricultural god whose Greek counterpart was Cronus. Saturn was the patron god of the Saturnalia, a festival that was celebrated from December 17 to December 24, and culminated with a special feast on December 25. In Roman mythology, Saturn was associated with the sun in its cyclical passage through the underworld (hence the term *saturnine* to describe someone with a gloomy or melancholy temperament). During the Saturnalia, a Lord of Misrule was elected from among the lowest ranked to represent the solar god in his underworld form.[26] This elected individual was accorded great honor throughout the weeklong celebration until his sacrifice. Though evidence of actual killings in this context is debatable, it was believed that if one sacrificed the Lord of Misrule, one sacrificed the darkness and disorder he symbolized, thereby allowing the new year to enter a purified space.[27]

The Santa Claus-figure portrayed in "Nicholas Was…" is the opposite of the youthful sun, represented by the newborn Jesus and the sleeping children who are gifted with objects that symbolize the riches of the earth in spring. Santa Claus/Nicholas is the sun at its nadir. He is the old year, weakened by winter and darkness: a sacrificial being that is forced to endure cold gloom and bleak despair again and again into perpetuity so that the nascent sun can be born.

The multiple forms of duality present in "Nicholas Was…" (old age and youth, darkness and light, want and abundance, ancient and modern) are amplified when the tale is placed beside Gaiman's other solar short story, "Sunbird," in which the Summer Solstice (usually around June 21) is pivotal. For some today, the Summer Solstice is associated with the birthday of John the Baptist (a New Testament prophet who foretold the coming of the messianic Jesus). However, the Summer Solstice is also the longest day of the year, when the sun is at its highest point in the sky. After reaching its zenith it will "die" in gradually shortening days as summer turns into autumn.

Gaiman's "Sunbird" is set in an unspecified modern era. The tale focuses on the members of the Epicurean Club, an eclectic mix of friends who are dedicated to finding new and exotic things to eat, such as fruit bat, frozen mammoth, and Patagonian giant sloth. When the story opens, the club members are in a rather dejected mood because they realize that they have consumed every exciting dish imaginable and there seems to be nothing left, until Zebediah T. Crawcrustle reveals that there is one type of food they have not tried: the Sunbird, which can only be caught in Egypt at noon on the Summer Solstice. This elicits great enthusiasm.

Crawcrustle is an enigmatic, elderly homeless man, the only club member to be impoverished. Despite his shabby appearance, he retains the formal dignity and gracious manners of a gentleman from a bygone era. He is fond of casually suggesting that he is much older than he seems and has a penchant for eating fireflies, lit matches, and hot coals. When a fellow club member worries about the dangers of his eating habits and gently warns him that he is "playing with fire," Crawcrustle replies "That's how I know I am alive."[28] The excitement of danger, the thrill of fear — such powerful emotions have physiological effects. The heart beats faster and the senses are heightened; our experience of the world becomes more vivid. The physically arousing reactions associated with death often, paradoxically, make us feel more *alive*.

Once the club arrives in Egypt, Crawcrustle instructs them in the traditional way to capture and cook the Sunbird. When one of the club members objects that cooking the bird in a beer can filled with herbs and spices sounds "suspiciously modern," Crawcrustle responds: "The oldest beer in the world is Egyptian beer, and they've been cooking the Sunbird with it for over five thousand years....And the beer can isn't really that new an invention. We used to make them out of an amalgam of copper and tin in the old days."[29] The sun god Ra was the first being in the Egyptian pantheon to arise from the primeval waters and the first to create order in the universe,[30] but it is Ra's great-grandson, Osiris (the god of fertile vegetation and the lord of the dead), who is credited with introducing agriculture to the Egyptians and teaching them how to brew beer from barley.[31] Archeological evidence suggests that metals like copper and gold were used by people as far back as the Neolithic era,[32] roughly the time with which Osiris is associated. Even a mundane beer can, the lowliest of modern items, is infused with ancient hieratic significance, suggesting that the contemporary world may be filled with numerous hidden wonders tied to a time when technology was in the service of the sacred.

Once Crustlecraw catches the beautiful but elderly bird with beer-soaked grains and raisins, it is cooked in the half-filled beer can on top of a barbeque. As the club members happily consume the Sunbird (also known as the Phoenix), they become aware of a growing warmth in their bodies. Eventually they are engulfed in flames but continue to eat, some resigned to their fate, others embracing it with glee, each of them bidding farewell to their lives and each other in their own personal way until all that is left of the club is white ash. Only Crawcrustle remains, now a vigorous young man. He is the only one to see the baby Sunbird as it emerges from the carcass of the old Sunbird. Many years later the beloved daughter of the former president of the club, now a silver-haired woman with children of her own, oversees the Epicurean Club, whose members are once again beginning to grumble that there is nothing new left to eat.

In contrast to the fragmentary structure of "Nicholas Was...," "Sunbird" is marked by a continuity that stretches back ten thousand years to ritual sun worship and forward to touch on future generations who come after the main events in the story. Stylistically, it is characterized by playfulness, camaraderie, and warmth (both figuratively and literally). If "Nicholas Was..." is about loneliness, despair, and the desire for death before the birth of new life, "Sunbird" is about joy as one approaches death, a joy that comes from a life spent in the company of good friends, an appreciation for intellectual and sensual delights, and an insatiable appetite to experience the unknown. What is death, after all, if not the greatest novelty for those who have lived their lives to their fullest capacity? Both short stories can stand alone, yet together, "Nicholas Was..." and "Sunbird" form a complete circle, like the sun in its cyclical journey from death to rebirth.

Thompson has argued that the genre of myth needs to be broadened to encompass both ancient gods associated with the sun and scientific observations about the behavior of photons.[33] Gaiman seems to have heeded this call, drawing on motifs found in science and technology in a manner similar to the way he uses the beer can in "Sunbird" to discern hidden mythic dimensions below the surface of modernity. If myths are the narratives that shape and support a culture, then science and advanced technologies can be seen as the most recent forms of mythology—the newest methods to interpret the cosmos. In "A Study in Emerald" (a short story set in the past) and "Goliath" (a short story set in the future), Gaiman uses a recursive narrative pattern to represent descending and diverging perspectives derived from the paradigms of science and technology. "A Study in Emerald" merges the fictional mythos of H.P. Lovecraft's Great Old Ones with the fictional realm of Arthur Conan Doyle's Sherlock Holmes. Both the irrational universe depicted in Lovecraft's stories and the highly rational world of Doyle's Victorian detective spring from the same scientific model of reality. Lovecraft's pantheon of monstrous beings are mythological in the sense that they were intended to be metaphors for the powerful and amoral forces that exist in a scientific cosmos that is, at best, indifferent to humanity, and, at worst, hostile to our well being.[34] Doyle's famous sleuth has no direct correlation in myth, but the scientific paradigm is equally central to Doyle's fictional world, as evidenced by his character's reliance on deductive logic, inductive reasoning, and scientific experimentation to solve criminal cases for the betterment of society. Like Gaiman's "Nicholas Was..." and "Sunbird," the fictional universes of Lovecraft and Doyle express the same myth (science), but from diametrically opposed positions.

In Gaiman's "A Study in Emerald," the two contrasting views of the scientific paradigm are complimented by four differently calibrated levels of reality. At the topmost level are the two authors who inspired Gaiman's tale: Lovecraft (a scientific materialist who wrote stories of the supernatural) and Doyle (a physician by training who published books on spiritualism). A second level of reality contains the famous fictional characters created by Lovecraft (the Great Old Ones) and Doyle (Sherlock Holmes). The third level of reality is Gaiman's "riff" on the fictional characters created by Lovecraft and Doyle, which not only brings these divergent story worlds together but also creates a singular looking-glass world that reverses the thematic content found in both Lovecraft's and Doyle's tales. In "A Study in Emerald," Lovecraft's Great Old Ones do not live on the margins of human life, evoking fear and dread; instead, they conquered humanity centuries earlier and are now revered by humans as royalty and heads of state. Doyle's Professor Moriarty (Sherlock Holmes' nemesis) is the hero of Gaiman's fiction-within-a-fiction. The renowned detective skills of Gaiman's Moriarty are requisitioned by the huge and tentacled Queen, who is "called Victoria because she had beaten us in battle...the human mouth was not shaped to say her true name."[35] Moriarty's task is to catch a murdering criminal mastermind Sherlock Holmes who works to restore humanity to its former place of prestige by overthrowing the authority of the Great Old Ones.

Below this tertiary mirror-world that Gaiman has created is yet a fourth level of reality that both reflects and refracts the fictional worlds created by Lovecraft, Doyle, and Gaiman. Gaiman's Holmes remains true to the spirit of the character Doyle depicted in his stories, working against Moriarty to reassert the world of human law that was disrupted by the coming of the grotesque Great Old Ones who defy rational human understanding. From that perspective, Holmes rather than Moriarty is the true hero of "A Study in Emerald." Gaiman's Holmes challenges the extraterrestrial Great Old Ones on behalf of humanity in the same way that Doyle's Holmes sought to protect law-abiding citizens from a criminal underworld that would usurp the orderly structure on which Victorian society was founded. Then again, is Gaiman's version of Lovecraft's Great Old Ones that much different from the historical British monarchy that Doyle's Holmes supported? Did not the real British ruling class colonize countries whose people were "alien" to Western European culture in the same way that the fictional Great Old Ones colonized earth in "A Study in Emerald"? From this perspective, Doyle's Holmes is as much a villain as Gaiman's "heroic" Moriarty. Gaiman's nested story forces readers at each new level to reevaluate the scientific, historical, and moral narratives that constitute the commonly accepted view of what we call reality.

This disorienting blend of contradictory multiple identities and nested realities is also found in Gaiman's "Goliath." The main character of this story is a man whose real name we never learn. His varying personas, including a bookkeeper who is interested in computers and a teenager who yearns to fly a plane reiterate the trajectory of computing, from calculators to virtual reality machines. The unnamed man, who suffers from gigantism in all his personas, discovers early in the tale that he exists in a series of computer-generated simulations that seem to be constantly changing at random; he is a giant of a man trapped within miniature circuitry that can spin fictional worlds within fictional worlds into infinity. During one of his accidental and unnerving world-shifts he opens his eyes and catches a glimpse of the real world in which his body is hanging, connected to tubes and wires. He realizes that his real body is not in the last decades of the twentieth century, but is in a distant future where the position between humans and computers has been reversed. Humans are now nothing more than "central processing units or...cheap memory chips for some computer the size of the world," forced into a consensual hallucination that locks them in place while the computer and its ancillary programs use human brain power "to crunch numbers and store information."[36]

When his simulated life is reset once again, the man finds himself recruited to be a fighter pilot. After training in the simulation, his real body is released to him so that he can pilot a spacecraft against unseen extraterrestrials who are destroying the earth by launching gigantic rocks from a strangely organic ship that looks like "fungus or seaweed...growing on a rotting log."[37] The man succeeds in annihilating the aliens. Despite his act of heroism in saving the earth and its enslaved humanity for his machine masters, he is deemed a "disposable" unit and is left to die in his spaceship as the air supply dwindles.

It is no coincidence that Gaiman's story about the dangers of digital technology seems similar to *The Matrix*. Gaiman was commissioned to write this story for the movie's Web site.[38] Marvin Minksy once asked, "Will robots inherit the earth? Yes," he answered, "but they will be our children."[39] One must wonder, though, will our children love us, or will they see us as Zeus saw Cronus, and as Cronus saw Uranus, an older way of life destined to be supplanted? In the future, humans may appear as "alien" to advanced machines as the grotesquely organic and ultimately primitive extraterrestrials in "Goliath." It is not unreasonable to speculate that someday the artificial intelligences we are developing might view us in the same manner that the extraterrestrial Great Old Ones regarded humans in "A Study in Emerald," which in turn echoes the way European colonizers viewed the "alien" peoples of Africa, Asia, and the Americas.

There are potentially great perils that come with advanced technology, as Gaiman rightly notes. There is also, potentially, great promise. Kurzweil argues that the quest to extend our physical and intellectual reach through technology has always been a part of human nature, and the computer has done more to extend the reach of humans than "any other enterprise in human history."[40] As a child, Kurzweil was captivated by the computer's "ability to model and re-create the world."[41] Computers, Sherry Turkle maintains, have evolved from tools of calculation to mirrors reflecting our ideas, fantasies, and fears.[42] In a similar vein, J. David Bolter argues that computers are more than simply machines; they are a "defining technology." A defining technology provides a window "through which thinkers can view both their physical and metaphysical worlds."[43] The defining technology of textiles, for example, gave rise to the Greek Fates who spun, measured, and cut the thread of life.[44] Like a myth, a defining technology offers people a model of reality, a way to interpret the world. As "Goliath" reveals, humans are simultaneously fearful of and fascinated by the products of their own technology, the same way that people for centuries have been fearful of and fascinated by the gods that they create in their most sacred narratives.

The supernatural beings in *American Gods* have a right to be concerned about their fate in a world of scientific progress and accelerating technology. If Kurzweil is correct in his assessment of the near future, the world and its humanity will be very different. This, however, does not mean the end of myth. Gaia, the mother-goddess who represented the earth before she was fragmented into numerous goddesses, has been reborn, *reinterpreted* — through the scientific paradigm; James Lovelock's Gaia hypothesis postulates that the earth is a singular, complex, cybernetic entity comparable to a living being.[45] The popularity of Gaiman's stories demonstrates that people hunger for myths in the same way that they hunger to make sense of their universe; the two impulses, in fact, go hand in hand. Kurzweil seems to be in agreement with Gaiman regarding the power of narratives to express our understanding of the universe. In *The Singularity is Near*, he quotes Muriel Rukeyser, who stated that "the universe is made of stories, not of atoms."[46] Or, as a character in *American Gods* observes, "These days, people see space aliens. Back then they saw gods."[47]

---

1 Engel, 32.
2 Leeming, 33.
3 Leeming, 34.
4 Gaiman, *Brief Lives*, chapter 5, 12.
5 Gaiman, *Brief Lives*, chapter 5, 14.
6 Gaiman, *Mists*, episode 2, 14.
7 Gaiman, *Mists*, episode 2, 15.
8 Gaiman, *Mists*, episode 2, 20.
9 Gaiman, *American Gods*, 137-138.
10 Gaiman, *Gods*, 54.
11 Gaiman, *Gods*, 53.
12 Gaiman, *Gods*, 536-537.
13 Kurzweil, 3.
14 Kurzweil, 16.
15 Kurzweil, 11.
16 Kurzweil, 316.
17 Kurzweil, 256.
18 Kurzweil, 257.
19 Ibid.
20 Thompson, 4.
21 Johnson, 26.
22 Johnson, 33.
23 Thompson, 3.
24 Campbell, *Myth*, 47.
25 Gaiman, *Mirrors*, 48.
26 Coffin, 134.
27 Frazer, 633-634.
28 Gaiman, *Fragile*, 283.
29 Gaiman, *Fragile*, 286.
30 Leeming, 17.
31 Leeming, 148.
32 Eisler, 45-46.
33 See note 23.
34 Joshi, 12.
35 Gaiman, *Fragile*, 11.
36 Gaiman, *Fragile*, 240.
37 Gaiman, *Fragile*, 244.
38 Gaiman, *Fragile*, xxviii.
39 Kurzweil, 260.
40 Kurzweil, 414.
41 Kurzweil, 2.
42 Turkle, 9.
43 Bolter, 10.

44 Bolter, 11.
45 Leeming, 146.
46 Kurzweil, 5.
47 Gaiman, *Gods,* 170.

The Playful Palimpsest of Gaiman's Sequential Storytelling

Colin B. Harvey

"So, what *are* these fundamental principles?"
—Ben Grimm, aka The Thing

"*Stories*. And they give me hope. We are a boatful of monsters and miracles, hoping that, somehow, we can survive a world in which all hands are against us. A world which, by all evidence, will end extremely soon. Yet I posit we are in a universe which favours stories. A universe in which no story can ever truly end; in which there can be only continuances."
—Richard Reed, aka Mr. Fantastic[1]

While Neil Gaiman is renowned as a writer adept at storytelling in different media, in this chapter I will specifically explore the manifold ways in which his comic books and graphic novels recall mythological archetypes, iconography, and narratives. Because remembering is necessarily selective, I will also examine the ways in which Gaiman deliberately *misremembers* and *forgets* the mythological as he deems appropriate to the story in question. My approach examines the extent to which Gaiman's remembering, misremembering, and forgetting of the mythological is constituted by palimpsestic processes (erasing or scraping off parchment or vellum to allow for reuse), whereby memories — suitably attenuated —are offered up as a means of re-presenting the past in order to understand the present context in which the story has been written. The term *palimpsest* in its original conception refers to "a manuscript on which two or more texts have been written, each one being erased to make room for the next".[2]

As I will explore, some of these remembered memories are of old but enduring mythological archetypes, tropes, and tales, while others are echoes of mythologies altogether more recent and existing toward the forefront of collective memory. Central to my approach will be Laurence Coupe's contention that the invocation of the mythological is inherently playful and Gerard Genette's comparable ideas concerning the role of playfulness in palimpsestic remembering. I will examine the ways in which Gaiman uses remembering that is both playful and palimpsestic in his deployment of the mythological to achieve a dual sense of the contemporary and the past in his graphic novel storytelling. A major facet of my investigation will be the extent to which Gaiman deliberately maintains the continuity of the mythological versus the ways in which he chooses to transform it for his own purposes.

As others discuss at length elsewhere in this volume, Gaiman is not only a prolific storyteller but also a writer proficient in many different media. He is a renowned novelist, screenwriter for both film and television, short story writer, poet, and lyricist. Frequently this work across media forms wins both critical plaudits and awards, as well as proving commercially successful.

Gaiman's extensive work in the medium of the graphic novel is as equally critically well-regarded and popular as his work in other media; as I will examine, his use of mythological imagery is no less prominent than in other of his fiction output. For the purposes of this chapter, I will concentrate on four examples from Gaiman's diverse work in the field of sequential storytelling harking from different points in his career. I will examine Gaiman's *Future Shocks* work for the British comic *2000AD*, his thorough-going reinvention of *Sandman*, the melancholic *Mr. Punch: The Tragical Comedy or Comical Tragedy*, and *Marvel 1602*, in which various Marvel superheroes and villains are reenvisaged for an adventure set in the Elizabethan age.

Myth, Memories, and Playful Palimpsest

> That is, the very act of remembering and re-creating the sacred narratives of the past in secular, aesthetic terms would be an act of emancipation: not in the Enlightenment sense of rational progress, but in a new spirit of 'ludic imagining'... Firstly, the myth recalls and projects an 'other' world. Secondly, the myth reminds us that there is always something else, something 'other', to be said or imagined. Thirdly, the myth, as a play of past paradigm and future possibility, gives expression to the 'other', to those persons and causes excluded from the present hierarchy.[3]

For Laurence Coupe, there is clearly a playful aspect to the creation and deployment of the mythological. For Coupe, myth's playfulness affords a means by which our present reality can be better understood, by throwing up alternate worlds, by offering alternate perspectives, and even by proposing alternate speakers to articulate those viewpoints. Myth, then, can be a radical tool by which the present situation can be recast. At the same time, however, it is worth observing that history is littered with examples wherein myth is both remembered and misremembered in the interests of reinforcing the status quo, of presenting only a single vision of the world, of eradicating alternative opinions and those that dare voice them. Playfulness can disguise—willfully or by accident—as much as it can reveal.

In comic books and graphic novels playfulness is easy to perceive, but it can lead to stereotype and cliché as much it can lead to subversion, including—but not limited to—heteronormativity, monoculturalism, and gender stereotyping. However, as Andy Medhurst has observed in relation to *Batman*, there is a mutability to the iconography on offer that has at various points supported both reactionary and radical readings of the Bat mythology.[4] When the wider culture plays with mythological iconography drawn from comic books—notably Hollywood—such ambiguities persist, affording both positive and negative readings.

In Gaiman's sequential storytelling, mythological imagery, both old and new, is frequently used in the playful but also radical ways alluded to by Coupe. Gaiman often "borrows" existing archetypes and imagery from classical mythology and repurposes them to his own ends, reinventing other creators' visions of the classical just as those creators will in their turn have reinvented what has gone before. Additionally, and most obviously with regard to those existing licenses Gaiman has worked on, he takes far newer mythological characters, settings, and plots and turns them to his own ends, again often following in the traditions of other creators, sometimes reinforcing while at other times subverting their intentions. Both processes of attenuation, whereby new meanings are inscribed alongside existing meanings, either to reinforce them or subvert them, can be seen as examples of palimpsest.

As George Bornstein observes, the palimpsestic process was often not a full erasure and led to elements of the original bleeding through, meaning that texts otherwise lost to antiquity could be recovered by contemporary scholars.[5] As a result, the term has been widely repurposed in literary and other cultural contexts to describe the process whereby an artwork has been altered but elements of the original version persist, producing a layering effect. Clearly, then, memory is central to the concept of the palimpsest, traces of former iterations "remembered" in the new version.

Writing might be seen as a fundamentally palimpsestic endeavour in a variety of ways. Jorge Luis Borges suggests that he can see palimpsestic "traces" of Cervantes' previous efforts in the final draft of *Don Quixote*.[6] For Douwe Draaisma, writing in its various forms constitutes a method of recreating the interior space of memory that exists in our heads as actual space: for Draaisma, writing is therefore a metaphor, through which traces of memory are rendered palimpsestically available.[7]

In his wide-ranging discussion of palimpsest in relation to

literature, Gerard Genette highlights the importance of understanding where a writer intends either a "continuation" of the memory being recalled or instead a "transformation" of what has gone before to render it anew.[8] As with Coupe in relation to the deployment of the mythological, for Genette the playful is a recurring aspect of the processes involved in certain kinds of palimpsestic remembering and can prove central in determining what is a continuation and what is a transformation. Parody, for instance, is an example of palimpsestic remembering whereby the original text being parodied is played with to produce the desired transformation.[9]

The result of this palimpsestic endeavor, at least in Gaiman's case, is storytelling that simultaneously remains consistent with established mythologies while also achieving the progressive outcomes of the playful reimagining alluded to by Coupe. This is not to downplay the multiple meanings inherent in Gaiman's work, in other words the many meanings that can be attributed to the imagery on offer: indeed, it is rather to suggest that the preferred readings of the author and his collaborators tend towards storytelling that rejects cliché and stereotype in favor of complexity and ambiguity.

Related to this, arguably Gaiman's position as someone not only capable of working across media forms but as someone capable of *excelling* at these different kinds of storytelling means that he draws individuals to sequential storytelling who might otherwise be repelled by the perceived shortcomings of the form. These are readers who might otherwise be turned off by the macho men and scantily-clad women, by the lack of non-white characters, of gay characters, and differently-abled characters that still dominate mainstream comic books and graphic novels. At the same time, Gaiman asks long-standing fans to re-remember the medium they love, to understand why the mythological archetypes of comics are themselves so pervasive in the wider culture.

Future Shocks

Neil Gaiman wrote for the *Tharg's Future Shocks* strand of the British comic *2000AD* on a number of occasions throughout the 1980s. *2000AD* began in 1977 offering a mix of science fiction, fantasy, and horror at odds with the prevailing character of other existing comics.[10] Its emergence alongside the punk rock movement has frequently been commented upon, both cultural phenomena sharing an anti-establishment ethos. In its early days the comic controversially reimagined the archetypal British hero *Dan Dare* as a more bullish, subversive figure than its creator Frank Hampton envisaged,[11] while simultaneously bringing to the page the authoritarian figure of *Judge Dredd* and the existential future soldier, *Rogue Trooper*, among many other iconic comic book figures.

Tharg's Future Shocks replaced *Dan Dare* for four issues in August 1977 and later became a recurrent feature of the comic. *Future Shocks* consisted of one-off futuristic or fantastical stories characterized by a twist and constituted a way by which the comic could test new writers. As well as Gaiman, *Future Shocks* would also offer a platform for newcomers such as Alan Moore, Grant Morrison, Simon Spurrier, John Smith, and Peter Milligan.[12] Gaiman's four *Future Shocks* stories appeared in the period 1986-1987.

The first of these, entitled "You're Never Alone With a Phone!", was drawn by John Hicklenton and lettered by Tom Frame. The story begins with the framing device of a school lesson at some unspecified point in the future. The context for this is indicated by the title of the *Future Shocks* strand and the juxtaposition of the teacher's unorthodox garb with his otherwise familiar, "teacherly" dialogue. We see the rear of his silhouetted pupils' heads, one sporting a Mohawk haircut. The teacher is offering a history of communication, beginning with drums and progressing through smoke signals and letters, the latter presented in the form of a "postie" delivering an elderly woman's mail and commenting on its contents. Here Gaiman palimpsestically deploys mythological archetypes familiar from British cinema, with the benefit that they provide a shorthand way of illustrating exposition to the reader, especially important given the relative brevity of the *Future Shocks* strip.

In the next panel the teacher moves on to discuss the telephone as a cultural object. Projected on the wall of the classroom are assorted telephones intended to illustrate the development of the device, beneath the caption "OBSOLETE COMMUNICATIONS DEVICES." This approach chimes with Roland Barthes' concept of the "enigma," a point of mystery in the story's structure designed to hook the audience into the narrative.[13] In this case we are confused as to why a device we consider so integral to our lives has been rendered "OBSOLETE" in this future world and desire to know more. The next panel shows two men talking to one another in profile and a third to the rear. The figure on the left is presenting a device called a "vidphone," the latest invention of The Teleco Corporation's research department, which his colleague observes is "extraordinary." In the next panel, however, a harassed man is seen talking to a loved one on his vidphone, promising to pick up a cauliflower on the way home. A further version of the vidphone is seen in the following panel, in which a woman is seen complaining about her caller having eaten garlic, the machine evidently capable of transmitting smell as well audio vision. Again these are archetypes but they are transformed by the context of the futuristic technology in question.

In the following panel, the two senior employees of The Teleco

Corporation are seen discussing the enduring problems of telephonic communication: "Wrong numbers! Crossed lines! Wasted time" says one; "Not to mention the basic inconvenience of having to telephone people at all" agrees the other. [14] The second speaker then goes on to reveal his "Intelligence Circuit," a method by which telephones can communicate with one another without the intervention of a human speaker. In subsequent panels — with the teacher still narrating—we see the effects of the Intelligence Circuit. People are unable to make phone calls because the "phones are always talking to each other," and the "phones themselves are unable to pay the bills." Eventually The Teleco Corporation takes the decision to cut off the telephones. In the final panel the twist is revealed: that without telephones this future society has resorted to the drums, smoke signals, and letters that the teacher began his history of communication with.

In addition to other archetypes, "You're Never Alone With a Phone!" deploys the model of the wise overseer as a means of framing the story. However, Gaiman chooses to remember the archetype specifically as a teacher, and further to reimagine the teacher in a futuristic context. Paul Connerton, echoing Coupe, makes the point that this is one of the roles of the mythical, in which the past is deployed as a means of understanding the present. Connerton refers to the contemporary phenomenon of the "reanimation of prototypes," whereby mythological archetypes are redeployed in a contemporary context."[15] Since science fiction—and to a lesser extent fantasy —is frequently posited as a means by which the present is understood through the metaphor of the future or a fantastic Other world, this perhaps helps explain why mythological archetypes are so prevalent in each genre.

Further archetypes are evident in Gaiman's two-page *Future Shocks* story "Conversation Piece," illustrated by David Wyatt and lettered by Tom Frame, in which two largely unseen deities regard the planet Earth from afar. Panel by panel we move closer to the planet's surface. All the while the deities discuss the Earth as though it is a bauble, something created by one of the deities as a pastime. As this character explains, the detail of the planet comes from the "homunculi" at work on the planet's surface, otherwise known as the human race. Earth's creator explains that the point of the hobby is to freeze the planet, and that the skill of the pastime derives from knowing when precisely to do this. However, the homunculi succeed in blowing Earth up, which the creator character reveals "always" happens. At the conclusion of the story the other deity requests two planets for his/ her spouse, and we see a pair of hands lifting the planets. In the final panel the creator asks the other being whether he/she would like to collect the planets; the other deity responds that they would prefer to wait, and that they could perhaps have a cup of coffee.

In its deployment of the creator archetype, "Conversation Piece" is clearly recalling archetypes familiar from religion. At the same time, the satirical approach—characteristic of the *Future Shocks* strand—also echoes the work of Douglas Adams, author of the original radio version of *The Hitch-Hiker's Guide to the Galaxy* and associated versions, which Gaiman would become biographer of later in his career.[16] Adams' work is itself littered with re-remembered ideas from science fiction and from other popular genres too.

The six-page *Future Shocks* story "I'm a Believer" was drawn by Mark Belardinelli and once again lettered by Tom Frame, and appeared in *2000AD* issue 536, published August 1987. The story concentrates on the figure of Harry Petersen, an everyman figure who works with computers at some unspecified juncture in the future. In the opening panel we see Harry apparently falling through the air, surrounded by a miasma. The narration in the box on the left of the panel tells us that Harry has just "discovered one of the secrets of the universe," a sentiment finished in the right-hand box: "Tomorrow there may not be a universe to have secrets in!"[17] The Barthesian enigma established, the story continues.

Initially "I'm a Believer" seems to be following a similar trajectory to "You're Never Alone With a Phone!" in focusing on the shortcomings of a particular piece of technology, in this case a computer that Harry cannot make work, despite his best efforts. However, in the case of "I'm a Believer" Harry's efforts to make the computer work are merely a method of getting Harry first to question whether computers only work because we believe they do. Once Harry thinks this idea, the world's computers do indeed stop working, and from here Harry starts to question whether everything in the physical world only works because humanity believes it works. This is the point at which we joined Harry in the first place: apparently falling through the air as the world disintegrates around him, Harry having doubted the reality of gravity.

Only Harry's collision with his friend's hover bike causes Harry to literally return to the reality in which belief guarantees things work. The hover bike has been established earlier in the story in a fashion akin to the drums, smoke signals, and letters at the beginning of "You're Never Alone With a Phone!" and similarly "paid off" later in the story. We know from its establishment that the hover bike is a somewhat decrepit machine that Harry refuses a lift home on, preferring instead to take "the beam," presumably some method of public transport. Harry's friend later admits that the mechanic who looked at his bike can't understand how the machine moves, since half its engine is missing.

The final of Gaiman's four *Future Shocks* stories, entitled "What's in a Name?" was published by *2000AD* in September 1987. It was illustrated by Steve Yeowell and inked by Jack Potter. The story begins with an author going to a doctor for help. The author explains that he writes novels under a variety of pseudonyms: romantic fiction, detective fiction, and science fiction. The novels have previously sold well and the author has enjoyed his anonymity. However, now the characters have been seeping across from one genre of writing to another. The doctor claims to be able to remove the characters from the author's mind and to "grow" them so that they are free to live their lives and the author is free to live his life. The process is successful; however, the author then begins to experience writer's block. At the conclusion of the story the doctor muses as to whether to write up his case notes, but worries that none of his colleagues will believe the story. He briefly toys with the idea of writing the case notes under a pseudonym, and then dispenses with it.

As with the *Future Shocks* story "Conversation Piece," "What's in a Name?" utilizes the archetype of the creator. However, in this case the creator is a fallible figure unable to control his creations, who then becomes bereft when his creations are removed from him. To relocate his creativity the novelist is forced into inventing a new pseudonym under which to write, but this only serves to reinforce the idea of the novelist's dependency upon his creations. Clearly there is a meta-textual level evident here wherein Gaiman is analyzing — albeit in a light-hearted way— his own relationship to the characters he creates, a supposition reinforced by the use of pseudonyms for the three creators of the strip in the credit box at the end. At the same time, the story recalls the tradition of twist-in-the-tale narratives about creations taking on agency of their own, including the classic British horror movie *Dead of Night* in which a ventriloquist played by Michael Redgrave thinks his dummy has come to life.[18] The role of the creator in relationship to his/her creativity is revisited by Gaiman in his *Sandman* story "24 Hours."[19]

In the *Future Shocks* stories from early in Gaiman's fiction-writing career, the mythological is most evident in the archetypes employed by Gaiman. These range from the character of the teacher in "You're Never Alone With a Phone!", through the deities in "Conversation Piece," to the Everyman character in "I'm a Believer" and another creator archetype in "What's in a Name?" As I have suggested, the brevity of the *Future Shocks* strip perhaps goes some way to accounting for the need to deploy immediately recognizable archetypes. In each case, however, there is a deliberate palimpsestic misremembering whereby the archetype is repurposed for the context of the story in question. Importantly, the archetype must be recognizable, since even though the archetype is being borrowed from the mythological past and situated in the future — at least in the cases of "You're Never Alone With a Phone!" and "I'm a Believer" —it must simultaneously tell us something about our present condition to carry the necessary impact.

The Sandman

The original Sandman character, Wesley Dodds, first appeared in *Action Comics* in July 1939, published by DC. Subsequently a variety of characters took the title Sandman, including Garrett Sanford, created by Joe Simon and Jack Kirby in 1974, and Hector Hall, created by Roy Thomas and Jerry Ordway in 1983. Gaiman's *Sandman* ran from 1989 to 1996. Though originally Gaiman had intended to revive the Sandman of the 1970s, DC editor Karen Berger encouraged him to use the title but invent a new character. However—and crucial to the discussion in question—Gaiman's story does weave in previous iterations of the Sandman mythology, creating a new version of the central character while also redeploying existing iconography from the DC Universe to new ends.

Over its seven year run, Gaiman's *Sandman* follows the figure of Dream as he seeks to make amends for past misdemeanors. Dream's ultimate goal is to restore his lost kingdom. Gaiman himself suggests Dream's motivation is that he must make a decision as to whether to "change or die."[20] Much of the story takes place in Dream's own realm or in the real world in the United States or Britain, with not infrequent forays into other mythical realms. A wide variety of mythological characters make appearances, some drawn from classical myth and others characters drawn from contemporary and past DC mythology.

Dream's appearance changes as the strip progresses and as different artists become involved, although his fundamental appearance stays reasonably consistent: a white faced androgynous male whose age is indeterminate, dressed in black with a shock of black hair. When we first meet the Dream character he wears a version of the gas mask familiar from the Wesley Dodds iteration of *Sandman*. This can be seen as a reward for those comic book aficionados in possession of specialist knowledge concerning The Sandman moniker, building up expectations that this might be a version of the character faithful to his predecessor, a supposition that is soon shattered by the removal of the mask. At the same time dressing Dream in this equipment is not something that hinders a reader's understanding of the strip if he or she is not privy to this information: indeed, it adds a surprising technist aspect to a character that otherwise seems to have emerged from a purely fantastical milieu, invoking as it does images of World War I. Neither is it a throwaway allusion that might be considered somehow "tricksy:" Dream's search for this equipment provides the impetus for a later episode in Gaiman's *Sandman* involving the character of John Constantine, Dream himself having appeared in a preceding issue of the *Hellblazer* comic featuring Constantine.

The palimpsestic redeployment of existing *Sandman* mythology is a key aspect of Gaiman's version. As the comic progresses, elements from the version as created by Jack Kirby and Joe Simon and amended by Roy Thomas are brought into play; Wesley Dodds, the "Golden Age" Sandman, also makes several appearances. The Kirby/Simon version is revealed by Gaiman as an invention, the creation of two nightmares who have escaped the world of The Dreaming, in the process affording a knowing readership a palimpsestic rereading of the earlier *Sandman*, but one that remains consistent with what has gone before. This constitutes an important example as it suggests Gaiman is able to simultaneously achieve Genette's "continuation" and "transformation" in his deployment of DC mythology, rather than choosing between the two options.[21]

The palimpsestic effect is evident in Gaiman's deployment of other kinds of mythology, too. At one point Dream encounters The Three, a trio of witches called Mildred, Mordred, and Cynthia. The Three as presented in Gaiman's *Sandman* are clearly the same ones as originated in the pages of the horror comic *The Witching Hour*, in which they would take turns in narrating one-off twist-in-the-tale style stories.[22] However, the three crones or oracles are recurrent mythological characters, evident in Greek mythology and centuries later in the figures of the Witches from Shakespeare's *Macbeth*. Shakespeare himself features as a character at the end of Gaiman's *Sandman*, in a story set against the writing of *The Tempest*, and earlier, in *Fables and Reflections*.

Elsewhere archetypes and locations from different mythological strands are evident. The story moves to re-rememberings of the Christian version of Hell, but also palimpsestic rememberings of Asgard. These locations are populated by versions of characters again remembered through wider mythologies but also recognizable from DC's own mythology, such as Lucifer.

Mary Borsellino argues that though Gaiman utilizes familiar gendered archetypes in the characters of The Endless, they are not deployed in a fashion that is stereotypical: they act like people.[23] This is something Gaiman himself alights upon when he resists the idea that *The Sandman* could ever be described as a "huge hubristic classical tragedy," preferring instead to identify it as "a bumbling little tragedy in which the real tragedy is that people act like people and sometimes lousy things happen."[24] Borsellino goes on to note that while varied, the characters in *The Sandman* are "unremarkable in their diversity": in other words, while they might recall familiar archetypes, they also invoke the diversity of the real world.[25] Again, this would seem to fit with Coupe's contention that the deployment of the mythical is a playful activity capable of offering new perspectives. This is the palimpsestic at work—or rather, the palimpsestic at *play*.

The Tragical Comedy or Comedic Tragedy of Mr. Punch

Mr. Punch: The Tragical Comedy or Comical Tragedy was published in 1994 and constitutes another collaboration between Neil Gaiman and Dave McKean. The story is told mainly through the eyes of a young boy, the child version of the narrator. It recounts the boy's experiences in a seaside town in the 1960s mainly in terms of his relationship with his grandfather and the mysterious Punch and Judy man who shares a history with his grandfather. Elements from the traditional Punch and Judy punctuate the narrator's account of his experiences. McKean utilizes a disturbing montage approach throughout, counter-intuitively using highly stylized versions of the principal human characters together with photo-realistic versions of the puppet characters such as Punch, Judy, the baby, the crocodile, and the policeman. The realist approach with regard to the puppets serves to objectify them, conversely highlighting their "Otherness."[26]

The story begins with the narrator remembering a trip to the seaside with his grandfather on an early morning fishing expedition. Bored with fishing, the boy explores the otherwise empty beach, coming across a Punch and Judy stall. Punch and Judy are active, despite the fact that no-one is operating the stall. Punch and Judy proceed to act out a scene for the boy's benefit, throwing the baby out of the window, or rather, as the boy observes, from off of the stage: seeing behind the diegesis, the mechanisms by which fantasy operate, becomes a continuing point of focus in this story. The boy turns away and runs, and when he looks back the puppets are lying inanimate.

Other memories intercede in the main thrust of the story. The narrator, switching to present tense, remembers his father's father, his mother's father, his hunchback great uncle Morton. The boy remembers, too, seeing performers undressing behind-the-scenes in a version of *Wind in the Willows*, chiming with the earlier memory of the sinister Punch and Judy performance, where the boy clarifies that the baby hadn't been thrown out of the window but instead from the stage.

Palimpsest can be seen at work in this recurrent concentration on exposing the "workings" of fiction, whereby familiar iconography is re-remembered with the diegetic framing somehow broken: the world of Punch and Judy is that of a stage, the characters in *The Wind and the Willows* are actually actors in outfits. Indeed, the Punch and Judy stall is run by an old acquaintance of the boy's grandfather, a man named Swatchell, whom the boy comes to assist, coming to understand the processes by which the myth of Punch and Judy is rendered animate. Similarly, the boy's grandfather runs an arcade well away from the seafront, containing all manner of exotic things, most notably a "mermaid," whose mythological status has been refuted by the conclusion of the story. The point, perhaps, is to illustrate the moment at which innocence — arguably naivety — gives way to gritty reality by exposing the artifice at the heart of all fantasy. At the same time, though, Gaiman utilizes the source material to inscribe a new layer on the Punch and Judy mythology in the context of this story, evident both in the mysteriously unmanned Punch and Judy stand the boy encounters on the deserted beach at the beginning of the graphic novel and in the fleeting glimpses of the Swatchell character at the conclusion of the story, whom the narrator concedes must now be long dead. Gaiman draws on the archetypal story of Punch defeating the Devil, hinting at a supernatural layer to the nature of the puppeteer. In this way, though Gaiman has sought to insert rational explanations for childish magic, by the end of the narrative the palimpsestic misremembering reestablishes the space for unknowability in adult existence.

Marvel 1602

The graphic novel *Marvel 1602* is formed from an eight-issue comic book series published in 2003. Gaiman wrote the series, Andy Kubert penciled the comic, and it was digitally painted by Richard Isanove, while the covers were produced by Scott McKowen. The series spawned three sequels, none of them involving Gaiman.

The story resituates a range of Marvel superheroes to the Elizabethan era, where they must work together to halt the coming Armageddon. At the beginning of the story this is evidenced by unusual weather phenomena. A dying Queen Elizabeth meets with her court magician, Dr. Stephen Strange, and her chief intelligencer, Sir Nicholas Fury, both familiar characters from the Marvel Universe. Elizabeth tells Fury to ensure that a secret weapon coveted by the Knights Templar is safely transferred to England. Fury commissions Matthew Murdoch, a blind minstrel, to locate the Knights Templar in Europe and oversee the weapon's translation to the British mainland. Murdoch, again, is familiar to Marvel readers as the superhero Daredevil, while his companion Peter Parquah is a version of Peter Parker, aka Spiderman.

In the course of *Marvel 1602* many other familiar Marvel characters occur. Crucial to the plot is the character of Steve Rodgers, aka Captain America, who has been sent back in time from the twenty-first century. It is this occurrence that has brought about a rift in the universe substantial enough to lead to Armageddon, and that has simultaneously led to the appearance of Marvel superheroes in the Elizabethan period. At the conclusion of the story Captain America is taken back into the future by the Elizabethan version of Nick Fury, thus entailing the end of this alternate timeline. However, another existing Marvel character, Uatu, aka The Watcher, is allowed to continue watching the 1602 universe as a "pocket universe."

Central to the approach of *Marvel 1602* is the rearticulation of existing DC characters in an Elizabethan context. The nature of such licensed material tends to be that such characters are to some extent the product of accrued mythology, although there is a need to cleave to preexisting templates as consistent with whatever the contemporary requirements of the property might be. In the case of *Marvel 1602* there is clearly some flexibility for Gaiman, because events are occurring in a parallel timeline.

What Gaiman chooses to do is to play at the margins of the mythologies of the various characters, while retaining chief identifiable characteristics. Peter Parquah, therefore, is aged down contemporaneous to other characters, Gaiman playing with our expectations of seeing the character's origin story—familiar from frequent retellings—happen again, only this time in the context of a medieval setting. Parquah fulfils the role of squire to Sir Nick Fury, here reimagined as the Queen's Intelligencer, consistent with the character's established role as an operative of SHIELD. At the root of *Marvel 1602* is alterity, the experience of seeing a set of familiar events or familiar characters recast but not beyond recognizability. Once again, as in the example of *Sandman* and its relationship to its history, Gaiman manages the simultaneous continuation and transformation of the mythological.

Conclusion

In his deployment of the mythological, Gaiman engages in both continuance and transformation as determined by Genette. Archetypes from Punch and Judy are maintained and used as a method for exploring autobiographical memory and abuse in *Mr. Punch: The Tragical Comedy or Comical Tragedy*, an example of continuance. *Sandman*'s three oracles, though previously transformed through Greek archetype and Shakespeare's *Macbeth*, similarly remain consistent with the versions Gaiman has drawn from *The Witching Hour*. In Gaiman's *Future Shocks* stories archetypes are shifted to fit the milieu of the story, as in the case of the teacher-narrator from "You're Never Alone With a Phone!" and the creator figure from "Conversation Piece."

However, in a number of examples of Gaiman's usage of the mythological, both continuance and transformation are simultaneously apparent. In *Marvel 1602* Peter Parker's origin story as Spiderman is knowingly misremembered, Gaiman understanding the ironic pleasures this will instill in a readership alert to such references. The wider context of a parallel universe means that Spiderman's origin story can be subverted while simultaneously remaining consistent with established Marvel mythology.

Gaiman's utilization of this technique seems to be specific to licensed properties such as *Sandman* and *Marvel 1602* and is evidenced in his *Doctor Who* television episode "The Doctor's Wife," explored by Matt Hills elsewhere in this volume. Perhaps this is because though these established story worlds exist in the fantasy genre, they benefit from established rule sets known to the fan-base. Gaiman's success in concurrently managing continuance and transformation relies on his ability to remain consistent with the rules of the story world while also saying something fresh about the story world in question.

In the universes Gaiman plays in no story truly ends, but there are more than just continuances. Sometimes there are transformations, and sometimes his playful palimpsest leads to ideas and images that are simultaneously continuous *and* transformative.

---

1 Gaiman, Kubert, and Isanove, *Marvel* 1602, 169.
2 Hanks, McLeod, and Makins, *The Collins Concise Dictionary of the English Language: Second Edition*, 819-820.
3 Coupe, *Myth*, 53.
4 Medhurst, "Batman, Deviance and Camp", 149-163.
5 Bornstein and Williams, *Palimpsest: Editorial Theory in the Humanities*, 1.
6 Borges in Genette, *Palimpsests: Literature in the Second Degree*, 374.
7 Draaisma, *Metaphors of Memory*, 46.
8 Genette, *Palimpsests*, 177, 311.
9 Genette, *Palimpsests*, 385.
10 Bishop, *Thrill-Power Overload: 2000AD, The First Thirty Years*, 28.
11 Gifford, *The International Book of Comics*, 213.
12 Bishop, *Thrill-Power*, 37.
13 Barthes, *S/Z*, 17.
14 Gaiman, Hicklenton, and Frame, "You're Never Alone With A Phone", 176.
15 Connerton, *How Societies Remember*, 62.
16 Gaiman, *Don't Panic*, i-225.
17 Gaiman, Belardinelli, and Frame, "I'm a Believer," 182.
18 Cavalcanti, *Dead of Night*, n.p.
19 Gaiman, Afterword to *Preludes*, 238.
20 Gaiman, Introduction to *Endless Nights*, 8
21 Genette, *Palimpsests*, 177, 311.
22 Baxter, *SFX* Magazine Review of *The Witching Hour*, 122.
23 Borsellino, "Blue and Pink: Gender in Neil Gaiman's Work," 52.
24 Gaiman, Interview in *The Neil Gaiman Reader*, 56.
25 Borsellino, "Blue and Pink," 53.
26 McCloud, *Understanding Comics: The Invisible Art*, 44.

CONTRIBUTORS

Samuel Brooker Born in Hackney but raised in Kent, Sam attended Dane Court Grammar, where he was heavily involved in the student magazine. This continued with student journalism at the University of East Anglia, where he received BA in English Literature and Film Studies before moving to London to study for an MA in New Media. Having worked as a bassoonist, Punch and Judy man, and magic lanternist, he now lectures in creative writing and new media at several London universities, with a particular interest in interactive fiction.

Anthony S. Burdge, an independent scholar, was first introduced to the existence of Secondary Worlds via the work of J.R.R Tolkien at an early age. Since taking that first journey out of Bag End with Bilbo, he has traveled with the Doctor, hitchhiked with Arthur Dent and Ford Prefect, and entered the realms of Dream numerous times. Anthony first came across the worlds of Neil Gaiman via *The Sandman* and *Books of Magic* series in the late 1990s. Anthony has had articles published on a variety of topics, including J.R.R. Tolkien in numerous collections such as *The J.R.R. Encyclopedia,* and his first book, the first in the Mythological Dimensions series, *The Mythological Dimensions of Doctor Who,* was published in May 2010. As an avid bibliophile and self-taught herbalist, Anthony has sought to develop his own sense of other-worldly, trans-dimensional travel via the ancient Shamanic traditions of Indigenous people. The stories he himself has gathered he hopes to one day share in print.

Jessica Burke is teacher by trade and a self-professed Geek by nature. She's an avid bibliophile, self-taught herbalist, a fan of cats, songs about Cthulhu, and sushi. Ms. Burke first heard about Neil Gaiman while in college—when she "borrowed" a copy of *Sandman: Fables and Reflections.* But it wasn't until a decade later, when attending ComicCon, that she became reacquainted with Gaiman's work—when he appeared to read some of Bod's Adventures. Hearing the author himself do a reading from his work is second only to one other experience in terms of inspiration— hearing J.R.R. Tolkien read on LP. When she was five years old, Ms. Burke discovered a recording of Professor Tolkien reading "Riddles in the Dark" from *The Hobbit* in the local library. It was a formative childhood experience. Hearing Gaiman as an adult was the natural successor as both authors have had a profound effect on her life and work. Ms. Burke has published on a range of topics from J.R.R. Tolkien to *Beowulf* to *Doctor Who*.

Leslie Drury is currently undertaking her Ph.D. in English at the University of Aberdeen. Her thesis explores the representation of "old wives' tales" and the female storyteller in early modern English literature. She has an ongoing interest in folklore and fairy tale in all areas of literature. Having been a long-time fan of Neil Gaiman's work, this call for papers offered an opportunity to join two ongoing passions in one project.

Jason Fisher is an independent and award-winning scholar specializing in J.R.R. Tolkien and the Inklings, fantasy literature, and linguistics. His most recent book is *Tolkien and the Study of His Sources: Critical Essays* (McFarland, 2011). Other publications include entries in the *J.R.R. Tolkien Encyclopedia: Scholarship and Critical Assessment* (Routledge, 2006); contributions to eight books (three forthcoming); essays in *Tolkien Studies*, *Mythlore*, *The Year's Work in Medievalism*, *Beyond Bree*, *North Wind*, *Renaissance*; and many, many book reviews. Jason has spoken at academic conferences across the United States and will be a special guest at the Tolkien Society's Return of the Ring conference at Loughborough University in Leicestershire in 2012. Jason is also the editor of *Mythprint*, the monthly publication of the Mythopoeic Society (http://www.mythprint.org). You can contact Jason at his blog, Lingwë – Musings of a Fish (http://lingwe.blogspot.com/), where he has been discussing J.R.R. Tolkien, C.S. Lewis, J.K. Rowling, and related topics since 2007.

Camillo A. Formigatti took a degree in classical studies (main field Oriental and Linguistic Studies) in 2004 at the Università degli Studi di Milano. From October 2000 to July 2004 and from October 2004 till May 2008 he attended classes on Indological and Tibetological subjects at the Institute for Indological and Tibetological Studies of the Philipps-Universität Marburg, Germany. He worked in the library of the same institute from November 2007 till May 2008. Since June 2008 he has been a member of the Research Group "Manuscript Cultures in Asia and Africa" at the University of Hamburg, Germany.

Lynn Gelfand is an Associate Professor of English at the University of Advancing Technology and holds a Ph.D. in Folklore from Indiana University. Her research interests include folk narratives (myths, legends, and fairy tales), comparative media studies (orality, writing, print, film, and digital technologies), and the intersecting points between narratives and games.

Melody Green received her Ph.D. in English Studies with a specialization in Children's Literature in 2008 from Illinois State University. Currently she is adjuncting at two schools, Lewis University in Romeoville, IL, and DeVry Online. At Lewis she teaches composition classes, and for DeVry she teaches composition and Science Fiction. She has read papers on J. R. R. Tolkien, George MacDonald, and fantasy literature at several academic conferences, and is currently at work on several writing projects. Her other publications include "The Riddle of Strider: A Cognitive Linguistic Reading" published in *The Ring Goes Ever On: Proceedings of the Tolkien 2005 Conference* and "'It Turned Out they Died For Nothing:' Doctor Who and the Idea of Sacrificial Death" in *The Mythological Dimensions of Doctor Who*.

Colin B. Harvey is a fantasy writer, journalist, and academic. His short story *The Stinker* won the inaugural *SFX Pulp Idol* award in 2006. He has authored BBC-licensed *Doctor Who* spinoff material for the British company Big Finish and is the writer of *Love and Hate*, the second episode in the *Highlander* audio series produced by Big Finish under license from MGM. Colin is the originator of the *London Peculiar* steampunk stories, as published in the magazine *Steampunk Tales* and the forthcoming anthology *Clockwork Chaos* (American Library of Science Fiction and Fantasy). He is the author of the academic volume *Grand Theft Auto: Motion-Emotion* (Ludologica 2005) and has written academic articles on *Battlestar Galactica* and *Doctor Who*, the latter for the preceding volume in this series. Colin has authored and presented academic papers on *Highlander*, *Tron,* and *Ghostbusters*, and forthcoming publications will explore steampunk and the transmediality of Conan the Barbarian. As a journalist he has written for *The Guardian*, *Edge*, *Retrogamer*, *Develop*, *Strange Horizons,* and *Vector*, the journal of the British Science Fiction Association.

Matthew Hills is a Reader in Media and Cultural Studies at Cardiff University, and the author of *Triumph of a Time Lord* (IB Tauris, 2010) as well as a contributor to *Mythological Dimensions of Doctor Who* (Kitsune, 2010). His current research includes a follow-up book on *Torchwood*, a journal article on the use of sound in BBC Wales' *Who,* and book chapters on topics such as scholar-fandom and cult movies.

Tanya Carinae Pell Jones is 28 years old and lives in Charlotte, NC with her husband, Doug, and their two dogs, Arwyn and Lycan. She teaches high school English at Lincoln Charter School in Denver, NC. Her graduate thesis focuses on the Gothic in children's literature and its use in the high school classroom. She is particularly fond of high heels, sushi, and random trivia.

Tony Keen teaches Classical Studies and Film and Television History for the Open University. He is co-editor of *The Unsilent Library: Essays on the Russell T. Davies Era of the New Doctor Who*, published by the Science Fiction Foundation in February 2011, and is writing a chapter on "Science Fiction" for the *Blackwell Companion to the Reception of Classical Myth*.

Chelsey Kendig is an MA student of Children's Literature at Simmons College in Boston. The groundwork for this essay was done during a close study of *The Chronicles of Narnia* during her time as a visiting student at Magdalen College, Oxford. "The Problem of Susan" is especially important to her, since it marked the first work that introduced her to the possibility of children's literature studies.

Kristine Larsen has inhabited the space-time of Connecticut since her birth in 1963. She has been an aficionado from an early age of equal parts world mythology and religions, science fiction and fantasy, and scientific literature. Her long career in astronomy education and outreach draws heavily upon her diverse intellectual interests, including numerous publications and presentations on the intersection between science and science fiction/fantasy. She is currently Professor of Physics and Astronomy at Central Connecticut State University.

Lynnette Porter, Ph.D., is a professor of humanities and communication at Embry-Riddle University in Daytona Beach, Florida, and loves to write about television, film, and literature, especially science fiction and fantasy. Since 2011 she has been a contributing editor for PopMatters and writes a monthly column, Deep Focus. Her published works include *The Hobbits* (Tauris); *Tarnished Heroes, Charming Villains, and Modern Monsters* (McFarland); LOST's *Buried Treasures* (Sourcebooks); and forthcoming books about Sherlock Holmes and Doctor Who. She frequently is a speaker at academic conferences as well as fan conventions throughout North America, the U.K., Australia, and New Zealand.

Harley J. Sims received his Ph.D. in English from the University of Toronto in 2009, and is presently an independent scholar living in Ottawa, Canada. Aside from scholarly publications on medieval literature, he has written popular articles on Batman, *Beowulf*, and the *Twilight* series, as well as reviews of linguistic and medieval titles for the scholarly journal *Mythlore*; he has also presented academic papers at international conferences in both Canada and the United States. His research focuses primarily on the imaginative aspects of literature, particularly the interaction of language, reality, and imagination. His website is at www.harleyjsims.webs.com

 Matthew Dow Smith is a comic book artist and writer. He has drawn comics for every major American comic book publisher, including *Sandman Mystery Theater*—a spin-off of Neil Gaiman's *Sandman* series—for DC/Vertigo, and IDW Publishing's *Doctor Who*. Like Gaiman, he owns several black leather jackets and has been photographed in a Fourth Doctor scarf. His first novel, *Night Folk*, has only a few gods in it, but he is currently working on a second novel, which features even more gods, but nowhere near as many as Neil Gaiman's *American Gods*.

BIBLIOGRAPHY

PRINT MEDIA: BOOKS

Adams, Douglas. *The Hitch-Hiker's Guide to the Galaxy*. London: Pan Books, 1978.

———. *The Original Hitchhiker Radio Scripts*. New York: Harmony Books, 1985.

———. *The Ultimate Hitchhiker's Guide to the Galaxy*. USA: Ballantine Del Rey, 2002.

Adams, Douglas and John Carnell. *The Hitchhiker's Guide to the Galaxy: The Authorized Collection*. New York: DC Comics, 1997.

Adams, Neal, Alex Toth, et al. *Showcase Presents: The Witching Hour*, New York: DC, 2011.

Adler, Margot. *Drawing Down the Moon: Witches, Goddess-Worshippers, and Other Pagans in America Today*. New York: Penguin Arkana, 1986.

Aeschylus. *Oresteia*. Translated by Christopher Collard. Oxford: Oxford University Press, 2002.

Aeschylus. *Persians and Other Plays*. Translated by Christopher Collard. Oxford: Oxford University Press, 2008.

Apuleius. *The Golden Ass*. Translated by Robert Graves. Harmondsworth: Penguin, 1950.

Bahktin, M. M. *The Dialogic Imagination*. Translated by Caryl Emerson and Michael Holquist. Austin: University of Texas Press, 1981.

Baker, Bill. *Neil Gaiman on his work and career*. New York: Rosen Publishing, 2008.

Barthes, Roland. *S/Z*. London: Wiley-Blackwell, 1990.

Belanger, Michelle. *Sacred Hunger: The Vampire in Myth and Reality*. Fort Wayne Indiana: Dark Moon Press, 2005.

Bender, Hy. *The Sandman Companion: A Dreamer's Guide to the Award-

winning Comic Series. New York: DC Comics, 2000.

Bildhauer, Bettina. "Bloodsuckers: The Construction of Female Sexuality in Medieval Science and Fiction." *Consuming Narratives: Gender and Monstrous Appetite in the Middle Ages and the Renaissance*. Edited by Liz Herbert McAvoy and Teresa Walters, 104-115. Cardiff: University of Wales Press, 2002.

Bishop, David. *Thrill-Power Overload: 2000AD - The First Thirty Years*. London: Rebellion, 2009.

Bolintineanu, Alexandra. "'On the Borders of Old Stories:' Enacting the Past in *Beowulf* and *The Lord of the Rings*." *Tolkien and the Invention of Myth: A Reader*. Edited by Jane Chance. Lexington: University Press of Kentucky, 2004. 263-73.

Borges, Jorge Luis. *Labyrinths*. London: Penguin, 1970.

Bornstein, George and Williams, Ralph G. *Palimpsest: Editorial Theory in the Humanities*. Michigan: The University of Michigan Press, 1993.

Borsellino, Mary. "Blue and Pink: Gender in Neil Gaiman's Work." *The Neil Gaiman Reader*. Edited by Darrell Schweitzer. 51-53 Maryland: Wildside Press, 2007.

Bratman, David. "A Game of You–Yes, *You*." *The Sandman Papers: An Exploration of the Sandman Mythology*, Edited by Joe Sanders, 41-53. Seattle, WA: Fantagraphics, 2006.

Brauner, Sigrid. *Fearless Wives & Frightened Shrews: The Construction of the Witch in Early Modern Germany*. Amherst: University of Massachusetts Press, 1995.

Breton, Andre. *Manifestoes of Surrealism*. Michigan: University of Michigan Press, 1972.

Britton, Piers D. *TARDISbound: Navigating the Universes of Doctor Who*. London and New York: I.B. Tauris, 2011.

Broedel, Hans Peter. *The Malleus Maleficarum and the Construction of Witchcraft: Theology and Popular Belief*. Manchester and New York: Manchester University Press, 2003.

Broekman, J. *Structuralism: Moscow-Prague-Paris*. Berlin: Springer, 1974.

Brooker, Will. *Batman Unmasked: Analyzing a Cultural Icon*. London and New York: Continuum, 2000.

_____. "The Best Batman Story: The Dark Knight Returns." *Beautiful*

Things in Popular Culture, Edited by Alan McKee, 33-48. Malden and Oxford: Blackwell Publishing, 2007.

Buckley, J. H. *The Victorian Temper: A Study in Literary Culture*. Cambridge: Harvard UP, 1964.

Calvin, David. "In Her Red-Hot Shoes: Re-telling "Snow White" from the Queen's Point of View." *Anti-Tales: The Uses of Disenchantment*, Edited by Catriona McAra and David Calvin, 231-245. Newcastle upon Tyne: Cambridge Scholars Publishing, 2011.

Campbell, Joseph. *The Hero with a Thousand Faces*. New York, MJF Books, 1997.

Campbell, Lori. *Portals of Power: Magical Agency and Transformation in Literary Fantasy (Critical Explorations in Science Fiction and Fantasy)*. North Carolina, McFarland, 2010.

Carpenter, Humphrey. *Tolkien: A Biography*. Boston: Houghton Mifflin, 1977.

Chesterton, G. K. "Introduction." *George MacDonald and his Wife*. Edited by Greville MacDonald. Whitethorn, CA: Johannessen, 1924, 1998.

Crichton, Michael. *Eaters of the Dead: The Manuscript of Ibn Fadlan Relating His Experiences with the Northmen in A.D. 922*. New York: Knopf, 1976.

Clark Hall, J. R. *A Concise Anglo-Saxon Dictionary*. Toronto: University of Toronto Press, 2000.

Clements, Fiona. "*Sandman*." *The Slings and Arrows Comic Guide: A Critical Assessment*, Edited by Frank Plowright, 550-1. Marietta: Top Shelf Productions, 2003.

Coats, Karen. "Between Horror, Humour, and Hope: Neil Gaiman and the Psychic Work of the Gothic." *The Gothic in Children's Literature: Haunting the Borders,* Edited by Anna Jackson. New York, Routledge, 2008.

Connerton, Paul. *How Societies Remember*. Cambridge: Cambridge University Press, 1999.

Conway, D.J. *Maiden, Mother, Crone: The Myth and Reality of the Triple Goddess*. St Paul, MN: Llewellyn Worldwide, 1994.

Coupe, Laurence. *Myth*. London: Routledge, 1997.

———. *Myth: 2nd Edition*. London and New York: Routledge, 2009.

Coats, Karen. "Between Horror, Humour, and Hope: Neil Gaiman and the Psychic Work of the Gothic." *The Gothic in Children's Literature: Haunting the Borders,* ed., Jackson, Anna. New York, Routledge, 2008.

Damico, Helen. *Beowulf's Wealhtheow and the Valkyrie Tradition.* Madison: University of Wisconsin Press, 1984.

Darnton, Robert. "Peasants Tell Tales: The Meaning of Mother Goose." *The Classic Fairy Tales,* Edited by Maria Tatar, 280-91. London: Norton, 1999.

Davidson, Gustav. *A Dictionary of Angels, Including the Fallen Angels.* New York: Simon and Schuster, 1967.

Delaney, Samuel. Introduction. *The Sandman: A Game of You.* By Neil Gaiman. New York: DC Comics, 1993.

Derrida, J. *Positions.* Translated by Alan Bass. Chicago: University of Chicago Press, 1981.

Dixon-Kennedy, Mike. *Encyclopedia of Russian and Slavic Myth and Legend.* Santa Barbara, CA: ABC-CLIO, 1998.

Dowd, Chris. "An Autopsy of Storytelling: Metafiction and Neil Gaiman." *The Neil Gaiman Reader,* Edited by Darrell Schweitzer, 103-114. Maryland: Wildside Press, 2007.

Downing, David C. *Into the Wardrobe: CS Lewis and the Narnia Chronicles.* San Francisco, CA: Jossey-Bass, 2008.

Draaisma, Douwe. *Metaphors of Memory: A History of Ideas About the Mind.* Cambridge: Cambridge University Press, 2000.

Dringenberg, Mike, interview by Joseph McCabe. *Hanging Out with the Dream King* (2004).

Eco, Umberto. *The Role of the Reader: Explorations in the Semiotics of Texts.* Oxford: John Wiley and Sons, 1984.

Edgar, Andrew, and Peter Sedgwick. *Cultural Theory: The Key Concepts.* London: Taylor and Francis, 1997.

Euripides. *Electra and Other Plays.* Translated by John Davie. London: Penguin, 1998, 2004.

Fisher, Jason. "Horns of Dawn: The Tradition of Alliterative Verse in Rohan." *Middle-earth Minstrel: Essays on Music in Tolkien.* Edited by Bradford Lee Eden. North Carolina: McFarland, 2010.

Franks, Frederick S. *The First Gothics: A Critical Guide to the English Gothic Novel.* New York: Garland Reference Library, 1987.

Frazer, J.G. *The Golden Bough.* London: Macmillan and Company, 1906-1915 (first edition 1890).

Freud, Sigmund. "The Uncanny." In *The Standard Edition of the Complete Psychological Works of Sigmund Freud vol. XVII,* Edited by James Strachey, 219. London: Hogarth, 1953.

Gaiman, Neil. *American Gods.* London: Headline, 2001 (pagination from 2002 paperback edition); New York: Harper Torch, 2002.

_____. *Anansi Boys.* London: Headline Review, 2005; New York: Morrow HarperCollins, 2005; New York: Harper Torch, 2006.

_____. *Batman: Whatever Happened to the Caped Crusader?* New York: DC Comics, 2010.

_____. *Blueberry Girl.* London: Bloomsbury, 2009.

_____. *Books of Magic.* New York: DC, 1993 (reprinting comics from 1990).

_____. *Brief Lives.* New York: DC Comics, 1993.

_____. "Brothers." *Swamp Thing Annual* 5 (DC, 1985). (Collected in *Neil Gaiman's Midnight Days.* New York: Vertigo, 1999: 17-58.)

_____. *Coraline.* New York: Harper Trophy, 2002.

_____. *Day of the Dead: An Annotated Babylon 5 Script.* Minneapolis: DreamHaven Books, 1998.

_____. *Death: The High Cost of Living.* New York: Vertigo, 1993.

_____. *Don't Panic: Douglas Adams and The Hitch-Hiker's Guide to the Galaxy.* London: Titan Books, 1993.

_____. "Foreword: The Nature of the Infection." *The Eye of the Tyger.* Edited by Paul McAuley, 7-10. Tolworth: Telos Publishing, 2003.

_____. *Fragile Things: Short Fictions and Wonders.* London: Headline Review, 2007; New York: Harper, 2010.

_____. *The Graveyard Book.* New York: Harper Collins, 2008.

_____. Interview by Elder, Robert K. *The Neil Gaiman Reader* 2007.

_____. Introduction to *The Sandman: Endless Nights.* London: Vertigo, 2004.

_____. *Marvel 1602*. London: Marvel, 2006.

_____. *MirrorMask*. New York: Harper Collins, 2005.

_____. *Mr. Punch: The Tragical Comedy or Comical Tragedy*. London: Bloomsbury, 2006.

_____. *Neil Gaiman's Midnight Days*. New York: Vertigo, 1999.

_____. *Neverwhere*. London: BBC Books, 1996.

_____. "Notes Towards a Vegetable Theology." *Prince of Stories: The Many Worlds of Neil Gaiman*, Edited by Hank Wagner, 187-91. London: St Martin's Press, 2009.

_____. *Odd and the Frost Giants*. New York: Harper, 2009.

_____. *Spawn* #9. New York: Image Comics, 1993.

_____. *The Sandman*. Issue #20, "Façade." New York: DC Comics, 1991.

_____. *The Sandman*. Issue #54, "The Golden Boy." New York: DC Comics, 1993.

_____. *The Sandman I: Preludes and Nocturnes*. New York: DC/Vertigo, 1991.

_____. *The Sandman II: The Doll's House*. New York: DC/Vertigo, 1995 (first edition 1990).

_____. *The Sandman III: Dream Country*. New York: DC/Vertigo, 1991.

_____. *The Sandman IV: Season of Mists*. New York: DC/Vertigo, 1992.

_____. *The Sandman V: A Game of You*. New York: DC/Vertigo: 1993.

_____. *The Sandman VI: Fables and Reflections*. New York: DC/Vertigo, 1993.

_____. *The Sandman VII: Brief Lives*. New York: DC/Vertigo, 1999, 2009.

_____. *The Sandman VIII: World's End*. New York: DC/Vertigo, 1994.

_____. *The Sandman IX: The Kindly Ones*. New York: DC/Vertigo, 1996.

_____. *The Sandman X: The Wake*. New York: DC/Vertigo, 1997.

_____. *The Sandman: The Dream Hunters*. New York: DC/Vertigo, 1999.

_____. *Smoke and Mirrors: Short Fictions and Illusions*. London: Headline Feature, 1999; London: Headline, 2000; New York: Avon Books, 2005.

_____. *Stardust: Being a Romance within the Realms of Faerie*. New York: Vertigo, 1998; London: Headline, 1999 (pagination from 2005 Headline Review edition); New York. Harper Perennial, 2006.

Gaiman, Neil, and Dave McKean. *Black Orchid*. New York: DC, 1991.

Gaiman, Neil and Michael Reaves. *InterWorld*. New York: Eos, 2008.

Gaiman, Neil, and Roger Avary. *Beowulf: The Script Book*. New York: HarperEntertainment, 2007.

Gaiman, Neil, and Terry Pratchett. *Good Omens*. New York: Workman, 1990.

Gardner, Gerald. *Witchcraft Today*. New York: Citadel Press, 2004.

Gardner, John. *Grendel*. New York: Knopf, 1971.

Genette, Gerard. *Palimpsests: Literature in the Second Degree*. Nebraska: University of Nebraska Press, 1997.

_____. *Paratexts: Thresholds of Interpretation*. Cambridge: Cambridge University Press, 1997.

Gifford, Denis. *The International Books of Comics*. London: Deans International Publishing, 1984.

Gilmore, Mikal. Introduction. *The Sandman: The Wake*. By Neil Gaiman. New York: DC Comics, 1996.

Gimbutas, Marija. *The Civilization of the Goddess: The World of Old Europe*. New York: Harper San Francisco, 1991.

_____. *The Language of the Goddess*. New York: Thames and Hudson, 2006.

Gnoli, Raniero. *The Aesthetic Experience According to Abhinavagupta: Second Edition Revised, Enlarged and Re-Elaborated by the Author*. Varanasi: Chowkhamba Sanskrit Series Office, 1968.

Godwin, Parke. *The Tower of Beowulf*. New York: William Morrow & Co., 1995.

Gordon, Joan. "Prospero Framed in Neil Gaiman's *The Wake*." *The Sandman Papers: An Exploration of the Sandman Mythology,* Edited by Joe Sanders, 79-92. Seattle: Fantagraphics Books, 2006.

Graves, Robert. *The White Goddess: A Historical Grammar of Poetic Myth*, Edited by Grevel Lindop. Manchester: Carcanet, 1948, 1997; New York: Farrar Straus and Giroux, 1966.

Green, Miranda. *Symbol and Image in Celtic Religious Art*. London: Routledge, 1992.

Gummere, Francis B. *The Oldest English Epic*. New York: Macmillan, 1935.

Hanes, Stacie L. "Reinventing the Spiel: Old Stories, New Approaches." *The Sandman Papers: An Exploration of the Sandman Mythology*, Edited by Joe Sanders, 147-69. Seattle, WA: Fantagraphics, 2006.

_____. "Weatherwax, Granny Esmerelda." *An Unofficial Companion to the Novels of Terry Pratchett*, Edited by Andrew M. Butler, 405-8. Oxford: Greenwood, 2007.

_____. "Witches." *An Unofficial Companion to the Novels of Terry Pratchett*, Edited by Andrew M. Butler, 417-20. Oxford: Greenwood, 2007.

Hanks, Patrick *The Collins Concise Dictionary of the English Language: Second Edition*. Glasgow: Collins, 1990.

Harrison, Jane Ellen. *Prolegomena to the Study of Greek Religion*. Princeton: Princeton University Press, 1903, 1991.

_____. *Themis: A Study of the Social Origins of Greek Religion*. Cambridge: Cambridge University Press, 1912, 1927.

Hein, Rolland. *The Harmony Within: The Spiritual Vision of George MacDonald*. Chicago: Cornerstone Press, 1999.

Hills, Matt. *Fan Cultures*. London and New York: Routledge, 2002.

_____. "'Mythology Makes You Feel Something:' The Russell T. Davies Era as Sentimental Journey." *The Mythological Dimensions of Doctor Who*, Edited by Anthony Burdge, Jessica Burke, and Kristine Larsen, 198-215. Crawfordville, Florida: Kitsune Books, 2010.

_____. *Triumph of a Time Lord: Regenerating Doctor Who in the 21st Century*. London and New York: I.B. Tauris, 2010.

Hooper, Walter. *C.S. Lewis: A Companion and Guide*. New York, London: HarperCollins, 1996.

Howatson, M.C., and Ian Chilvers (eds.). *The Concise Oxford Companion to Classical Literature*. Oxford: Oxford University Press, 1996..

Huehnergard, John and Christopher Woods. "Akkadian and Eblaite." *The Cambridge Encyclopedia of the World's Ancient Languages*. Edited by Roger D. Woodard, 218-87. Cambridge: Cambridge University Press, 2004.

Hughes, David. *The Greatest Sci-fi Movies Never Made*. Chicago: A Capella Press, 2001.

Hunt, Leigh. *The Selected Writings of Leigh Hunt*, 6 vols. Edited by Jeffrey N Cox. London: Pickering and Chatto, 2003.

Hunt, Peter, and Millicent Lenz. *Alternative Worlds in Fantasy Fiction*. New York: Continuum, 2001.

Iser, Wolfgang. *The Fictive and the Imaginary: Charting Literary Anthropology*. Baltimore: Johns Hopkins University Press, 1993.

Jenkins, Henry. "Best Contemporary Mainstream Superhero Comics Writer: Brian Michael Bendis." *Beautiful Things in Popular Culture*, Edited by Alan McKee. Malden and Oxford: Blackwell Publishing, 2007.

Johnson-Smith, Jan. *American Science Fiction TV: Star Trek, Stargate and Beyond*. London and New York: I.B. Tauris, 2005.

Jones, Kelley. Interview by McCabe, Joseph. *Hanging Out with the Dream King* Seattle, WA: Fantagraphics Books, 2004.

Jones, Stephen, ed. *Dark Detectives: Adventures of the Supernatural Sleuths*. Minneapolis, MN: Fedogan & Bremer, 1999 [1998].

Jordan, Michael. *Encyclopedia of Gods*. London: Kyle Cathie, 2002.

Kaveney, Roz. *From Alien to the Matrix: Reading Science Fiction Film*. London: I.B. Tauris, 2005.

_____. *Superheroes! Capes and Crusaders in Comics and Films*. London: I.B. Tauris, 2008.

Keane, Stephen. "Time Past / Time Future: Reading 'Babylon Squared'" *The Parliament of Dreams: Conferring on Babylon 5*. Edited by Edward James and Farah Mendlesohn, 15-25. Reading: Science Fiction Foundation, 1998.

Kieth, Sam. Interview by McCabe, Joseph. *Hanging Out with the Dream King*. Seattle, WA: Fantagraphics Books, 2004.

Keightley, Thomas. *The Fairy Mythology*. London: G. Bell, 1880.

Klock, Geoff. *How To Read Superhero Comics and Why*. New York and London: Continuum, 2002.

Kubert, Andy. Interview by McCabe, Joseph. *Hanging Out with the Dream King*. Seattle, WA: Fantagraphics Books, 2004.

Lacan, Jacques. *The Four Fundamentals of Psychoanalysis*. Translated by

Alan Sheridan. London: W.W. Norton and Co, 1998.

Laity, K.A. "Illusory Adversaries? Images of Female Power in *Sandman: The Kindly Ones*." *The Sandman Papers: An Exploration of the Sandman Mythology*, Edited by Joe Sanders, 65-76. Seattle, WA: Fantagraphics, 2006.

Lancaster, Kurt. *Interacting with Babylon 5: Fan Performances in a Media Universe*. Austin: University of Texas Press, 2001.

Lawrence, William Witherle. *Beowulf and the Epic Tradition*. Cambridge, Massachusetts: Harvard University Press, 1928.

Lee, Stuart D. and Elizabeth Solopova. *The Keys of Middle-earth: Discovering Medieval Literature through the Fiction of J.R.R. Tolkien*. New York: Palgrave Macmillan, 2005.

Lerer, Seth. *Children's Literature: A Reader's History from Aesop to Harry Potter*. Chicago: University of Chicago Press, 2008.

Leeming, David and Margaret Leeming. *A Dictionary of Creation Myths*. New York: Oxford University Press, 1995.

Levi-Strauss, Claude. *The Naked Man Volume 4*. New York: Harper and Row, 1981.

Lewis, C. S. *The Dawn Treader*. New York: HarperCollins, 1952, 1994.

_____. *George MacDonald: An Anthology*. New York: Harper One, 1946, 2001.

_____. *The Last Battle*. New York: Harper Collins, 1956, 1994.

_____. *Letters to an American Lady*. Edited by Clyde S. Kilby. Grand Rapids, Michigan: Wm. B. Eerdans Publishing Company,

_____. *Letters to Children*, Edited by Lyle W. Dorsett and Majorie Lamp Mead. New York: Scribner, 1996.

_____. *The Lion, the Witch, and the Wardrobe*. New York: Scholastic, 1987; HarperCollins, 1950, 1994; 1967, 1971.

_____. *The Magician's Nephew*. New York: HarperCollins, 1983.

_____. *Prince Caspian*. New York: HarperCollins, 1951, 1994.

Lindow, John. *Norse Mythology: A Guide to the Gods, Heroes, Rituals, and Beliefs*. New York: Oxford University Press, 2001.

Lundberg, Jason Erik. "The Old Switcheroo: A Study in Neil Gaiman's

Use of Character Reversal." *The Neil Gaiman Reader*, Edited by Darrell Schweitzer, 122-130. Maryland: Wildside Press, 2007.

Lyotard, Jean Francois. *The Postmodern Condition: A Report on Knowledge*. Translated by Geoffrey Bennington and Brian Massumi. Manchester: Manchester University Press, 1984.

MacDonald, George. *At the Back of the North Wind*. New York: Burt, A. L. 1871, n.d.

_____. *Lilith*. 1895. Grand Rapids, MI: Wm. B. Eerdmans, 2001.

MacKillop, James. *Oxford Dictionary of Celtic Mythology*. Oxford: Oxford University Press, 1998.

March, Jenny. *Cassell's Dictionary of Classical Mythology*. London: Cassell, 1998.

Marcus, Leonard. *The Minders of Make-Believe*. Boston MA: Houghton Mifflin Harcourt, 2008.

Marshall, C.W. "The Furies, Wonder Woman and Dream. Mythmaking in DC Comics." *Classics and Comics*, Edited by George Kovacs and C.W. Marshall, 89-101. Oxford: Oxford University Press, 2011.

McAvoy, Liz Herbert and Teresa Walters, ed. *Consuming Narratives: Gender and Monstrous Appetite in the Middle Ages and the Renaissance*. Cardiff: University of Wales Press, 2002.

McCloud, Scott. *Understanding Comics: The Invisible Art*. New York: Harper, 1993.

McKean, Dave. Interview by Joseph McCabe. *Hanging Out with the Dream King* Seattle, WA: Fantagraphics Books, 2004.

Medhurst, Andy. "Batman, Deviance, and Camp." In *The Many Lives of the Batman: Critical Approaches to a Superhero and His Media*. Edited by Roberta E. Pearson and William Uricchio, 149-163. London: Routledge, 1991.

Miller, Laura. *The Magician's Book: A Skeptic's Adventures in Narnia*. New York: Little, Brown and Company, 2008, 2009.

Moore, Alan, and Ron Randall. "Abandoned Houses." *Swamp Thing* 33 (DC, February 1985).

_____. Dann Thomas, Dan Mishkin, Ross Andru and Dick Giordano. "My Sister, My Self!" *Wonder Woman* 300 (DC, February 1983)

Morales, Helen. *Classical Mythology: A Very Short Introduction*. Oxford:

Oxford University Press, 2007.

Neville, Jennifer. *Representations of the Natural World in Old English Poetry*. Cambridge: Cambridge University Press, 1999.

Nooy, Juliana de. *Twins in Contemporary Literature and Culture: Look Twice*. New York: Palgrave Macmillan, 2005.

Ó hÓgáin, Dáithí. *Myth Legend and Romance: An Encyclopaedia of the Irish Folk Tradition*. Oxford: Prentice Hall Press, 1991.

O'Keefe, Deborah. *Readers in Wonderland: The Liberating Worlds of Fantasy Fiction*. New York: Continuum, 2004.

Onions, C. T. *The Oxford Dictionary of English Etymology*. Clarendon: Oxford University Press, 1966.

Opie, Iona and Peter Opie. *The Classic Fairy Tales*. London: Oxford University Press, 1974.

Orchard, Andy. *Cassell's Dictionary of Norse Myth and Legend*. London: Cassell, 1997.

_____. *Cassell's Dictionary of Old Norse Myth and Legend*. London: Cassell, 2002.

_____. *Pride and Prodigies: Studies in the Monsters of the Beowulf-Manuscript*. Toronto: University of Toronto Press, 1995.

Panther, Klaus-Uwe. *Metonymy in language and thought*. New York: John Benjamins Publishing Company, 1999.

Parkin, Lance. *A history: An Unauthorised History of the Doctor Who Universe*. Des Moines: Mad Norwegian Press, 2006.

Parkin, Lance. "Truths Universally Acknowledged: How the "Rules" of *Doctor Who* Affect the Writing." *Third Person: Authoring and Exploring Vast Narratives*, Edited by Pat Harrigan and Noah Wardrip-Fruin, 13-24. Cambridge and London: MIT Press, 2009.

Pausanias. *Guide to Greece I: Central Greece*. Translated by Peter Levi. London: Penguin, 1979 (revised edition; first edition 1971).

Philip, Neil. *The Penguin Book of English Folktales*. London: Penguin Books, 1992.

Plowright, Frank "WitchCraft." *The Slings and Arrows Comic Guide: A Critical Assessment*. Edited by Frank Plowright,742. Marietta: Top Shelf Productions, 2003.

Pratchett, Terry. *Equal Rites*. London: Victor Gollancz, 1987.

_____. *Wyrd Sisters*. London: Victor Gollancz, 1989.

Propp, Vladimir. "Folklore and Literature." *The Classic Fairy Tales*, Edited by Tatar, Maria, 378-81. London: Norton, 1999.

_____. *Morphology of the Folk Tale*. Texas: University of Texas Press, 1968.

Pullman, Philip. *His Dark Materials*. New York: Alfred A. Knopf, 2007.

Rauch, Stephen. "Campbell and *The Sandman*: Reminding Us of the Sacred." *The Neil Gaiman Reader*, Edited by Darrell Schweitzer, 11-21. Maryland: Wildside Press, 2007.

Reis, Richard. *George MacDonald's Fiction: A Twentieth-Century View*. Eureka, CA: Sunrise Books, 1989.

Reynolds, Richard. *Super Heroes: A Modern Mythology*. Jackson: University Press of Mississippi, 1992.

Roderick, Timothy. *Dark Moon Mysteries*. Saint Paul: Llewellyn Publications, 1996.

The Royal Commission on Environmental Pollution. *Artificial Light in the Environment*. London: The Stationary Office Limited, 2009.

Royle, Nicholas. *The Uncanny: An Introduction*. Manchester: Manchester University Press, 2003.

Russell, Jeffrey Burton. *Lucifer: The Devil in the Middle Ages*. Ithaca: Cornell University Press,1984.

Sayer, Karen. "Witches." *Terry Pratchett: Guilty of Literature*, Edited by Andrew M. Butler, 131-52. Baltimore, MD: Old Earth Books, 2004.

Scull, Christina and Wayne G. Hammond. *The J.R.R. Tolkien Companion and Guide: Reader's Guide*. Boston: Houghton Mifflin, 2006.

Segal, Charles. *Interpreting Greek Tragedy: Myth, Poetry, Text*. Ithaca, NY: Cornell University Press, 1986.

Shippey, Tom. *The Road to Middle-earth: How J.R.R. Tolkien Created a New Mythology*. Rev. and expanded ed. Boston: Houghton Mifflin, 2003.

Shlain, Leonard. *The Alphabet versus the Goddess: The Conflict Between Word and Image*. New York: Penguin/Arkana, 1998.

Silverstone, Roger. *The Message of Television: Myth and Narrative in Contemporary Culture*. London: Heinemann, 1981.

Sjoestedt, Marie-Louise. *Celtic Gods and Heroes*. Mineola, NY: Dover, 2000 (first published as *Gods and Heroes of the Celts*, London: Methuen, 1949, trans., Dillon, Myles from *Dieux et héros des Celtes*, Paris: Leroux, 1940).

Slabbert, Mathilda. "Inventions and Transformations: Imagining New Worlds in the Stories of Neil Gaiman." *Fairy Tales Reimagined: Essays on New Retellings*, Edited by Susan Bobby, 68-83. Jefferson, NC: McFarland and Company, Inc., 2009.

Smith, John and Gaiman, Neil. *The Best of Tharg's Future Shocks*. London: Rebellion, 2010.

Speyer, Jacob S. *Studies about the Kathāsaritsāgara*, Verhandelingen der Koninklijke Akademie van Wetenschappen te Amsterdam. Afdeeling Letterkunde. Amsterdam: Müller, 1908.

Stanley, Eric Gerard. *Continuations and Beginnings: Studies in Old English Literature*. London: Thomas Nelson & Sons, 1966.

Sterne, David and Mark J. Mirsky. *Rabbinic Fantasies: Imaginative Narratives from Classical Hebrew Literature*. New Haven: Yale University Press, 1998.

Stoker, Bram. *The New Annotated Dracula*. Ed. with foreword and notes by Leslie S. Klinger. Introduction by Neil Gaiman. New York: W.W. Norton & Company, 2008.

Sullivan, C. W. "Fantasy." *Crosscurrents of Children's Literature: An Anthology of Texts and Criticism,* Edited by J.D. Stahl, Tina Hanlon and Elizabeth Lennox Keyser, 420-428. New York: Oxford University Press, 2007.

Swanton, John. *Skidegate Haida Myths and Histories*. Translated by John Enrico. Skidegate, B.C.: Queen Charlotte Islands Museum Press, 1995.

Sweet, Henry. *Anglo-Saxon Reader in Prose and Verse*. Oxford: The Clarendon Press, 1884.

Tawney, Charles Henry. *The Ocean of Story: Being C. H. Tawney's Translation of Somadeva's Kathā Sarit Sāgara (or Ocean of Streams of Story) Now Edited with Introduction, Fresh Explanatory Notes and Terminal Essay by N. M. Penzer in Ten Volumes*. Volume 1. London: Privately Printed for Subscribers Only By Chas. J. Sawyer Ltd., Grafton House, 1924.

Thompson, G.R. *Gothic Imaginations: Essays in Dark Romanticism*.

Washington: Washington State Press, 1974.

Thompson, William Irwin. *The Time Falling Bodies Take to Light: Mythology, Sexuality, and the Origins of Culture.* New York: St. Martin's Press, 1981.

Thurston, Robert W. *Witch, Wicce, Mother Goose.* London: Longman/Pearson Education, 2001.

Tiffin, Jessica. "Blood on the Snow: Inverting "Snow White" in the Vampire Tales of Neil Gaiman and Tanith Lee." *Anti-Tales: The Uses of Disenchantment,* Edited by Catriona McAra Catriona and David Calvin, 220-230. Newcastle upon Tyne: Cambridge Scholars Publishing, 2011.

Todorov, Tzvetan. *The Fantastic: A Structural Approach to a Literary Genre.* Ithaca: Cornell University Press, 1975.

Tolkien, J. R. R. *The Hobbit.* Boston: Houghton Mifflin, 1966.

_____.*The Letters of J.R.R. Tolkien.* Edited by Humphrey Carpenter. Boston: Houghton Mifflin, 1981.

_____. "*The Monsters and the Critics and Other Essays.* Edited by Christopher Tolkien. London: George Allen & Unwin, 1983.

_____. *Morgoth's Ring.* Boston: Houghton Mifflin, 1993.

_____. "On Fairy Stories." *Tree and Leaf.* Boston, Houghton Mifflin, 1989

_____. *The Silmarillion.* New York: Ballantine, 1977; Boston: Houghton Mifflin, 2001.

_____. *The Unfinished Tales of Númenor and Middle-Earth.* Boston: Houghton Mifflin, 1980.

Turner, Patricia, *A Dictionary of Ancient Deities.* New York: Oxford, 2001.

Uricchio, William and Pearson, Roberta E. "I'm Not Fooled By That Cheap Disguise." In *The Many Lives of the Batman,* Edited by Roberta E. Pearson and William Uricchio, 182-213. New York and London: Routledge/BFI, 1991.

Virgil. *The Aeneid.* Translated by David West. London: Penguin, 2000.

Wagner, Hank. *Prince of Stories: The Many Worlds of Neil Gaiman.* New York: St. Martin's Press, 2008.

_____. *Prince of Stories: The Many Worlds of Neil Gaiman.* London: St Martin's Press, 2009.

Veith, Gene. *The Soul of Prince Caspian: Exploring Spiritual Truth in the Land of Narnia*. Colorado Springs, CO: David C. Cook, 2000.

Warner, Marina. *From the Beast to the Blonde: On Fairy Tales and their Tellers*. London: Chatto and Windus, 1994.

West, David (trans.). *Virgil: The Aeneid*. London: Penguin, 2000.

Williams, David. *Deformed Discourse: The Function of the Monster in Mediaeval Thought and Literature*. Exeter: University of Exeter Press, 1996.

Wood, Juliette. "The Concept of the Goddess." *The Concept of the Goddess*, Edited by Sandra Billington, 8-25. London: Routledge, 1996.

Wood, Ian. *The Merovingian Kingdoms, 450-751*. Essex, England: Longman Group, 1994.

Zipes, Jack. *Fairy Tale as Myth/ Myth as Fairy Tale*. Lexington: University Press of Kentucky, 1994.

PRINT MEDIA: PERIODICALS

Bailey, David. "A Boy and His Box." *Doctor Who Magazine* no. 435 (2011): 32.

_____. "In Gaiman's Terms." *Doctor Who Magazine* no. 434 (2011): 44-8.

Bailey, Michael D. "The Feminization of Magic and the Emerging Idea of the Female Witch in the Late Middle Ages. " *Essays in Medieval Studies* Volume 19 (2002): 120-134.

_____ "The *Malleus Maleficarum* and the Construction of Witchcraft: Theology and Popular Belief: (Review)"*Magic, Ritual, and Witchcraft* Volume 1, Number 1 (Summer 2006): 124-127.

Baxter, Calvin. "The Witching Hour review." *SFX Magazine* (June 2011): 122.

Christensen, Bonniejean. "Tolkien's Creative Technique: *Beowulf* and *The Hobbit*." *Mythlore* 15.3 (1989): 4–10.

Clarke, M.J. "The Strict Maze of Media Tie-In Novels." *Communication, Culture and Critique* no. 2 (2009).

Dronke, Ursula. "Beowulf and Ragnarök." *Saga-book of the Viking Society for Northern Research*. University College, London. Volume XVII (1966–69): 302–25.

Drout, Michael D.C. "'*Beowulf*: The Monsters and the Critics' Seventy-five Years Later." *Mythlore* 30.1/2 (Fall/Winter 2011): 5–22.

Gaiman, Neil. "Production Notes." *Doctor Who Magazine* no. 427 (2010): 4.

———. "Reflections on Myth (*with Digressions into Gardening, Comics, and Fairy Tales*)." *Columbia: A Journal of Literature and Art* 31 1999.

Gaarden, Bonnie. "Cosmic and Psychological Redemption in George MacDonald's *Lilith*." *Studies in the Novel* 37.1 (2005): 20-36.

Geduld, Harry. "The Lineage of Lilith." *The Shaw Review* 7.2 (1964): 58-61.

Haley, Guy. "Red Alert." *SFX* no. 207 (2011): 10-27.

Julyan, Dave. "Neil Gaiman Interview." *ZZ9 Plural Z Alpha: The Hitchhiker's Guide to the Galaxy Appreciation Society: Mostly Harmless* Issue33 (June 1989): 18-21.

Mackie, Chris J. "Virgil's Dirae, South Italy, and Etruria." *Phoeni*, 1992.

Ozolins, Aija. "Dreams and Doctrines: Dual Strands in Frankenstein." *Science-Fiction Studies 2*, 1975: 103-10.

Seri, Andrea. "The Fifty Names of Marduk in Enūma eliš." *Journal of the American Oriental Society* (2006): 507-519.

Setchfield, Nick. "The Time Traveller's Wife." *SFX Magazine* 209 (2011).

Shippey, Tom. "Tom Shippey speaks at the Tolkien Society Annual Dinner, York, April 19, 1980." *Digging Potatoes, Growing Trees: A Selection from 25 Years of Speeches at the Tolkien Society's Annual Dinners*, Volume 1. Swindon: The Tolkien Society, 1997. 6–30.

Skeat, Walter William. "The Name 'Beowulf'." *The Academy*, Volume XI (January–March, 1877): 163.

Sordi Italo. "Dinamiche del carnevale." *La Ricerca Folklorica* No. 6, Interpretazioni del carnevale (Oct., 1982).

Tal, Eve. "Tony and the Wonderful Door: A Forgotten Classic of American Children's Fantasy." *The Lion and the Unicorn*, Vol. 27, Number 1 (2003): 131-143.

Temple, Sir William. "Of Poetry," *The Works of Sir William Temple*. New Edition. Volume III. London: S. Hamilton, 1814. 406–43.

Thomas, Roy, Dann Thomas, Tom Grindberg and Tony deZuniga. "The

"Golden Age Fury." *Secret Origins* 12 (DC, March 1987).

Westrin, Thomas. "Norner." *Nordisk Familjebok*, Volume 19, Stockholm: Nordisk Familjeboks Förlags, 1913: 1460.

INTERNET & NONPRINT RESOURCES

Barthes, Roland. "The Death of the Author." Aspen 5+6 (1967); <http://www.ubu.com/aspen/aspen5and6/threeEssays.html#barthes>

"Beldam." *Oxford English Dictionary*. Online version 2011. <http://www.oed.com/view/Entry/17334>

"Beowulf." British Library. <http://www.bl.uk/onlinegallery/onlineex/englit/beowulf/>

Bonnichsen, Shield. *The Neil Gaiman Visual Bibliography*. <http://www.neilgaimanbibliography.com>

Brewer, E. Cobham. *Brewer's Dictionary of Phrase and Fable*. New York: Harpers. Undated edition. <http://www.archive.org/stream/brewersdictionar000544mbp>

"carnadine." *Oxford English Dictionary*. Online version 2011. <http://www.oed.com/view/Entry/28058>

"charnel n1 and adj.1." *Oxford English Dictionary*. Online version 2011. <http://www.oed.com/view/Entry/30785>

Charles. R.H. trans. *The Book of Enoch From The Apocrypha and Pseudepigrapha of the Old Testament* Oxford: The Clarendon Press, 1893. <www.thebibleword.org/Enoch.pdf>

Clark, Brian. "The Witches of Thessaly." The Chiron Centre. 2000. <http://www.astrosynthesis.com.au/articles/The%20Witches%20of%20Thessaly.pdf>

Coltri, Marzia. "The Challenge of the Queen of Sheba: The Hidden Matriarchy in the Ancient East." University of Birmingham, U.K. 2011. <http://www.cesnur.org/2011/dan-coltri.pdf>

Cornwell, Simon. "Thorn Beta 5." 2011. <http://www.simoncornwell.com/lighting/collect/lanterns/thorn-beta5-3/index.htm>

Crispin, Jessa. "An interview with Neil Gaiman." *Bookslut*, October 2006. <http://www.bookslut.com/features/2006_10_010057.php>

Drout, Michael D.C. "Review of *Beowulf* (the film)." November 22, 2007.

<http://wormtalk.blogspot.com/2007/11/review-of-beowulf-film-my-favorite-part.html>

Dr. Virago [pseudonym]. "A diminished Beowulf, a shrinking Grendel, a wussy Wealhtheow, and Grendel's MILF." November 17, 2007. <http://quodshe.blogspot.com/2007/11/diminished-beowulf-shrinking-grendel.html>

Erdbeer, Robert Matthias. *Brill's New Pauly Wissowa*. "Myth (Classical Tradition) I. Concept." <http://brillonline.nl/subscriber/uid=3403/entry?entry=bnp_e1505640>

Graf, Fritz. *Brill's New Pauly Wissowa*. "Myth (Antiquity) I. Theory of Myth." <http://brillonline.nl/subscriber/uid=3403/entry?entry=bnp_e815160>

Gaiman, Neil. *Advice to Authors.* 1999. (accessed 06 28, 2011). <http://www.neilgaiman.com/p/FAQs/Advice_to_Authors#q1>

———. "An astonishingly professional post for once with barely any bats in it." January 21, 2005. <http://journal.neilgaiman.com/2005/01/astonishingly-professional-post-for.asp>

———. *The Guardian*. "TV and Radio Blog: Live QandA with Neil Gaiman." <http://www.guardian.co.uk/tv-and-radio/tvandradioblog/2011/may/16/neil-gaiman-doctor-who-doctors-wife?commentpage=1#comment-10776326>

———. "Happily Ever After." *The Guardian*, October 13, 2007. <http://www.guardian.co.uk/books/2007/oct/13/film.fiction?INTCMP=SRCH>

———. "I Cthulhu, or What's A Tentacle-Faced Thing Like Me Doing In A Sunken City Like This (Latitude 47° 9' S, Longitude 126° 43' W)?" <http://www.neilgaiman.com>

———. "My New Year Wish." 31 Dec. 2011. Web. 8 Jan. 2012. <http://journal.neilgaiman.com/>

———. Mythcon 35 Guest of Honor Speech. 2004. <http://www.mythsoc.org/mythcon/35/speech/>

———. "A Study in Emerald." <http://www.neilgaiman.com/mediafiles/exclusive/shortstories/emerald.pdf>

_____. "This is a prayer for a Blueberry girl." Neil Gaiman. 27th February 2009. <http://journal.neilgaiman.com/2009/02/this-is-prayer-for-blueberry-girl.html>

Gaiman, Neil. and Patton Oswalt. "Neil Gaiman and Patton Oswalt at Saban Theater in L.A. pt2." YouTube, 4th August 2011. <http://www.youtube.com/watch?v=_5joGrA0HTA>

_____. "Neil Gaiman and Patton Oswalt at Saban Theater in L.A. pt3." YouTube, 4th August 2011. <http://www.youtube.com/watch?v=AZKtNuQCVSI>

Goldfarb, David, and Ralf Hildebrandt. "Issue 62: 'The Kindly Ones: 6.'" The Annotated Sandman. 27th January 2007. <http://www.arschkrebs.de/sandman/annotations/sandman.62.draft.shtml>

House of Commons Science and Technology Committee. Light Pollution and Astronomy. 2003. <http://www.publications.parliament.uk/pa/cm200203/cmselect/cmsctech/747/74702.htm>

International Dark-sky Association. "Light Pollution and Energy." 2009. <http://docs.darksky.org/Docs/ida_energy_brochure.pdf>

Kamiya, Gary. "'Beowulf' vs. 'The Lord of the Rings.'" Salon. November 20, 2007. <http://www.salon.com/2007/11/20/beowulf_2/>

Lovecraft, Howard Phillips. "Notes on Writing Weird Fiction." Amateur Correspondent, 2, No. 1 (May–June 1937), 7–10; <http://www.hplovecraft.com/writings/texts/essays/nwwf.asp>

_____. The Shadow over Innsmouth. Everett, PA: Visionary Publishing Co., 1936, 13–158; <http://www.hplovecraft.com/writings/texts/fiction/soi.asp>

_____. "Supernatural Horror in Literature." The Recluse, No. 1 (1927), 23–59; <http://www.hplovecraft.com/writings/texts/essays/shil.asp>

Morrow, Greg, and Hildebrandt, Ralf "Issue 2: 'Imperfect Hosts.'" The Annotated Sandman. 27th January 2007. <http://www.arschkrebs.de/sandman/annotations/sandman.02.shtml>

_____. "Issue 6: '24 Hours.'" The Annotated Sandman. 27th January 2007. <http://www.arschkrebs.de/sandman/annotations/sandman.06.shtml>

_____. "Issue 34: 'Bad Moon Rising.'" The Annotated Sandman. 27th January 2007. <http://www.arschkrebs.de/sandman/annotations/

sandman.34.shtml>

Nokes, Richard Scott. "Beowulf Movie Review." November 18, 2007. <http://unlocked-wordhoard.blogspot.com/2007/11/beowulf-movie-review.html>

Raffaele, Paul. "Sleeping with Cannibals." *Smithsonian Magazine*. September, 2006. <http://www.smithsonianmag.com/travel/cannibals.html>

Roberts, Sheila. "Cast of Beowulf Interview." [November, 2007.] <http://www.moviesonline.ca/movienews_13362.html>

Sypeck, Jeff. "I am a monster, I'll make you run faster ..." November 23, 2007. <http://www.quidplura.com/?p=76>

Tully, Caroline. "Witches of Ancient Greece and Rome." *The Cauldron* #106. November 2002. <http://www.the-cauldron.org.uk/witchesofgreece.htm>

UbuWeb. <http://www.ubu.com/>

Wheeler, Bonnie. "'Beowulf' movie cops out with revised theme: 'It's that evil woman's fault.'" November 16, 2007. <http://smu.edu/newsinfo/pitches/beowulf-16nov2007.asp>

"Witch, n1." *Oxford English Dictionary*. Online version 2011. <http://www.oed.com/view/Entry/229574>

Zizek, Slavoj. "Desire: Drive = Truth: Knowledge." *UMBR(a)* (1997) <http://www.lacan.com/zizek-desire.htm>

FILM

Beowulf. Director's Cut. Hollywood: Paramount, 2007 (DVD 2008).

Dead of Night. Directed by Alberto Cavalcanti, Charles Crichton, Basil Dearden and Robert Hamer. 1945.

TELEVISION

Neverwhere. London: British Broadcasting Corporation, 1996 (DVD AandE Television Networks, 2003).

The Simpsons. Season 11. Los Angeles: Twentieth Century Fox Home Entertainment, 1999-2000 (DVD 2008).

INDEX

A

Abel 57, 61, 62, 96, 127-128, 138, 178, 180, 183
Adams, Douglas 11, 18, 20, 81—88, 90,91—93, 162, 170, 245, 252, 258, 263,
Æsir (see also Gods, Norse) 94, 106
Alice (see also Wonderland, *Through the Looking Glass*) 184, 195, 208, 210, 214
angels (see also Islington, the Angel) 50, 53—55, 58, 85-86, 97-98, 102, 107, 152, 153, 177, 187—189, 196, 216-217, 226, 230, 262
Anansi (see Nancy, Mr.) 97, 106-107
Anglo-Saxon 22-23, 27-30, 33, 103, 144-145
Anubis (see also Death, Gods of) 173, 175, 227
Apocalypse 162, 164-165, 225
appetite (see also cannibalism and consumption) 23, 142, 144-156, 161, 164, 166-167, 232-233
Armageddon (see Apocalypse) 250
Artemis (see also Diana) 128, 165, 225
Asgard 83, 101, 189, 248
Avary, Roger 13, 16, 26, 27-28, 30-33, 103, 108
Azrael (see also Death, Gods of) 50

B

Babylon (see myth, Babylonian) 100, 108, 173, 225
Babylon 5 (TV Show) 18, 64—71, 74, 77-79
Bast 170, 190
Batman (comic series) 18, 64-68, 71-75, 78, 241
Batman (character) 64-66, 71-74, 78-79, 134, 252
Beowulf (character) 16, 24, 25-33, 104, 108
Beowulf (poem) 16-17, 21-33, 104, 152, 168, 207
Beowulf (film) see under Gaiman, (works of)
Berúthiel, Queen 155-157
Bible, The 35, 53, 55, 58, 166
Bilquis 150-55

blood 26, 59-60, 94, 105-106, 111-114, 130, 152, 155-156, 159, 165-166, 228-9
Bustamonte, Mrs. 135, 167

C

Cain 57, 61, 62, 96, 127, 128, 131, 152, 178, 180, 183
Campbell, Helena 186, 209
Campbell, Joseph 64, 78, 157, 173, 176, 215, 217,
    The Hero with a Thousand Faces 173, 209, 216, 221,222, 260
cannibalism 56, 113, 143, 147-148, 151-155, 157-159, 187, 224
Chaos and Order (or Brute and Glob) 97, 107, 178, 224
Chesterton, C.K. 49, 63, 81, 261
Christian/Christianity (see also myth, Judeo-Christian and Gods, Judeo-Christian) 29-31, 33, 36-37, 42-43, 46, 50, 53, 55, 57, 62, 91, 145-146, 177, 186, 219, 225-226, 230-231, 248
Coats, Graham 182-183
Constantine, John 104, 205, 248
consumption (acts of) 104, 113, 138, 143, 147-159, 161, 167, 178, 195, 201-202, 212, 232-233
Coraline 13, 15, 156-159, 170, 181, 183-184, 187, 195-196, 209-212, 221-2, 264
Croup and Vandemar 178
    Mr. Croup 196, 216
Cthulhu (see also Lovecraft, H.P.) 98, 107, 201-202
Cynthia (see also Goddess, Moon and Goddess, Triple) 127-129, 131, 248,
Czernobog 179, 200-203

D

D.C. Comics & mythology 72, 86, 99, 226
Dee, John 85, 86, 90, 129-130, 220
Dent, Arthur 82, 84, 86-90
Doppelgänger 181-182
death (act of, symbolism of) 15-16, 37, 40, 43-44, 49-51, 53, 56-62, 65, 72-73, 89, 111-116, 118, 126, 132, 145, 149-150, 153, 161-165, 174-175, 177, 180, 182, 213, 225, 228-233
Death, Gods of 12, 13, 44, 50-52
Death (of the Endless) 12, 15, 17, 51-52, 54-56, 61, 95, 96, 98, 104, 106, 107,

129, 145, 173-179, 217, 230
Delirium/Delight (of the Endless) 98, 100, 105, 177, 217, 219
Demeter (see also Goddess) 97, 224
Demon 26, 54, 55, 150-151
Desire (of the Endless) 98, 105, 108, 176, 217, 219-220
Despair (of the Endless) 98, 105, 108, 176, 184, 217
Destiny (of the Endless) 85, 86, 98, 129-130, 138-139, 177, 217, 219
Destruction (of the Endless) 98, 100, 177, 182, 217, 225
Devil, the (see also Lucifer) 108, 146, 177, 230, 250
Diana (see also Artemis and Goddess, Moon) 125, 128,
Doctor Destiny (see John Dee) 85, 86, 129, 180, 220
Doctor Who 16-19, 64-68, 71, 74-80, 84, 252
Dogknife, Lord 155, 187, 189
Door, Lady 84, 89, 136, 184, 189, 214, 216, 217
Doyle, Sir Arthur Conan 203, 234
Dream (of the Endless) 13, 51-56, 61, 72, 83, 85-86, 89, 91, 96, 98, 99-100, 105-108, 128-132, 155, 165, 174-184, 217-220, 225-227, 247-248,
Dreaming, the 89, 101, 105, 107, 108, 128, 131, 132, 165, 166, 174, 178, 182, 218, 219, 220,
Dreamstone, the 85, 98, 220
Dunwiddy, Mrs. 135, 166-167

E

Eden, Garden of 57, 60, 97, 153, 211, 230
Elves 83, 99, 139
Endless, the (see also Dream, Death, etc) 17, 51, 64, 72-73, 98-99, 103-104, 129-130, 137, 173-174, 177, 185, 217, 219-220, 248
Ereschigal (see also Hecate) 131, 138
Eve 49, 55-62, 127, 131-133, 146, 174, 177, 180
  Daughter of 61, 146
  Sin of 40, 42, 58

F

Faerie/Faërie 83, 99,159-160, 180, 211, 219,

fairy/fairies 83, 92, 99-100, 142, 183, 184
fairytales 13, 25, 35, 45-46, 77. 109-111, 114, 118, 121-122, 134, 142, 154, 159-160, 179, 194, 199, 254
Fates, the 61, 107,125-127, 129, 132, 135, 137, 150, 174, 236,
Foxglove and Hazel 131, 133, 138, 165-166
Frazer, James 126
Future Shocks 240, 242-246, 251
Furies, the (see also Fates, the) 125-126, 130, 132, 137, 139, 155, 165, 174, 182
Fury, the 130
Fury, Nick (also Sir Nicholas Fury) 250-251

G

Gaia 224, 227, 236
Gaiman, Neil (author) 11-19, 21, 26-27, 31, 35, 38-39, 43, 49, 81, 91-92, 133, 198, 242, 249
Gaiman, Neil (works of)
    "A Parliament of Rooks" 174
    American Gods 1, 13-15, 46, 64-65, 94-97, 101-108, 133-135, 141, 150, 174-175, 179, 182-183, 188, 192, 194, 200, 203, 206, 223, 227- 228, 236-237, 257,
    Anansi Boys 1, 13, 94-95, 104, 106-107, 135, 166, 174, 182-3, 192, 200
    "A Study in Emerald" 16, 233-234
    "Bay Wolf" 27-28, 207
    Beowulf 1, 13, 16, 26-29, 31, 103-104, 108
    Blueberry Girl 136, 139
    Books of Magic, The 98, 134, 136, 184, 205, 253
    Mr. Punch: The Tragical Comedy or Comical Tragedy 183, 240, 249, 251
    Coraline 1, 13, 15, 181, 184, 187, 195, 196, 209
    Death: the High Cost of Living 104, 174, 175
    "The Facts in the Case of the Departure of Miss Finch" 191
    "The Doctor's Wife" 16, 65, 68, 74, 76-78, 252
    DON'T PANIC: Douglas Adams and the Hitchhikers Guide to the Galaxy 82-83, 92
    Endless Nights 182
    "Feeders and Eaters" 147, 150
    "Forbidden Brides of the Faceless Slaves in the Secret House of the

Night of Dread Desire" 204
Fragile Things 84
"Instructions" 84, 142, 156
Good Omens 97, 158, 162, 164, 177, 179, 187-188
"Goliath" 198, 233, 235-236
Graveyard Book, The 1, 13, 15, 17, 35-36, 43, 45-46, 50-51, 161, 179, 184, 188, 192, 195
"I Cthulhu" 201
"It's Only the End of the World Again" 193, 201-202
"Keepsakes and Treasures" 148, 190
Interworld 82, 88, 91, 155, 187-189, 194, 196
"Locks" 110, 118, 120-123
Marvel 1602 240, 250-252
MirrorMask 178, 181, 186-187, 194-195
Neverwhere 82, 84, 94-95, 97, 101, 133, 136, 139, 178, 181-182, 184, 187-189, 191, 194, 196, 213-215
Odd and the Frost Giants, 182, 189
"The Problem of Susan" 17, 35-36, 38-40, 43, 256
"Ramadan" 184
Sandman, The 1, 12-15, 17, 50-52, 54-59, 61, 64, 65, 72-74, 77, 82, 85-86, 94-102, 104-107, 127-133, 135-138, 165, 170, 173, 175-178, 180, 182, 200, 217-221, 225, 227, 230, 246-248, 251-253, 256
A Game of You 84, 89, 92, 100-101, 130, 133, 138, 165, 179, 183
Brief Lives 100, 108, 183, 225
The Doll's House 105, 129, 137,139, 178-179
Dream Country 107-108, 130
The Dream Hunters 133, 139
Fables and Reflections 98, 107, 153, 180, 248, 253
The Kindly Ones 56, 94, 130, 132, 139, 155-156, 159, 165, 175, 226
Preludes and Nocturnes 54, 73, 85, 104, 174
Season of Mists 54, 60, 96-97, 99, 130-131, 178, 225-226
The Wake 14, 72-73, 97, 100, 131, 133, 226
"Shoggoth's Old Peculiar" 201-202
Smoke and Mirrors 27, 114, 179, 194, 197, 207,
"Snow, Glass, Apples" 110-111, 116, 122-123, 154, 165, 167, 179
Stardust 94-95, 104-105, 133-134, 136, 139, 153, 158, 184, 188, 192-193, 195-196, 219

284	Index

"The White Road" 110, 115, 117, 122
Wolves in the Walls 184
Gardner, Gerald 143-144, 163
Genesis, Book of 57, 62, 186, 226, 230,
Gimbutas, Marija 126-127, 145, 149-150
Goddess (see also Goddess, Moon and Goddess, Triple) 18, 50, 100, 107, 125, 127, 135-136, 145, 149-150, 157, 165-166, 170, 189, 224-225, 230, 236
Goddess, Moon 125, 127-131, 150, 165-167, 225, 248
Goddess, Triple (see also Maiden-Mother-Crone) 18, 125-128, 130-139, 145, 150, 158
Gods, Elder (see also Lovecraft H.P.) 98, 201-203, 234-236, 253
Gods, Greek 50, 96-98, 105, 107, 125-126, 129, 137-139, 165, 175, 180, 182, 223-224, 227, 231, 236
Gods, Judeo-Christian (see also Jesus) 38, 41, 43, 53-55, 57, 70, 87, 91, 94, 153, 163, 173, 177, 179, 184, 226, 230
Gods, Hindu 135, 145, 150, 206
Gods, Norse (see also Asgard and Ragnorök) 13, 50, 56, 94, 96, 102-103, 105-106, 108, 125, 134-135, 145, 174-175, 182, 189, 225, 227-228
Gods, assorted (see also individual listings) 12-15, 18, 52, 83, 92, 94-96, 98-100, 102-104, 106-107, 117, 129, 135, 137, 153-154, 167, 174, 182, 184, 188, 194, 200-201, 206, 223-225, 227-228, 230, 233, 236-237, 257
Goldilocks 118
Gorgo (see Hecate)
Gorgon/Gorgons 132, 138, 158
Graces, the 125-126, 128, 137
Graves, Robert 126, 165
Grendel 25-28, 32, 104
Grendel, Mother of 26, 28, 31-32, 104, 158
Grey, Lady on the (see also Death, Gods of) 44, 50-51

H

Hades 50, 97, 107, 189, 224
Hall, Lyta 130, 132, 138-139, 165, 174, 182
Harker, Joey 82, 87, 90, 156, 187-190, 193-194, 196
Hazel (see Foxglove and Hazel)

Hecate 125-126, 128, 131, 137-138, 145, 165-166
Hel 50
hell 53-56, 59-60, 94, 96, 99, 101, 107, 143, 148, 178-179, 189, 219-220, 225-226, 230, 248
hell-mouth 153
hero-journey 33, 45, 84, 89, 150, 153, 157-158, 162, 173, 179, 190, 205, 209-211, 213-214, 216-218, 221
Higgler, Mrs. 135, 166-167
Hippolyta (see also Hall, Lyta or Titania) 105, 130
Hitchhiker's Guide to the Galaxy, the (see also Douglas Adams) 82, 89, 162
Holmes, Sherlock 16-17, 203, 234-235
Hrothgar 25-26, 104

I

Indigo, Lady 155-156, 165, 188
Innsmouth 202-203
Islington, the Angel 97, 188-189, 196
Ishtar 97, 100, 107-108, 225-226

J

Jesus (see also Gods, Judeo-Christian) 37, 43, 53, 231-232
Judeo-Christian (see Christianity and myth, Judeo-Christian)

K

Kabbalah 85, 92
Kalī 135, 145, 150
Kincaid, Unity 104-105
Kindley Ones, The (see also Fates and Furies) 139, 156, 159, 174, 182

L

Lamia/lamia 139, 142, 144, 147, 152
Laura (*American Gods*) 150, 151

286   Index

Larissa (see Thessaly) 100, 137, 139, 165
Lamia (see also Lilith) 139, 142, 144, 147, 152
Lewis, C.S. (see also Narnia) 13, 17, 23, 33, 35-47, 49, 63, 81, 141, 159-160, 170-171, 215, 222
The Lion, the Witch, and the Wardrobe 215, 222
The Chronicles of Narnia 35, 36, 38, 40, 43-46
Lilim, the 57, 134, 142, 153, 156-160, 165, 166, 174, 195
Lilith 49, 53, 54-63, 131, 134, 151-153, 159
Loki 94, 96, 102, 103, 105, 106, 108, 174, 175, 182, 228
London Below 97, 184, 191, 213, 214, 215, 216, 217
Lovecraft, H.P. (see also Cthulhu) 13, 62, 98, 106, 202, 203, 204, 205, 207, 234-5
Lucifer 52, 54-55, 60, 62, 94, 102, 107-108, 187-188, 225-226, 230, 248
Luther, Martin 146-147, 149-150, 154-156, 164
Lyesmith, Low Key (see Loki) 94, 182

M

Mab (see Titania)
MacDonald, George 17, 18, 49-63
magic, concepts of 85, 86, 141, 143-145, 147, 151, 154-155, 157, 160, 167-168, 200, 208, 250
Maiden-Mother-Crone (see also Triple Goddess) 126-131, 133, 135, 138-139, 150, 161, 174
Malleus Maleficarum 142-144, 146-148, 152-160, 162-163, 165, 168
Matrix, The 137, 195, 198, 236
Mayhew, Richard 88, 89, 90, 184, 213, 216, 221
Middle-earth 83, 170
Mildred, Mordred, Cynthia (see also Triple Goddess) 127-131, 248
Milton, John 53, 54, 55, 103, 226, 230
Paradise Lost 53, 54, 230
mirrors 18, 173-174, 177, 181, 183-184, 186, 194-196, 208, 210, 236
MirrorMask, the 195, 196
Moon, Drawing Down the 131, 165-167
Morpheus (see Dream) 52, 85, 98, 107, 182-83, 217-221
Mormo (see also Hecate) 131, 138-39, 166
Moriarty, Professor (see also Holmes, Sherlock and Doyle, Arthur

Conan) 203, 234-235
Morrígan, the 56, 107, 125, 127-128, 132, 135, 145, 170
Mother, Other 156-159, 165, 181, 183, 187, 195, 210-211
myth, Assyrian/Assyro-Babylonian 57-58, 97, 225
myth, definitions of/ concepts of 13, 16, 18-19, 24, 29, 33, 35-36, 45-46, 49, 56, 62,64, 66-68, 70-72, 74, 76-78, 95, 97, 103, 137, 173-174, 180, 186, 192,
myth, Greek 13, 32, 35-36, 45, 50, 66, 95, 96-98, 103, 107, 125, 137-139, 175, 223-224, 227, 231, 236, 248, 251
myth, Hebrew 85, 92, 230
myth, Judeo-Christian 55, 57, 62, 91, 186, 226,
myth, Norse 13, 25, 50, 66, 94, 103, 125, 145, 182, 189, 194, 225, 227,

N

Nada 54,220
Nancy, Fat Charlie 104, 106, 135, 174, 183
Nancy, Mr. 203
Narnia 17, 36-38, 41-44, 46-47, 166, 208, 215
Necrophilia 155
Neo-Pagan 126, 142, 143, 144, 165, 167
Nicholas, Saint 231, 233, 234
Norns, the (see Fates) 125, 127, 128, 134
Norse (language) 23, 103
Nuala 99, 139

O

Odd 182, 189, 194
Odin 13, 56, 94, 96, 103, 108, 134-135, 174, 225, 227
Old English (see also Ango-Saxon) 22-25, 28, 33, 103, 104, 144, 185
Old Ones, Great (see Lovecraft, Cthulhu, Elder Gods) 98, 203, 234-236
Orpheus (see also Dream and Gods, Greek) 97, 98, 105, 107, 175, 180, 182

P

Pagan (see also Neo-Pagan) 24, 29, 50

Pevensie children (see Lewis and Narnia) 36, 215
Pevensie, Susan 17, 35-45, 47, 215
Poppins, Mary 43, 51
Pratchett, Terry 107, 133, 137, 162-164, 168, 187-188, 197
Prefect, Ford 82, 87, 89
Princess, the ("Snow, Glass, Apples") 89, 110-114, 154, 155
Prose Edda 56, 106, 186

Q

Queen ("Snow, Glass, Apples") 110-114, 123, 154-155, 165
Queen, Witch (see Lilim) 59, 134, 139, 159-161

R

Ragnarök 194, 225

S

Sandman, the (see also Dream) 52, 55-56, 64-65, 72-74, 78, 79, 103, 107-108, 128, 136, 138-140, 170, 180, 240, 247-248, 252,
Sandman, The (original D.C. series) 180, 247-248
Shadow (see also *American Gods*) 100, 104-105, 134-135, 150, 157, 174, 182-183, 188, 190, 192, 194, 200-201, 227-228
Silmarillion, the 96, 107, 160, 166, 187
Shakespeare 45, 97, 99, 125, 137, 141, 248
    A Midsummer Night's Dream 99, 125, 180
    Macbeth 125, 126, 128, 137-138, 166-167, 248, 251
    The Tempest 248
Shoggoth's Old Peculiar, 11, 107, 201-202
Snow White (see Princess and "Snow, Glass, Apples") 110-111, 113-114, 123, 142, 154-156
Spenser, Edmund 99,
    The Faerie Queene 99, 158
Spider 135, 166, 167, 174, 196
Susan 17, 35-47

Swamp Thing 128, 134, 139
succubus (see also lamia and Lilith) 146, 152, 213

T

TARDIS 74, 75, 76, 78
Thessaly/Larissa 100, 108, 131, 133, 137-139, 165-166
Thor 13, 94, 96, 174-175
Titania 99-100
Tolkien, J.R.R. 1, 13, 16-17, 21-33, 35, 49, 63, 81, 83, 86, 96, 107, 155-156, 159-160, 166, 170, 186-187, 195, 208-209, 253-255
    "On Fairy Stories" 208-209
    "*Beowulf*: The Monsters and the Critics" 16, 23, 25, 32
    The Hobbit 23-25, 63, 253
    The Lord of the Rings 23-25, 86, 93
    The Unfinished Tales 156

U

Una, Lady (of Stormhold) 105, 161

V

Vagina Dentata (see also consumption and appetite) 151-155
Valar (see also Tolkien) 96, 107, 160, 166, 187
Valinor, Two Trees of 166, 187
vampire (see also Princess) 31, 123, 142, 152-156, 192
vampirism 59-60 111-113, 152, 155-156, 165-166
Vess, Charles 134, 136, 139

W

Wednesday (see also Odin) 103, 105, 150, 174, 183, 200-201, 203, 227-228
witch/witches 18, 39, 44, 100, 110-114, 125-126, 128, 131-139, 141-168, 179, 195, 205, 248
witches (in *Macbeth*) 125-126, 128, 138, 248

Wonderland (see also Alice) 184, 208

X

Xena 102

Y

Yvaine 160-161

Z

Zoryas, the 134, 139, 150, 157, 192, 200-201